The Complete Guide to Thematic Units

Second Edition

The Complete Guide to Thematic Units

Creating the Integrated Curriculum

Second Edition

Anita Meyer Meinbach
Anthony D. Fredericks
Liz Rothlein

Christopher-Gordon Publishers, Inc.
Norwood, Massachusetts

Credits

Every effort has been made to contact copyright holders for permission to reproduce borrowed material where necessary. We apologize for any oversights and would be happy to rectify them in future printings.

Chapter 2:
Excerpts from *Miss Rumphius* by Barbara Cooney (New York: Puffin Books, © 1982) used with permission of the publishers.

"K-W-L: A teaching model that develops active reading of expository text," by Donna Ogle, reprinted with permission of the International Reading Association.

Chapter 3:
The Developmental Inventory, from Ruddell, M. R., (1993). Teaching content reading and writing, is reproduced with permission from M. R. Ruddell, 1993.

Thematic Unit: Folktales from Around the World:
Pages from *Frantic Frogs and Other Frankly Fractured Folktales for Readers' Theatre* © 1993 are used with the permission of the publisher, Teacher Ideas Press, 800-237-6124.

Christopher-Gordon Publishers, Inc.
1502 Providence Highway, Suite 12
Norwood, MA 02062
(800) 934-8322

Printed in the United States of America

10 9 8 7 6 5 4 3 2 1   03 02 01 00

ISBN: 1-929024-10-X
Library of Congress Catalogue Number: 99076809

Dedication

To Lawrence Annis, my sixth grade teacher
whose creativity inspired many of the activities in this book
and whose encouragement helped shape my life.

—A.M.M.

To the next generation of teachers—
May their classrooms be filled with
love, imagination, and the joys of discover!

—A.D.F.

To Jay Jensen, a dedicated teacher, friend, and colleague.

—L. R.

Contents

Introduction xi

PART I
Thematic Units: Structure and Design 1

Chapter 1
Developing and Using Thematic Units 3

    Thematic Teaching and Multiple Intelligences 6
    Additional Advantages of Thematic Instruction 8
    Thematic Teaching: A Sample Plan 10
    Planning Thematic Instruction 15

Chapter 2
Strategies for Success 35

    Strategies You Can Use 39
    Before Reading 39
    During Reading 50
    After Reading 55

Chapter 3
Authentic Assessment 65

    The Nature of Assessment 66
    Portfolio Assessment 68
    Student Self-Assessment 77
    Criterion Checks 80
    Multiple Options 81

Chapter 4
Parent and Community Involvement 85

    Involving Parents 86
    Community Field Trips 92

PART II
Thematic Units: Primary Units 99

The Changing Earth 101
    Overview 101
    How it Works 101
    Literature Related Activities 103
    Culminating Activity 108

Supplemental Literature 109
Mini-Themes 111

Insects/Bugs 115

Overview 115
How it Works 115
Literature Related Activities 118
Culminating Activity 124
Supplemental Literature 124
Mini-Themes 126

Dinosaurs 129

Overview 129
How it Works 129
Literature Related Activities 131
Culminating Activity 135
Supplemental Literature 135
Mini-Themes 138

Growing Up 143

Overview 143
How it Works 143
Literature Related Activities 146
Culminating Activity 151
Supplemental Literature 152
Mini Themes 154

Holidays and Celebrations 159

Overview 159
How it Works 160
Literature Related Activities 165
Culminating Activity 170
Supplemental Literature 170
Mini–Themes 175

Folktales from Around the World 179

Overview 179
How it Works 179
Literature Related Activities 183
Culminating Activity 188
Supplemental Literature 192
Mini-Themes 198

The Caldecott Award 203

Overview 203
How it Works 203
Literature Related Activities 205
Culminating Activity 211
Supplemental Literature 212
Mini-Themes 219

Counting and Computations 223

Overview 223
How it Works 223
Literature Related Activities 225
Culminating Activity 229
Supplemental Literature 230
Mini-Themes 232

Measurement and Sizes 235

Overview 235
How it Works 235
Literature Related Activities 237
Culminating Activity 241
Supplemental Literature 242
Mini-Themes 244

Intermediate Thematic Units 249

Oceans 251

Overview 251
How it Works 251
Literature Related Activities 255
Culminating Activity 265
Supplemental Literature 265
Mini-Themes 269

Space: The Final Frontier 273

Overview 273
How it Works 273
Literature Related Activities 277
Culminating Activity 282
Supplemental Literature 283
Mini-Themes 285

Becoming A Nation 291

Overview 291
How it Works 291
Literature Related Activities 294
Culminating Activity 298
Supplemental Literature 299
Mini-Themes 300

The Wild, Wild West 303

Overview 303
How it Works 303
Literature Related Activities 306
Culminating Activity 312
Supplemental Literature 312
Mini-Themes 315

Poetry: The Words And The Music 319

Overview 319
How it Works 319
Literature Related Activities 324
Culminating Activity 329
Supplemental Literature 329
Mini-Themes 333

Biography: Making a Difference 339

Overview 339
How it Works 339
Literature Related Activities 341
Culminating Activity 347
Supplemental Literature 348
Mini-Themes 349

Meet The Newberys 353

Overview 353
How it Works 353
Literature Related Activities 356
Culminating Activity 362
Supplemental Literature 362
Mini-Themes 369

Fractions 375

Overview 375
How it Works 375
Literature Related Activities 377
Culminating Activity 381
Supplemental Literature 381
Mini-Themes 382

Geometry 385

Overview 385
How it Works 385
Literature Related Activities 386
Culminating Activity 392
Supplemental Literature 392
Mini-Themes 394

Art 397

Overview 397
How it Works 397
Literature Related Activities 399
Culminating Activity 405
Supplemental Literature 405
Mini-Themes 406

Title Index 409

Subject Index 413

Introduction

WOW! We could not have anticipated the enthusiastic response and emphatic support of the first edition of *The Complete Guide to Thematic Units*. We were gratified to learn how the plans, procedures, and units in that edition engaged teachers, stimulated students, and "energized" classroom learning environments from north to south, and east to west. The profusion of positive letters and supportive messages we received was a testament to our belief that a literature-rich classroom is a classroom that encourages, supports, and celebrates the role of literature throughout every aspect of the elementary curriculum.

With that in mind we wanted to create a new edition—an edition that would extend, expand, and elaborate on the principles and practices that were celebrated in the first book. We know that this is an exciting time to be a teacher! The infusion of children's literature throughout the elementary curriculum and the invitational classrooms being established in schools all over the country make this a vibrant and fascinating time to be in education. With more than 60 years of combined teaching experience between the three of us, we have seen the ebb and flow of several educational "movements." But, what is happening in elementary classrooms at the start of the 21st century represents some of the most exciting "reforms" we have seen in our professional careers.

What we find so dynamic and stimulating about the curricular changes taking place today is that they are not new! The concepts behind invitational classrooms were first proposed by John Dewey and his colleagues in the 1920's. The foundation for literature-based reading programs were advocated and delineated by Louise Rosenblatt in the 1930's. What is happening in today's classrooms is a renewal of the ideas and strategies that have "been around" for many years. The research is not new; it is how it is being used that is so electric!

We believe that learning through children's literature, in authentic invitational classrooms, can be intensely exciting and magnificently stimulating. As classroom teachers and reading specialists we have had the pleasure of working with hundreds of youngsters—helping them experience the joys of a book sumptuously savored or a story richly shared. We have had the honor of working with fellow teachers throughout the country as they seek to convey the magic of literature to their students in new and dynamic ways. And, we have experienced the thrill of working with pre-service teachers—sharing with them the excitement and enthusiasm of a literature-rich reading program and a student-centered learning environment. Indeed, it is an exciting time to be a teacher!

As authors, we have also had the honor of sharing our zeal about teaching and our zest for learning with fellow educators around the country. We hope that this second edition of *The Complete Guide to Thematic Units* will not only demonstrate the magical experiences possible in literature-rich learning environments, but also promote a belief of ours that the best teachers are those who are willing to learn alongside their students—exploring new territories and examining new vistas. Indeed, we are strong advocates of the idea that the best teachers are those who have as much to learn as they do to teach. In fact, we approached this edition as a new and exciting learning experience—seeking new ways to use children's literature, exploring new dimensions of literature-rich classrooms, and examining new ideas about the learning process and the role of teachers. We believe that that process has helped us to grow as writers and has surely helped us grow as teachers. We hope that our discoveries along the way may be guide-posts for your professional development and certainly increase your students' growth as lifelong readers and learners.

We have worked hard to fill the pages of this edition with a plethora of ideas and a host of practical strategies for your classroom and your students. We sincerely hope that you find our recommendations and suggestions appropriate in building exciting frameworks for your entire curriculum. We believe that thematic teaching and thematic units offer a wealth of learning opportunities for learners of all ages—opportunities without limits and without restrictions. As you and your students set your sails for new lands and new destinations, we hope that this book will serve as a guide for those journeys and a companion for the literature-rich discoveries along the way. May your classroom be filled with all the excitement that thematic units can bring; and may your students be filled with all the wonder and imagination books can offer.

—Anita M. Meinbach
Anthony D. Fredericks
Liz Rothlein

PART I

Thematic Units:
Structure and Design

Chapter 1

Developing and Using Thematic Units

Long strings of Pacific Giant Kelp hung down from every possible light fixture and corner of the room. An array of blues and greens were splashed across the walls and down the window panes. Illustrations of sharks, jellyfish, and octopuses and photos of sunfish, lobsters, and seahorses were arrayed throughout the room. The distant cries of dolphins and humpback whales filled the air with a medley of sounds. Occasionally, the orchestral lyrics of shoreline waves could be heard ebbing and flowing throughout the room. Sea life of every dimension, size, and shape could be seen swimming and surging overhead, while unseen deep-water creatures arched their way across the blackened expanse of an oversized bulletin board. A paper mache coral reef populated by immense sea stars, iridescent tropical fish, and menacing stonefish snaked its way across the floor. The lyrical gurgling of an aquarium pump mixed with oceanic audio tapes to create an melodious blend of ancient rhythms that swept into every corner of the room. To any visiter it was evident that this was a place filled with a rich diversity of life—and an incredible assortment of learning opportunities.

Carol Dutton has been a fourth grade teacher in southern New Mexico for the past eight years. Visitors entering her classroom often feel as though they have been transported to some enormous aquarium or vast underwater kingdom. Carol, along with her students, has transformed the room into an oceanic wonderland awash in magnificent sights and sounds. This simulated ocean environment is so authentic that one might expect a moray eel to lunge out of a rocky outcropping or a school of reef sharks to swim innocently by.

Carol knows that a study of the world's oceans is critical to her students' understanding of the varied ecosystems throughout the world. She also knows that the oceans of the world, as well as many of the inhabitants, are seriously endangered and that the next generation of kids must work together to help preserve the flora and fauna that live in this over-polluted, over-fished, and over-commercialized ecosystem.

In order to actively involve her students in a host of positive learning experiences, increase their awareness of this valued environment, and offer "hands-on, minds-on" activities and projects, Carol presented them with a thematic unit on "Oceans" (see p. 251). Let's take a few moments and look in on Carol's class as her students explore some of the mysteries and marvels of this magical world:

A small group of youngsters were comparing notes on information they had obtained from back issues of *International Wildlife* and *Wildlife Conservation* about the status of selected endangered species in the Pacific Ocean. Terri and Maria had elected to contact various environmental organizations throughout the country (e.g. American Oceans Campaign [725 Arizona Ave., Suite 102, Santa Monica, CA 90401]; Center for Marine Conservation [1725 DeSales St., NW, Suite 500, Washington, DC 20036]; Coastal Conservation Association [4801 Woodway, Suite 220 West, Houston, TX 77056]; The Coral Reef Alliance [809 Delaware St., Berkeley, CA 94710]) to obtain information on each organization's efforts to preserve and conserve marine animals.

Carlos, Peter, Ernest, and Tyrone were working with the school librarian to assemble a bibliography of ocean-related literature that could be shared with their "pen pals" in another fourth grade class in Santa Fe.

Fernando, David, and Hecter were constructing miniature aquaria in order to study the life cycles of individual and isolated animals such as sea shrimp, neon tetras, and mollusks. Their observations were being recorded in handmade journals—each shaped like the organisms they were studying. The finished products would be prominently displayed in a school display case. The aquaria were set up on the window sill and the growth of their life forms were being tracked and recorded over a period of several weeks.

April, Martin, and Isabel were in the process of drafting a letter to various political leaders sharing their concerns about overfishing. Virgil and Sharon were collecting, cataloging, and assembling information they had obtained from various whale conservation groups (e.g. American Cetacean Society [P.O. Box 1391, San Pedro, CA 90733]; Cetacean Society International [P.O. Box 953, Georgetown, CT 06829]; Pacific Whale Foundation [101 North Kihei Road, Kihei, HI 96753]).

Amanda and Carole were creating a series of posters focusing on representative animals that live in each of the five major oceans of the world.

One group of students was beginning preparations for a short video on the ecology of coral reefs. Wally, Alix, Louise, and Sylvia were interviewing other fourth grade students for a list of questions to pose to the environmental sciences professor who would be visiting from the New Mexico State University the following week. Nella and Darryl began looking through several books to collect information about the life of the Great White Shark and other dangerous animals that lived in the ocean. Johanna, Lucrecia, and Irma were logging on to several ocean-related web sites (e.g. [http://www.nos.noaa.gov/], [http://www.actwin.com/fish/species.cgi], [http://www.oceans.net/preserve.html]) in order to obtain information on the preservation and protection of the world's oceans.

Enthusiasm echoed throughout the classroom. Students were excited by the opportunities to share information, discuss ideas for presenting data with other classes, and make decisions on how their knowledge could be used in productive ways. Some students choose to pursue independent activities while others worked quietly in small groups. Cooperative learning was evident throughout the room as students assembled ideas and shared possibilities in an atmosphere of mutual respect and support. Competition was scarcely evident, as students helped each other with ideas, resources, and extensions of activities. It was clearly apparent that this was a true "community of learners"—one in which students were all working toward common goals, making and following through on decisions, and taking responsibility for how they learned as much as for what they learned.

Carol's students were engaged in a series of well-planned and thoroughly engaging learning opportunities wrapped around a *thematic unit*. The thematic unit was designed to assist students in learning about specific aspects of ocean life, help them appreciate the various oceans around the world, and become aware of environmental threats. Carol had introduced the unit with a collection of children's literature about oceans—including those dealing with flora and fauna, explorations, ecological hazards, medicines obtained from the oceans, and some of the most unusual and dangerous animals found anywhere in the world. Her primary resource was *Exploring the Oceans: Science Activities for Kids* by Anthony D. Fredericks (Golden, CO: Fulcrum Publications, 1998). Other books included *Watch Out for Sharks* by Caroline Arnold (New York: Clarion, 1991); *Exploring an Ocean Tide Pool* by Jeanne Bendick (New York: Holt, 1994); *The Magic School Bus on the Ocean Floor* by Joanna Cole (New York: Scholastic, 1994); *I Wonder Why the Sea is Salty and Other Questions About the Ocean* by Anita Ganeri (New York: Kingfisher, 1995); *Ocean* by Ron Hirschi (New York: Bantam, 1990); *Ocean* by Miranda MacQuitty (New York: Knopf, 1995); *Is This a House for a Hermit Crab* by Margaret MacDonald (New York: Orchard, 1990); *The Underwater Alphabet Book* by Jerry Pallotta (Watertown, MA: Charlesbridge, 1991); and *A Swim Through the Sea* by Kristen Joy Pratt (Nevada City, CA: Dawn Publications, 1994). While these books were the impetus for the unit, Carol was also able to offer her students a wide-ranging assortment of hands-on experiences, activities, experiments, and projects that provided engaging and exciting learning opportunities for several weeks. Some of these extending activities included:

a. The creation of an undersea poster covering one wall of the classroom.

b. The "invention" of a homemade desalinization device.

c. A "semantic octopus" which recorded new words and terms learned throughout the unit.

d. Life-size illustrations of blue whales and other large ocean creatures on the school playground.

e. A scrapbook of amazing facts and figures.

f. A video series devoted to the changing ecology of various sections of the southern California coastline.

g. A display of letters written to various scientific groups and universities.

h. Surveys of family members and relatives on environmental concerns related to oceans.

i. A photographic collection (with annotations) of tide pool life.

j. A skit on the life and death of various ocean creatures.

k. A set of brochures on currents and tides and their effect on land masses.

Carol and thousands of other teachers have discovered that a thematic learning environment has enormous possibilities for "energizing" the elementary curriculum. A classroom that provides a variety of stimulating activities, a classroom overflowing with books and opportunities to read those books in a productive way, and a classroom overflowing with meaningful and productive activities is a classroom that facilitates learning and values the depth and breadth to which students can become immersed in their own scholastic endeavors.

In Carol's classroom learning comes alive—the curriculum is "energized" and students understand the natural connections that exist between reading, language arts, science, social studies, math, and the creative arts. Carol's students are also provided with opportunities to take responsibility for their learning by making choices, making decisions, and making judgements on the material and processes used throughout a designated unit. In essence, Carol's classroom is one in which children's literature provides both a foundation and a launching pad for her students' self-initiated discoveries. A thematic unit provides breadth and depth to the entire curriculum by offering innumerable opportunities for students to become immersed in the dynamics of their own education. In short, a thematic unit is the epitome of holistic teaching: students use language productively to answer self-initiated questions and satisfy their own inherent and natural curiosity about the world around them.

THEMATIC TEACHING AND MULTIPLE INTELLIGENCES

Thematic instruction offers a host of opportunities for students to actively engage in a constructivist approach to learning. It offers a variety of meaningful learning opportunities tailored to students' needs and interests. Children are given the chance to make important choices about *what* they learn, as well as about *how* they learn it. Thematic instruction provides the means to integrate the entire elementary curriculum while involving students in a multiplicity of learning opportunities and ventures.

Incorporated into thematic explorations are opportunities for students to take advantage of, hone, and build upon one or more of their multiple intelligences. According to Howard Gardner (*Frames of Mind: The Theory of Multiple Intelligences.* New York: BasicBooks, HarperCollins Publishers, 1985), each individual possesses eight different intelligences (see Figure 1-1, "The Eight Human Intelligences") in varying degrees. These intelligences (as opposed to a single intelligence quotient as traditionally reported via many standardized intelligence tests) help determine how individuals learn and how they fare in their daily lives. Gardner defines an "intelligence" as consisting of three components:

- The ability to create an effective product or offer a service that is valuable in one's culture.
- A set of skills that enables an individual to solve problems encountered in life.
- The potential for finding or creating solutions for problems, which enables a person to acquire new knowledge.

Individuals differ in the strength (or weakness) of each of the eight intelligences in isolation, as well as in combination. For example, whereas some indi-

Figure 1-1

The Eight Human Intelligences

According to Howard Gardner, individuals possess these eight intelligences in varying degrees.

1. *Verbal-Linguistic Intelligence* involves ease in producing language and sensitivity to the nuances, order, and rhythm of words. Individuals who are strong in verbal-linguistic intelligence love to read, write, and tell stories.

2. *Math-Logic Intelligence* relates to the ability to reason deductively or inductively, and to recognize and manipulate abstract patterns and relationships. Individuals who excel in this intelligence have strong problem-solving and reasoning skills and ask questions in a logical manner.

3. *Musical Intelligence* encompasses sensitivity to the pitch, timbre, and rhythm of sounds as well as responsiveness to the emotional implications of these elements of music. Individuals who remember melodies or recognize pitch and rhythm exhibit musical intelligence.

4. *Spatial Intelligence* includes the ability to create visual-spatial representations of the world and to transfer them mentally or concretely. Individuals who exhibit spatial intelligence need a mental or physical picture to best understand new information. They are strong in drawing, designing, and creating things.

5. *Bodily-Kinesthetic Intelligence* involves using the body to solve problems, make things, and convey ideas and emotions. Individuals who are strong in this intelligence are good at physical activities, eye-hand coordination, and have a tendency to move around, touch things, and gesture.

6. *Intrapersonal Intelligence* entails the ability to understand one's own emotions, goals, and intentions. Individuals strong in intrapersonal intelligence have a strong sense of self, are confident, and can enjoy working alone.

7. *Interpersonal Intelligence* refers to the ability to work effectively with other people and to understand them and recognize their goals and intentions. Individuals who exhibit this intelligence thrive on cooperative work, have strong leadership skills, and are skilled at organizing, communicating, and negotiating.

8. *Naturalist Intelligence* includes the capacity to recognize flora and fauna; to make distinctions in the natural world; and to use this ability productively in activities such as farming and biological science.

---

viduals learn best through linguistic means, others are more kinesthetic learners, and still others are spatial learners. Suffice to say, that no two people learn in the same way, nor should they be taught in the same way.

The research on multiple intelligences has revealed that teaching aimed at sharpening one kind of intelligence will carry over to others. There is also mounting evidence that learning opportunities involving a variety of intelligences allow students to take advantage of their preferred intelligence(s), as well as strengthen weaker intelligences. In short, thematic instruction provides something for everyone.

Thematic instruction allows you to extend, expand, and take advantage of students' intelligences. Thematic instruction also provides you with many opportunities to combine the intelligences of your students with the resources, information, and concepts of your entire curriculum. In short, thematic teaching celebrates multiple intelligences, offering learning opportunities that provide students with a meaningful and balanced approach to learning. Above all, thematic instruction supports and emphasizes the varied relationships that exist among investigative inquiry, a process approach to learning, and the exercise of multiple intelligences in a positive and supportive environment.

ADDITIONAL ADVANTAGES OF THEMATIC INSTRUCTION

Let's take a look at some other advantages of thematic units—for teachers (Figure 1-2) as well as for students (Figure 1-3).

Figure 1-2

Advantages of Thematic Teaching
For Teachers

- There is more time available for instructional purposes. Material does not have to be crammed into artificial time periods, but can be extended across the curriculum and across the day.

- The connections which can and do exist between subjects, topics, and themes can be logically and naturally developed. Teachers can demonstrate relationships and assist students in comprehending those relationships.

- Learning can be demonstrated as a continuous activity—one not restricted by textbook designs, time barriers, or even the four walls of the classroom. Teachers can help students extend learning opportunities into many aspects of their personal lives.

- Teachers are able to relinquish "control" of the curriculum and assist students in assuming a sense of "ownership" for their individual learning opportunities.

- Teachers are free to help students look at a problem, situation, or topic from a variety of viewpoints, rather than the "right way" frequently demonstrated in a teacher's manual or curriculum guide.

- The development of a "community of learners" is facilitated and enhanced through thematic teaching. There is less emphasis on *competition* and more emphasis on *collaboration and cooperation.*

- Opportunities for the teacher to model appropriate learning behaviors in a supportive and encouraging environment is enhanced.

- Assessment is more holistic, authentic, and meaningful and provides a more accurate picture of students' progress and development.

- Authentic use of all the language arts (reading, writing, listening, and speaking) is encouraged throughout all curricular areas.

- There is more emphasis on *teaching* students; less emphasis on *telling* students.

(continued)

- Teachers are provided with an abundance of opportunities for integrating children's literature into all aspects of the curriculum and all aspects of the day.
- Teachers can promote problem solving, creative thinking, and critical thinking processes within all aspects of a topic.
- Teachers can promote and support children's individual autonomy and self-direction offering students control over their learning.
- Teachers are also engaged as *learners* throughout the development and implementation of a thematic unit.

Figure 1-3

**Advantages of Thematic Teaching
For Students**

- Focuses on the *processes* of learning more so than the *products* of learning.
- Breaks down the "artificial barriers" that often exist between areas of the curriculum and provides an integrative approach to learning.
- Provides a child-centered curriculum—one tailored to their interests, needs, and abilities; one in which they are encouraged to make their own decisions and assume a measure of responsibility for learning.
- Stimulates self-directed discovery and investigation in and outside of the classroom.
- Assists youngsters in developing relationships between ideas and concepts enhancing appreciation and comprehension.
- Offers realistic opportunities for children to build upon individual backgrounds of information in developing new knowledge.
- Respects the individual cultural backgrounds, home experiences, and interest levels of children.
- Stimulates the creation of important concepts through first-hand experiences and self-initiated discoveries.
- Students are encouraged (and supported in their efforts) to take risks.
- Students develop more self-direction and independence through a variety of learning activities and opportunities.
- Students understand the "why" of activities and events instead of just the "what."
- Students are encouraged to make approximations of learning, rather than focus on the absolutes of learning.
- Children have sustained time and opportunity to investigate topics thoroughly and to engage in reflective inquiry.

THEMATIC TEACHING: A SAMPLE PLAN

As indicated in Figures 1-2 and 1-3, thematic units offer teachers and students some unique opportunities to examine all the dimensions and ramifications of holistic learning. Thematic units are not, however, a simple hodgepodge of random activities or an "Irish Stew" of cross-curricular projects. We would like to offer a definition of thematic units we have used in a previous book—a definition we have found particularly useful in designing and implementing our own units:

> A thematic approach to learning combines structured, sequential, and well-organized strategies, activities, children's literature, and materials used to expand a particular concept. A thematic unit is multidisciplinary and multidimensional; it knows no boundaries. It is responsive to the interests, abilities, and needs of children and is respectful of their developing aptitudes and attitudes. In essence, a thematic approach to learning offers students a realistic arena in which they can pursue learning using a host of contexts and a panorama of literature.
>
> Fredericks, Meinbach, & Rothlein; 1993

In short, we like to think of thematic units as an instructional device to *expand* the learning opportunities of students and the teaching opportunities of teachers.

Perhaps, you're wondering how thematic teaching works. That is, how does a thematic unit work within the structure of daily lesson plans and curriculum guides. To assist you we have provided a daily plan from Laurice Childer's thematic unit on "The Changing Earth." Laurice is a fourth grade teacher in northern Louisiana and has been developing and using thematic units for five years. She has discovered that thematic teaching provides her with a multitude of teaching opportunities that not only excite her students, but get her excited as well. As a result, she has developed several units for various areas of her fourth grade curriculum. Since the district requires all teachers to follow a specific curriculum guide in each subject area, there are selected objectives Laurice must include in her lessons. She has found that these can be easily incorporated within the parameters of a thematic unit and, in fact, provide some of the framework for developing a unit.

The daily plan which follows illustrates how Laurice has captured the spirit and excitement of thematic teaching for an entire day. Please note how subjects have been integrated, how students are able to take responsibility for their own learning, how Laurice can act as a facilitator for learning, and how literature is a stimulant for the events that can and do happen in Laurice's classroom.

	Theme: The Changing Earth (Day #4—Volcanoes)
8:30–8:50 Opening	After putting away their book bags, students assemble around a table on which are several different daily newspapers (e.g. *San Francisco Chronicle*, *Los Angeles Times*, *New York Times*). Students are invited to look through the newspapers for articles regarding changes in the earth (volcanic eruptions, earthquakes, landslides, etc.). Selected articles are cut out and assembled into an on-going journal. One small group of students is creating a dictionary booklet

	entitled "My Earth Book." These pupils are creating a page for each letter of the alphabet (i.e. A = Abyss; B = Biosphere; C = Chasm; D = Dangerous). This group is using the book *Earth Words* by Seymour Simon (HarperCollins, 1995) as a reference for their dictionary.
8:50–9:15 Whole Class Instruction	Laurice shows the video "This Changing Planet" (National Geographic Society, Washington, D.C.; Catalog No. 30352) [This film explains how the earth is constantly changing its surface through weather, erosion, earthquakes, and volcanoes]. Afterwards, she takes the students outside to the playground and constructs a chemical volcano as follows: She sets a soda bottle on the ground and builds up a mound of dirt around it so that only the top of the neck shows. She puts 1 tablespoon of liquid detergent in the bottle. She adds a few drops of food coloring, one cup of vinegar, and enough warm water to fill the bottle almost to the top. Very quickly, she adds 2 tablespoons of baking soda (that has been mixed with a little water) to the bottle. She invites students to discuss the similarities between their artificial volcano and the ones depicted in the video. Students record their discussions in their science journals.
9:15–9:45 Writing Process	**Facts on File**—One group of students goes to the school library to research various books for facts about volcanoes. They collect information about the location of major volcanoes around the globe as well as the damage done by each volcano. **Journals**—Several students have taken charge of monitoring the events surrounding Mount Kilauea in Hawaii as reported in the local newspaper. These students are recording those events in their individual journals and are also comparing notes on their individual interpretations of those events. **Newspaper**—A small group of students have designed a weekly newspaper which reports catastrophic events that happen around the world. Each event is "assigned" a reporter and is developed into an article. **Interviews**—A variety of students have initiated a series of interviews with graduate students and professors at San Francisco State University. The interviews have centered around recent volcanic eruptions in the South Pacific, an earthquake in Eastern Europe, an interpretation of the Richter scale, and the effects of wind erosion in the midwest.
9:45–10:30 Drama Time	Students have been divided into four separate groups. Each group uses various play houses and other models to create make-believe towns located near major volcanoes (Mt. St. Helens, Kilauea, Mt. Pinatubo). Each of these "towns" is assembled on a sheet of plywood along with a clay model of a volcano. Students create skits based on each of the three different types of volcanic eruptions (Hawaiian-type, Strombolian-type, and Vulcanian-type) and the "effects" on those "towns." Students are invited to make videotapes of their skits.
10:30–11:30 Required/Optional Activities	**Group 1**—Under the direction of the teacher's aide, students are observing her manipulate a paraffin block on a hot plate to simulate the formation of a "hot spot" volcano—the type which formed the Hawaiian Islands over thousands of years.

	Group 2—Students use the Internet (http://www.askanexpert.com/askanexpert/) to contact working volcanologists requesting information on the effects of volcanoes, eruption rates, and temperatures of different types of lava. The data will be collected in the form of charts and graphs.
	Group 3—Students have erected a "Graffiti Wall" outside the classroom and have invited students from other classes to record their information or research about volcanoes. Later, these ideas will be reconstructed in the form of a giant semantic web.
	Group 4—After viewing the video "The Violent Earth" (National Geographic Society, Washington, D.C.; Catalog No. 51234) students are composing a book of adjectives and descriptive phrases which have been used to describe various volcanoes around the world.
	Group 5—Students have obtained the address of Hawaii Volcanoes National Park (P.O. Box 52, Hawaii National Park, HI 96718). They have written requesting the park's newspaper, descriptive brochures, and information on recent eruptions of Kilauea. The data will be compared with information collected from a variety of library resources and newspaper clippings.
11:30–12:00 Lunch	
12:00–12:30 Sustained Silent Reading	Students obtain books from the collection offered by Laurice and disperse throughout the room. Books selected include *Earthquakes and Volcanoes* by Fiona Watt (New York: Usborne, 1993); *Mountains and Volcanoes* by Barbara Taylor (New York: Kingfisher, 1993); *Volcano and Earthquake* by Susanna Rose (New York: Knopf, 1992); *Surtsey: The Newest Place on Earth* by Kathryn Lasky (New York: Hyperion, 1992); and *Volcanoes* by Gregory Vogt (New York: Watts, 1993). Several groups of two and three students have formed to share their selected books in cooperative reading groups.
12:30–1:15 Teacher Directed Activities	**Opening**—Laurice decides to open the day's lesson with an Anticipation Guide. Using the book *Volcanoes* by Seymour Simon (New York: Morrow, 1988), she has created the following set of statements which are presented to students prior to the reading of the book: Before After _____ _____ 1. Volcanoes happen all over the world. _____ _____ 2. More volcanoes happen in Hawaii than in any other state. _____ _____ 3. A volcano is the most destructive natural disaster in the world. _____ _____ 4. Volcanoes always occur along tectonic plates. _____ _____ 5. Volcanoes are rare occurrences. Each student is provided with a duplicated copy of the Guide and is invited to record "True" or "False" in the "BEFORE" column depending on their personal beliefs.

	Class Discussion—The class discusses the responses made on individual Anticipation Guides. Agreements and disagreements are voiced and ideas are recorded on a special area of the chalkboard. Laurice invites students to make predictions about the book. **Selected Reading**—Laurice reads the book *Volcanoes* to the class. Prior to reading she invites students to listen for statements or information which may confirm or modify their responses to the Anticipation Guide statements recorded earlier. She also stops periodically throughout the reading and invites students to change or alter their original predictions based on data in the book. **Closure**—Laurice invites students to assemble in small groups and complete the "AFTER" column of the Anticipation Guide (based on the information learned in the book, students record "True" or "False" in the space in front of each statement). Later, she encourages students to share reasons for their responses and any changes they may have made in their original recordings. Laurice encourages students to confirm their ideas through additional reading in other pieces of literature.
1:15–1:35 Storytelling/Read-Aloud	The students all gather on the large "Reading Rug" in the back of the classroom to listen to Laurice read the book *What If . . . The Earth* by Steve Parker (New York: Watts, 1995). Afterwards, students discuss volcanoes and lithospheric plates (this discussion will form the basis for extending activities related to other natural changes on the surface of the earth—earthquakes, glaciers, and erosion).
1:35–2:10 Art/Music	The art teacher, Christine Borsa, has posted a large sheet of newsprint in the school cafeteria. Students, in small groups, have been invited to create a large mural of the events that would happen during and immediately after a volcanic eruption. Christine has shared slides of Diego Rivera's murals which have been painted on public buildings throughout Mexico (this will be extended in later days into a series of geography and history lessons on the land and culture of Mexico).
2:10–2:40 Self Selected Activities	**Group 1**—A small group of students has created models of each of the four different types of volcanoes (shield volcano [Mauna Loa], cinder cone volcano [El Misti], strato-volcano [Mount Fuji], and dome volcano [Mt. St. Helens]. The models will be displayed in the school library. **Group 2**—Students are constructing models of the two basic types of lava (*pahoehoe* and *aa*) using modeling clay and photographs from various books. These will be displayed in the classroom with appropriate labels. **Group 3**—Students are creating an extended time line of the major events related to the continuing eruption of Kilauea volcano in Hawaii. Events are

	selected from those reported on TV, those obtained from the Internet, as well as those which appear in the newspaper. **Group 4**—Students are writing letters to students at the University of California–Berkeley. The college students are being invited to share information learned during a recent course—"The Geology of North America." **Group 5**—Two small groups of students are each putting together bibliographies of current trade books related to "The Changing Earth." These bibliographies will be shared with teachers in other classes.
2:40–3:00 Responding to Literature	Students are completing the reading of the book *Volcano: The Eruption and Healing of Mount St. Helens* by Patricia Lauber (New York: Aladdin, 1986). The class has been divided into three separate groups. The first group is discussing the similarities between Mount St. Helens and a volcano erupting in the South Pacific. A second group is developing a "Story Map" which outlines the major elements of the book in a graphic representation. The third group is summarizing the major points of the book in the form of a newspaper article to be included in the class newspaper—*Earth Watch*.
3:00–3:15 Daily Closure	The class is divided into "teams" of three students each. The teams are invited to discuss some of the items they learned during the course of the day, items remaining for them to work on in following days, and those items for which they would still like to obtain additional information. Each team's recorder shares some of the discussion with the entire class. Students are invited to share their ideas with parents upon their return home.
3:15 Dismissal	

As you look over Laurice's plan for one day of her "The Changing Earth" unit you will note a variety of learning options for students. As you might suspect, the entire unit encompassed more than a single day—in fact, the unit is planned for three weeks of intensive investigation into all aspects of "The Changing Earth." Succeeding days included such topics and activities as:

- The world's most dangerous volcanoes
- The work of geologists
- Dangers of living near fault lines
- A guidebook on natural disasters
- A letter writing campaign to various universities
- Read-alouds by various community members including the town mayor
- Geological study of the local community
- Predicting natural disasters

- Creation of a diorama about glaciers
- Creation of an almanac of earthquake activity around the world over the past 100 years
- An investigation of rates of different types of erosion
- Creation of a salt map on the "Ring of Fire"

What is most striking about Laurice's thematic unit is not that it was based on a required component of the science curriculum (which she would have had to teach anyway), but rather that the events, activities, and projects included within the unit evolved from the suggestions and interests of her students. In a real sense, Laurice has created an "invitational" classroom—one in which students take an active role in the design, structure, and formation of any thematic unit. While Laurice may begin the process with the district's curriculum guide in a particular area, a collection of teacher resource books, input from colleagues and friends, or information collected at conferences and professional journals, it is her students who provide the bulk of the ideas and investigations Laurice builds into hers units. In so doing, she is offering her students an opportunity to take an active role in their own learning and an equal opportunity to assume a measure of responsibility for their own scholastic endeavors.

PLANNING THEMATIC INSTRUCTION

As you might expect, thematic teaching requires some planning and organization in order to make it successful. Our own experiences, as well as those of teachers with whom we have talked around the country, have indicated that there are five primary areas to consider in the design of an effective and successful thematic unit. These include:

1. Selecting the theme
2. Organizing the theme
3. Gathering materials and resources
4. Designing activities and projects
5. Implementing the unit

Let's take a look at each of those components in a little more detail. To assist you in designing your own units we will periodically share with you the processes Jean Ziebel, a fourth grade teacher in West Virginia, used in the development of a thematic unit on "The Environment."

1. Selecting the theme

The topics for thematic units can come from many sources. Here are a few to consider:

- **Curricular topics**—Themes or topics outlined in a basal textbook or in the district's curriculum guide(s).
- **Issues**—Local concerns or topics that affect students or their families directly.

- **Problems**—Concerns or questions which have a more universal application or appeal.
- **Special events**—A local or national celebration or holiday.
- **Student interests**—Special topics that capture student interest or reflect their hobbies and/or leisure activities.
- **Literary interests**—Genres of literature, author studies, or a special collection of related books.

The following chart provides you with a few possibilities to consider for the development of your own thematic units.

Theme Topics	Primary (Grades 1–3)		Intermediate (Grades 4–6)	
Curricular Areas	Animals The seasons Dinosaurs Weather Plants Staying healthy The changing earth Sun and moon Magnetism Simple machines	Light and Heat Neighborhoods Communities Transportation Growing up Family life Holidays Celebrations Sports Native Americans	Body systems Inventors The environment Oceanography Life cycles Work & energy Electricity Sound & light Solar system The changing earth	Space Mythology Geography Discovery Becoming a nation Pioneer life War & peace Multiculturalism Careers Ancient cultures
Issues	Homework Family matters Siblings Trash disposal Rules		Pollution Water quality Toxic wastes Air quality Nuclear power	
Problems	Energy use Crime Natural resources The environment Food		Ozone layer Starvation Population Oil spills Wildlife Solar power	
Special Events	Birthdays Winter holidays Circus Field trip Olympics Summer vacation		Shuttle launch Elections World Series Super Bowl Unusual weather Legislation	
Student Interests	Dinosaurs Monsters Sharks Airplanes Friends & neighbors	Vacations Space exploration Ocean creatures Scary things	Computers Famous people Ecology Environment Sports heros/heroines	Sports Relationships Clothes Vacations
Literary Interests	Nursery rhymes Fairy tales Sports stories Adventure Mystery	Poetry Fiction Books by a favorite author	Romances Legends Mysteries Autobiographies Sports heros/ heroines	Horror stories Outer space Books by a favorite author

The chart on the previous page is only a partial listing of potential topics which can be developed into thematic units. The textbooks you use in your classroom, your school district's curriculum guides in various subjects (and the policies related to the use of those guides), and your students' interests and suggestions can all be used as resources for the selection of thematic topics.

2. Organizing the theme

Once you have selected a theme topic your next step is to determine the skills and objectives for the unit, as well as the activities which will be used to foster an understanding and appreciation of those elements.

We have found two strategies to be particularly useful at this stage—one is called "Themewebbing;" the other "Bookwebbing."

Themewebbing

Themewebbing provides you with an outline form with which you can interrelate and integrate aspects of the elementary curriculum with a specific thematic topic. In so doing, you can offer students an opportunity to understand the universality of a topic as well as how that topic can be expanded and enlarged within each curricular area.

Indicated below is the outline Jean used as she began developing her thematic unit on "The Environment." She began by placing the title of her thematic unit in the center space on the *Unit Planning Form* (Figures 1-4 and 1-5). For each of the curricular areas, she brainstormed some possible activities and projects related to the general theme. She also invited her students to participate in this brainstorming effort too, offering them opportunities to suggest whole language activities which might expand their understanding or participation in the unit. What Jean discovered, as you will, is that whenever students are offered sincere opportunities to contribute to the learning milieu, they are more inclined to participate in that environment and, hence, learn from that environment. Thus, the successful planning of a unit involves input from your students as much as it involves input from you.

> You will note on the "Unit Planning Forms" (Figures 1-4 through 1-7) that there is a space to record the skills to be taught during a thematic unit. Thematic teaching does not mean the elimination of skill work for students. Instead, it means that skills are still taught, but in a more meaningful, realistic, and holistic manner. Depending on where you are teaching, you may be required to adhere to a district curriculum guide or a publisher's scope and sequence chart of skills. Using a thematic unit does not negate the teaching of skills, rather it offers a host of teaching possibilities for sharing those skills with your students and assisting students in using their newly learned skills in "real-life" situations and authentic literature. The "Sample Plan" presented earlier in this chapter is an example of how the grammatical skill of adjective use was incorporated into the structure of a thematic unit. We encourage you to consider the utilization of skills as a requisite part of the thematic units you create or the thematic units you use from this book.

Figure 1-4

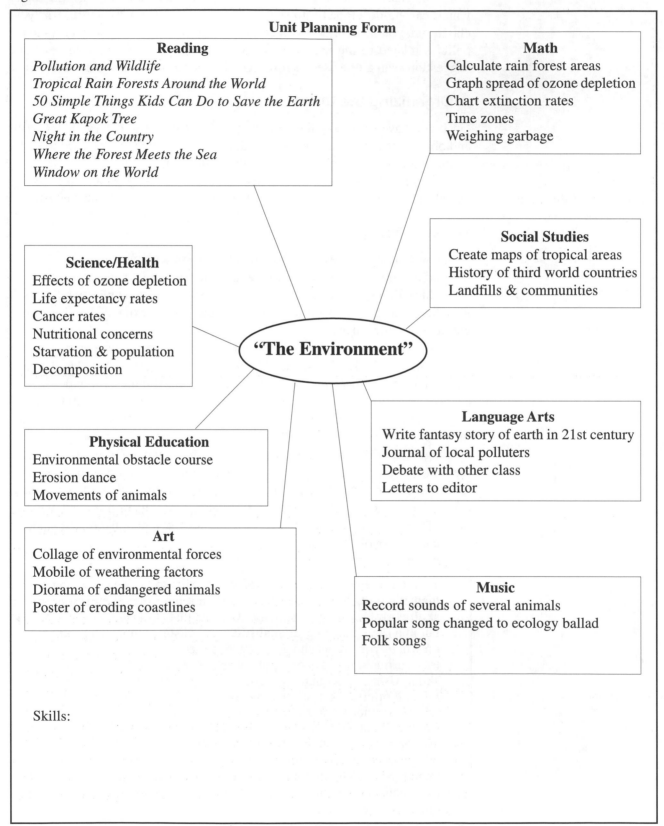

Unit Planning Form

Reading
Pollution and Wildlife
Tropical Rain Forests Around the World
50 Simple Things Kids Can Do to Save the Earth
Great Kapok Tree
Night in the Country
Where the Forest Meets the Sea
Window on the World

Math
Calculate rain forest areas
Graph spread of ozone depletion
Chart extinction rates
Time zones
Weighing garbage

Science/Health
Effects of ozone depletion
Life expectancy rates
Cancer rates
Nutritional concerns
Starvation & population
Decomposition

Social Studies
Create maps of tropical areas
History of third world countries
Landfills & communities

"The Environment"

Physical Education
Environmental obstacle course
Erosion dance
Movements of animals

Language Arts
Write fantasy story of earth in 21st century
Journal of local polluters
Debate with other class
Letters to editor

Art
Collage of environmental forces
Mobile of weathering factors
Diorama of endangered animals
Poster of eroding coastlines

Music
Record sounds of several animals
Popular song changed to ecology ballad
Folk songs

Skills:

Figure 1-5

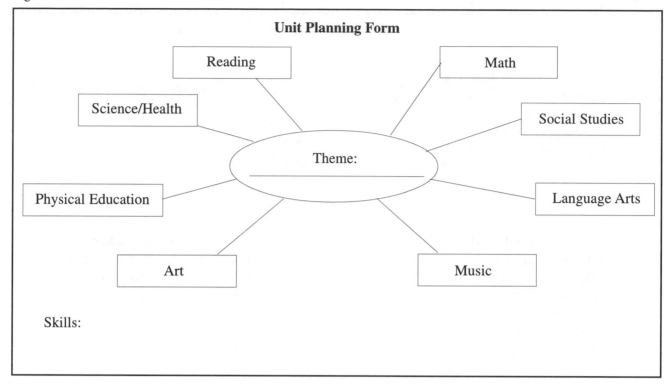

Unit Planning Form

Reading

Math

Science/Health

Social Studies

Theme:
_____

Physical Education

Language Arts

Art

Music

Skills:

Bookwebbing

Another strategy Jean uses to plan thematic units is called "Bookwebbing." Bookwebbing is similar to Themewebbing except in this strategy a literature selection is selected as the central focal point for the webbing procedure. That is, curricular extensions are tied to the material in a book—providing students with opportunities to expand the information in a book into all the other areas of the elementary curriculum.

Figure 1-6 is an example of how Jean used the book *The Great Kapok Tree* by Lynn Cherry (New York: Gulliver, 1990) as an initial literature selection for her "The Environment" thematic unit. It should be noted that "Bookwebbing" can be done with several related books selected for a unit. For example, Figure 1-7 is a preliminary outline for a *single book* within a larger thematic unit. To continue the development of the thematic unit, Jean would also use "Bookwebbing" with two or three other similarly related books (see Figure 1-8, "Unit Guide"). For example, she may wish to "bookweb" additional books such as *The Wump World* by Bill Peet (Boston: Houghton Mifflin, 1970); *One Day in the Tropical Rainforest* by Jean Craighead George (New York: Crowell, 1990); and *Going Green: A Kid's Handbook to Saving the Planet* by John Elkington (New York: Puffin, 1990). All four of these respective "bookwebs" could then be combined and assembled into a well-rounded and thorough thematic unit on "The Environment."

Figure 1-6

Book Planning Form

Reading
Where the Forest Meets the Sea
Rain Forest Secrets
Planet Earth
Tropical Rain Forests
The Giving Tree
The Wump World

Math
Visit recycling center—figure trees saved
Compare heights of trees
Count tree rings
Graph growth of trees at school

Science/Health
Classroom terrarium
Medicines obtained from trees
Health needs of Amazonian Indians
Adopt an animal
Growth rates of trees
Field trip to nursery

Social Studies
Location of rain forests around world
Companies that make life jackets
Initiate an "Ecology Club"

"The Great Kapok Tree"

Physical Education
Rain forest games
Rain forest obstacle course
Leap frog
Games played by Brazilian Children

Language Arts
Change ending of story
Write thank you letters to man from each
    animal
Share tree poetry
Letters to the editor
Obtain brochures from National Wildlife
    Federation

Art
Create "Save Our Home" posters
Make a collage of all animals in book
Create cardboard Kapok trees
Create rain forest environment in classroom

Music
Play Brazilian folk songs
Invent an "ecology song" using tune from
    popular song

Skills:

Figure 1-7

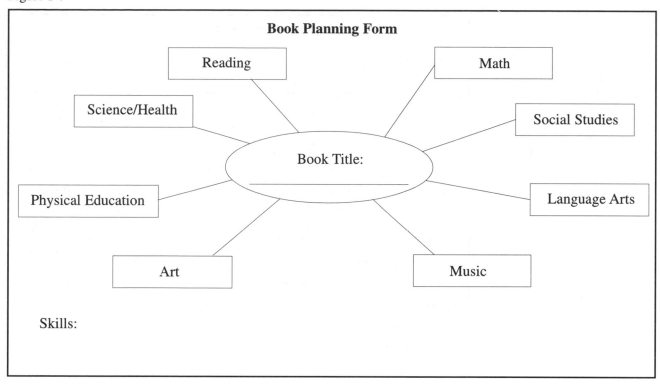

In planning activities for a book you will find it advantageous to consider:

1. "Pre-reading Activities"—those activities which "tap into" students' background knowledge and allow them to relate that knowledge to the information in a selected book.

2. "During" or "After" whole language activities that students can pursue within or across selected curricular areas (see Chapter 2).

3. A selection of open-ended questions used as "discussion starters" between yourself and students or among students. Obviously, these questions are not intended to "test" students on what they have read, but to help students think about the implications and ramifications of a piece of literature as it relates to the general theme.

The "Literature Log" (Figure 1-9) provides you with an easily duplicated planning sheet to assist you in this process. You may wish to consider this sheet as a supplement to, or a replacement for, the "Book Planning Form." Please feel free to use both or either one according to your own teaching or planning style.

Many teachers have discovered that "Bookwebbing" is an easy and practical way with which to design thematic units. Unit construction begins with a single book—then, two or three additional books are "linked" to the initial literature selection to create the basic structure for a thematic unit. The most advantageous aspect of this strategy is that students can be invited to actively participate in the design of the unit—particularly when they have been exposed to a plethora of children's literature and other thematic units. Their contribu-

Figure 1-8

Unit Guide

Theme: _____

Focus: _____

Objectives: 1. _____

                2. _____

                3. _____

Initiating Activities (whole language activities shared with students at the beginning of a unit and prior to the reading of any literature selections):

_____

_____

_____

_____

_____

Literature Selections:

Book #1:	Book #2:
Book #3:	Book #4:

Specific Skills: _____

_____

Culminating Activity (one or more whole language activities used to "round out" a unit and bring closure for students):

_____

_____

Mini-Themes (one or more mini-units related to the larger unit. These can be used in place of, or as a supplement to, the larger unit):

Mini-Theme #1:	Mini-Theme #2:
Mini-Theme #3:	Mini-Theme #4:

Evaluation/Assessment Strategies:

_____

_____

_____

Figure 1-9

Literature Log

Book Title:_____

Author:_____

Pre-Reading Activity:_____

_____

_____

_____

_____

Cross-Curricular Activities (related to book):

Reading:	Math:	Science/ Health:	Social Studies:
Physical Education:	Language Arts:	Art:	Music:

Specific Skills:_____

_____

_____

_____

_____

Open-Ended Questions:

1. _____
2. _____
3. _____
4. _____
5. _____

tions in the form of ideas and related activities help make the planning process meaningful and relevant, and the eventual thematic unit a positive addition to any content area. Some teachers have discovered that students can be major developers in the preliminary design of an unit—a factor that contributes to its eventual impact and success.

3. Gathering Materials and Resources

Thematic units differ from textbook-based units not only in their design, but also in the variety and types of materials used. Suffice it to say that thematic units can encompass a host of materials and resources—thus ensuring an abundance of opportunities for students to experience a "hands-on, minds-on" approach to learning. Obviously, your first consideration will be the types of literature you wish to use within a unit. After that, you and your students can work together suggesting and planning any number of materials and resources for use within a unit. Indeed, when students are provided with active opportunities to suggest resources, then they will be more inclined to use those items throughout the duration of a unit.

Here are some possible resources for you to consider in designing your own units:

Printed Resources

newspapers	brochures	letters
pamphlets	flyers	maps
notices	encyclopedias	advertisements
travel guides	dictionaries	catalogs
junk mail	magazines	
journals	booklets	

Visual Resources

videos	films	slide programs
filmstrips	CD-ROM	overhead transparencies
computer software	movies	

Literature Resources

1. Printed

    a. *Eyeopeners* by Beverly Kobrin (New York, NY: Penguin Books, 1988)

    b. "Outstanding Science Trade Books for Children" (March issue of *Science and Children*).

    c. "Notable Children's Trade Books in the Field of Social Studies" (April/May issue of *Social Education*).

    d. "Children's Choices" (October issue of *The Reading Teacher*).

    e. *Science Through Children's Literature* by Carol Butzow and John Butzow (Englewood, CO: Teacher Ideas Press, 1989).

    f. *Social Studies Through Children's Literature* by Anthony D. Fredericks (Englewood, CO: Teacher Ideas Press, 1991).

    g. *More Social Studies Through Children's Literature* by Anthony D. Fredericks (Englewood, CO: Teacher Ideas Press, 2000).

    h. *Science Adventures with Children's Literature: A Thematic Approach* by Anthony D. Fredericks (Englewood, CO: Teacher Ideas Press, 1998).

  i. *From Butterflies to Thunderbolts: Discovering Science with Books Kids Love* by Anthony D. Fredericks (Golden, CO: Fulcrum Publishing, 1997).

  j. *The Literature Connection: Using Children's Books in the Classroom* by Liz Rothlein and Anita Meinbach (Glenview, IL: Scott, Foresman and Co., 1991).

  k. *LEGACIES: Using Children's Literature in the Classroom* by Liz Rothlein and Anita Meinbach. New York: Harper Collins, 1996).

  l. *Booklist Magazine* published by The American Library Association (50 E. Huron St., Chicago, IL 60611).

  m. *Children's Books in Print* (Ann Arbor, MI: Bowker, annual).

  n. *Through the Eyes of a Child: An Introduction to Children's Literature* by Donna Norton (Columbus, OH: Merrill, 1995).

  o. *The WEB: Wonderfully Exciting Books* (The Ohio State University, 200 Ramseyer Hall, Columbus, OH 43210) (periodical).

2. Librarians

  a. Your school librarian
  b. The public librarian
  c. College librarian

3. Book Clubs

  a. *Scholastic Book Clubs.* 2931 East McCarty St., P.O. Box 7500, Jefferson City, MO 65102.

  b. *Troll Book Clubs.* 320 Route 17, Mahwah, NJ 07498.

  c. *The Trumpet Club.* P.O. Box 604, Holmes, PA 19092.

  d. *Weekly Reader Paperback Clubs.* 4343 Equity Dr., P.O. Box 16628, Columbus, OH 43272.

Technology Connection

It is safe to say that education no longer takes place solely within the four walls of a classroom. Technology has opened incredible doors to learning and teaching that expand the curriculum and enhance the educational parameters of any school. We, too, are great admirers and users of technology in our own classrooms knowing that what students can learn, and what we can teach, are both enhanced immeasureably.

The units in this book have all been designed with the best in children's literature and the most current resources and activities available. But, our knowledge base changes rapidly and, so too, should a thematic unit. The Internet offers you and your students marvelous opportunities to keep the ideas in this book fresh, current, and exciting. We encourge you to take advantage of this technology and incorporate it into the dynamics of any unit—those within these pages or those you create yourself. The result will be "energized" units and students who will understand and appreciate the relevancy of thematic instruction in their everyday lives.

To assist you in creating *evolutionary* thematic units we offer the following World Wide Web sites. These web sites can provide you with valuable background information, a wealth of literature resources, scores of up-to-date lesson plans, and numerous tools for expanding any area of your language arts curriculum. They can become important adjuncts to any literature-based reading program and can be used by teachers and students alike.

> *Note:* These Web sites were current and accurate as of the writing of this book. Please be aware that some may change, others may be eliminated, and new ones will be added to the various search engines that you use at home or at school.

http://www.afredericks.com
This Web site is designed to provide busy classroom teachers with the latest information, the newest activities, and some of the most creative ideas for using children's literature across the curriculum—with a special emphasis on the science curriculum. It's updated frequently with hundreds of exciting projects.

http://www.acs.ucalgary.ca/~dkbrown
This is the ultimate compendium of literature resources. It includes book awards, authors on the web, book reviews, recommended books, book discussion groups, children's literature organizations, best sellers, and scores of teaching ideas.

http://www.carolhurst.com/
This site has a wonderful collection of reviews of great books for kids, ideas of ways to use them in the classroom, and collections of books and activities about particular subjects, curricular areas, themes, and professional topics.

http://www.scils.rutgers.edu/special/kay/childlit.html
Here you'll find lots of resources and valuable information on how to effectively use children's literature in the classroom. The focus is on multiple genres and various methods for promoting good books to all ages and all abilities.

http://www.users.interport.net/~fairrosa/
Here are articles, reviews, lists, links, authors, discussions, and monthly updates about the best in children's literature and how to share it with kids. This is a great site for the always busy classroom teacher.

http://www.ipl.org
This is the Internet Public Library—an overwhelming assembly of collections and resources of a large public library. This site covers just about every topic in children's literature with an incredible array of resources.

http://www.ccn.cs.dal.ca/~aa331/childlit.html#review
This site is dedicated to reviewing WWW resources related to children's literature and youth services. These resources are aimed towards school librarians, children's writers, illustrators, book reviewers, storytellers, parents, and teachers.

http://i-site.on.ca/booknook.html
This site is a repository of book reviews for kids written by other kids. The reviews are categorized by grade level: K–3, 4–6, 7–9, and 10–12. It's a great way to find out what's popular among young readers.

http://www.armory.com/~web/notes.html
This site provides reviews of children's literature written by teachers and others who love kid's books. It's an electronic journal of book reviews concentrating on how well books are written and how well they entertain.

Artifacts

Depending on the nature and scope of your thematic unit you can use a variety of artifacts within that unit. For example, if you and your students were designing a unit on "Simple Machines" you might bring in artifacts such as a screwdriver, a pair of pliers, a knife, a doorknob, a small pulley, a can opener, and a small piece of wood. A unit on "Insects" might include artifacts such as a pair of tweezers, a magnifying lens, pins, display mounts, and a microscope. Obviously, the types of artifacts appropriate for a unit will depend on the topic of the unit. However, here are some resources who can assist you in obtaining and selecting necessary artifacts:

parents (see Figure 1-10, "Parent Letter")	students
school media specialist	computer specialist
colleagues	teachers in other districts
pen pals	relatives
community members	guest speakers
college professors	local high school teachers
public officials	social agencies
shop/store owners	senior citizens

4. Designing Activities and Projects

As you will note in the preceding sections, whole language activities are the crux of a well-designed and fully functioning thematic unit. We have discovered that the first few thematic units we have written have been the most difficult, simply because we were trying to organize a vast amount of information, ideas, and resources into a systematic and sequential framework. However, we also discovered, as have many other teachers, that once the first few units have been written, the rest become increasingly easier. That's not to say, however, that every unit will be straight-forward and easy. It does mean that practice in designing units makes the creation of future units that much more uncomplicated.

Here are some suggestions we have learned "along the way." We hope you find these useful in designing the activities and projects you wish to include in your units. Activities should:

- Incorporate one or more of the language arts—reading, writing, speaking, listening.

- Be holistic in nature.

- Emphasize a "hands-on, minds-on" approach to learning.

- Be cross-curricular in nature.

- Result from the ideas and suggestions of students.

Figure 1-10   Parent Letter

Dear Parents:

One of the sections of the local newspaper many people turn to for information is the weather report. The weather report is also a staple of the evening news on television. Indeed, most of us are very interested in the weather and often plan our outings and social events around the predicted weather for the day or weekend.

Children, too, are very interested in the weather. In fact, we are about to begin a science unit in our classroom entitled "The Weather and You." We would like to invite you to help us in this unit by donating some common household objects and items. Your child has checked the items below which he/she feels you might be able to share with all the students in our class. We hope that you might be able to contribute some or all of these items. Please feel free to contact me if you should have any questions. Thanking you in advance.

Sincerely,

_____

_____ soda bottle	_____ plastic wrap
_____ plastic cups	_____ measuring cup
_____ straws	_____ string
_____ cotton balls	_____ spray bottle
_____ spoons	_____ toothpicks
_____ various thermometers	_____ cardboard strips
_____ cellophane	_____ food coloring
_____ shoe boxes	_____ paper plates
_____ lunch bags	_____ eye dropper
_____ wax paper	_____ balloons
_____ funnel	_____ rubber bands

P.S. If you are interested, here are some children's books on "The Weather" you and your child may wish to check out from the school library or local public library:

Kahl, Jonathan. *Hazy Skies: Weather and the Environment*. Minneapolis, MN: Lerner Publications, 1997.

Kramer, Stephen. *Eye of the Storm: Chasing Storms with Walter Faidley*. New York: Putnam, 1997.

Lauber, Patricia. *Hurricanes: Earth's Mightiest Storms*. New York: Scholastic, 1996.

Simon, Seymour. *Lightning*. New York: Mulberry, 1999.

Sipiera, Paul. *Thunderstorms*. New York: Children's Press, 1999.

- Focus on the relationship(s) between a piece of children's literature and the "real world".

- Allow students to "tap into" their background knowledge and relate that information to what they are learning.

- Be based in a meaningful format that engages students in productive work (as opposed to "busy work").

- Be designed to last for differing periods of time (e.g. one hour, one day, one week).

- Be both instructional and motivational in nature.

- Relate to the general topic of the unit or the specific topic of a piece of literature.

It is important to point out that a thematic unit is *not* an arbitrary collection of random activities. It is a well orchestrated assembly of whole language activities designed to help students appreciate and comprehend a specific topic or a general idea. To do so requires an attention to the *types* of activities, the *variety* of activities, and the *purpose* of the activities selected. In other words, there must be a specific reason for the use of selected activities within a unit.

5. Implementing the Unit

Teaching thematically is not necessarily an "all or nothing" proposition. By that we mean that it is not necessary to use a thematic unit for a full day, a full week, or a full month. What it does mean is that you will have several options to consider in terms of how you will want to present a thematic unit to your class, how much you want it to dominate your daily curriculum, and how involved you and your students want to be. Obviously, your level of comfort with thematic teaching and the scope and sequence of your classroom or district curriculum may determine to degree to which you utilize (or do not utilize) a thematic unit. We offer the following options for your classroom. This listing, however, is only a partial collection of ideas. The dictates of your own particular teaching situation, personal experience, and student needs may suggest other possibilities or other alternatives to this register of ideas.

- Teach a thematic unit throughout a school day and for an extended period of several school days (see "Thematic Teaching: A Sample Plan" presented earlier).

- Teach a thematic unit for one-half a day for several days in succession.

- Use a thematic unit for two or more subject areas (e.g. science and math) in combination and the regular curriculum for the other subjects.

- Use a thematic unit as the "curriculum" for a selected subject area (e.g. science, social studies) and the regular curriculum for the other subjects.

- Teach a thematic unit for an entire day and follow up with the regular curriculum in succeeding days.

- Use a thematic unit as a follow-up to information and data presented in a textbook or curriculum guide.

- Provide students with a thematic unit as independent work upon completion of lessons in the basal textbook.

- Teach cooperatively with a colleague and present a thematic unit to both classes at the same time (this can be done with two classes at the same grade or two different classes—each at a different grade level).

- Use a thematic unit intermittently over the span of several weeks.

How you use the thematic units you and your students design will be determined by any number of factors. It is safe to say that there is no ideal way to implement thematic units into your classroom plans. We would like to suggest, however, that you consider a multiplicity of options—not only in the design of units, but also in their use.

The following Lesson Planning Forms, Figures 1-11, 1-12, and 1-13, will help you organize your thematic units in terms of your particular classroom and curricular parameters. Figure 1-11 provides a framework for considering various whole language options and the ways in which each can be used to enhance your thematic unit. The planning form in Figure 1-12 considers classroom dynamics, group planning and content area instruction, while Figure 1-13 offers an open-ended plan in which you can designate time frames for activities thus enabling you to plan thematically for extended periods of time—day, week or month.

Figure 1-11

Lesson Planning Form—I

Theme: _____

Opening (Time:_____ to _____):_____

_____

_____

Required Activities (Time:_____ to _____):_____

_____

_____

Optional Activities (Time:_____ to _____):_____

_____

_____

Sustained Silent Reading (Time:_____ to _____)

Writing Process (Time:_____ to _____):_____

_____

_____

Read-Aloud/Storytelling (Time:_____ to _____):_____

_____

_____

Teacher Directed Activities (Time:_____ to _____):_____

_____

_____

Responding to Literature (Time:_____ to _____):_____

_____

_____

Recess/Sharing (Time:_____ to _____)

Lunch (Time:_____ to _____)

Special Classes (Time:_____ to _____)

Teacher Directed Lesson (Time:_____ to _____):_____

_____

Daily Closure (Time:_____ to _____):_____

_____

Additional Activities:

(Time:_____ to _____):_____

(Time:_____ to _____):_____

Figure 1-12

Lesson Planning Form—II

Date:_____   Theme:_____

Introduction:_____

_____

_____

_____

Whole Group:_____

_____

_____

Mini-Lesson(s):_____

_____

_____

Learning Centers

Reading:_____

_____

Writing:_____

_____

Music/Art:_____

_____

Listening:_____

_____

Math:_____

_____

_____

Science:_____

_____

_____

Social Studies:_____

_____

_____

Closing:_____

_____

_____

_____

Figure 1-13

Lesson Planning Form—III

MONDAY _____

_____
_____
_____
_____
_____
_____
_____

TUESDAY _____

_____
_____
_____
_____
_____
_____
_____

WEDNESDAY _____

_____
_____
_____
_____
_____
_____
_____

THURSDAY _____

_____
_____
_____
_____
_____
_____

FRIDAY _____

_____
_____
_____
_____
_____
_____

Chapter 2
Strategies for Success

Aimeé Roerden has been a third grade teacher for nearly 11 years. Teaching in an inner city school in Los Angeles has given her a unique perspective on the experiences and needs of her students. Recently, she had grown frustrated at her inability to transform the facts and concepts of her third-grade curriculum into meaningful and relevant learning experiences for her students. She would "cover" the textbooks, but many of her students finished the year with poor attitudes, poor self-concepts, and poor mastery of the science concepts Aimeé felt they should know.

One spring Aimeé was given the opportunity to travel to the Annual Convention of the National Science Teachers Association. While there, she attended several sessions and workshops on thematic teaching and began to sense the enormous possibilities a thematic approach could offer her students. In talking with teachers from throughout the United States and Canada, Aimeé became equally aware of the energy and enthusiasm evident when thematic teaching was used throughout the day. Throughout the convention, Aimeé collected an array of ideas, techniques, and strategies for using thematic units and could hardly wait to return home to Los Angeles to plan for the following school year.

Aimeé realized that the best kinds of thematic units would be those she "built" with her students. That is, Aimeé wanted to offer her students these four basic concepts:

1. Active involvement—an opportunity for students to pursue their own questions within a the context of a thematic unit.

2. Empowerment—providing her students with a sense of "ownership" that would be both motivational and intellectually stimulating.

3. "Active learning contexts"—using thematic instruction to facilitate effective teaching and learning in every curricular area.

4. Personal connections—emphasizing the experiences and background knowledge her students brought to class while assisting each individual to become actively engaged in selected themes.

As the next school year began, Aimeé introduced her students to the concept of thematic instruction in science, as well as every other instructional area. She knew that the success of any thematic unit would be highly dependent upon a collaborative approach—an "invitational process" in which students are encouraged to contribute ideas and possibilities for exploration which are then "blended" into the instructional approaches, classroom methodology and teaching strategies proffered by Aimeé herself. The result would be a curriculum that engaged students in the dynamics of reading, as well as the dynamics of a truly integrated program—one which celebrates the "power" of children's literature and is founded on the utilization of all the language arts in a concert of holistic activities. What Aimeé and thousands of other elementary teachers have discovered is that thematic units help students use their developing literacy skills in meaningful contexts and as "tools" for further explorations and investigations.

Aimeé is one of a growing legion of elementary teachers who subscribe to the notion that reading involves an active and energetic relationship between the reader and the text. That is, the reader-text relationship is reciprocal and involves the characteristics of the reader as well as the nature of the materials. This philosophy of reading, often referred to as a *transactional approach to reading* is based on the seminal work of Louise Rosenblatt (1978) and has particular applications for teachers integrating literature into the curricular framework of any subject area. As you might expect, it serves as a foundation for the construction, implementation, and effectiveness of thematic units. Here are some principles of *reading instruction* and *reading literature* (adapted from Rosenblatt, 1978) particularly useful for classroom teachers:

1. Reading is a lived-through experience or event. The reader "evokes" the text, bringing a network of past experiences with the world, with language and with other texts.

2. The meaning is neither in the reader nor in the text, but in the reciprocal transaction between the two.

3. There is no single correct reading of a literary text.

4. In any specific reading activity, given agreed upon purposes and criteria, some readings or interpretations are more defensible than others.

In brief, this suggests that we all have our own unique backgrounds of experience which we bring to any reading material. As a result, we will all have our own unique and personal interpretation of that material—an interpretation which may or may not be similar to the interpretations of others reading the same text. Thus, reading a piece of literature opens up interpretive possibilities for youngsters and provides opportunities for extending that literature in personal and subjective ways. The point we wish to defend is that children's literature (within the context of a thematic unit) enhances the curriculum and enhances children's thinking, interpretation, and appreciation of that curriculum in meaningful and personally reflective ways.

Encouraging youngsters to become actively and meaningfully engaged with text demands a systematic approach to reading instruction. Traditional practices (e.g. Directed Reading Activity) have placed the burden of responsibility on the shoulders of teachers who directed much of the learning and much of the interpretation of textual material. Current views (e.g. transactional views) place a great deal of responsibility on the shoulders of students. Two differing models predominate here and are illustrated in Table 2-1 (adapted from Pincus, 1986).

The transactional approach described in Table 2-1 organizes instruction in three phases:

Before Reading: Strategies designed to link students' background knowledge and experiences to the text.

During Reading: Strategies designed to help students read constructively and interact with text.

After Reading: Strategies designed to deepen and extend students' responses to text.

Table 2-2 illustrates each of these three divisions along with suggested activities and strategies teachers can promote and students can examine independently. This list, while not finite, suggests possibilities for the literature you use within your reading program and within the context of any thematic unit. Suffice it to say, you would not want to utilize all of these ideas; rather, you may wish to consider possibilities within each of the three major areas as options for

Table 2-1

Traditional vs. Transactional Teaching	
Traditional Directed Reading Activity	**Transactional** Before, During, After Paradigm
Readiness & Motivation • Teacher sets purposes for reading • Teacher talk predominates • Teacher discusses vocabulary and predetermined concepts • No writing is involved	*Before* • Students make predictions about story • Teacher helps activate prior knowledge • Students share in multiple grouping formats • Students write, talk, listen, and read with each other
Oral/Silent Reading • Students read silently • Sometimes students read in round robin situations	*During* • Teacher may read aloud or students may read silently • Students relate what they are reading to prior experiences • Students annotate while they read (i.e. questioning, journaling, comparing)
Follow-up Activities • Students answer comprehension questions (with pre-determined answers) • Teacher selects writing topics • Students complete worksheets (with pre-determined answers) • Teacher teaches specific skills	*After* • Students discuss and share what they have read • Students engage in problem solving activities • Students participate in self-initiated activities • Students initiate discovery activities

Table 2-2

CONTEXT	Before, During, and After Activities and Strategies	
	Teacher Responsibilities	**Student Tasks/Activities**
Before Reading	• Encourage students to activate background knowledge • Help students establish purposes for reading • Encourage students to generate questions • Invite students to make predictions about text • Encourage students to construct semantic webs • Stimulate prediction-making • Encourage journal entries • Present skills	• Brainstorm concepts and key ideas • Journal past experiences • Categorize, web, and map • Establish own purpose for reading • Create self-initiated questions • Survey material • View film, filmstrip, slides, video • Make predictions • Draw, build, sketch • Link with previous readings
During Reading	• Model metacognitive and cognitive processes • Invite students to verify and/or reformulate predictions • Encourage students to integrate new data with prior knowledge • Help students think about what they are reading • Invite students to summarize text • Read aloud • Encourage additional questions • Incorporate skills	• Locate answers to self-initiated questions • Role playing • Silent reading • Journaling • Partner reading • Read aloud • Ask questions • Add information and concepts to previously constructed webs • Taking notes • Re-reading as necessary • Small group sharing
After Reading	• Encourage retellings • Encourage students to reflect on what was read • Invite students to evaluate predictions and purposes • Promote closure between pre-reading and post-reading • Develop questions that guide reading • Encourage students to respond to text through a variety of holistic endeavors • Assist students in linking background knowledge with text knowledge • Encourage students to seek additional information • Reflect on skills	• Retellings • Discussions • Debates • Panel discussions • Dramatization • Reader's theatre • Simulations • Role playing • Oral presentations • Mapping • Journaling • Pen pals • Reading related materials • Viewing slides, videos, etc. • Interviews • Library research • Storytelling • Response groups • Writing conferences • Puppetry • Book talks • Story mapping • Problem solving

the design of any literature-based lessons. In so doing, you will be assisting your students in becoming responsible readers and will be encouraging them to interact with all the dimensions of text.

What is evident from Table 2-2 is that children's literature provides a vehicle through which students can begin to assume some responsibility for their own learning and through which teachers can become facilitators for that process. When literature is organized within the framework of a thematic unit, youngsters are provided with a multitude of learning possibilities and a plethora of reading discoveries.

STRATEGIES YOU CAN USE

If you support the notion of children's literature woven throughout the elementary curriculum, then it seems likely that you would want to use that literature in ways which stimulate reading development and conceptual understandings in a host of contexts. We would like to share with you some techniques and strategies you may find helpful, not only in terms of specific books and reading selections, but also in terms of the overall impact of a thematic unit within a particular subject area. Periodically, we would like to share with you how selected strategies have been used effectively by various classroom teachers. We invite you to use their experiences as models for the implementation of a *transactional approach to reading* in your classroom.

We do not mean to suggest that all of these ideas should be used at one time with a single book. Instead, our intent is to offer you a selection from which you can choose and begin to build meaningful and lasting experiences with all sorts of literature—either singly or within the framework of a thematic unit. As before, this is not intended to be a finite list but, rather, a starting point from which you can create lesson plans that assist your students in becoming competent and energetic readers.

BEFORE READING

Semantic Webbing

One method used as a framework for making linkages between prior knowledge and knowledge encountered in text is semantic webbing. Semantic webbing is a graphic display of students' words, ideas, and images in concert with textual words, ideas, and images. A semantic web helps students comprehend text by activating their background knowledge, organizing new concepts, and discovering the relationships between the two.

Semantic webbing includes the following steps:

1. A word or phrase central to the story is selected and written on the chalkboard.

2. Students are encouraged to think of as many words as they can that relate to the central word. These can be recorded on separate sheets or on the chalkboard.

3. Students are asked to identify categories that encompass one or more of the recorded words.

4. Category titles are written on the board. Students then share words from their individual lists or the master list appropriate for each category. Words are written under each category title.

5. Students should be encouraged to discuss and defend their word placements. Predictions about story content can also be made.

6. After the story has been read, new words or categories can be added to the web. Other words or categories can be modified or changed depending upon the information gleaned from the story.

David McManus uses semantic webbing in his classroom for individual books, thematic units, or topics and ideas he wishes to explore with his students. For the "Communities" unit, David wrote the word *communities* on the chalkboard and invited his students to brainstorm for all the words or concepts they knew about communities. After the chalkboard had been covered with words, David invited students to work in small groups to organize the words into several selected categories and to provide a title for each category. Afterwards, David asked separate groups to record their categories on the board and to explain their choice of words within groupings to the entire class. Discussion then centered on selecting the most representative categories for the forthcoming unit. A "Master Web," developed by the students, was drawn on the chalkboard. The identified category titles were drawn in white chalk, and the items selected for each category were recorded on the radiating "spokes" in yellow chalk (see Figure 2-1). During the course of the unit, as new ideas and concepts were being learned, students added more words and ideas to the "Master Web" in pink chalk. Thus, students were able to see the relationships that can exist between their background knowledge (yellow chalk) and what they were learning within the thematic unit (pink chalk).

Figure 2-1   Master Web Sample

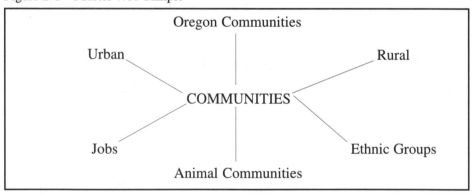

Student Motivated Active Reading Technique (S.M.A.R.T)

S.M.A.R.T. is a comprehension strategy providing students opportunities to become personally involved in reading—both expository and narrative. Self-initiated questions and concept development underscore the utility of S.M.A.R.T. throughout a wide range of reading situations and abilities.

S.M.A.R.T, which is appropriate for individuals, as well as small and large groups, can be organized as follows:

1. A book, story, or reading selection is chosen for the group to discuss.

2. The title of the book is recorded on the chalkboard and the group members are encouraged to ask questions about the title of the contents of the selection. All questions are recorded.

3. The group makes predictions about the content of the selection. Students decide on the questions they feel to be most appropriate for exploration.

4. Any illustrations found in the book or story are examined and additional questions are proposed. The initial prediction(s) is modified or altered according to information shared on the illustrations.

5. The group reads the selection (either orally or silently) looking for answers to the recorded questions. Also, new questions may be generated for discussion as well. As answers are found in the text, the individual or group talks about them and attempts to arrive at mutually satisfying responses.

6. The procedure continues throughout the remainder of the selection: (a) seeking answers to previously generated questions, and (b) continuing to ask additional questions. Upon completion of the book, all recorded questions and answers provided in the selection are discussed. The group decides on all appropriate answers. Questions that were not answered from the text are also shared. Students are encouraged to refer back to the book to answer any lingering questions.

Concept Cards

Concept Cards allow students to tap into their background knowledge about the topic of a book, share that information with classmates, and make predictions about the content of a piece of literature. At the same time, students can manipulate their vocabulary and share ideas related to word study and comprehension of text. Although this strategy works particularly well with non-fiction materials, it can also be used with narrative text.

1. Before students read a book, select 20–25 words from throughout the book. It is preferable to have words from the front, middle, and back of the book. Include words you know students are familiar with, words essential to comprehension of text, and a few unknown words.

2. Print each set of words on index cards and distribute each set to a small group of students.

3. Invite students to assemble the cards into categories of their own choosing (NOTE: Do not tell them a specific number of categories or the number of "word cards" that should be in each grouping). Encourage students to place words in categories according to their own knowledge of those words or their predictions of how those words might be used in the forthcoming text.

4. Invite student groups to share their various categories and grouping and provide rationale for the placement of word cards within specific groups.

5. Invite students to read the text looking for the words on the index cards. After reading, encourage students to rearrange cards or manipulate words into new categories or groupings based on the information gleaned from

the text. Afterwards, invite students to discuss reasons for any rearrangements and compare their placements with those of other groups.

As part of the unit on "African Animals," Holly Piccone and her students wanted to investigate some of the fauna of different regions of the African continent. Holly was able to introduce her students to a wide range of literature describing the animal life of Africa. One of the books she used was *Elephants for Kids* by Anthony D. Fredericks (Minnetonka, MN: NorthWord Press, 1999) [This book provides young readers with fascinating information about African and Asian elephants as narrated by a Kenyan boy]. In preparation for their study of the book, Holly prepared several sets of Concept Cards. She selected 25 words from the book and typed each word on five separate index cards (thus creating five sets of 25 words each). Holly selected words from throughout the book including words known by her students, as well as additional vocabulary important to their overall comprehension. The words illustrated in Figure 2-2 are those Holly used with her students.

Figure 2-2

Concept Card Words

Kenya	bull	cow	species	India
savanna	gestation	forest	herd	calf
female	male	matriarch	leader	migration
memory	trunk	muscle	organ	pregnant
tusk	incisor	ivory	zoologist	herbivore

Holly presented each of five separate groups of students with a set of Concept Cards and invited them to arrange their cards in categories of their own choosing. Afterwards, each group was invited to share their categories and groupings with the entire class. Discussion centered on some of the differences between the groups and the various types of background information shared within groups.

Later, Holly read the book to her students, inviting them to listen for the words identified on the Concept Cards. Upon finishing the book, Holly asked her students to rearrange and reassemble the cards according to the information they learned in the book. As before, students worked in groups, sharing and comparing data and facts learned from the book. Students were encouraged to discuss any differences between the arrangement of cards before the reading of the book and new arrangements made after hearing Holly read the book aloud. Students were amazed to discover the ways in which their background information could be combined with the book information to create a host of new categories and groupings.

K-W-L

K-W-L (Ogle, 1986) is a three step framework which helps students access appropriate information in expository writing. It takes advantage of student's background knowledge and helps demonstrate relationships between that knowledge and the information in text.

K-W-L (What I *Know*, What I *Want* to Learn, What I *Learned*) involves students in three major cognitive steps—accessing their background knowledge about a topic, determining what students would like to learn about that subject, and evaluating what was learned about the topic. Figure 2-3 sets up a paradigm through which teachers and students can begin to read expository text. The following steps can be utilized (each number is keyed to the Strategy Sheet in Figure 2-3):

Figure 2-3

K-W-L STRATEGY SHEET

1. K—What we know	4. W—What we want to find out	6. L—What we learned & still need to learn

2. *Categories of information we expect to use:*

A.   E.

B.   F.

C.   G.

D.   H.

3. *Predictions on the information included in the text:*

A.

B.

C.

D.

5. *Answers to self-initiated questions discovered in the text:*

SOURCE: Adapted from Ogle, D. "K-W-L: A Teaching Model That Develops Active Reading of Expository Text", *The Reading Teacher*, February 1986, pp. 564–570. Reprinted with permission The International Reading Association.

---

1. Invite students to talk about what they already know about the topic of the text. This information should be freely volunteered and written on the chalkboard or in the first section (K—What we Know) of the chart (which can be duplicated and given to the class).

2. Encourage students to categorize the information they have volunteered. This can be done through various grouping strategies such as semantic webbing. These groupings can be recorded in Section 2 on the chart.

3. Invite students to make predictions about the types of information the text will contain. These predictions should be based on their background knowledge as well as the categories of information elicited in Section 2.

4. Encourage students to generate their own questions about the text. These can be discussed and recorded in the "W—What we want to find out" section of the chart.

5. Invite students to read the text and record any answers to their questions. Students may wish to do this individually or in small groups.

6. Upon completion of the text provide students with an opportunity to discuss the information learned and how that data relates to their prior knowledge. Talk about questions posed for which no information was found in the text. Help students discover other sources for satisfying their inquiries.

Anticipation Guide

Anticipation Guides alert students to some of the major concepts in textual material before it is read. As such, students have an opportunity to share ideas and opinions, as well as activate their prior knowledge about a topic before they read about that subject. It is also a helpful technique for eliciting students' misconceptions about a subject. Students become actively involved in the dynamics of reading a specified selection because they have an opportunity to talk about the topic before reading about it.

1. Read the story or selection and attempt to select the major concepts, ideas, or facts in the text. For example, in a selection on "Weather" the following concepts could be identified:
   a. There are many different types of clouds.
   b. Different examples of severe weather include tornadoes, hurricanes, and thunderstorms.
   c. Precipitation occurs in the form of rain, snow, sleet, and hailstones.
   d. Many types of weather occur along "fronts."

2. Create 5-10 statements (not questions) that reflect common misconceptions about the subject, are ambiguous, or are indicative of students' prior knowledge. Statements can be written on the chalkboard or photocopied and distributed. [Using concepts for oceanography, the statements indicated in Figure 2-4 could be used.]

3. Give students plenty of opportunities to agree or disagree with each statement. Whole class or small group discussions would be appropriate. After discussions, let each individual student record a positive or negative response to each statement. Initiate discussions focusing on reasons for individual responses.

4. Direct students to read the text, keeping in mind the statements and their individual or group reactions to those statements.

5. After reading the selection, engage the class in a discussion on how the textual information may have changed their opinions. Provide students with a opportunity to record their reactions to each statement based upon what they read in the text. It is not important for a consensus to be reached, nor that the students agree with everything the author states. Rather, it is more important for students to engage in an active dialogue which allows them to react to the relationships between prior knowledge and current knowledge.

As part of Ted Pringle's 5th grade unit on "Oceanography" students had expressed an interest in learning about some of the dangers facing the world's oceans. The effects of a recent oil spill off the New Jersey coast had received front page coverage in the *New York Times* and had sparked students' curiosity about how oil spills and other environmental hazards affected the local flora and fauna. Based on his students' interests, Ted introduced his class to the book *Exploring the Oceans: Science Activities for Kids* by Anthony D. Fredericks (Golden, CO: Fulcrum Publishing, 1999) [This book contains dozens of hands-on projects and activities that help students learn and appreciate this important ecosystem.]. In preparation for their study of Chapter 8 of the book, Ted prepared the Anticipation Guide as seen in Figure 2-4.

Figure 2-4

Oceanography Anticipation Guide

Directions: Look at the sentences on this page. The statements are numbered from 1 to 6. Read each sentence; if you think that what it says is right, print *Yes* on the line under the word BEFORE. If you think the sentence is wrong, print *No* on the line under the word BEFORE. Do the same thing for each sentence. Remember how to do this because you will do it again *after* you read the selection.

BEFORE   AFTER

_____   _____   1. There is only one way to clean up an oil spill.

_____   _____   2. An oil spill is dangerous to sea and land creatures, but not birds.

_____   _____   3. Untreated sewage is dumped directly into the ocean.

_____   _____   4. Bottom-feeding fish eat cigarette butts.

_____   _____   5. Laundry detergent is a pollutant.

_____   _____   6. The oceans of the world are in serious danger.

Working as a class, students responded to each of the statements on the Anticipation Guide. Class discussion centered on reasons for their choices and predictions about what they might discover in the forthcoming chapter. Ted then provided multiple copies of the book to students and invited them to read and locate confirming data related to each of the identified statements. Afterwards, students completed the AFTER column of the guide and shared their reasons for placing *Yes* or *No* on each line. Follow-up discussions revealed some differences of opinion, yet the conversation was lively as well as supportive. Students found that they each brought different perspectives to a book, yet they could all benefit from those differences in a mutually stimulating learning environment.

Anticipation Guides are also appropriate for use with fiction material. In Figure 2-5, note how the book *The Salamander Room* by Anne Mazer (New York: Knopf, 1991) could be developed into an anticipation guide [as part of a thematic unit on "Animals" or "Ecology"].

Figure 2-5

Salamander Anticipation Guide

Directions: Look at the sentences on this page. The statements are numbered from 1 to 5. Read each sentence; if you think that what it says is right, print *Yes* on the line under the word BEFORE. If you think the sentence is wrong, print *No* on the line under the word BEFORE. Do the same thing for each sentence. Remember how to do this because you will do it again *after* you read the book *The Salamander Room*.

BEFORE   AFTER

_____   _____   1. Salamanders live under dried leaves.

_____   _____   2. Most salamanders are orange in color.

_____   _____   3. Salamanders eat crickets and other insects for food.

_____   _____   4. The diet of salamanders is similar to the diet of frogs.

_____   _____   5. Salamanders are an important part of the ecology of the forest.

_____   _____   6. People should not remove animals from their natural Habitat.

Semantic Feature Analysis

This strategy provides opportunities for students to share ideas about word concepts and vocabulary used in a piece of literature. It can assist students in making decisions about how words are related and stimulates discussions about the features of both familiar and unfamiliar vocabulary.

1. Identify a major topic from a forthcoming book. Using the SFA Grid in Figure 2-6, select a category of words which can be described with multiple features (e.g. The topic is "Transportation"—words could be: *bus, motorcycle, airplane, barge, skateboard,* etc.; features might be *on land, on water, in the air, motorized, no wheels, four wheels, more than four wheels*, etc.

2. Invite students to brainstorm for words which relate to the general category. These words should be listed down the left hand side of the SFA Grid (e.g. *bus, motorcycle*). Then, encourage students to brainstorm for features of some of those words—these should be listed across the top of the grid (e.g. *on land, on water*).

3. Invite students to match a word with a feature by placing a "+" (match) or "-" (no match) in the place where a row and a column intersect.

4. Upon completion, invite students to discuss words with common features or features represented by more than one word. Encourage conversation about any agreements or disagreements.

A blank SFA Grid can be found in Figure 2-7.

Figure 2-6

SFA GRID

TRANSPORTATION

FEATURES --->	ON LAND	ON WATER	IN THE AIR	ON TRACKS	MOTORIZED	HAS WHEELS	CAN CARRY MORE THAN 3 PEOPLE AT A TIME		
MOTORCYCLE	+	-	-	-	+	+	-		
AIRPLANE	-	-	+	-	+	+	+		
BARGE	-	+	-	-	-	-	+		
SKATEBOARD	+	-	-	-	-	+	-		
BUS	+	-	-	-	+	+	+		

Figure 2-7

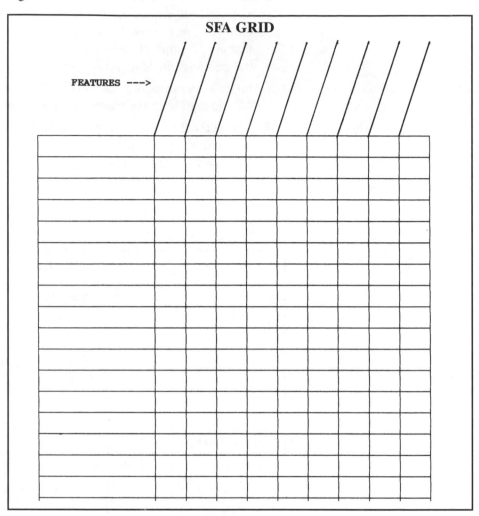

Reflective Sharing Technique

The Reflective Sharing Technique demonstrates the interrelationships that naturally exist between the language arts *and* specific curricular areas. This strategy stimulates children to use language as a basis for learning across the curriculum. The Reflective Sharing Technique encourages students to share and discuss ideas that are important to them; while, at the same time, reacting in positive ways to each other.

1. Choose a book or story appropriate to the interests of your students or their developing reading abilities. Record the general subject area of the story on the chalkboard.

2. For approximately 3–5 minutes invite students to brainstorm for as many ideas, concepts, or items that could be included in that subject area. These items can be recorded on the chalkboard. Brainstorming should stimulate a free flow of ideas, irrespective of their quality. The emphasis should be on generating a quantity of ideas and a wide range of responses.

3. Ask each student to select one of the brainstormed ideas from the list on the board. Invite each student to write about his/her selected item for about five minutes (this time limit can be adjusted according to the age or ability levels of students).

4. Sharing what each person has composed is the most important part of this activity.

   a. Students are divided into groups of four (it is very important to have groups of four for the sharing process). In each group of four, members take specific roles:

      1. Person #1—Reads what he/she wrote.

      2. Person #2—Summarizes what Person #1 read.

      3. Person #3—Tells what he/she liked about what Person #1 read.

      4. Person #4—Tells something else he/she would like to know about the subject upon which Person #1 wrote.

      Note 1: This completes Round 1.

      Note 2: If you can't get four students in every group (even with you as a participant) eliminate role #3 or #4 in one or two groups.

   b. After one round of sharing, the process is repeated until four rounds are completed and everyone has taken on all four roles (see Figure 2-8).

Figure 2-8

Reflective Sharing Technique Chart				
ROLE	Round 1	Round 2	Round 3	Round 4
Reads what he/she wrote	Person #1	Person #2	Person #3	Person #4
Summarizes reader's story	Person #2	Person #3	Person #4	Person #1
Tells what he/she liked	Person #3	Person #4	Person #1	Person #2
Tells something else he/she wants to know	Person #4	Person #1	Person #2	Person #3

5. Provide the groups with an opportunity to share some of the ideas discussed in their sessions(s) with the entire class (it is not necessary to have every group share; since some ideas will be redundant). Point out to students the wealth of information they already have about the subject of the book or story even before they begin to read it. You may wish to invite students to discuss how their backgrounds of experience melded with ideas in the book.

6. At this point you may wish to invite students to read the book independently or share the book with them in an oral format.

   Note: With younger students you may wish to conduct the Reflective Sharing Technique as an oral activity. Designated students are selected to talk about special interests. The entire class takes on the roles of summarizer, positive reactor, and those asking about other things they would like to know.

DURING READING

Directed Reading-Thinking Activity (DRTA)

The DRTA (Stauffer, 1969) is a comprehension strategy that stimulates students' critical thinking of text. It is designed to allow students to make predictions, think about those predictions, verify or modify the predictions with text, and stimulate a personal involvement with many different kinds of reading material.

DRTA's are guided by three essential questions which are inserted throughout the reading and discussion of a book. These include:

- *What do you think will happen next?* (Using prior knowledge to form hypotheses)

- *Why do you think so?* (Justifying predictions; explaining one's reasoning)

- *How can you prove it?* (Evaluating predictions; gathering additional data)

Vacca and Vacca (1989) outline a series of general steps for the DRTA.

1. Begin with the title of the book or with a quick survey of the title, subheads, illustrations and so forth. Ask students, "What do you think this story (or book) will be about?" Encourage students to make predictions and to elaborate on the reasons for making selected predictions ("Why do you think so?").

2. Have students read to a predetermined logical stopping point in the text (this should be located by the teacher before students read). This point can be a major shift in the action of the story, the introduction of a new character, or the resolution of a story conflict.

3. Repeat the questions from Step #1. Some of the predictions will be refined, some will be eliminated, and new ones will be formulated. Ask students, "How do you know?" to encourage clarification or verification. Redirect questions to several students (if working in a group situation).

4. Continue the reading to another logical stopping point. Continue to ask questions similar to those above.

5. Continue through to the end of the text. Make sure the focus is on large units of text, rather than small sections which tend to upset the flow of the narrative and disrupt adequate comprehension. As students move through the text be sure to encourage thoughtful contemplation of the text, reflective discussion, and individual purposes for reading.

Asking Divergent Questions

Use of some of the following questions throughout the discussion of text can help students appreciate the diversity of observations and responses they can make to literature. The intent is not to have students all arrive at "right answers", but rather to help them look at the diversity of thinking that can take place within a piece of literature.

Initially, you will want to ask students these questions as part of a whole class discussion of a children's book. The basic intent is to have students begin asking themselves these questions as they become more accomplished readers.

1. List all the words you can think of to describe _____.
2. What are all the possible solutions for _____?
3. List as many _____ as you can think of.
4. How would _____ view this?
5. What would _____ mean from the viewpoint of _____?
6. How would a _____ describe _____?
7. How would you feel if you were _____?
8. What would _____ do?
9. You are a _____. Describe your feelings.
10. How is _____ like _____?
11. I only know about _____. Explain _____ to me.
12. What ideas from _____ are like _____?
13. What _____ is most like a _____?
14. What would happen if there were more _____?
15. Suppose _____ happened, what would be the results?
16. Imagine if _____ and _____ were reversed. What would happen?

Prior to, and during, the reading of the book *Exploring the Oceans: Science Activities for Kids* by Anthony D. Fredericks (Golden, CO: Fulcrum Publishing, 1998) fourth grade teacher Carmella Lopez shared some of the following questions with her students. According to Carmella, "I was not my intent to force students into right or wrong answers. Rather, I wanted to help them think about the information we were learning from the book, how it related to their own lives, and how selected facts could be looked at from a number of viewpoints." Here are some of Carmella's queries:

- Make a list of all the words you can think of that describe an ocean.
- How would a seagull describe an ocean? How would a shark describe that same ocean?
- How would you feel if you were a piece of driftwood floating on the surface of the ocean?
- How are ocean currents like a river?

- You are a sea urchin. Describe your feelings about the rise and fall of tides.
- What do you think would happen if there were more salt in the oceans of the world?
- Suppose all the icebergs melted, what do you think might happen?
- Imagine that you had to live on a boat in the ocean for the next year. What habits would you need to change?

Carmella's intent was to assist her students in becoming active thinkers during the reading of selected literature throughout the thematic unit. While her initial focus was to provide students with books and activities on "Oceanography", a secondary goal was to help her students use reading as a vehicle for learning in any area or endeavor. The use of divergent questions helps students process information instead of just committing it to memory.

Self-Questioning

Providing students with opportunities to initiate their own questions throughout the reading process can be a valuable goal of reading instruction. Figure 2-9 provides you with a list of questions accomplished and mature readers tend to ask themselves. Here is a modeling procedure you may wish to follow:

1. Select a piece of children's literature.
2. Ask yourself (out loud) some of the *Pre-Reading* questions and provide answers for yourself (again, out loud).
3. Read the book aloud to the class.
4. Periodically through the reading continue to ask yourself questions (this time from the *During Reading* list.
5. Complete the oral reading and once more ask yourself a sampling of questions from the *Post-Reading* section.
6. After several readings, ask a student to come forward and model similar processes for the entire class.
7. Invite several students to demonstrate the steps outlined above.
8. Encourage students to select several questions from each of the three sections and respond to them in writing in their journals. After the reading of a piece of literature, use their questions and responses as discussion points in individual conferences.

Cooperative Learning

One of the ways students can be supported in their literature adventures is through cooperative learning.

Following are some brief examples of cooperative learning methods. It will be important to note how these methods can become integral elements of thematic units. Indeed, when students are provided with opportunities to learn from each other in the pursuit of mutual goals then the vitality and purpose of thematic units is enhanced and strengthened.

Figure 2-9

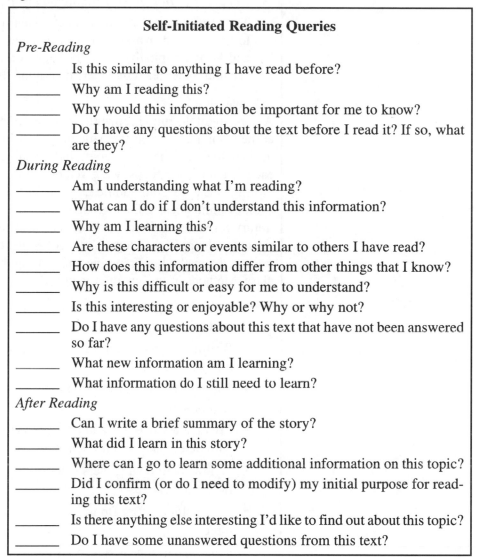

Examples of Cooperative Learning Methods

1. *STAD (Student Teams—Achievement Divisions)*

   Students are assigned to four-person teams, each of which is mixed according to ability, gender, and ethnicity. After the presentation of a teacher-directed lesson students work in their teams to master that lesson. Individual quizzes are given to each team member.

2. *TGT (Teams-Games-Tournaments)*

   This is similar to STAD, however quizzes are replaced with weekly tournaments in which teams compete against each other. Teammates help one another prepare for the tournaments through instruction, sharing, and coaching techniques.

3. *Cooperative Integrated Reading and Composition*

Teams are composed of individuals of varying ability levels. Groups work to read through an assignment and engage in productive activities (see #1 and #2) that capitalize on all the language arts. Students do not take quizzes until other team members determine that they are ready.

Example

As a result of the initial semantic web created by David McManus's students at the beginning of their thematic unit on "Communities" (see p. 40), David decided to divide the class into six individual groups of four and five students each. Each of the groups was given one of the original topics (e.g. "Urban," "Rural," "Ethnic Communities," "Animal Communities," "Jobs," and "Oregon Communities."). Each group was encouraged to investigate a variety of library resources and other printed materials to collect data and information related to their assigned topic. After collecting the necessary data, each group proposed a method of preparing and sharing the information with the whole class. Methods of presentation included:

- Preparing a group diary of essential information collected over a period of time.
- Writing a series of letters to students in another class about information learned.
- Putting together an informational brochure to be contributed to the school library.
- Creating a videotape and accompanying information packet to share with other classes in the school.
- Writing their own readers theatre script for presentation to one of the first grade classes.
- Assembling a "Big Book" of important facts and data related to their topic.

Each of the groups was responsible for collecting, evaluating, and presenting the information related to their assigned topic. In so doing, each group was able to work together on a clearly defined topic and assist other class members in comprehending that aspect of the larger theme.

4. *Jigsaw*

Students are assigned to six-person teams to work on material that has been divided into sections. Team members read and study their respective sections. Next, members of different teams who have studied the same material meet in "expert groups" to share their findings. Then the students return to their team and teach their teammates about the information.

5. *Web Weavers*

Three or four students work together prior to reading or discussing a story. A large piece of poster paper or chart pack paper is given to each group. Each member of the group is provided with a different color pen or felt tip marker. A preliminary semantic web for the story is drawn on the paper by the teacher and each student (in turn) records his or her background knowledge, or prior experiences around the categories designated on the web. Students discuss any similarities and/or differences. As the story is read, new data is recorded on the web.

6. *Prediction People*

Students are organized into groups of three or four and are provided with a prediction "map" (a large sheet of paper). Each member of the group is encouraged to write a prediction (for a forthcoming story) on the map and discuss his/her reasons for recording that information. The group talks and arrives at a common prediction. As the story is read, students are invited to stop at selected spots and change, modify, or rewrite their initial predictions. The groups' prediction is also changed, modified, or rewritten.

7. *Reader's Roundtable*

The class is divided into several small groups and assigned the same piece of reading. Each group is responsible for dividing the reading into several parts (as in "reader's theater") and assigning readings to individual members of the group. Afterwards, each group can share their interpretation with other members of the class. It would be important to discuss the differences in interpretation with class members.

AFTER READING

Continuums

The Character Continuum (Figure 2-10) is a delightful post-reading strategy which helps students discuss information related to the qualities and characteristics of selected characters in a story. With the following minor modifications, this strategy can also be used to help students focus on the setting a story.

1. Ask students to brainstorm for all the words they can think of that can be used to describe one or more characters in a story. Write all the words on the chalkboard or overhead projector.
2. Invite students to suggest antonyms for most, or all, of the recorded words.
3. Place each word pair at opposite ends of a continuum (see Figure 2-10). For primary level youngsters 6–8 lines are sufficient; for intermediate students 8–12 lines are adequate.
4. Invite students to work in pairs, small groups, or as a whole class to place an "X" on each line indicating the degree to which an identified character exhibits a particular trait (there are no right or wrong answers).
5. Encourage students to discuss their rationale for placement of the "X's." Rereading of portions of the book may be necessary to verify information or assumptions.

Figure 2-10

```
┌─────────────────────────────────────────────────────────────┐
│                   Character Continuum                        │
│ Book Title:_____   │
│ Character:_____   │
│                                                              │
│                                                              │
│ Friendly .............................................. Unfriendly │
│ Happy ...................................................... Sad │
│ Popular ............................................... Unpopular │
│ Wise ................................................... Foolish │
│ Outgoing ................................................... Shy │
│ Unselfish................................................ Selfish │
│ Sociable ............................................ Unsociable │
│ Ambitious .............................................. Lazy │
│ Neat ..................................................... Messy │
│ Honest................................................ Dishonest │
│ Brave ................................................. Cowardly │
│ Kind .................................................... Cruel │
└─────────────────────────────────────────────────────────────┘
```

6. Students may wish to create a "Master Continuum" which can be duplicated and used repeatedly with other characters in other stories. Separate continuums also can be developed for story settings.

Figure 2-11 is a Character Continuum that Ward Kessler's third grade students created for the book *The Island-below-the-Star* by James Rumford (Boston: Houghton Mifflin, 1998) [This is an engaging story about five brothers, each with a special skill, who set sail across the vast Pacific Ocean to the islands now known as Hawaii]. One of the major characters is Manu; and the continuum was created after Ward read the first part of the book to the class.

After students completed the Character Continuum, Ward read the rest of the book to them. He then invited them to consider repositioning any of their "X's" on the Continuum as a result of hearing the second half of the story. In this way, Ward helped his students understand that characters change, grow and develop throughout a story.

Figure 2-12 is an example of a Setting Continuum which can be used with students. The words and their antonyms have all been suggested by students in Mitch Gersten's third grade classroom. You are encouraged to invite your students to suggest their own words (and their opposites) for continuums used in your classroom.

A modification of the Character Continuum is the "Facts/Attitude Continuum" which is appropriate for use with non-fiction material. The procedure

Figure 2-11

Character Continuum

Book Title: *The Island-below-the-Star*

Character: *Manu*

Friendly ..... X .... Unfriendly

Happy ...X .... Sad

Popular .... X .... Unpopular

Wise ....X .... Foolish

Outgoing .... X .... Shy

Unselfish .... X .... Selfish

Sociable .... X .. Unsociable

Ambitious ..... X .... Lazy

Neat ....X .... Messy

Honest .... X ... Dishonest

Brave .... X .... Cowardly

Kind .... X .... Cruel

Figure 2-12

Setting Continuum

Book Title:_____

Setting:_____

Hot .... Cold

Urban .... Rural

Friendly .... Hostile

Flat .... Hilly

Near Ocean .... Far from Ocean

Colorful .... Plain

New .... Old

---

is similar to that outlined above, except that students are encouraged to suggest facts about a topic, as well as their attitudes or perceptions of that topic. These items (and their accompanying antonyms) are arranged on continuum lines like those shown in Figure 2-12. Students are invited to complete these after reading a book. [*Note:* This is also appropriate as a pre-reading strategy, too, with students suggesting ideas based on their background knowledge of a forthcoming topic.]

Figure 2-13 is an example of a Facts/Attitude Continuum created by Abby Heliker's second grade students in preparation for reading the book *Slugs* by Anthony D. Fredericks (Minneapolis, MN: Lerner Publications, 2000).

Figure 2-13

Facts/Attitude Continuum

Book Title: *Slugs*

Topic: *Slugs*

Author: *Anthony D. Fredericks*

Publisher: *Lerner, 2000*

Strong	.... X	Weak
Neat	.... X	Yuccy
Useful	.... X	Harmful
Eat Meat	.... X	Eat Plants
Important	.... X	Worthless
Live Birth	.... X	Eggs
Not Poisonous	.... X...	Poisonous
Fun	.... X.............................	Boring
Industrious	.... X	Lazy
Underground	.... X	Above Ground

Plot Graph

The Plot Graph allows students to design a graphic representation of the plot of a story. In so doing, they are able to use selected math skills in concert with a pictorial display of the sequence of events in a story or book. This post-reading strategy is particularly useful in helping students understand the utility of charts and graphs in realistic situations, as well as comprehend the "flow" of a story from beginning to end.

1. Provide students with graph paper and invite them to select four or five of the major events of a story to record (in sequence) at the bottom of the sheet.

2. Encourage students to record numbers up the left hand side of the graph indicating degrees of intensity.

3. After a story has been completed invite students to plot each of the selected events on the graph according to their own perceptions of intensity (see Figure 2-14).

4. Students may wish to use their Plot Graphs as an aid to journal writing or summarization activities.

Figure 2-14   Sample Plot Graph

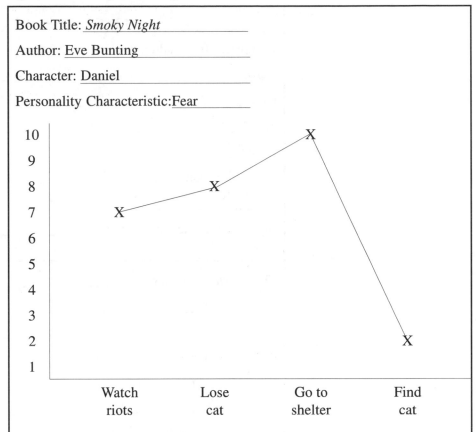

Book Title: _Smoky Night_

Author: Eve Bunting

Character: Daniel

Personality Characteristic:Fear

Summary: Daniel and his mother are caught up in the Los Angeles riots—something Daniel doesn't fully understand. During the rioting Daniel's cat is lost. He and his mother are sheparded to a local shelter where they meet many interesting people. Daniel is finally reunited with his cat.

Literature Log

A Literature Log provides students with opportunities to think about what they have read and to organize that information into a systematic piece of writing. These should not be interpreted as "worksheets" since there are no right or wrong answers to any Literature Log. They can be used by individuals or small groups of students as a way to record information and thoughts about a particular book. As such, you may find them important to use as assessment tools or as summary sheets to be maintained in each student's portfolio.

The first Literature Log (Figure 2-15) is appropriate for use at the conclusion of a book or story. The second log (Figure 2-16) can be used by students prior to, during, and after the reading of a book.

Figure 2-15

LITERATURE LOG—I

Complete after reading book.

Name:_____

Date:_____

Title:_____

Author:_____

My favorite part was: _____

_____

My least favorite part was: _____

_____

The central problem was: _____

_____

_____

Some important words were: _____

Words I need to learn are: _____

My favorite character was: _____

My least favorite character was: _____

I didn't understand: _____

I will never forget: _____

I would recommend this book to _____ because _____

_____

_____

Creative Questioning

Creative Questioning is a framework which stimulates children to think about common occurrences and events in creative and unusual ways. It is set up in the form of a paradigm using each of the letters in the word "CREATIVE" as a key to questions or writing activities which help students use traditional forms of grammar in different ways. The intent is not to have all youngsters reach the same conclusions, but rather to provide students with thinking activities that support their creativity and allow them to "play with" language in new and different way.

Figure 2-16

LITERATURE LOG—II

Complete prior to, during, and after reading book

Name:_____ Date:_____
Title:_____ Author:_____

Before Reading
Why I want to read this book:_____
_____

What do I know about this topic?_____
_____

What questions would I like to ask before I read?_____
_____
_____

What I think the book is about:_____
_____

During Reading
What am I learning as I read this book?_____
_____

What did I do when I didn't understand something in the book? _____
_____

Will I want to finish this book?_____
Why?_____
_____

Am I finding answers to some of my questions?_____
Is the main character(s) similar to any other(s) I have read about?_____
_____

How?_____
_____

After Reading
Why did the author write this book?_____
_____

Am I satisfied with this story?_____
Why?_____
_____

Can I write a brief summary of the story?_____ Here it is:_____
_____
_____

Would I want to read this story at another time?_____
What questions do I still need answers to?_____
_____

How can I find that information?_____
_____

Here's how the author could have made this a better book:_____

Figure 2-17 illustrates types of writing activities, discussion questions, and grammatical concepts that enhance childrens' appreciation of the varied uses of language.

Figure 2-17

CREATIVE Questioning Paradigm

C—*Combine:* Blend two or more details together.
"What would be the consequences if Snow White and the witch had the same personality?"
R—*Rearrange:* Change the order of events.
"What would change if the enchanted frog had been a princess instead of a prince?"
E—*Eliminate:* Remove one or more details.
"How would 'Curious George' stories (by H. A. Rey) be different if he didn't have a tail?"
A—*Adapt:* Use data from another source.
"What if Robin Hood had a gun instead of a bow and arrow?"
T—*Take advantage of:* Use story details in a different way.
"What would have happened if Goldilocks had eaten all of the porridge?"
I—*Insert something else:* Substitute new ideas.
"What would have happened if Mary had taken an elephant to school one day?"
V—*Vary:* Make changes in factual information.
"What would have been the consequences if Charlotte (in *Charlotte's Web*) had been a tarantula?"
E—*Exaggerate:* Magnify events or details.
"What would you have to change around your house if your dog was as large as Clifford (the Big Red Dog)?"

Cloze Technique

In the cloze technique, the teacher prepares sentences or paragraphs in which selected words have been omitted. The teacher may wish to delete every fifth or every tenth word, for example. Or, the teacher may wish to delete all the nouns or all the adjectives from a written piece of work. The written piece could be a student paper or a selection from a popular book.

When the teacher has decided on the words to be deleted from the piece, it is retyped leaving blank spaces for the deleted words (it is suggested that each blank be the same length so that students cannot infer words based solely on their length). The retyped piece can then be used with students as part of a group lesson or individual activity. The advantage of cloze is that it allows you to focus on specific grammatical concepts within the context of a familiar and contextually appropriate piece of writing. Students are then encouraged to work together, or by themselves, to replace the missing words with words that "sound right" or that make sense in the selection.

Following is a cloze piece developed by Laura Rubin for her third grade students. She took a portion of text from the book *Miss Rumphius* by Barbara Cooney (New York: Puffin, 1982) and retyped it onto a sheet of acetate for projection on the overhead projector. As she prepared the piece she deleted selected nouns and replaced each one with a blank of ten spaces. She then projected the story sample on the screen and invited students to contribute nouns which would help restore a sense of meaning to the original story (Laura was not interested in having students replicate the exact words he had deleted from the text, but rather wanted them to focus on a specific part of speech within a familiar book).

CLOZE Technique

Then my Great-aunt Alice set out to do the three things she had told her _____ she was going to do. She left _____ and went to live in another _____ far from the sea and the salt _____. There she worked in a _____, dusting books and keeping them from getting mixed up, and helping _____ find the ones they wanted. Some of the _____ told her about far-away _____.

Story Frames

A story frame (Fowler, 1982) is a basic outline of a story that is designed to help the reader or writer organize his or her thoughts about a story. A "frame" consists of a series of extended blanks (similar in nature to the cloze procedure) which are linked together by transition words or phrases. Story frames differ from cloze in that students are provided longer blanks to complete and are given more latitude in selecting appropriate words or phrases. Following is a story frame which could be used in helping students focus on a particular character in a story.

Story Frame

This story is about_____

_____

who is an important character. _____

tried to _____

_____

_____

The story ends when _____

_____.

Story frames, when completed, can serve as discussion starters for the components of good stories as well as an outline for students who need a support structure for the creation of their own stories. Obviously, the intent is not to have all students arrive at an identical story, but rather provide them with the freedom they need to create stories within appropriate grammatical contexts. The following examples offer additional story frames you may find appropriate for your classroom.

Plot Frame

In this story the problem starts when _____
_____
_____. After that _____
_____.
Next, _____
_____
_____. Then, _____
_____. The problem is finally
solved when _____
_____
_____.

Information Frame

This story was written to teach us about _____
_____. One important
fact I learned was _____
_____. Another fact I
learned was _____
_____. A third important fact I learned was ____
_____.
If I were to remember one important thing from this story, it would
be _____
_____ because _____
_____.

Character Analysis Frame

_____ is an important character in
this story. _____ is important because
_____
_____. Once, he/she _____
_____.
Another time, _____
_____.
I think that _____ is _____
because _____
_____. He/she is also _____
_____ because _____
_____.

The strategies you select for use with the literature within a thematic unit
can assist youngsters in becoming accomplished and interested readers. We do
not mean to suggest, however, that every book you share with your students
should be used as part of a reading/language arts lesson. It is equally important
that students be exposed to a wide variety of literature simply for the sheer
enjoyment of reading a book independently or hearing you read aloud to the
entire class. Thematic units provide a framework in which literature can be
shared in a host of venues, situations, and instructional settings. Be sure to blend
pleasurable book experiences with instructional experiences, too.

Chapter 3

Authentic Assessment

Bright sunlight peeked around the shades in Kenny Bachman's third grade classroom echoing off the walls and dancing across the posters, murals, triramas, and hand-made books that hung from every corner. A casual observer would have a difficult time locating Kenny in the groups of students who covered the floor, crowded into two of the corners of the room, or congregated around the classroom library or ten gallon aquarium on the science table. In fact, that same visitor would have a difficult time locating the walls of the classroom—a true print-rich environment on which, and from which, every manner of student work and creation hung. It would be interesting to note that not a single teacher-created bulletin board display or announcement was displayed on any surface—each entry bore the unmistakable signature of one or more of Kenny's third graders.

There was a constant noise in the room—not loud, but at a level signaling a great deal of activity and animation as students shared ideas, discussed strategies, or debated the merits of a shared book. Erin, Marcia, and Karyn were discussing the tribulations faced by Emmeline in *Prairie Songs* (by Pam Conrad [New York: Harper and Row, 1985]); Peter and Kwasi were working on a salt map of the American midwest; Lawrence, José, and Katrina were preparing a series of letters to be sent to the Departments of Tourism in selected midwestern states; and William, Arthur, Natalie, and Kwan were working on a reader's theatre adaptation of *Grasshopper Summer* by Ann Turner (New York: Macmillan, 1989). The room was buzzing with enthusiasm as students actively participated in self-selected activities related to their thematic unit on "Midwestern America."

Kenny, himself, was sprawled out on the floor under the display table near the closet. In front of him was Hector, a large manila portfolio, and an assortment of papers, charts, hand-made books, letters, and other items.

"Tell me, Hector," Kenny asked, "why did you want to include this book on Native American life in your portfolio?"

"Well, you see, Mr. Bachman, I did a lot of research in the books you got from the library and I interviewed Maria's mother after she showed us some of her weavings and I spent a long time writing the story about Lone Bear . . . well, anyway, Mr. Bachman, I think it shows all the hard work I put into the project. It sort of sums up a lot of what I learned."

"So what you're saying to me then, Hector, is that this entry in your portfolio is there because it's a good representation of some of the independent work you did in our unit."

"Yea, that's right, Mr. Bachman."

"O.K., then what would you like to write on your 'Reflection Sheet' for your portfolio?", Kenny asked.

"I'm going to say that I'm including this because I learned a lot about the hardships the early settlers had in the midwest. I also learned about some of the customs and traditions faced by Native Americans in that area, something that I never knew before. I would also like to put down that I found some new books to read that I didn't know about before."

"That sounds fine," Kenny replied, "and I think I'll record that your self-made book shows that you have learned several new things about the midwest especially about its climate, you developed an interest in the ceremonies of Native Americans which you researched through letters to my sister in Iowa, and are going to read some new books from the classroom library and share some of them with the class. How does that sound, Hector?"

"That's great, Mr. Bachman. Now I'm going to work with Julie and Bryan on that mural about different houses on the prairie. See ya later!" And off he scampered.

"See you, Hector," Kenny replied to the disappearing figure.

The conversation between Kenny and Hector was not by chance—it was systematic and planned. It had been scheduled on the large "I'm ready for a Conference" chart (a laminated sheet of poster board on which students affix Post-it? notes with their names whenever each feels the need to conference with the teacher). But, most important, that conversation was indicative of a new perspective on assessment—one which is student-driven, reflective, and holistic. Kenny sincerely believes that students should have input into the methods and procedures by which they are evaluated. He also believes that portfolio assessment encourages children to take personal responsibility for their individual progress and achievement within and throughout the language arts program. Kenny has discovered that this approach to assessment, not only expands the variety of ways in which student progress can be gauged, but also allows Kenny opportunities to take a more facilitative role in the thematic projects, activities, and discussions in which his students participate. Kenny believes that the information collected in each student's portfolio becomes a more accurate representation of involvement and growth than end-of-chapter quizzes and standardized tests. Significant, too, is the fact that students view assessment as an on-going process in which they are a participant, rather than an event controlled by the teacher and administered at the conclusion of a unit of study.

THE NATURE OF ASSESSMENT

To be effective, evaluation must be a continuous process. So too, must it engage students in the design of their own learning objectives and provide both teachers and students with useful data which can be used to enhance learning opportunities. In that light, evaluation is much, much more than the traditional pen and paper tests of yesterday; rather, it is more a *process* of reaction, reflection, and redirection. It is certainly much more than the simple administration of a test and the recording of resultant scores. It is a combination of factors and forces that should have a positive impact on children's literacy growth and development.

Let's take a moment and look at some of the purposes of assessment, particularly as they relate to thematic units. We believe that effective assessment:

- is a cooperative activity between teachers and students. In other words, assessment is not something done *to* students, but rather an activity done *with* students.

- provides opportunities for students to assume a sense of responsibility for their own learning. When actively engaged in evaluation, students become less teacher-dependent and more student-independent.

- respects the child and preserves and enhances the self-esteem of every child.

- should be used to improve instruction and gauge progress; not simply assign numerical scores to academic achievement.

- offers teachers and students viable opportunities to examine the learning process and make individual modifications as necessary.

- provides opportunities for teachers and student to work towards common curricular goals—both short-term and long-term.

Effective assessment is integrated into all aspects of a thematic unit, providing both teachers and students with data useful in gauging progress and determining the effectiveness of materials and procedures. In that light, it is important to consider assessment as a positive feature of thematic units—one woven into all its dimensions. This means that assessment is important during the initiation of a thematic unit, during the sharing of the unit, and even at the end of a unit.

Here are some considerations you may wish to keep in mind as you start designing your own units, use the ones provided for you in this book, or introduce commercial units. We like to think of these as the "Success Factors"—factors that can make assessment a positive feature of any thematic unit.

Assessment success factors include:

- Assessment should be continuous and ongoing—a constant process of evolution.

- Effective assessment utilizes a variety of evaluative measures—both formal and informal.

- Meaningful assessment should be child-centered.

- Successful assessment offers students active opportunities to self-evaluate throughout all aspects of a thematic unit.

- A well-designed assessment program promotes a collaborative spirit between teacher and students, as well as between students and students.

- Assessment should emphasize students' strengths and how students can build upon those strengths to become better learners.

- Good assessment is authentic in nature—it emanates from the literacy activities pursued by students, not from the artificial tests designed by large publishing houses.

- One of the most effective assessment tools is teacher observation—the interpretation of what children do, how they do it, and what they learn from their activities can be the cornerstone of a successful assessment program.

- Student portfolios (see below) are an efficient and effective way of tracking student progress over time and responding to the instructional needs of students in a variety of contexts.

It should be evident that effective assessment is more complex than writing a test, giving it to a group of students, scoring it, and handing it back with a numerical grade. It involves a combination of procedures and designs that gauge students' work while helping them grow in the process.

There are many forms of assessment that can be used with thematic units in this book or units you design on your own.

Consider the following as suggestions for use in your classroom. Obviously, we do not mean to suggest that you use all of these within the context of a single thematic unit; rather, the intent is to provide you with an assortment from which to choose according to the nature of a particular thematic unit, your own philosophy of teaching, the needs and interests of your students, and the data you and your students believe will be most useful in fostering academic progress.

PORTFOLIO ASSESSMENT

Most professional artists have portfolios—collections of their best work which can be shown to galleries and art dealers. A portfolio is a coordinated assembly of past and present work which provides the viewer with a definitive and representational look at the artist's work and talent. Through a portfolio an artist can collect a variety of work to reveal the depth and breadth of his or her talent.

Portfolios are also useful in thematic units. They exhibit the talents and skills of individual students—a demonstration of their growth and progress over a period of time. Portfolios are accurate and informative collections of students' work and academic development in a systematic assembly.

Types of Portfolios

There are three basic types of portfolio designs you should consider for classroom use. Well-rounded portfolios will include elements from all three of these designs in order to achieve a balance in design and function.

- *Showcase.* This type of portfolio focuses on work selected exclusively by the student. As such, the student has an opportunity to choose his/her best and most representative work for inclusion in the portfolio.

- *Descriptive.* The items included in this variety of portfolio include a majority chosen by the classroom teacher. The work represents selections predetermined by the teacher and measured against standards established primarily by the teacher.

- *Evaluative.* All of the items in an evaluative portfolio are scored, rated, ranked, or evaluated. This is a very directed type of portfolio and is indicative of a quantitative approach to assessment.

It seems practical and logical to create portfolios which embody elements of all three designs. In that way you and your students will be able to assemble materials which highlight different aspects of academic growth and development and are instructive as well as illustrative.

Contents of Portfolios

A portfolio can be as simple as a single file folder or accordion file for each student. They can be as complex as a series of mailbox compartments set up in a corner of the classroom or painted soda pop boxes stacked along one wall of the classroom. Included in each portfolio can be some of the following:

Anecdotal Records

By their nature, anecdotal records are subjective assessments of students. However, they have the advantage of "tracking" students over many occasions and many learning opportunities. In this way, they serve as an accurate record of performance which can be shared with administrators and parents. We would like to suggest the following guidelines in using anecdotal records:

1. Identify four or five youngsters and concentrate on those individuals for a day.

2. Keep your comments short and to the point.

3. Maintain separate file folders on each student.

4. Plan time at the end of the day to discuss your observations and anecdotes with each identified student.

Checklists

Use of a pre-designed checklist allows you to gauge students progress against a pre-determined set of observational criteria. In other words, as you watch students participate in a project or activity you can check off items on a checklist according to how those students perform or behave. This data is similar in some respects to the information gleaned via anecdotal records; however, it does provide a series of constants against which all students can be assessed. Figure 3-1 is a checklist which can be used to assess reading performance.

Examples of the student's work in progress

Each piece is stamped with a "Work in Progress" notation (rubber stamps can be made up at most stationary stores or local printing firms) and included in a separate file folder.

Dated observational notes written by the teacher

These can include brief notes by the teacher on a special form (see Figure 3-2) or a series of anecdotal comments recorded throughout the length of a thematic unit.

Figure 3-1

Developmental Inventory

Name: _____ Dates: _____

U = Usually   O = Occasionally   R = Rarely

Guides Self Through Text

1. Makes predictions.	U	O	R
2. Supports predictions with logical explanations.	U	O	R
3. Uses both prior knowledge and text information to support predictions.	U	O	R
4. Changes and refines predictions as reading proceeds.	U	O	R

Knows How Text Works

5. Demonstrates knowledge of common story/text elements and patterns.	U	O	R
6. Draws inferences from spoken and written text.	U	O	R
7. Understands similarities and differences between spoken and written text; narrative and expository text.	U	O	R

Understands Social Aspects of Meaning Construction

8. Is aware and tolerant of others'? interpretation of spoken and written text.	U	O	R
9. Supports and maintains own position in face of opposition.	U	O	R
10. Engages in interactions to negotiate meaning construction.	U	O	R

Uses Range of Strategies While Listening/Reading

11. Raises questions about unknown information.	U	O	R
12. Uses illustrations and/or other environmental information to construct meaning.	U	O	R
13. Relocates and uses specific information to support predictions, inferences, and conclusions.	U	O	R
14. Revises meaning as new information is revealed.	U	O	R
15. Uses a functional system to gain meaning for unknown words (e.g. context-structure-sound-reference).	U	O	R

Source: Adapted from Martha Rapp-Haggard Ruddell, Developmental Inventory?—Listening, Reading, unpublished document, Sonoma State University: Rohnert Park, CA, 1991

Dated progress notes written by the student

Self-evaluative questionnaires, checklists, and narrative summaries would be important to include in any portfolio. The form shown in Figure 3-3 offers students an opportunity to track reading materials throughout a thematic unit.

Figure 3-2

Teacher Observation Sheet

Student Name: _____ Date(s): _____

	(low) 1	(high) 10

1. Active Participation:
   Comments:

2. Interaction With Others:
   Comments:

3. Level of Enthusiasm:
   Comments:

4. Making Progress:
   Comments:

Student's Comments and/or Reactions:

Future Goals (designated by student):

Student's signature _____ Teacher's signature _____

Work samples selected by the students

Students are encouraged to include work with which they are especially proud and which they feel is illustrative of their progress. Along with each piece selected, students may elect to attach a Reflection Sheet (see Figure 3-4).

Photographs/illustrations of completed projects

Take photographs of student work (a display, bulletin board creation, clay model, etc.) and include them in a portfolio. This provides students (and their parents) with a permanent record of the activities and projects completed during a thematic unit.

Audio or video tapes of selected work

Students may wish to tape-record speeches, dramatic presentations, or choral readings to demonstrate their progress in oral reading activities. Audio tapes also have the added advantage of indicating reading progress, especially if recordings are made periodically throughout the year.

Figure 3-3

Books I have read, shared, and written about				
Date	Book Title & Author	Read	Shared	Written About

Figure 3-4

Student Reflection Sheet for Portfolio Entries

Student Name:_____ Date:_____

Thematic Unit Topic:_____

Type of product or assignment:_____

_____

I have chosen to place this item in my portfolio because:_____

_____

_____

_____

From this assignment I have learned:_____

_____

_____

_____

One thing I want to tell you about this assignment/project is:_____

_____

_____

_____

Teacher Comments: _____

_____

Teacher signature _____

Thematic Logs

As students begin a thematic unit encourage them to record their predictions and background knowledge about the topic on a special form (see Figure 3-5). The Thematic Log can also be used to record information used and data learned upon completion of the unit.

Figure 3-5

Thematic Log

Name:_____ Date:_____

Topic:_____

Some things I already know about this topic:_____

_____

_____

Where I learned that information:_____

_____

Some questions I have about the topic:_____

_____

_____

Things I would like to know:_____

_____

_____

What I learned from participating in this unit:_____

_____

_____

What I still need to find out:_____

_____

_____

Where I can go to get the answers:_____

_____

_____

Tests, quizzes, and/or exams

The teacher and student should work together in selecting formal evaluation measures for inclusion in a portfolio. Although you may not be using a large number of the more traditional forms of evaluation (i.e. standardized tests, basal reader progress tests, skills tests) they can be included as *one element* of a student's portfolio.

Writing samples

It is not necessary (nor is it practical) to include everything a student has written in his or her portfolio. However, a representative sampling of compositions selected by the teacher and student together should be considered. Writing samples could include:

- Selected journal entries
- Content area writing samples
- Diary entries or personal logs
- Student-initiated questionnaires, surveys, forms
- Literature extension activities
- Teacher-student conference records

Cooperative group assignments

Whenever students work together in cooperative groups it may be appropriate for a designated member of each group to complete a survey form similar to the Journal Entry Sheet shown in Figure 3-6. Copies of completed sheets can be included as entries in each group member's portfolio.

Figure 3-6

Journal Entry Sheet

Topic/Subject:_____

Date:_____

What we knew:_____

_____

_____

_____

_____

What we discovered:_____

_____

_____

_____

_____

Books or media where information was found:_____

_____

_____

Would we like to learn more?   Yes   No

The most interesting fact we learned:_____

_____

_____

Signed_____ (Group/Class Secretary)

The major criterion for items that can be included in a portfolio is that they be representative samples of each student's work over time. It is equally important that the selection of portfolio items be the result of a joint decision between teacher and student. It is ultimately valuable that "ownership" of the portfolio remain with the student.

Suggestions for Portfolio Management

The following ideas will assist you in managing your portfolio assessment program. You should feel free to modify or alter these suggestions according to the design and dynamics of your own language arts curriculum, the specific needs and abilities of your students, school or district policy, and your own level of "comfortableness." These ideas are not presented in a particular order, but can assist you in the design and development of a systematic and functioning portfolio project.

- Limit the portfolio contents to 2 to 3 items of each kind.
- Review, with each student, the contents of his or her portfolio on a regular basis.
- Include samples from a specific academic area (i.e. language arts) or examples from a variety of curricular areas.
- Date all samples and arrange them chronologically within the portfolio or within designated sections of the portfolio.
- Invite students to participate in the identification and selection of work samples to be included in the portfolio.
- Retain only those items (over a designated period of time) which demonstrate growth over that period of time (e.g. marking period, whole year).
- Encourage students to self-evaluate the contents of their individual portfolios on a periodic basis.
- Invite students to review selected portfolio entries periodically with a *Portfolio Progress Sheet* (see Figure 3-9 at the end of the chapter).
- Return work to a student as soon as it is no longer needed for assessment purposes.
- Invite parents to review the contents of a student's portfolio on a regular basis. Have portfolios available for parents at parent-teacher conferences.
- Use portfolios as an adjunct to report card grades. Use portfolio entries to clarify grades, identify student strengths, point out areas of concern, or note progress.
- Invite students to clarify any entries and add explanatory comments when necessary.
- Include an appropriate balance of formal and informal measures of academic achievement and progress. You may wish to use the *Evaluation Portfolio Contents* form in Figure 3-7.

Figure 3-7

Evaluation Portfolio Contents	
Contents	**Comments**
Tests	
————————————	————————————
————————————	————————————
Student Inventories	
————————————	————————————
————————————	————————————
————————————	————————————
Checklists	
————————————	————————————
————————————	————————————
————————————	————————————
Reading Log/Book Report	
————————————	————————————
————————————	————————————
————————————	————————————
Student Writing Samples	
————————————	————————————
————————————	————————————
————————————	————————————
Other	
————————————	————————————
————————————	————————————
————————————	————————————

- Portfolio entries should provide answers to the following three questions:
  - ♦ Where did the student begin?
  - ♦ Where is the student going?
  - ♦ Is the student achieving success?
- A student's portfolio should center on his or her individual accomplishments rather than on comparisons with the class.
- Consider whether students' portfolios will be shared with the next year's teachers or presented to each child's parents.

Rationale for Portfolios

Below are two "Top Ten" lists for you to consider in deciding on the utility of portfolio assessment for thematic units or for any other aspect of your language arts curriculum. You may wish to duplicate these lists and share them with colleagues, parents, or administrators who are curious about your use of portfolios.

> **Top Ten Reasons Why Teachers Should Use Portfolios**
>
> 1. Respects student ownership of their work.
> 2. Facilitates discussion that reflects student strengths, versatility, interests, and efforts.
> 3. Shows development over time.
> 4. Establishes a safe place to store collections that support student interests, decision making, and collaboration.
> 5. Invites parents to be involved.
> 6. Asks students to explain their reasons for including particular works.
> 7. Updates happen at regular intervals.
> 8. Gives teachers time to review progress.
> 9. Showcases work for parents and peers.
> 10. Demonstrates aspects of student work for discussion with parents and district personnel.

> **Top Ten Reasons Why Portfolios Help Students**
>
> 1. Make a collection of meaningful work.
> 2. Reflect on their strengths and needs.
> 3. Set personal goals.
> 4. See their own progress over time.
> 5. Think about ideas presented in their work.
> 6. Look at a variety of work.
> 7. See effort put forth.
> 8. Understand their versatility as a reader and a writer.
> 9. Feel ownership.
> 10. Feel their work has personal relevance.

The advantage of portfolios is that they provide teachers, students, administrators, and parents with a concrete representation of student growth over a designated period of time. They also offer a forum to discuss that growth as well as procedures and processes which might stimulate further growth. Although portfolios are useful in parent/teacher conferences, they are even more beneficial in teacher/student conferences. Portfolios personalize the evaluation process, making it dynamic and relevant to the lives of children and useful in the planning and design of future thematic units.

STUDENT SELF-ASSESSMENT

We strongly believe that an effective thematic unit is one that involves youngsters in each and every aspect of that unit—including assessment. When students can participate in evaluating their own progress within a thematic unit they begin to develop an internal sense of responsibility which helps them assume some degree of control over their own learning. A thematic unit which promotes student self-assessment is one where teachers and students can work in harmony to promote and evaluate activities and processes on an individual basis.

Self evaluation can take many forms. Simplest of all would be in the context of student/teacher discussions. Teacher/student conferences allow you to pose several types of questions which provide opportunities for students to "look inward" and gauge their learning. Wasserman and Ivany (1988) have provided several examples of these types of questions:

1. Tell me about the way you worked.
2. Tell me about some discoveries you have made.
3. Tell me about some of the things that did not go well for you.
4. Tell me about some of the things that gave you trouble.
5. What comments would you like to make about your behavior?
6. What were some of the things you could do for yourself?
7. What were some of the things you needed help with?
8. Where do you think you need help from me?
9. What did you discover about the materials you worked with?
10. What were some of the decisions you made, and how did they work for you?
11. What questions do you have about what happened?
12. Tell me how you think this thematic unit is going for you.

Other formats for self evaluation include data sheets and self report forms. There are many variations of these you can design and use in your classroom. Figures 3-8 and 3-9 are two examples that would be appropriate in a variety of settings and situations.

Listed below are some additional ideas and activities you can use to help students assume some degree of self evaluation within thematic units.

- Provide opportunities for students to establish their own goals for an activity. Afterwards, encourage them to decide if those goals were attained.

- Design a formal evaluation instrument for a thematic unit. Instead of having students respond with answers, ask them to indicate (for each question) whether they: (a) positively know the answer; (b) are mostly sure of the answer; (c) have some idea of the answer; or (d) have no idea what the answer is. Discuss and share reasons (via individual conferences) why students responded as they did.

- Ask students to evaluate the questions in the Teacher's Edition of the textbook. Encourage them to design a system that rates the queries in terms of difficulty, appropriateness, level of cognition, or any other criterion.

- Encourage students to explain their reasons for selecting answers to specific questions.

- Stimulate the development of student-generated questions throughout any activity or experiment.

Figure 3-8

Student Self-Report Form

Name:_____ Date:_____

Thematic Unit Topic:_____

Directions: Please complete this report about your activities in our thematic unit this week. Your comments will form the basis for a discussion with me later.

1. These are some of the things I learned this week:

_____
_____
_____
_____

2. These are some of the things that gave me trouble this week:

_____
_____
_____
_____

3. I believe I have improved this week. Here's why:

_____
_____
_____
_____

4. Here are some things I'd like to learn more about:

_____
_____
_____
_____

5. Here is how I would rate my performance this week:

_____
_____
_____
_____

6. This is what I'd like to do next week:

_____
_____
_____
_____

- Model your own metacognitive processes as you share information with students.

- Provide opportunities for students to explain the reasons why they understood or did not understand parts of an activity.

- Allow students to state their own expectations or criteria for assignments.

Figure 3-9

Portfolio Progress Sheet

Name:_____ Date:_____

Some things I have learned since the last "visit" to my portfolio
include:_____

_____

_____

_____

My favorite entry is:_____

_____ Because:_____

_____

My work shows that I have:_____

_____

_____

But, I still need to:_____

_____

_____

I want to learn more about:_____

_____

_____

Here are some additional items I'd like to include in my portfolio before my
next "visit": _____

_____

- Provide opportunities for students to write lists of things they learned from a unit as well as things they did not understand. Take time to discuss those lists.

- Permit students to rate any one of your thematic units in terms of *their* level of comprehension. In other words, did the unit promote understanding and interest? Discuss *your* reactions in terms of *their* perceptions.

- Provide a variety of self-correcting assignments within each unit.

CRITERION CHECKS

Providing children with opportunities to become personally involved in the dynamics of a thematic unit and to sense their active role in that unit can be accomplished through the use of criterion checks. A criterion check is a question, situation, or mini-activity placed periodically throughout a unit which allows children to assess their progress and the teacher a chance to monitor student progress.

Inform students that these checks are not for grading purposes, but instead provide you and them with guideposts with which the progress of a lesson can be gauged. Here are some possibilities:

1. Ask students several open-ended questions such as the following:

   "What have you learned so far in this unit?"

   "Why is this information important?"

   "How does this information relate to any information we have learned previously?"

   "How do you feel about your progress so far?"

   "What do you think might happen next?"

   "How do you think this will turn out?"

   "Is there something you don't understand at this point?"

2. Have students provide a brief summary (in 25 words or less) about what they have learned up to a specific point of time.

3. Direct students to prepare a brief written summary. Direct them to keep a record of these summaries in a journal for review after the lesson is over.

4. If small group work is being done, have each group appoint a reporter who briefly summarizes the work of the group.

5. Have students make a preliminary sketch of one major piece of information they have learned.

6. Ask students to describe what information they would need at a particular point if they were teaching or tutoring another students about the unit concepts.

Criterion checks should be "dropped into" a lesson periodically. In so doing you provide yourself, as well as your students, with several checkpoints that indicate if the thematic unit is progressing smoothly and is in line with your stated objectives.

MULTIPLE OPTIONS

In order to give you a flavor for the many types of evaluative measures you may wish to consider for your thematic units, we suggest some of the following options. You will need to decide which of these (or any others not on this list) would be appropriate for a specific unit. Of course, as you become more practiced in the design of thematic units you will develop personal preferences as well as other options not listed here. Once again, we would encourage you to invite your students to take an active role, not only in the evaluative process, but in deciding on the assessment measures that could be considered for any developing unit.

- Students can determine beforehand an established number of books that should be read throughout the unit.
- Each student should create an original language art product to include a play, skit, narrative, diary, or other appropriate creation.

- Each student can create a bank of five to eight questions to be placed in a central location. All students can draw from this bank and respond to the questions of their classmates.

- Small groups of students can each create an original quiz on the information shared in class. Duplicate and randomly distribute these quizzes to the groups for completion.

- Have each student prepare a simple outline of the significant points covered in the unit. Post these on the bulletin board.

- Have each student make a tape recording of the four or five most important pieces of information they learned in the unit. The tapes can be evaluated according to pre-determined objectives.

- Read student journal entries to determine how students are organizing their thoughts, integrating new data, and drawing important conclusions.

- Schedule frequent conferences with students or groups of students. Provide them with opportunities to share and discuss the information they are learning and using.

- Direct students to act as interviewers of other students. What has been learned? What are the implications? What else would you like to know?

- Have students write a letter to their parents summarizing what they have learned during various parts of the unit.

- Have a small group of students present a mini-lesson to another class.

- Direct students to write a critical review of one of the segments in the unit, including what they think would have made it a better lesson.

- Have an "Expert Day" and let students report to the class about various and specific aspects of a unit.

- Have students create their own bulletin boards using relevant and pertinent material from a unit.

- Encourage students to make a "ratings list" of the concepts they felt were most critical to the entire unit.

- Direct students to create a certain number of research folders summarizing the concepts learned throughout the unit.

- Actively "kidwatch" and evaluate their progress in group and individual work.

- Have students construct a book or booklet about what they would want to teach other students about the concepts within the unit.

Table 3-1 illustrates an assortment of assessment options categorized according to function. Consider these, too, in the development of your thematic units.

Assessment should be an integral part of the learning process and an important part of the thematic units you design and use in your classroom. As

Table 3-1

Assessment Strategies	
Building Background	**Responding to Literature**
quick write think-pair-share story mapping prediction chart knowledge chart graphic organizer teacher observation student resource book discussions brainstorming word web	story frame monitoring comprehension sheet literature log teacher conferences (individual, small group, casual) discussing and sharing peer response group journal pages story retellings story summary character map Venn diagram dramatic activities story pyramid writing samples teacher observation plot relationship charts story chart anecdotal records of observation think-pair-share K-W-L chart literature discussion circles personal responses
Reading the Literature	**Developing Strategies and Skills**
guided reading monitoring comprehension sheet oral reading teacher observation audio taping of oral reading shared reading discussions cooperative reading reading notes in journal use of strategies checklists	journal pages writing samples students resource pages discussions self-evaluation peer evaluation monitoring comprehension sheet students modeling teacher observation teacher conferencing

such, assessment must be sensitive to the needs, attitudes, and abilities of individual students as well as the class as a whole. Be careful that you do not over-rely on one or more forms of assessment just because they are easy or convenient for you. In other words, *what* you evaluate is just as important as *how* you evaluate! The "Assessment Data Planning List," Figure 3-10, will help you use a variety of assessments.

Figure 3-10

Assessment Data Planning List

Student's Name:_____

Theme: _____

	Type/Example	Comments
_____ Anecdotal Records		
_____ Checklists		
_____ Portfolio		
_____ Student Self-Evaluation		
_____ Others		

Chapter 4

Parent and Community Involvement

Nancy Danyo has been teaching fourth grade in a school district in the Texas panhandle for almost nine years. An active and energetic teacher, Nancy is a strong believer in the value and impact of thematic teaching. While in college, her professors had prepared her by requiring her to create several thematic units and to "test" those units during her student teaching placement. What Nancy discovered was an exciting way to involve students in all the dynamics of learning using children's literature as the primary vehicle.

During student teaching, Nancy also discovered that the local community offered a plethora of opportunities for extending and expanding thematic units. While presenting a unit on "Dangerous Animals", Nancy discovered that one of her students' parents had worked as a veterinarian's assistant in New Mexico; another had an extensive collection of photographs from a safari in Africa; and still a third had a degree in Wildlife Biology. Nancy also discovered that there were some community resources she could use in the development of her unit—including the local chapter of the Audubon Society, the resources of the local high school Biology Club, and various members of a local senior citizen center and their recollections of trips around the world. The librarian at the town library recommended some books for Nancy's unit including *Cannibal Animals: Animals That Eat Their Own Kind* by Anthony D. Fredericks (Danbury, CT: Grolier Publishing, 1999); *Dangerous Animals* by John Seidensticker and Susan Lumpkin (New York: Time-Life Books, 1996); *Living Monsters: The World's Most Dangerous Animals* by Howard Tomb (New York: Simon and Schuster, 1990); *Animal SharpShooters* by Anthony D. Fredericks (Danbury, CT: Grolier Publishing, 1999); and *Animal Monsters: The Truth About Scary Creatures* by Laurence Pringle (New York: Marshall Cavendish, 1997). What had begun as a class assignment for a course on "Teaching Elementary Language Arts" had mushroomed into a multifaceted thematic unit that continued to grow and expand throughout Nancy's twelve weeks of student teaching.

Nancy also saw the impact and power of parents and community involvement in the design of thematic units for her own classroom. For example, while developing a science unit on "The Rainforest," Boyd was able to enlist (1) several parents for a field trip to a local game preserve, (2) members of a chapter of The Sierra Club to speak to the class, (3) parents who were willing to create a listening library of tape-recorded books, and (4) a teller at the local bank who was an amateur wildlife photographer to present a selection of her photographs to the class. The reference librarian at the public library provided Nancy with the addresses of several environmental groups (e.g. Rainforest Action Network, Rainforest Alliance, Save the Rainforest and the Rainforest Preservation Foundation). The local senior citizen center had two residents who had traveled extensively throughout Central and South America and were able to share their experiences with students. A parent of one of the students contributed a selection of environment-related books (purchased by her older children) including *Exploring the Rainforest: Science Activities for Kids* by Anthony D. Fredericks (Golden, CO: Fulcrum Publishing, 1996); *Yanomami: People of the Amazon* by David Schwartz (New York: Lothrop, Lee & Shepard, 1995); *Nightwatch: Nightlife in the Tropical Rainforest* by Peter D. Riley (New York: Reader's Digest, 1999); *Monteverde: Science and Scientists in a Costa Rican Cloud Forest* by Sneed Collard (Danbury, Ct: Grolier Publishing, 1997); and *The Shaman's Apprentice: A Tale of the Amazon Rain Forest* by Lynn Cherry (San Diego, CA: Gulliver Books, 1998).

It became clear to Nancy that the creation and implementation of an effective thematic unit was based, in large measure, on the involvement of individuals outside the school—namely parents and other community members. While Nancy sometimes struggled with the creative aspects of designing a thematic unit from scratch, she quickly found that when the resources of others in the local area were included as factors in any thematic unit, then the design of that unit could be facilitated considerably. Parents and community members provided a wealth of resources, activities, designs, documents, and experiences that Nancy could not provide on her own. In essence, Nancy was able to extend and expand the impact of any thematic unit simply through the use of the experiences and expertise of other adults in the community. Nancy was able to make learning much more than a classroom event—it became an experience to be shared and enjoyed by those outside the four walls of her classroom. Quite naturally, when parents were offered sincere opportunities to become active participants in the development of any unit, they were more aware of the types of experiences their children were participating in as well as ways in which they could actively support those experiences. In short, parent involvement became much more than overseeing the completion of workbook pages and drilling multiplication tables—it became an opportunity for the entire family to take an active role in the whole learning process.

In the design of your own thematic units you will want to consider the role of parents and other community members. So too, will you want to provide opportunities for students to learn from the community and environment outside the classroom—encouraging students to develop relationships between classroom work and "real-life" situations.

INVOLVING PARENTS

Inviting parents as partners in the education of children presents many interesting possibilities for educational enrichment. Soliciting parent involvement not only opens up lines of communication between home and school, it also provides a vehicle through which parents and educators can work hand-in-hand towards the scholastic success of all youngsters.

(Fredericks & Rasinski, 1990)

Developing a successful outreach effort to solicit parent involvement within and throughout your thematic units is not always an easy proposition. It demands some planning and an attention to specific factors that can ensure the success of those efforts. Following are some principles which can aid you in the development of successful outreach efforts and equally successful thematic units:

- *Regular Daily Time*. It is important that parents be provided with activities and designs which will help them take an active role in the learning process on a regular and consistent basis.

- *Purpose and Motive*. Parents and children must understand the relevance of any home-based activities. That is, how does a particular unit relate to the day-to-day lives of youngsters? Completing workbook pages may have little relevance to childrens' lives—collecting water samples from a nearby stream or interviewing one's older relatives can!

- *Support and Encouragement*. Parents should understand that the activities and ideas you suggest to them are backed by a system of support. Parents like to know that should they have any concerns or questions, they are free to contact you to resolve any problems. Simply giving parents a project to complete with their children is not the best way to solicit their support.

- *Informality*. Spontaneity should be a prime consideration in any parent involvement effort. Parents should realize that learning happens in any number of informal situations, as well as formal ones. For example, when parents and children talk about the eating habits of a family pet they are involved in an informal science activity. So too, when parents and children discuss their ethnic heritage they are involved in informal learning activities that can have far-reaching and positive effects.

- *Interaction*. Whatever activities or projects you suggest to parents as extensions of your classroom program keep in mind that there should be a maximum of parent-child interaction built into those activities. Parents should not be asked to *tell* their children what to do, but rather *encouraged* to interact with their children in meaningful discussions and conversations.

Success Tips for Parent Involvement

Following is a compilation of additional ideas which can be made part of any thematic unit—strategies which ensure sustained family involvement throughout a unit. Garnered from a host of effective thematic units from around the country, this is a collection of ideas you can consider in developing your thematic units.

- Outreach efforts need to offer life-like activities that capitalize on the natural and normal relationships between parents and kids. In other words, don't offer suggestions that are a repetition of school-like activities, but rather provide opportunities for families to interact in mutually supporting pursuits.

- Encourage parents to participate continuously throughout the length of a thematic unit.

- Be patient with parents. Some may be reluctant to get involved with your efforts due to any number of extenuating circumstances. Keep trying and never give up on *any* parent.

- Encourage parents to participate in the affairs of the unit through volunteering, observing, or sharing their hobbies, vocations, or vacations. Keep this process as non-stressful as possible and provide a host of sharing opportunities throughout the year.

- Make a regular effort to communicate with parents through a brief phone call or short note (this is particularly appropriate for those parents who do not participate regularly).

- Parents must know that your outreach efforts are a natural and normal part of the unit.

- Get kids involved in any thematic unit—use them as "recruiters" for their own parents. Solicit their ideas as much as possible.

- You must be a good role model for parents—that is, be enthusiastic and committed to the idea of parent engagement. That desire will rub off on families and stimulate greater participation.

- Communicate to parents the fact that their involvement in a thematic unit is ultimately for the benefit of their children.

- Whenever possible, try to get any and all family members involved in a thematic unit. Moms, dads, grandparents, siblings, and extended family members can all lend an air of credibility to a project and help promote its benefits.

- Make sure parents are rewarded and/or recognized for their efforts, however small. Everyone likes to receive some form of recognition and parents are no exception. Certificates, awards, letters of commendation, or blue ribbons are all possible in rewarding parent participation.

- Coordinate your outreach efforts with some local community agencies (churches, social service, fraternal). They can be most effective in creating "contacts" for materials or resources.

- When sending any written information to parents be careful that you do not use educational jargon. Keep your tone informal and to the point— don't talk down to parents and don't insult their intelligence.

- It is vitally important that you be friendly, down to earth, and truly interested in parents and their children. A sincere interest to work together will provide the fuel for any type of outreach effort.

Ideas to Implement

Helping parents understand their roles and actively participate in the dynamics of a thematic unit can be a significant (if not overwhelming) task for many teachers. Terms such as "whole language", "integrated curriculum", and "literature-based reading program" may leave many parents confused and frightened. Yet, when we demonstrate to parents that many of the activities and interactions they naturally have with their children each day can support the goals and objectives of any thematic unit, then we can help them appreciate their valuable and significant role in the total scholastic development of their children. In doing so, we can assist parents in becoming supporters of whole language classrooms through regular, daily activities in a relaxed and comfortable learning environment—the home.

Following are a variety of activities—most of which can be suggested to parents as extensions of many thematic units.

- Set up a special series of workshops on the topic of a scheduled thematic unit.
- Write a letter to the editor of the local newspaper requesting resources and information about a thematic topic.
- Hold a monthly "Parent Tea" after school hours to share ideas with parents and discuss various parts of a thematic unit.
- Call one parent each week to relay some good news about what their child is doing in a thematic unit.
- Set up a lending library of resource books and extra theme-related materials for parents to check out and use at home.
- Provide parents with lists of theme-related books and literature which they can share with their youngsters at home. Also provide sources (library locations, teacher supply stores, bookstores, etc.) for obtaining that information.
- Invite parents into the classroom to share their theme-related interests, recent trips, or hobbies.
- Encourage parents to schedule "Family Field Trips" in which all members of the family can travel together to a particular site or exhibit. Consult local agencies or the yellow pages for locations of special places in the local community.
- Provide parents with a periodic newsletter (see Figure 4-1) updating them on unit activities and projects (The sample provided could be used as part of a thematic unit on "Communication.").
- Keep abreast of upcoming TV shows related to a particular theme and provide parents with information on those programs.
- Have students prepare a calendar of upcoming events in the unit. These can be sent home on a regular basis—once a week or once a month.
- Interview parents about some of their theme-related interests, hobbies, activities, or vacations. Prepare this information in the form of a special classroom newsletter.
- Many popular magazines frequently carry theme-related articles. You may wish to clip these and distribute them to parents.
- Every two weeks or so have your students prepare special "homework packets" consisting of theme-related articles, games, pertinent worksheets, upcoming TV programs, museum exhibits, and the like.

- Have parents tape record a book (related to a theme) or portion of a book so that the child can listen to it again and again.

- Parents and children can make a collage of important events related to a theme. Pictures from old magazines can be cut out and pasted on sheets of construction paper.

- Encourage parents to have their children write a letter to a friend about what they're learning in a unit.

- Encourage parents to read several different books on the same theme.

- Ask parents and children to make up a fictitious newspaper about a thematic unit.

- Parents can help their children adapt thematic events into a news report or TV program.

- Parents and children can create a glossary or dictionary of important words related to a theme.

- Encourage parents and children to create a scrapbook about important places, people, and events discovered as part of a thematic unit.

- Encourage parents and children to interview outside "experts" in the local community about information or data related to a theme.

- Have parents and children create time lines of thematic events.

- Have parents work with their children to put together a time capsule of objects mentioned in a thematic unit.

- Families can set up a "museum" of theme artifacts in one corner of the living room.

- Parents can help their children design and create a diorama of significant events in a unit.

- Ask parents to take photographs of scenes (similar to those from selected thematic unit books) within the local community and arrange them into an attractive display.

What makes any thematic unit successful is the creative vision of educators and parents working together in a spirit of mutual cooperation and support. Strong thematic units are those which, not only integrate all aspects of the elementary curriculum, but also integrate parents into the designs and delivery systems of those units, too. The bonds established between home and school can be powerful ones in terms of the effectiveness of any thematic unit. When parents are "employed" as partners in a thematic unit, students are afforded a wealth of exciting educational possibilities.

Figure 4-1

Parent Newsletter
Questions and Answers about Thematic Units

Dear Parents:

There's an exciting "revolution" taking place in schools today. It's called *Thematic Teaching or teaching with thematic units* and it offers youngsters exciting possibilities in terms of their reading growth and development. Your child may have been talking about some of the exciting activities taking place in our classroom and you may have some questions about this approach to teaching and learning. Here are some of the questions (and accompanying answers) parents are asking:

What is a thematic unit? A thematic unit is a series of lessons developed around a single theme—usually a theme in science or social studies. The unit encourages students to use their language arts skills (reading, writing, speaking, and listening) in a host of stimulating and supportive activities. Units are built around an abundance of children's literature related to the theme and whole language activities which encourage youngsters to investigate all the dynamics of that theme. Thematic units are a way in which regular writing activities, an abundance of children's literature, and a host of communication activities are used in all subject areas. Thematic units focus on the individual learning needs of each child in the classroom and offers a natural learning environment in which students can begin to assume some responsibility for their own learning.

What do students do? In a thematic unit, students are given choices to explore aspects of a particular theme through the use of one or more of the following: daily writing time, silent reading time, book sharing experiences, read-alouds by the teacher, sharing opportunities between students, teacher-modeled writing, lots of children's literature in every subject area, reading conferences and small group coopera-tive work, and frequent book-oriented discus-sions. Thematic teaching provides opportunities for the teacher to concentrate on the individual learning needs of each student and opportuni-ties for the students to examine and explore several aspects of a selected topic or theme, thereby gaining a broad-based exposure to, and appreciation of, a particular subject area.

What about skills? In a thematic unit skills are presented to children in a context that is meaningful to them. Typically, children do not fill in a lot of workbook pages or skill sheets. Instead, the teacher uses children's language (what they have said or written) and children's literature to focus on the skills needed by each individual child. For example, the teacher may have children write a journal entry about some of their favorite plants (as part of a science-related theme). The teacher may decide to focus on each child's use of capital letters and punctuation (as part of an English lesson). Each child's writing then become his or her own "lesson materials" for the identified skills. The skill lessons the teacher designs can then be supplemented with quality literature and textbook materials.

What can I do? The success your children achieves in all subject areas can be maximized by your support and involvement. In fact, you are probably doing many things at home already that support your child's involvement in a particular thematic unit. These include:

- Sharing with your child (e.g. reading aloud) books related to a certain theme.

- Talking with your child about the ideas and concepts that are discussed in class.

- Buying books for your child or visiting the local public library to locate additional books related to a particular theme.

- Listening carefully as your child tells you about events related to a thematic unit.

- Helping your child maintain a journal, notebook, or diary of thoughts and ideas related to a theme.

- Encouraging your child to create puppets, models, posters, or dioramas of characters and events from selected books.

- Inviting your child to become an author and create some original stories related to a theme and display them in the family library.

- Taking your child on field trips or excursions to sites in the local community which are related to a current theme.

- Encouraging your child to talk with experts and other community people about concepts and facts related to a certain theme.

Thematic units are a wonderful opportunity for your child to explore and examine a particular topic through a host of positive learning experiences. By taking an active role in your child's discoveries you will be helping him or her become an accomplished learner and an active participant in a variety of scholastic opportunities.

COMMUNITY FIELD TRIPS

Field trips provide youngsters with marvelous opportunities to expand and enlarge concepts taught within a particular thematic unit. In addition, field trips can enhance and promote your entire curriculum, providing students with important new information often unobtainable in textbooks. Most important, however, is the fact that students begin to see any subject as something more than a textbook topic or collection of "memorizeable" facts. Field trips can be a positive and dynamic part of the entire curriculum—particularly when they are considered as an important element of any thematic unit.

There is no limit to the places and sites that should be considered for a thematic unit field trip. The possibilities for field trips are only limited by a teacher's imagination. Figure 4-2 provides you with some possibilities to consider for the curricular areas of science, social studies, math, and language arts.

You can enhance any field trip by working with your students in preparing a guidebook. A guidebook becomes a creative, "real-life" extension of any language arts-based thematic unit. This guidebook not only provides students with some relevant information on the site they are to visit, but also allows them to record impressions and information gathered during the trip. Just as important, it can become an important record of one or more field trips taken during the year—a record that can be referred to throughout the year. The guidebook should be prepared well in advance of any field trip and can be done individually by students or in small groups. You may wish to have students construct a separate guidebook for each field trip or a permanent guidebook for all field trips taken during the year. The following items can be included in a guidebook prior to a field trip:

- Brochures or other printed materials available from the field trip site (write in advance for these).

- Students can write a brief capsule description of the site and the reasons for visiting that place.

Figure 4-2

Possible Field Trip Locations		
Science	hospital forest lumber yard garden center pet store dairy farm natural history museum aquarium nature center college biology department river, stream, swamp police crime lab generating station	machine shop music store service station fix-it shop manufacturing plant water treatment plant dumps recycling center hydroelectric plant planetarium radio station hobby store local astronomy club

Social Studies	different neighborhoods
	social service agency
	city hall
	local/county government
	   agency
	manufacturing plant
	chamber of commerce
	cultural organization/club
	museum
	historical display
	college geography department
	police/fire station
	Red Cross Center
	volunteer recruitment center
		newspaper
		state department of
		   transportation
		telecommunications center
		graveyard
		shipyard
		festivals
		church/temple/synagogue
		historical site
		nursing home
		ethnic restaurants
		sanitation areas
		train station/airport

Math	precision instrument company cartographer surveying company bank, credit union bakery any small business pizza parlor music store meteorologist weather station	college math department high school computer lab manufacturing plant architect pool hall artist or art studio flea market supermarket hospital hardware store symphony/orchestra
Language Arts	book store library author book binding plant stationary store paper manufacturer	newspaper or magazine publisher computer store live plays/theater printer post office

- Student-generated questions about the site and what might be seen (have students provide space under the questions for responses).

- A list of safety rules and expected form of behavior during the trip.

- Blank pages for students to record observations and illustrations of significant points or observations.

- A summary page for students to write a brief wrap-up of the trip (this should be done prior to boarding the bus back to school).

Success Tips

Any teacher who has taken a class of kids on a field trip knows that field trips are much more than loading students on a school bus, traveling to some distant site, having an "expert" dispense a variety of facts and figures, wolfing down a semi-stale peanut butter and jelly sandwich, and trying to make it back to school with one's sanity still intact. Successful and effective field trips take planning and preparation—they do not come about overnight. Teachers should consider the following items as important elements in any meaningful field trip.

Before

What is done prior to the actual field trip often determines the success of the trip itself. Planning involves much more than sending out parental permission slips and arranging for bus transportation. Consider these activities as part of the preparation process:

- If possible, obtain some brochures or other literature about the site you are visiting or the topic(s) that will be discussed. Many museums, planetariums, and the like have all sorts of printed materials you can obtain and share with students prior to the trip.

- Discuss with students the reasons for the trip, what they can expect to discover, and any additional highlights. Talk about how the planned trip is correlated with information discussed in a thematic unit.

- Provide students with examples of children's literature in advance of the scheduled field trip. Use of children's literature before a field trip can provide students with the necessary background information they need to fully understand and appreciate what actually takes place during the field trip.

- If possible, visit the site yourself in advance of the scheduled field trip. Talk to the people in charge, pick up some literature, and ask some questions. This "dry run" will provide you with important points and observations which can be shared with students prior to the trip.

During

To be successful a field trip must provide students with opportunities to become actively engaged in learning new information or in reinforcing previously learned material. The following guidelines provide kids with opportunities to become participants rather than just observers:

- Invite students to discuss the questions they generated before the trip. Encourage students to generate additional questions throughout the trip, too.

- Help students understand the relevance of the exhibit, display, or venue to the materials and information they are studying in a thematic unit.

- Invite students to record their thoughts, impressions, or drawings of important information or concepts. It is advisable to stop every so often to review what has been seen and allow children to make notations on newly learned information.

After

After a field trip, invite students to participate in a "debriefing" session in which important points are discussed, misconceptions are cleared up, and relationships are drawn between the outside world and the concepts in a thematic unit. Invite students to share their perceptions of the field trip, the important or unimportant points, and how specific features relate to the thematic unit. Encourage students to create drawings, models, dioramas, posters or some other artistic (and permanent) display of the information they learned during the trip (See Table 4-1).

Table 4-1

Post-Field Trip Activities

class newspaper	news broadcast
bulletin board display	book of "world records"
collage	letter to the editor
videotape summary	read follow-up literature
newsletter	song with new lyrics
map	mini lesson
thank you notes	"Jeopardy!" game
brochure on trip site	word puzzles
class survey on favorite items	poetry
photo album	skit or play
picture book (share with younger class)	big book
	showcase display
field trip magazine	cartoon strips
"Flip book"	school experts

- Integrate the field trip into the thematic unit by providing students with opportunities to create plays, stories, dances, poems, lyrics, and video or audio recordings of portions of the field trip.

- Invite students to review the purposes for the trip and ask them to decide if those purposes were met.

- Provide opportunities for students to understand the relevance of the field trip to all areas of the curriculum. For example, how can the information gathered during the trip be used in social studies, reading, art, or physical education.

Mini Field Trips

We like the idea of mini field trips. These are field trips you can take around the school or in the immediate community. They require little planning, no money, and a host of possibilities for students to integrate classroom information with the world around them.

Design several short (10–20 minutes each) investigations of the environment around the school. Each of these ideas should be recorded separately on individual index cards and kept in a card file in the classroom. The activities can be used for individuals, small or large groups, or as "homework" assignments. Here are some mini field trip ideas, each of which could be embedded in a relevant thematic unit:

Plants
Go outside and see how many different leaves you can collect in ten minutes. What are some similarities? What are some differences?

Weather
Go outside and record the temperature, wind speed, and humidity. Do this during the day at one hour intervals. What do you notice?

Measurement
Go home and collect three different measurement instruments from the kitchen, the garage, or your bedroom. Make a list of the similarities and differences between the instruments.

Geometry
Use several different grocery bags and collect objects representing each of several basic geometric shapes, for example: sphere—baseball, cube—block, rectangle—letter.

Writing
Ask selected adults in your family or neighborhood to contribute selected examples of writing ("To do" lists, order forms, grocery lists, etc.) they use in their everyday work. Categorize those writing by types and purpose.

Communication
Take a walking field trip around the school and list all the ways in which people communicate with each other (e.g. signs, billboards, letters, etc.).

Families
Interview three different adults and obtain their definitions of the word "Family." What similarities are there in the definitions.

Geography
Pretend you are an ant and had to travel from one end of the playground to the other. Record all the geographical features you would encounter on your trip.

Effective thematic units offer students unique opportunities to work with their parents and other community members to enhance and expand their knowledge base. When families and the local environment are intertwined into the dynamics of a thematic unit, students are afforded learning opportunities that far exceed the objectives of textbooks or curriculum guides. We sincerely hope that the units you create for your classroom will include a host of individuals, organizations, and situations—helping students understand the relevance of classroom experiences to those experiences beyond the classroom.

PART II

Thematic Units

The thematic units included in this section emphasize key concepts in Science, Social Studies, Language Arts, Mathematics, and the Arts. In addition, the activities included within each unit integrate skills from a variety of disciplines to ensure a unique, multidisciplinary, interdisciplinary unit of study with a strong literature component. Looking back in Chapters 1–4 you will find a wide spectrum of methodology to help you plan and implement thematic units to match your classroom dynamics.

The following chart lists the focus for each thematic unit, along with the various mini-themes that have been developed for each unit. These mini-themes, which can be used alone or in conjunction with other mini-units, extend the focus and concepts developed through the main thematic unit. Each mini-theme includes activities, questions, and related works of literature to provide you with a variety of choices through which to develop specific content objectives and skills.

The wide scope of activities developed for each unit illustrates the tremendous possibilities from which you can select to provide students with a framework that best meets their individual needs and interests. While each unit also develops a number of literary works, you may choose to use only one or two selections or you may wish to substitute other titles.

As students become involved in the various units, we suggest that you guide them in developing other activities based on teaching/learning styles. For learning to be meaningful, it must have relevance. We urge you to adapt the strategies described in Chapter 2, along with activities included in the units and mini-units, to create a challenging learning environment that will arouse each student's natural curiosity and encourage students to pursue new ideas and formulate their own connections.

The scope of activities in the thematic units and the outcomes developed will allow you to employ a wide variety of assessment techniques that not only gauge students' work but also help them grow in the process. The journals, anecdotal records, portfolio assessment, checklists, conferences, student self-evaluations, and so forth described in Chapter 3 provide authentic assessments that will provide an accurate evaluation of students' learning and progress. We hope you will encourage your students to take an active role in both the assessment process and in determining the assessment measures for any developing unit.

Primary Thematic Units:

Themes and Mini-Themes

Unit	Focus	Mini-Themes
I. The Changing Earth (Science)	Students will learn about the ever-changing nature of the earth's surface and the impact these events have on humans.	Water Rocks and Soil
II. Insects/Bugs (Science)	Students will learn some of the common characteristics of insects and spiders.	Caterpillars, Butterflies, and Moths Ants
III. Dinosaurs (Science)	Students will explore prehistoric times to expand their knowledge of dinosaurs.	Why Dinosaurs Became Extinct Discovering Dinosaurs
IV. Growing Up (Social Studies)	Students will identify feelings about aging and recognize that growing up is individualistic and developmental.	Growing Up with Separation and Divorce Death and Dying
V. Holidays and Celebrations (Social Studies)	Students will expand their knowledge about holidays.	Martin Luther King, Jr., Day Birthdays
VI. Folktales from Around the World (Language Arts)	Through the readings and discussion of folktales from countries around the world, students will gain an appreciation for this literary form and become familiar with a variety of cultures.	Folktales of Native Americans Afro-American Folktales
VII. The Caldecott Award (Language Arts)	Students will become aware of the diversity of artistic media used to illustrate children's books and become familiar with those illustrators whose books have been awarded the Caldecott Award for the most distinguished picture book published in the U.S.	Ed Young Leo and Diane Dillon
VIII. Counting and Computation (Math)	Students will develop an intuitive feeling for numbers and their various uses and interpretations.	Addition and Subtraction Money
IX. Measurement and Sizes (Math)	Students will become familiar with the various aspects of measurement and how it relates to mathematics.	Time Months and Seasons

The Changing Earth

OVERVIEW

Focus

Students will learn about the ever-changing nature of the earth's surface and the impact these events have on humans.

Objectives

Upon completion of this unit, students will:

1. Learn that the surface of the earth is constantly changing.
2. Understand how changes in the earth affect people living on the surface.
3. Appreciate the different types of forces which affect the earth.

HOW IT WORKS

Initiating Activity

Invite students to share their thoughts and feelings about living through a violent earthquake (such as the one which occurred in Los Angeles on January 17, 1994, a recent one, or an imaginary one), or a volcanic eruption. Invite each student to record his or her thoughts in a personal journal. Students may elect to share their thoughts and feelings in small or large group settings. Afterwards, encourage students to select one or more of the following activities to do by themselves or with one or more partners:

1. Invite students to create a "graffiti wall" which records personal feelings about the aftermath of an earthquake or volcanic eruption. Students may post a long sheet of newsprint on one wall of the classroom and invite classmates and others to record their thoughts, feelings, and ideas.

2. Invite students to create a short skit about a make-believe earthquake or volcano in their neighborhood. What events happened in the neighborhood? How did the local residents react to those events? Was there a memorable incident which happened nearby?

3. Invite students to create a mock news broadcast about an imaginary earthquake or volcano. Selected students can each take on the roles of newscaster, interviewer, local citizens and interested bystanders and recreate the events which occurred in their neighborhood.

4. Invite students to each create a collage (using photos cut out of the newspaper or selected news magazines) which replicate the major events of a recent earthquake or volcano. Encourage students to share

their finished products with the class and arrange them into an appropriate display in the classroom (bulletin board, poster, collage, etc.). Students may wish to include appropriate captions for selected photos using ideas from their individual journals.

5. Invite students to interview adults in their neighborhood concerning the adults' feelings and emotions about an earthquake or volcano. What would they do? How would they feel? How do the emotions expressed by adults differ from those recorded in students' journals. Students may wish to discuss any similarities or differences.

6. Invite students to use play houses and other models to create a make-believe town located on a fault line. Encourage students to assemble a town on a large sheet cake (see "Cakequake! An Earth-Shaking Experience" by Garry Hardy and Marvin Tolman in *Science and Children* Vol. 29, No. 1 [September 1991], pp. 18—21). Invite students to make a videotape of the effects of their earthquake.

General Activities

1. Invite students to create a dictionary booklet entitled, "My Earth Book". Students may wish to create a page for each letter of the alphabet (For example: A = abyss; B = biosphere; C = chasm; D = dangerous).

2. Share one or more videos from the following list. After viewing a selected film invite students to create a review of the film to be included in an ongoing unit newspaper: *Earth Watch* (specific activities for each film are also suggested).

   a. *This Changing Planet* (Catalog No. 30352) available through National Geographic Society, Washington, D.C. Explains how the earth is constantly changing its surface through weather, erosion, earthquakes, and volcanoes. After viewing, invite students to choose one of the ways described in the movie and draw an illustration regarding the event using appropriate captions.

   b. *The Violent Earth* (Catalog No. 51234) available through National Geographic Society, Washington, D.C. The video tours active volcanoes throughout the world. After viewing encourage students to make a replica of a volcano from modeling clay or paper mache. Invite students to model their volcanoes after one or more of those in the film.

3. Invite students to maintain an "Earthquake Journal" which includes an ongoing chart of the Richter Scale readings for the aftershocks which occur in the days and weeks following an earthquake, photographs or illustrations of the damage observed in various neighborhoods, interviews with adults and other students, and lists of earthquake related books located in the local library.

Discussion Questions

1. Why is it important for scientists to be able to predict natural disasters such as earthquakes, volcanic eruptions, and the like?

2. Of all the natural disasters, which ones do you think are most destructive?

3. Why do you think people continue to live in areas that are prone to natural disasters such as volcanoes and earthquakes? What types of special precautions do these people need to take in their daily lives?

4. Why are humans so fascinated by natural disasters?

5. If you could interview a volcanologist or seismologist, what would you like to ask that person (NOTE: Students may wish to e-mail a working scientist such as a volcanologist or seismologist through the following web site: http://www.askanexpert.com/askanexpert/).

6. In your opinion, what is the most powerful "earth force" in nature?

LITERATURE RELATED ACTIVITIES

Title: *Earthquakes*

Genre: Non-fiction

Author: Franklyn Branley

Bibliographic Information: New York: Crowell, 1990.

Summary: This book contains information about earthquakes and how they affect our world. What causes earthquakes? How do earthquakes destroy the land? How do scientists measure and predict earthquakes?

Interest Level: Grades 1–3

Pre-Reading Activity

Show the film *The Great San Francisco Earthquake*, produced by PBS Video, 1988, or the video *Our Dynamic Earth* produced by the National Geographic Society (catalog No. C51162). Invite students to discuss the similarities between the events portrayed in the film(s) and those described in the book. Encourage students to create a Venn Diagram illustrating the similarities and differences.

Learning Activities

1. Invite students to write their own personal newspaper article about a recent earthquake. Afterwards, encourage students to form small groups and discuss their articles and how those pieces compare with the descriptions given in the book.

2. Invite students to construct a model of the different layers of the earth by painting a huge ball on a piece of poster board. The inside of the ball can be painted in three colors according to the three layers of the earth: the core, the mantle, and the crust. Afterwards, students may wish to use a globe of the world to plot selected countries on their illustrations. They

may also wish to plot the locations of some of the major earthquakes which have occurred during the past 25 to 50 years.

3. Encourage students to work in small groups and research other books about earthquakes. Each group may wish to prepare a brief summary on their findings, and present their discoveries to the rest of the class. Invite groups to each prepare a fact book about their collected data and present their finished products to the school library.

4. Invite selected students to work in small groups to construct their own makeshift Seismographs. Each group will need a ball of clay, a pencil, a string approximately one-foot long, tape, and a white piece of paper. Invite students to tie the string to the eraser end to their pencil and punch the tip of the pencil through a clay ball until just the lead point is sticking out of the clay. Invite one student in each group to tape a sheet of white paper to a desk. One group member can stage an earthquake by shaking the desk with another group member holding the string up steadily above the desk so that just the tip of the pencil is barely touching the paper. Invite students to observe how their makeshift seismograph records the waves of the "earthquake". Encourage students to compare the recordings they obtained with those found in various library books.

5. Provide each of several small groups of students with a shallow pan of water and a marble. Invite individual students to each drop a marble into the pan and describe the ripples which are sent out. Encourage students to compare the waves in their pans with those which might be sent out from the epicenter of an earthquake. Students may also wish to compare their ripples with waves in the ocean. What similarities do they notice? Invite students to record their observations in an appropriate journal.

Discussion Questions

1. Discuss why you would or would not want to live along a fault line.

2. Why do so many people continue to live along fault lines when they know of the dangers associated with that location?

3. What would you imagine to be the most frightening or scariest part about an earthquake?

4. What parts of the world are the most dangerous—as far as earthquakes go?

Title: *Volcanoes: Fire From Below*

Genre:	Informational
Author:	Jenny Wood
Bibliographic Information:	Milwaukee, WI: Gareth Stevens, 1991.
Summary:	Lots of photographs and dynamic illustrations highlight this book about volcanic activity. Readers learn a wealth of information about volcanoes, hot springs and geysers along with lots of scientific terms.
Interest Level:	Grades 1–3

Pre-Reading Activity

Prior to reading the book with students, provide them with photographs of Mt. St. Helens before its eruption. Invite students to imagine what the mountain must have looked like after the eruption and encourage them to each draw an illustration of how they think the mountain may have looked after the eruption. Later, invite students to compare their predictions with actual photos (the book *Volcano: The Eruption and Healing of Mt. St. Helens* by Patricia Lauber [New York: Aladdin, 1993] is an excellent resource). What differences do they note?

Learning Activities

1. Invite students to research other books about volcanoes. Students may wish to choose a volcano (ex. Mt. Fuji) to compare and contrast with Mt. St. Helens.

2. Invite small groups of students to each write a fictional story about how they were affected when a volcano erupted. What were some of the effects of the volcano's eruption on their daily lives? How did they survive? What did they do afterwards? Provide opportunities for students to share their creations with the class.

3. Demonstrate the gas pressure that builds up inside of volcanoes by shaking up a bottle of warm soda and then taking the cap off (use caution). Invite students to compare what they observed with the eruption of a recent volcanic eruption. Students may wish to discuss how the soda compares with the magma of another volcano.

4. Generate a class discussion on how the eruption of a volcano had an affect on the food-chain for the surrounding area. Encourage students to discuss such aspects as: How did the avalanches and mud slides affect the food-chain? What are some of the ways that the vegetation was able to rejuvenate after the eruption? Why were some animals able to escape harm from the eruption? Invite students to create individual journals to record their discussions.

5. Invite students to compare and contrast the environment immediately following the eruption to the environment two years after the eruption. Encourage students to take on the roles of news reporters and "interview" the plants and animals in the region about the processes they experienced during this transition phase.

Discussion Questions

1. What do you think is the most frightening aspect of volcanoes?
2. If you could ask a volcanologist just one question, what would it be?
3. If you could visit any volcano in the world, which one would you like to see?
4. Why are volcanoes an important part of the changing earth?

Title: *Volcanoes*

Genre: Informational

Author: Seymour Simon

Bibliographic Information: New York: Morrow, 1988.

Summary: Using clear and concise language, the author explains how volcanoes are formed, how they erupt, different types of lava, and how they affect the earth. Full color photographs are included throughout the text.

Interest Level: Grades 2–4

Pre-Reading Activity

Bring in samples of volcanic ash and/or lava and show them to students (these can be obtained through science supply companies such as Hubbard Scientific [P.O. Box 104, Northbrook, IL 60065—800-323-8368]; The Institute for Earth Education [P.O. Box 288, Warrenville, IL 60555—509-395-2299]; or Scott Resources [P.O. Box 2121F, Fort Collins, CO 80522—800-289-9299]). Ask students to discuss the feel of these substances in comparison with the descriptions in the book.

Learning Activities

1. Invite students to record the titles of each of the four different kinds of volcanoes on four separate sheets of oaktag. Encourage them to draw illustrations of selected volcanoes (from around the world) on each sheet of oaktag. Students may wish to consult other references.

2. Invite students to construct comparative charts of volcanoes according to different climatic regions of the world (e.g. how many active volcanoes are located in tropical regions vs. how many active volcanoes are located in polar regions?). Is there a relationship between climate and the location of active and/or inactive volcanoes?

3. Invite students to make charts of the dormancy periods of selected volcanoes. For example, which volcanoes have remained dormant the longest? Which volcanoes have had the most recent eruptions? Where are the most dormant volcanoes located? Where are the most active volcanoes located?

4. Invite students to compare the photographs in this book with volcano photos in other books. What similarities are there? What kinds of differences are noted? How can students account for the differences in photos of the same volcanoes? Encourage students to record their inferences in journals.

5. Invite students to speculate on what happens when a bottle of soda pop is vigorously shaken. How is that action similar to the action of a volcano? Are there other "actions" similar to those which take place inside a volcano?

6. Invite students to watch a video of a volcano erupting (e.g. "The Violent Earth" [National Geographic Society, Washington, D.C. 20036; catalog

No. 51234]). Afterwards, encourage students to pretend that they are at the site of one of the eruptions. Invite them to put together an "on the spot" newscast (videotape) recording their reactions during the "eruption."

7. Invite students to conduct some library research on famous volcanoes in history (i.e. Krakatoa, Mt. Fuji, Vesuvius, etc.). Collected data can be assembled into a large class book or presented via a specially prepared videotape.

8. Some students may be interested in investigating the myths and legends of volcanoes throughout history. How do those stories and tales compare with what modern science knows about volcanoes today?

Discussion Questions

1. What was the most enjoyable part of this book?

2. Some people have said that volcanoes are terrible destructive acts of nature. Do you agree with that statement?

3. What would be some of the benefits of predicting the eruption of selected volcanoes?

4. Why do so many kids enjoying learning about volcanoes?

Title: *The Pebble in My Pocket*

Genre: Historical fiction

Author: Meredith Hooper

Illustrator: Chris Coady

Bibliographic Information: New York: Viking, 1996.

Summary: This is an incredible book which traces the "life history" of a small pebble from the beginning of the earth's formation four and one-half billion years ago to the present day. A richly illustrated and magnificent book.

Interest Level: Grades 2–4

Pre-Reading Activity

Mix three tablespoons of sand with three tablespoons of white glue (you may need to adjust the mixture depending on the type of sand—it should have the consistency of stiff wet concrete.). Form the mixture into two or three "rocks" and allow to dry in a slow (250°F) oven for several hours. Place the "rocks" in a tumbler or sturdy cup filled with water. Cover the cup with a tight-fitting lid. Invite students to shake the cup vigorously for several minutes and note the results (The "rocks" will be worn down due to the eroding power of the water.)

Learning Activities

1. Soak pieces of sandstone in water overnight. Place a piece of saturated sandstone in a zip-loc bag and seal tightly. Put the bag in the freezer over-

night. Invite students to observe the results. (Water expands as it freezes causing the "rock" to split. The same type of weathering occurs in nature—breaking large rocks into smaller ones.)

2. Invite students to look for various types of erosion in and around their homes. Some examples to look for include (1) coins that are smooth from handling, (2) shoes with the heels worn down, (3) an old car tire with no tread, and (4) a counter top with the design or finish worn away. Invite students to compare these forms of erosion with those that naturally occur in nature (wind and water erosion).

3. Invite students to assemble a collection of rocks found in and around their homes or the school grounds. Can they identify the rocks collected? What is the most unusual rock? What is the most common rock? If possible, invite a science teacher from the local high school or college to share information about rocks commonly found in your area.

Discussion Questions

1. Have you ever found a rock or pebble that was special to you? Can you create an imaginary "time line" for that rock or any rock you have found?

2. How old do you think some of the rocks in your yard are? How would you be able to find out?

3. How did the illustrations in this book help you appreciate or understand the events that were taking place?

4. What do you imagine will happen to the pebble in the future?

CULMINATING ACTIVITY

Students will be invited to select one or more of the following activities and projects:

1. College students from a local university can be invited to share specially prepared lessons on the changing earth. Additionally, students majoring in geology at the university can be invited to share their expertise with the class. Invite students to interview the college students.

2. Students can be invited to initiate an "Earth Watch Newspaper"—a collection of stories about violent activities taking place on the earth's surface over a designated period of time. Periodic reports may be made to the class.

3. Individual students will be invited to create an advertisement (written or oral) for a volcano. Class members will be asked to describe the features which would be most necessary in the promotion (i.e. the sale) of an active volcano.

4. Invite students to create a play or reader's theatre adaptation of a story concerning the steps that need to be taken in case of a natural disaster. Encourage students to consult with the local Red Cross center for information necessary in preparing the presentation.

5. Invite students to work in small groups to create "Before" and "After" dioramas of the local area prior to and immediately after an imaginary

earthquake. Other groups of students may be invited to create "Before" and "After" dioramas of selected volcano eruptions, floods, or other natural disasters as a result of their readings. Encourage students to discuss their feelings about these events.

6. Invite students to create semantic webs of important information introduced in the unit and post the webs throughout the room. Encourage students to make two separate webs: "Natural Earth Changes" and "Changes Created by Humans". Plan time to discuss any similarities or differences.

SUPPLEMENTAL LITERATURE

Books

Primary (Grades 1–3)

Bourgeois, P. (1990). *The amazing dirt book*. Reading, MA: Addison-Wesley.
An engaging book that provides young readers with information and delightful text about dirt and all its components.

Branley, F. (1986). *Volcanoes*. New York: Harper.
This book explains how volcanoes are formed and how they affect the earth when they erupt.

Damon, L. (1990). *Discovering earthquakes and volcanoes*. Mahweh, NJ: Troll.
Provides readers with a basic introduction to earthquakes and their causes as well as the formation and eruption of volcanoes.

Griffey, H. (1998). *Volcanoes and other natural disasters*. New York: DK.
Kids learn about earthquakes, volcanoes, and tidal waves—and their effects on human populations.

Hiscock, B. (1988). *The big rock*. New York: Atheneum.
The story of a single rock in the Adirondack Mountains and the weathering, erosion, and mountain building that created it.

Lye, K. (1993). *Earthquakes*. Austin, TX: Raintree/Steck-Vaughn.
Discusses the phenomenon of earthquakes, including information on where and how they form.

Lye, K. (1998). *Volcanoes*. Austin, TX: Raintree/Steck-Vaughn.
Discusses the origin and nature of volcanoes—how they erupt and where they are found.

Moore, J. (1999). *I didn't know that quakes split the ground*. Brookfield, CT: Copper Beech Books.
A delightfully illustrated book that provides youngsters with fascinating facts and incredible information about earthquakes. A real winner!

Nirgiotis, N. (1996). *Volcanoes: Mountains that blow their tops*. New York: Grosset & Dunlap.
An easy-to-read introduction to one of nature's most spectacular forces.

Oliver, C. (1998). *I didn't know that mountains gush lava and ash*. Brookfield, CT: Copper Beech Books.

Filled with lots of mind-boggling illustrations, this book offers lots of engaging information about volcanoes.

Intermediate (Grades 4–6)

Bain, I. (1984). *Mountains and earth movements.* New York: Watts.
What are the effects of erosion, weathering, faulting, folding, and continental drift on the creation of mountains? This book describes all of them in detail.

Farndon, J. (1992). *How the earth works: 100 ways parents and kids can share the secrets of the earth.* New York: Readers Digest.
Lots and lots of experiments and projects designed to help kids learn about the earth.

Fredericks, A. D. (1995). *Simple nature experiments with everyday materials.* New York: Sterling.
Filled with more than 100 experiments and activities about earth, nature, and the environment, this book offers youngsters loads of investigative projects that will delight and inform.

Ganeri, A. (1991). *Forces of nature.* Racine, WI: Western Publishing.
Presented in a question and answer format, this book provides young scientists with basic information about the geology of the earth.

George, M. (1991). *Glaciers.* Mankato, MN: Creative Education.
Color photographs of glaciers and other natural phenomena are presented in dynamic two-page spreads. A fantastic addition to any young scientist's library.

Lasky, K. (1992). *Surtsey: The newest place on earth.* New York: Hyperion.
Lyrical prose and spectacular photographs recount the story of this newest volcanic island created off the coast of Iceland in 1963.

Levy, M. (1997). *Earthquake games: Earthquakes and volcanoes explained by games and experiments.* New York: Margaret McElderry.
Where do earthquakes and volcanoes come from. Through interactive games and activities students learn much about these natural phenomena.

Loeschnig, L. (1996). *Simple earth science experiments with everyday materials.* New York: Sterling Publishing.
Dozens of explorations, discoveries, and experiments designed to help youngsters learn more about their planet.

Pope, J. (1998). *Earthquakes.* Brookfield, CT: Copper Beech Books.
A delightful introduction to the forces and power of these natural occurrences.

Sattler, H. (1995). *Our patchwork planet.* New York: Lothrop.
This book provides the reader with an interesting excursion through present-day tectonic theory.

Taylor, B. (1993). *Mountains and volcanoes.* New York: Kingfisher.
A wonderfully illustrated text highlighted by informative details and stories about mountains and volcanoes.

Watt, F. (1993). *Earthquakes and volcanoes.* London: Usborne.
Lots of illustrations and a detailed text make this a fascinating book on volcanoes and earthquakes.

Zoehfeld, K. (1995). *How mountains are made.* New York: HarperCollins.
Mountain formation is described through the eyes of four children.

Web Sites

http://volcano.und.nodak.edu
http://www.k12.hi.us/~kapuhaha/volcanoes_of_the_world_mai.htm
http://hammer.ne.mediaone.net/earth_force/default.html
http://quake.wr.usgs.gov
http://www.crustal.ucsb.edu/ics/understanding/
http://www.ittybittyblackboard.com/science.htm

Audiovisual Selections

The Forces of Nature [filmstrip] (catalog no. C31012). Washington, D.C., National Geographic Society.

Our Ever Changing Earth [filmstrip] (catalog no. C30730). Washington, D.C., National Geographic Society.

MINI-THEMES

Water

We often take water for granted. Without question, it is certainly one of the most precious commodities on the face of the earth. It is necessary for our health and survival, important in business and industry, and needed for the sustenance of life in all its forms. One of the major concerns we have with water today is its purity. Pollution of our water sources and resources is an increasing social, economic, and environmental issue. Helping students appreciate the importance of water in their lives can help them in understanding their role in preserving this valuable resource.

Activities

1. Invite students to make a list of all the different ways in which water is used in their homes (cooking, drinking, bathing, etc.). How many different ways is water used around the house? Encourage students to compute the average amount of water used in the home each day. Students whose families use city water may be able to use their monthly water bill to compute a daily average.

2. Students may wish to create their own well. Invite them to obtain a large (#10) aluminum can (a coffee can works well). A cardboard tube (from a roll of paper towels) can be placed upright in the can. Pour a layer of gravel inside the can around the outside of the tube. Pour another equal layer of sand on top of the gravel. Pour in water until it reaches the top of the layer of sand. Invite students to notice what happens inside the tube. Explain to them that this is the same process used for obtaining well water.

3. Invite students to obtain several different water samples from in and around their homes (e.g. tap water, water from a standing puddle, rain water, etc.). Encourage students to place several coffee filters over each of several glass jars. Then, invite students to pour each of the water samples into a separate jar. Encourage students to note the impurities that have been "trapped" by each of the filters. Which type of water has the most impurities?

4. Obtain some chunks of sandstone from a neighborhood building supplier or hardware store. Soak the pieces in water for a few hours. Place individual pieces of (soaked) sandstone in sealable sandwich bags and seal them tightly. Place the bags in the freezer overnight. Take them out and invite students to note what has happened inside each bag (the sandstone has split apart because water expands as it freezes). Share with students the fact that this process is identical to a similar occurrence in nature when water seeks into the cracks and fissures in rocks. It freezes and (over time) begins to break them apart.

References

Ardley, N. (1991). *The science book of water*. New York: Harcourt Brace.

Arnold, C. (1985). *Bodies of water: Fun, facts, and activities*. New York: Watts.

Fredericks, Anthony D. (1995). *Simple nature experiments with everyday materials*. New York: Sterling Publishing.

Peters, L. (1991). *Water's way*. New York: Arcade Publishing.

Taylor, Barbara. (1990). *Sink or swim!: The science of water*. New York: Random House.

Taylor, B. (1991). *Water at work*. New York: Watts.

Rocks and Soil

There are three different kinds of rocks. **Igneous** rocks are those that form from melted mineral and can often be found near volcanoes. Granite is one type of igneous rock. **Sedimentary** rocks are those that are usually formed under water as a result of layers of sediment pressing down on other layers of sediment. Sandstone and limestone are examples of sedimentary rocks. **Metamorphic** rocks are those that result from great heat and pressure inside the earth's surface. Marble is an example of a metamorphic rock.

Soil is actually rocks which have been broken up into very fine pieces. Soil is usually created over several years (hundreds or thousands) and is the result of weathering, erosion, and freezing. Soil also contains air, water, and decayed matter (known as **humus**). Basically, there are three types of soil— clay, sandy, and loam (a rich mixture of clay, sand, and humus).

Activities

1. Provide students with several sealable plastic sandwich bags. Take a "field trip" through your town or neighborhood and invite students to collect as many different soil samples as possible. Upon your return to the classroom, invite students to gently pour each sample onto a white sheet of

paper. Provide students with some toothpicks and hand lenses (available at most toy or hobby stores). Invite students to carefully sift through each sample to determine its components. What "ingredients" are found in each sample? Are the samples distinctively different or about the same? How big or small are the particles in each sample? Which sample would be best for growing plants?

2. Invite a local gardener or employee of a local gardening center to visit your classroom to talk about soil conditions in your area. What recommendations would that person make for turning the native soil into the best possible growing medium? What special nutrients or additives should be added to the soil in order to begin a garden? What is distinctive about the native soil that makes it appropriate or inappropriate for growing vegetables, for example?

3. Obtain some organic clay and some modeling clay from a local arts and crafts store. Invite students to note the difference in the composition of the two clays. Encourage students to make a simple piece of pottery from each sample. Place each piece of pottery in the sun. After a few days, ask students to note the difference between the two pottery pieces. What has changed? What has remained the same? You may wish to share with students the fact that pottery pieces more than 5,000 years old have been found at various archeological sites around the world.

4. *Adult Demonstration Only:* Bring a small piece of brick to the classroom, soak it in water, and place it in a bowl. In a separate large container, mix together ½ cup of water, ½ cup of bluing (from the laundry section of the grocery store), and ½ cup of ammonia. Use a measuring cup to pour some of this mixture over the brick. Sprinkle the brick with salt and let it stand for 24 hours. The next day students will be able to see crystals forming on the surface of the brick. Continue to add some more of the water + bluing + ammonia mixture to keep the crystals growing. Explain to students that this is similar to a process in nature known as *crystallization*—a process in which crystals are formed over long periods of time (hundreds of years).

References

Bass, L. (1991). *Rocks*. Racine, WI: Western Publishing.

Barkin, J. (1990). *Rocks, rocks big and small*. Englewood Cliffs, NJ: Silver Press.

Bourgeois, P. (1990). *The amazing dirt book*. Reading, MA: Addison-Wesley.

Fredericks, A. D. (1995). *Simple nature experiments with everyday materials*. New York: Sterling Publishing.

Hiscock, B. (1988). *The big rock*. New York: Atheneum.

Parker, S. (1993). *Rocks and minerals*. New York: Dorling Kindersley.

Selsam, M. *First look at rocks*. New York: Walker, 1984.

Insects/Bugs

OVERVIEW

Focus

Students will learn some of the common characteristics of insects and spiders.

Objectives

On completion of this thematic unit, students will be able to:

1. Recognize and describe a variety of insects/bugs.
2. Describe the difference between spiders (arachnid) and insects. Spiders have two body parts and eight legs. Insects usually have 6 legs, if winged, four wings and three body parts.
3. Describe where insects/bugs live and what they eat.
4. Identify how some insects/bugs are helpful and how some are harmful.
5. Demonstrate how insects/bugs move.

HOW IT WORKS

Initiating Activity

Create a semantic web about insects by first asking the children to share with you what they know about insects as you record it on the web. After you have recorded what they know about insects, add the following facts and information about insects to the web such as:

- There are more than a million species of insects on the earth.
- All insects hatch from eggs.
- Bodies of insects have three parts: head, thorax, and abdomen (Show a diagram, if possible).
- Insects are food for birds, reptiles, some mammals, and other insects.
- Insects have no bones. They have an outside skeleton that protects their bodies.
- The mouth of an insect has teeth, a tongue, and a sucking tube used for eating.
- Most insects have two sets of eyes.

Example of a Semantic Web on Insects

```
thorax          head          abdomen

         three body parts          hatch from eggs

                      insects

         no bone               more than a million
                                species on earth
```

General Activities

1. Provide the students with some clay and an assortment of pipe cleaners in various sizes and colors, toothpicks or straws. Ask the students to make an insect of their choice, using a picture as a guide. The clay can be used to represent the bodies and the pipe cleaners, straws or toothpicks the legs and antennae. Provide an area where the insects can be displayed. Ask the students to label their insects by placing a small piece of paper beside it with the name of the insect and the student's name.

2. Obtain a medium-sized, wide-mouth jar in which you can secure a piece of netting or nylon stocking with a rubber band over it. Then take a nature walk outside to look for insects. The jar can become the habitat for an insect that the students find (e.g. a caterpillar, ant, etc.). Once the insect is caught, be sure to put a twig, leaves and other appropriate materials for that particular insect's environment in the jar and put the cover over the top. Allow the children to observe this insect for a few days, record findings, and then carefully return it to its original environment. See Activity 9 for additional information related to this activity.

3. Ask the children to select an insect for which they can demonstrate it's movement (e.g. for a bee, they could extend their arms and buzz around the room; for a caterpillar they could slither on the floor). Allow other children to guess the insect. It is the child who guesses correctly to act out the next movements.

4. Provide the children with an assortment of magazines that would contain pictures of insects. Encourage them to bring in old magazines from home. Then ask the children to make a class collage by pasting pictures of different insects on an insect graffiti wall.

5. As a class, write to *Ranger Rick's Nature Magazine*, [National Wildlife Federation, 1412 - 16th Street, N.W., Washington, DC 20036] asking them

to send you information about the materials they have available about insects. You may be able to obtain some free and/or inexpensive pictures and books that can be displayed and used in the classroom. If you do not subscribe to *Ranger Rick* or *Your Big Backyard,* ask for sample copies. Both magazines provide an excellent addition to your library.

6. Invite an entomologist to visit the class. Explain to the children that an entomologist is someone who studies insects. Many entomologists have collections of insects. Ask him/her if they have a collection of insects if they would be willing to share it with the class. Also, ask the entomologist to explain why they study insects and how they do it. Encourage the children to ask questions. (*Note:* Many museums also have insect collections.)

7. Have the children help make an "Insect Concentration Game." This can be done by purchasing two sets of insect stickers, putting one of each insect on two sets of cards so that you have a pair of each insect. Laminate the cards and turn the cards face down. Next, a player turns over two cards. If they match, he/she keeps the pair. The game continues until all cards are matched. The person with the most matched pairs is the winner. Matching cards can also be made by making sets of animals/insects and the food they eat; turtles eat bugs, bees for flowers, etc., or habitats with insects; bees with hive, ants with hills, caterpillars with cocoons. Pictures for cards can be drawn by children or cut from magazines.

8. Provide inked stamp pads and ask the children to use their thumb prints to make insect/spider bodies and then draw legs and antennae. Tell the children to also illustrate the environment in which you would find that particular insect(s). Display the illustrations.

9. Send a letter to the parents telling them that the children in your class are learning about insects. Ask them for their cooperation in helping their child find an insect to bring to the class. Caution them about how they need to be sure the insect is harmless and to be careful scooping it into a jar. Small plastic containers with small holes punched in the lid are safe containers to put insects in to transport to school. Be sure to remind them to include dirt, grass, leaves, and twigs to create an appropriate environment. Ask the children to bring in the different insects, identify them, place them on a "Science Table" with magnifying glasses, and allow the children time to observe them. Have a paper on the table where children can write out their observations.

10. Create a Semantic Feature Analysis (SFA) Grid (see Chapter 2, pp. 46–48) on which the children list insects with which they are familiar along the left-hand side of the grid and some features of insects across the top of the grid. (See example on p. 118) When grid is completed, encourage children to discuss insects that have common features.

11. Collect items for the classroom that reinforces information about insects such as the Smithsonian Insects Video, Backyard Bugs Giant Floor Puzzle, Bug Cookie Cutters, Insect Finger Puppets, The Bug Game, Very Hungry Caterpillar Game, Ant Farm, etc. The materials are available at a variety

Sample SFA Grid on Insects

If an insect matches with a feature, place an "x" under that feature. For example:

	colorful	eats plants	Eats other insects	helpful	harmful
Firefly	X	X		X	
Ladybug	X		X	X	
Aphid		X			X

of stores or from catalogs such as Insect Lore [P. O. Box 1535, 132 S. Beech Avenue, Shafter, CA 93263 (1-800-Live Bug)].

Discussion Questions

1. What are the differences between a spider and an insect? (Most insects have three body parts, six legs, and if winged, two wings. Spiders have two body parts and eight legs).

2. How can insects be helpful to humans?

3. How can insects be harmful to humans?

4. If you could be an insect, what would you be? Why?

LITERATURE RELATED ACTIVITIES

Title: *Fireflies in the Night*

Genre: Nonfiction

Author: Judy Hawes

Illustrator: Ellen Alexander

Bibliographic Information: HarperCollins Publishing, New York, 1991.

Summary: A young girl visiting her grandparents in the country finds out how and why fireflies make light and how to catch and handle them. She also finds out several uses for the light made by the fireflies.

Interest Level: Grades K–3

Pre-Reading Activitiy

Read the title of the book, *Fireflies in the Night*. Then turn to the first two pages (pp. 4 and 5) and show the children the illustrations as you read the text. Then initiate the K-W-L three step framework (see Chapter 2, pp. 42–44) by creating the following column on the chalkboard and asking the children to respond to the headings.

What I **K**now	What I **W**ant to Learn	What I **L**earned

Record what the children tell you they already know about fireflies and what they want to learn. Read the story and record what they have learned from reading the book.

Learning Activities

1. Obtain other books about fireflies such as P. Sturges' *Ten Flashing Fireflies* or J. Brinckloe's *Fireflies!*. Compare and contrast these books.

2. As a group, write an experience story about a night with some fireflies. Ask the children to pretend they are somewhere, like the little girl in *Fireflies in the Night*. What would they see? What would they do? How would they feel? When the story is completed, divide the text into different parts. Assign different parts or even one sentence to a small group of children to illustrate. Finally, put the text with the illustrations and put together to make a class book about fireflies.

3. Allow the children time to look at the illustrations. Then ask them to work in cooperative learning groups to write a Haiku poem about the firefly. Haiku is a form of Japanese poetry consisting of three lines. The first line has five syllables in it, the second line seven syllables and the third line five syllables, and usually the topic of the poem has to do with nature.

   For example:

   > Fire/flies light at night
   >   1   2   3   4   5
   > Beau/ti/ful and bright as stars
   > 1 2 3   4   5   6   7
   > Will you light my way
   >   1   2   3   4   5

4. Help the children create a crayon resist picture by drawing fireflies all over a paper and then coloring their tails bright yellow, wings brown and white. Remind them to press very hard with the crayons. Then using very thin black tempera paint, paint over the fireflies. The fireflies will look as if they are illuminating in the dark. Display pictures.

Discussion Questions

1. Do you think the little girl likes to visit her grandparents? Why or why not?

2. What part of this story did you like best? Why?

   What part of this story did you like least? Why?

3. What were some of the uses made of the light from the fireflies?

4. Do you think the little girl wanted to let the fireflies out of the jar? Explain. What do you think would have happened to the fireflies if they had not let them go?

5. Do you believe a doctor in Cuba used a firefly lamp in the operating room? Why or why not?

Title: *The Very Quiet Cricket*

Genre: Picture Book

Author: Eric Carle

Bibliographic Information: Philomel Books, New York, 1990.

Summary: A beautifully illustrated book about a very quiet cricket who wanted to make a sound. He meets many other insects that do make sounds. Finally, he meets another cricket and he is able to make a beautiful chirping sound.

Interest Level: Grades Pre School–2.

Pre-Reading Activity

Show the children the book and read the title. Ask the children to tell you what they know about crickets. Ask what kind of noises they make. Then read them the introduction about crickets. If possible, share additional information and pictures of crickets that you have collected.

Learning Activities

1. As a group, review all the different insects that are introduced in this book. Then ask them to make a large illustration of that insect and label it. Display the illustrations on a bulletin board that is labeled, "Our Insect Collection".

2. Divide the class into cooperative learning groups and assign each group an insect that was introduced in the book. Ask this group to work cooperatively to find out more about their insect, (e.g. What do they eat? Where do they live? Are they helpful to humans? Are they harmful to humans?) Resources such as the encyclopedia, *Ranger Rick* and *Your Big Backyard* magazines may be helpful. The children may be able to find some of the insects (except for the bumblebee!) and put them in jars. Finally, allow time for the groups to share what they found out about their assigned insect.

3. As a group, discuss what you think will happen now that the cricket met another cricket and he can chirp. Then write a language experience story as sequel to *The Very Quiet Cricket* and illustrate it.

4. Obtain other books by Eric Carle such as *The Very Hungry Caterpillar*; *The Grouchy Lady Bug; The Very Busy Spider;* and *The Honeybee and the Robber*. Allow time for the children to read these books. Then discuss the style of this illustrator/author. Also, discuss the different insects introduced in these stories and how Mr. Carle's presentation of the insects are similar or different. As a culmination of looking at Eric Carle's books, write him a letter, and send it via his publisher telling him what you like about his books.

Discussion Questions

1. What would be a good name for the cricket in this story? Why?

2. What do you think the other crickets thought when they said "Hello" and the cricket said nothing? How do you think the cricket felt?

3. Which of the insects that the cricket met would you like to meet?

4. Why was the cricket able to make a sound when he met the other cricket and not before?

Title: *The Best Book of Bugs*

Genre:	Informational
Author:	Claire Llewellyn
Bibliographic Information:	Kingfishers, New York, 1998.
Summary:	This book describes the habitats and life cycles of various insects and provides ways for identifying them in their natural habitats.
Interest Level:	Grades 1–4.

Pre-Reading Activity

Write the word bugs/insects on the chalkboard. Explain that another name for bugs is insects. Ask the children to name some bugs as you list them. After insects have been named, ask the children to describe what all these insects have in common (most of them are small, they have six legs, three body parts, etc.). Read the book and compare what the children said to the information provided in the book.

Learning Activities

1. Provide the children with an assortment of arts and crafts materials (paper, glue, yarn, pipe cleaners, glitter, small plastic moveable eyes, sequins, etc.). Ask the children to create an insect and label what it is. Display the insects.

2. Ask the children to think about and then create a make-believe insect that is yet to be discovered. The make-believe insect should be illustrated,

named, and a brief paragraph written telling where the insect would live, what it would eat, if it is helpful or pesty, etc. Allow time to share.

3. Read pp. 22–23 of *The Best Book of Bugs* and then demonstrate the stages of a butterfly by making the following sock puppet out of two socks. You will need one knee sock (preferably brown) and a small paper butterfly. Place the butterfly in your hand and pull the brown knee sock up over one arm. The long knee sock is the caterpillar. Next, pull the knee sock down over your hand and hold your hand down (looks like a cocoon hanging from a tree). Finally, shed the knee sock and in your hand will be the final stage: the butterfly. The students will be amazed and will want to try it themselves.

4. As a class, brainstorm (both positive and negative) about what the planet earth would be like if there were no insects. For example, imagine no more mosquito or bee bites, no more honey, no more flowers, no more butterflies, etc. Categorize these into "Positive effects of insects" and "Negative effects of insects" and list them on the chalkboard. Then write and illustrate a short story about the planet without insects.

Discussion Questions

1. Are spiders bugs? (No) Explain. (Spiders have eight legs instead of six and their bodies are divided into two parts instead of three)

2. What is meant by a complete metamorphosis? (When insects go through four stages of life to become an adult) Name one insect that goes through four stages.

3. What are the four stages a butterfly goes through? (egg, larva, pupa, butterfly)

4. How do insects help us?

5. What do insects eat?

Title: *Ladybug*

Genre:	Informational
Author:	Emery Bernhard
Illustrator:	Durga Bernhard
Bibliographic Information:	Holiday House, New York, 1994.
Summary:	This book follows the stages of development of the ladybug, from mating and hatching of the larvae, to the growth of the larvae into an adult ladybug. It contains realistic photographs and drawings.
Interest Level:	Grades K–3 (The text is written in two different levels).

Pre-Reading Activity

Read the title of the book and show the children the cover. Ask the children if they have ever seen a ladybug. If so, ask them to tell you about it. If not, ask them to tell you what they think a ladybug is like. Before reading the story, you may want to introduce some of the key words found in the glossary of the book.

Learning Activities

1. Have the children fold a piece of paper or draw lines so they have 4 boxes. Tell them to number the boxes 1-4. Ask the children to illustrate the first phase of the ladybugs life cycle in first box, second phase in next box, and so forth. Allowing them to review the illustrations in the book will help them. This paper could be cut apart and stapled to make a booklet that the children could take home.

1	2
3	4

2. Collect other books about ladybugs such as *Ladybug* by Barrie Watts, *The Ladybug and Other Insects* by G. Jeunesse, *Ladybugs Ball* by H. Heldman or *The Grouchy Ladybug* by Eric Carle. Allow time for the children to compare and contrast these books with *Ladybug* by Emery Bernhard.

3. Ladybugs live on aphids. Discuss how aphids suck juice from leaves and then the leaves die. Help the children find out more about aphids. Encyclopedias or other insect books can provide information. *The Grouchy Ladybug* by Eric Carle would be a good book to share with the children while you are discussing aphids.

4. Paint the outside of pry-off bottle caps with red nail polish so you have one for each child. When dry, use a black marker to draw the head and spots of the ladybug.

   See example to the right.

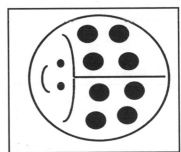

Discussion Questions

1. How do you think the ladybug got its name? Do you think it is a good name? Why or why not?

2. What is the most interesting thing you learned about ladybugs from reading this book?

3. The book indicated there are approximately 350 kinds of ladybugs in North America. Describe some of the other kinds of ladybugs (two-spotted, nine-spotted, spotless, ash gray). Have you ever seen any of these types of ladybugs? If so, describe what they look like.

4. Why do orange growers in California bring ladybugs into their groves (they protect the orange trees by eating the scale insects)?

CULMINATING ACTIVITY

Ask the children to each write three questions about insects for which they *do* or *do not* know the answer. Put all the questions on strips of paper that have been folded into a container. As a group, pull one at a time from the container and see if anyone knows the answer. If someone does, go to the next question. If no one knows the answer, assign two or three children to research the answer at a later time. Once all questions have been dealt with, allow a few days for the researchers to find answers for those questions not answered. Then reconvene the group and allow researchers to report their findings. Finally, compile all the questions with answers into a class booklet entitled, "Everything We've Ever Wanted to Know About Insects".

SUPPLEMENTAL LITERATURE

Books

Aardema, V. (1978). *Why mosquitoes buzz in people's ears*. New York: Dial Books.
A beautifully illustrated African tale that explains the origin of mosquitoes buzzing in people's ears.

Brinckloe, J. (1985). *Fireflies!* New York: Macmillan.
A beautiful story that captures the freedom of the fireflies on a summer night.

Broda, R. (1998). *Have you seen bugs*? Illustrated by Joanne F. Oppenheimer. New York: Scholastic Trade.
This book describes, in rhyming verse, a variety of bugs and how they look, behave, and improve our lives.

Carle, E. (1985). *The grouchy ladybug*. New York: HarperCollins.
A braggart becomes a better behaved bug as it learns something about getting along with others.

Facklam, M. (1994). *The big bug book*. Illustrated by P. Facklam. Boston: Little, Brown.
Describes thirteen of the world's largest insects, including the Great Owlet Moth and Hercules Beetle.

Feldman, H. L., & Hirashima, J. (1998). *Lady bugs ball*. Illustrated by Heather Lowenberg. New York: Random Library.
Join Lady Bug and her other winged guests as they get ready to dance the night away. Inchworms measure the dance floor, Duchess de Spider weaves decorations, and an ensemble of crickets provide the music.

Florian, D. (1998). *Insectlopedia: Poems and Paintings*. San Diego, CA: Harcourt Brace.
This book presents twenty-one short poems about insects such as the inchworm, termite, cricket, and ladybug.

Hepworth, C. (1998). *Bug off!: A swarm of insect words*. New York: Putnam Publishing Group Juv.
This book presents vocabulary words relating to insects, including bees, moths, and ants.

Hornblow, L., & Hornblow, A. (1989). *Insects do the strangest things*. New York: Random House.
> This book describes nineteen insects that have peculiar and strange characteristics such as the camouflage of the walking stick, bugs that row themselves like boats on the water's surface, etc.

Jeunesse, G., & de Bourgoing, P. (1989). *The ladybug and other insects*. Illustrated by Sylvie Perols. New York: Scholastic, Inc.
> The brightly painted transparent pages allows the reader to watch a ladybug lay eggs on a leaf, see larvae turn into mature insects, and more.

Lavies, B. (1991). *Wasps at home*. New York: Dutton.
> This book is a study of social wasps, paper wasps, and baldface hornets from a colony's beginnings in spring to its demise in autumn.

Lewis, J. P. (1998). *The little buggers: Insect and spider poems*. Illustrated by Victoria Chess. New York: Dial Books.
> Provides an assortment of poems about insects and spiders.

Mishica, F. (1998). *Billions of bugs*. Illustrated by Roberta K. Loman. New York: Standard Publishing.
> An easy-to-read book that provides characteristics of some of the ordinary, as well as unusual bugs in our universe.

Murphy, S. (1996). *The best bug parade*. Illustrated by H. Keller. New York: HarperCollins Publishing.
> A variety of bugs compare their sizes while going on parade.

Parker, N. W., & Wright, J. R. (1987). *Bugs*. New York: William Morrow.
> Includes general information, jokes, and brief descriptions of the physical characteristics, habits, and natural environment of a variety of common insects.

Porcaro, S. T. (1997). *The creepy, crawly critters, bugs and bees book*. Illustrated by Lynda Pelkey and Julie Hadden. New York: Huckleberry Press.

Pringle, L. (1990). *The golden book of insects and spiders*. Racine, WI: Western Pub. Co.
> Beautifully illustrated book that includes diagrams and information about various insects and spiders.

Ryden, H. (1996). *ABC of crawlers and flyers*. Boston: Clarion Books.
> An alphabet book that contains facts and close-up photographs about many insects that inhabit the world.

Ross, K. (1997). *Wild about insects*. Brookfield, CT. Millbrook Press.
> Introduces crawling and flying insects through twenty simple projects.

Souza, D. M. (1991). *Insects around the house*. Minneapolis, MN: Carolrhoda Books, Inc.
> Describes the life cycles and habits of various insects found around the house.

Sturges, P. (1995). *Ten flashing fireflies*. Illustrated by Anna Vojtech. New York: North-South Books, Inc.

A rhymed counting book that captures the joy of catching fireflies on a summer night.

Suben, E. (1998). *The big rescue*. New York: Golden Books Publishing Co., Inc. The story of how Flik and his warrior friends save little princess Dot from the big bad bird.

Watts, B. (1987). *Ladybug*. Morristown, NJ: Silver Burdett Publishing. Photographs, drawings, and text on two different levels of difficulty follow the stages of development of the ladybug. It also describes insects as a human food source.

Web Sites

WWW.CRICKETMAG.COM
WWW.INSECTLORE.COM.

MINI-THEMES

Caterpillars, Butterflies and Moths

Butterflies and moths come in many shapes, colors, and sizes. The adult butterfly and moth are not harmful. They mostly suck the nectar of flowers and particularly like juice from fruits, sap, and honey. They taste with special organs on the bottoms of their feet. Most butterflies fly during the day; whereas, moths mostly fly at night. The children will enjoy learning about how butterflies and moths change in form and structure—how they go through stages of metamorphosis: egg, larva, or caterpillar, pupa, and finally a butterfly or moth.

Activities

1. Read Eric Carle's, *The Very Hungry Caterpillar* or *Butterflies* by Claude Delafosse and then discuss four stages of a butterfly: egg, caterpillar, pupa, then butterfly. If possible, find a caterpillar and put it in a large jar that has nylon or netting secured over the top. Place leaves in the jar for the caterpillar to eat and put a twig or branch for it to hopefully build a cocoon. Tell the children to be patient because it takes several months for the metamorphosis to take place. Butterfly kits are available commercially and come with feeding kits. *Note:* Silkworm's metamorphosis takes less than two months.

2. Cut large sheets of paper into a simple butterfly shape. Then ask the children to write a brief paragraph that begins, "If I Were a Butterfly I . . ." Allow children to share their stories and then compile them into a class booklet.

3. Some people collect butterflies. Try to locate someone with a butterfly collection to bring into your class to share. If this is not possible, obtain copy of *Butterflies* by Gail Saunders-Smith or similar books that contain excellent illustrations of butterflies. Allow time for the children to look at the different kinds of butterflies. Discuss the differences and similarities in the butterflies.

4. As a follow-up to Activity 3, collect the appropriate materials and plan a creative art time in which children make butterflies. Demonstrate how they can make butterflies by putting a pipe cleaner around the middle of a sheet of tissue paper. The butterfly can then be decorated, if desired. Or have them place old crayon shavings onto wax paper, lay another sheet of wax paper over it, and press with an iron set on low heat (use caution with iron). Then mount the melted crayon under a butterfly shaped mat opening. Display the butterflies.

5. Cut egg cartons in half, lengthwise. Tell the children to paint the egg carton. When it is dry, make a face on one end and then insert pipe cleaners for feelers and you have a caterpillar!

6. Butterflies can be grown in the classroom by obtaining a "Butterfly Garden" from Nasco Co. [901 Janesville Avenue, Ft. Atkinson, WI 53538 (1-800-558-9595)].

References

Arvetis, C. (1987). *What is a butterfly?* Chicago: Childrens Press.

Carle, E. (1969). *The very hungry caterpillar.* New York: Putman.

Delafosse, C. (1997). *Butterflies.* Illustrated by Gallimard Jeunesse. New York: Scholastic Trade.

Fraser, J. (1998). *Abdullah's Butterfly.* Illustrated by Kim Gamble. New York: Scholastic.

French, V. (1993). *Caterpillar, caterpillar.* Cambridge, MA: Candlewick Press.

Heller, R. (1985). *How to hide a butterfly and other insects.* New York: Grosset and Dunlap.

Hines, A. G. (1991). *Remember the butterflies.* New York: Dutton.

Howe, J. (1992). *I wish I were a butterfly.* Illustrated by Ed Young. San Diego: Harcourt Brace Jovanovich.

Kalman, B., & Everts, T. (1994). *Butterflies and Moths.* New York: Crabtree Publishing.

Morgan, S. (1996). *Butterflies, Bugs, and Worms.* New York: Kingfisher Books.

Saunders-Smith, G. (1998). *Butterflies.* Chicago: Children's Book Press.

Suzan, G. (1997). *Butterfly boy.* Illustrated by Virginia L. Kroll. Honesdale, PA: Boyds Mills Publishers.

Whayne, S. S. (1995). *The big butterfly book.* Mahwah, NJ: Troll Associates.

Ziefert, H. (1998). *Bugs, beetles, and butterflies.* Illustrated by Lisa Feather. New York: Viking Children's Books.

Ants

Ants are known as social insects and they live together in organized communities called colonies. The female members of the ant colonies are workers, except for the queen who lays the eggs. The workers jobs are to search for food, build the nest, care for the young, and fight off enemies. The male ants' only job is to mate with the young queens and then they die soon after. Each queen starts her new colony after mating. Children will enjoy reading the recommended books and doing the suggested activities to find out more about how ants live.

Activities

1. Ant farms are available in some commercial catalogs as well as in many toy, hobby or pet stores. Purchase an ant farm and allow children to observe the ants as they dig tunnels, build roads and rooms, eat and store food, and so forth. If you would rather create your own ant farm, directions are provided in *Ant Cities* by Arthur Dorros.

2. After a few days of careful observation of the ant farm (or an outdoor ant hill) ask the children to write and illustrate a story in which they put themselves into the life of an ant. Ask them to title their stories, "My Life As An Ant." Allow time to share stories and then compile into a class booklet.

3. Ants have no voice and do not communicate with sounds. They give messages through secretions which they pass throughout the colony by touching each other. They also leave a trail of secretions to help other ants find food. Provide stamp pads, tempera paints, markers, and paper. Then ask the children to create an "ant message" by "secreting" any kind of trail they want. After they have finished secreting their message, ask the children to explain their message either verbally or in writing. Ask the children questions such as, "What are you trying to tell the ant?" "What will the ant find at the end?"

4. After reading books such as *Inside an Ant Colony* by Allan Fowler or *Ant Cities* by Arthur Dorros, provide the children with a large sheet of paper. Then ask them to pretend they are inside an ant hill and to draw a map of what it would look like. Tell them to label or illustrate the various rooms (e.g. room for queen to lay eggs, rooms for larva and pupae, rooms for food, etc.). Allow time to share.

References

Brimmer, L. D. (1997). *How many ants?* Illustrated by Joan Cottle. New York: Children's Press.

Chinery, M. (1991). *Ant.* Mahwah, NJ: Troll Associates.

Dorros, A. (1987). *Ant cities.* New York: Harper & Row.

Fowler, A. (1998). *Inside an ant colony.* Danbury, CT: Children's Press.

Grossman, P. (1997). *Very first things to know about ants.* Illustrated by John D. Dawson. New York: Workman Publishing Co.

Hoose, P. M., Hoose, H., & Hoose. Debbie T. (1998). *Hey, little aunt.* Berkeley, CA: Tricycle Publishing.

Korman, J. (1998). *A bug's life: Classic storybook.* New York: Mouse Works.

Losi, C. A. (1997). *512 ants on Sullivan Street.* Illustrated by Patrick Merrell. Madsion, WI: Demco Media.

Nickle, J. (1995). *The ant bully.* New York: Scholastic Trade.

Rowen, J.P. (1993). *Ants.* Vero Beach, FL: Rourke, Corp. Inc.

Van Allsburg, C. (1988). *Two bad ants.* New York: Houghton Mifflin.

Dinosaurs

OVERVIEW

Focus

Students will explore prehistoric times to expand their knowledge of dinosaurs.

Objectives

On completion of this thematic unit, students will be able to:

1. Define various dinosaur terms such as "extinct" and "fossil."

2. Give examples of animals from the past that are now extinct.

3. Explain how scientists learned about life long ago.

4. Compare/contrast life today to life when the dinosaurs existed.

HOW IT WORKS

Initiating Activity

Purchase 3 to 4 medium-sized watermelons and paint them white. These are then hidden in a "dinosaur nest" somewhere on the playground before the start of the lesson. Tell the students that they must find the dinosaur's nest in order to begin the dinosaur unit. Once the "eggs" are found, they can be cut open and shared with the group. After returning to the classroom, have the students draw pictures of imaginary creatures that may have laid the eggs.

General Activities

1. Prior to the lesson, use string to measure the height and length of various dinosaurs. Line the class up by height and choose the student in the center of the line to represent the average height. Trace this person's body on heavy butcher paper to get a pattern. On the playground, roll out the string to represent the size for one of the dinosaurs. Have students guess how many bodies long and high the dinosaur is. Have a child record the estimate and use the pattern to obtain an actual measurement. Do this for the other dinosaurs for which you cut string. Compare the sizes.

2. Have students develop different menus for various types of dinosaurs. What plants or meats must each dinosaur eat to stay healthy? How much food should a particular dinosaur eat each day?

3. Have students work in small groups to create a large wall mural showing what life was like when the dinosaurs existed. The mural can be drawn on heavy butcher paper and decorated with paints, crayons, construction paper, or other art materials selected by the students.

4. Make arrangements with the school's special teachers (music, art, physical education, etc.) so they become involved in the unit: the music teacher can teach songs related to dinosaurs; the art teacher can help students create dinosaur t-shirts using stencils and paint; the gym teacher can involve students in creating dinosaur movements; the librarian can read additional dinosaur stories and show filmstrips or movies related to dinosaurs and the age of dinosaurs.

5. Have students select a favorite dinosaur. As that dinosaur, have them write "dinograms" to another "dinosaur" in the class comparing life today with their lives during the age of dinosaurs.

6. Have students create graphs and charts that record the heights, weights, and sizes of various dinosaurs. Some library research will be necessary.

7. Invite a professor from a local college to make a short presentation on dinosaurs. Have your students prepare a list of questions beforehand to ask the visiting speaker.

8. Using known poems, songs, and stories, create frames and have the students make them into dinosaur poems and songs. For example, using *Brown Bear, Brown Bear, What Do You See?* by Bill Martin, Jr. (Holt, 1967), students can turn it into *Dinosaur, Dinosaur . . .* Or, students may wish to use the story, *If the Dinosaurs Came Back,* by Bernard Most (HBJ, 1978), as a model for their own story about what would happen if the dinosaurs again walked on earth.

9. Take a poll of the students' favorite dinosaurs and graph responses.

10. Share and choral read poems about dinosaurs, such as those in *Dinosaurs* (Hopkins, 1987), *Tyrannosaurus Was a Beast* (Mulberry, 1988), *Laugheteria* (Harcourt Brace) or *Dinosaur Dinner* (Random House). Have students collect their favorite dinosaur poems (both original and those published in books), illustrate them, and create a class anthology dedicated to the dinosaur.

Discussion Questions

1. What if dinosaurs were still living today? Where would they live?

2. What are some of the similarities between dinosaurs and some animals that live today? (Many animals have similar characteristics—for example, like the rhinoceros, triceratops walked on four legs and had horns. The hadrosaurus was a "duckbilled dinosaur" and had webbed fingers and toes. Porcupines are similar to the kentrosaurus, which was covered with sharp spikes. The pteranodon resembles the pelican—it lived by the sea and scooped up fish in a pelican-like beak. Lizards and alligators, both reptiles, have many characteristics that remind us of the dinosaurs of yesterday.)

3. How do scientists learn about animals that are no longer living? (By studying fossils and fossil tracks.)

4. How can we tell if a dinosaur ate meat or plants? (Generally, the meat eaters had much sharper teeth; some even had fangs.)

5. In what ways do you think dinosaurs were able to protect themselves from their enemies? (By using their sharp teeth, claws, horns, etc.)

LITERATURE RELATED ACTIVITIES

Title: *Dinosaur Skeletons*

Genre: Nonfiction

Author: Annie Ingle

Illustrated: Peter Barrett

Bibliographic Information: Random House, New York, 1993.

Summary: Many youngsters assume that all dinosaurs were big, lumbering creatures. Not so! Many types of dinosaurs were no bigger than the pets we have at home. This book presents some unique characteristics of both small and large dinosaurs.

Interest Level: Grades 1–3.

Pre-Reading Activity

Ask students whether they think it would be easier for a large dinosaur or a small dinosaur to survive. Discuss the special types of survival techniques a small dinosaur would need to compete with his bigger cousins. Read the book and compare their answers.

Learning Activities

1. Ask students to create a "testimonial" on the benefits of a small dinosaur over a large one.
2. Have students create various dinosaur skeletons with pipe cleaners.
3. Have students write and illustrate make-believe stories about going back in time to observe the age of dinosaurs.
4. Using an old board game, have students create rules and characters for a dinosaur game. For example, use an old "Candy Land" game board and write out cards that are facts about dinosaurs. Don't forget to have some free moves forward and some move backward cards.

Discussion Questions

1. What advantages do you think small dinosaurs have over larger ones? (They required less food; could hide more easily from enemies; could find food in certain areas inaccessible to larger dinosaurs.)
2. What would you enjoy most about living during the time of the dinosaurs?
3. What new information would you still like to learn about dinosaurs?
4. In your opinion, what is the most important thing we know about the dinosaurs?

Title: *Fossils*

Genre: Nonfiction

Author: John Howard

Illustrator: Lisa Bonforte

Bibliographic Information: Troll, New York, 1997.

Summary: Presents readers with valuable information regarding the painstaking process of digging up dinosaur fossils and reconstructing dinosaur skeletons. The book provides data on the work of paleontologists using a light and easy tone.

Interest Level: Grades 2–4.

Pre-Reading Activity

Provide small groups of children with a pile of chicken bones (be sure the bones have been boiled and dried thoroughly). Direct each group to arrange the bones in their original configuration. Discuss any problems they had in putting the skeleton back together—even though most know exactly what a chicken looks like. Discuss the difficulties scientists have in putting dinosaur skeleton together, particularly when no human has ever seen a live dinosaur.

Learning Activities

1. Have students imagine they are a certain dinosaur. Have them introduce themselves to the class by describing the important features of the dinosaur they have become. Ask other students to determine their identities.

2. Have students create their own dinosaur fossils. Provide small groups of students with pie plates half-filled with wet sand. Ask each group to place several chicken bones in the wet sand. Circular strips of cardboard can be placed around the bones and then plaster of Paris mixed and poured into the makeshift molds. After the plaster of Paris has dried, have students examine their "fossils" to note any similarities with dinosaur fossils.

3. Have students create their own dinosaur books. Ask each student to trace an outline of a favorite type of dinosaur on a sheet of construction paper and cut it out. Students should then trace that shape on another piece of construction paper, as well as several sheets of newsprint, and cut them out. All the sheets should be put together (with the construction paper sheets on the front and back) and stapled together. Have students write about their favorite dinosaur on the pages of their "dinosaur book."

4. Locate a photograph or illustration of a dinosaur skeleton. Direct students to count the number of bones in a leg, in the chest, or in other sections of the dinosaur body. Ask them to compare their count with the number of bones in a similar section of a human body or to bones in other animal groups.

Discussion Questions

1. How was our planet earth different during the dinosaur period than it is now? (The air was warmer and much of the land was low and swampy.)

2. What are some of the difficulties scientists have in reconstructing dinosaur bones? (Rarely is the entire dinosaur fossil found. Scientists have to piece together fossils like a puzzle.)

3. Why do you think people are so interested in learning about dinosaurs?

4. What do you consider to be the most interesting part of a paleontologist's job?

Title: *An Alphabet of Dinosaurs*

Genre: Nonfiction

Author: Peter Dodson

Bibliographic Information: Scholastic, New York, 1995.

Summary: With an abundance of illustrations and diagrams, this book provides young children with a captivating look at 26 different dinosaurs.

Interest Level: Grades 4–6.

Pre-Reading Activity

Ask each student to create an illustration of the *ideal* dinosaur. What would it look like? What size would it be in order to have the best chance for survival? What color would it be? Collect these illustrations and use them for comparison with illustrations in the book.

Learning Activities

1. Have students imagine they are reporters who have been transported back to the time of the dinosaurs. Direct them to create a news bulletin that describes an encounter between two or more dinosaurs, or a dinosaur and a person.

2. Have students create an original dinosaur dictionary. Direct them to collect dinosaur-related words (not dinosaur names) from this book and other resources and compile these words into a dictionary (cut in the shape of a dinosaur).

3. Using a long roll of butcher paper or newsprint, cover one wall of your classroom or a section of hallway outside your room. Have students create a mural that depicts the age of the dinosaurs.

Discussion Questions

1. Which dinosaur do you think would have the greatest chance for survival if it were to appear on earth today? Why? Which one would have the most difficult time surviving today? Why?

2. Which dinosaur do you believe is the most dangerous? Why?

3. Describe four dinosaurs and discuss how the dinosaurs are different from one another.

4. Why do people find dinosaurs so fascinating? Which dinosaur is your favorite? Explain.

Title: *I Wonder Why Triceratops Had Horns and Other Questions About Dinosaurs*

Genre: Informational

Author: Rod Theodorou

Bibliographic Information: Kingfisher, New York, 1997.

Summary: This book is full of interesting questions and lively answers about dinosaurs that inhabited our planet millions of years ago.

Interest level: Grades 1–4.

Pre-Reading Activity

Read the title of the book to the students and then ask them to devise questions about dinosaurs for which they would like to have answers.

Learning Activities

1. Discuss some of the theories used to explain the disappearance of the dinosaurs. After sharing the book with students, have them create their own books using titles such as, What Happened to (student's name) Dinosaur?

2. In groups have students create a skit about one of the dinosaurs presented in the book. The skit can be performed using puppets, masks, etc.

3. Have small groups of students choose a dinosaur. Ask them to take a familiar or popular song and rewrite the lyrics using dinosaur words. For example (to the tune of "I've Been Working on the Railroad"):

    I've been watching Stegosaurus

    All the live long day.

    I've been watching Stegosaurus

    Just to see what he would say.

    Can't you hear him munchin', crunchin',

    Rise up and start to eat a tree?

    Don't you ever try to meet him,

    'Cause he will make you flee.

4. Have students deliver a persuasive speech they would use to try to convince a parent to allow them to have a dinosaur for a pet.

Discussion Questions

1. What did you find out in this question and answer book that you thought was most interesting?

2. Imagine that you went out to play one day and found a dinosaur in your backyard. What is the first thing you would say to it? What would you do?

3. What if you found a clue that led you to believe a dinosaur was still living. What would you do?

4. Describe what a dinosaurs life was like. What did they eat, where did they live, what did they do, etc?

CULMINATING ACTIVITY

Plan a "Dinosaur Day." This day can include all or some of the following activities.

1. Have students wear dinosaur costumes or t-shirts they designed.

2. Have a dinosaur read-in by selecting and reading only dinosaur-related books only.

3. Have students write experience stories from the perspective of a dinosaur.

4. Make dinosaur models out of clay or dough mixture.

5. Play dinosaur games and sing dinosaur songs.

6. Show a dinosaur video such as *Jurassic Park*.

7. Have a dinosaur feast making dinosaur-shaped foods out of jello, cookie dough, etc.

8. Construct and break open a dinosaur piñata.

9. Invite a guest speaker from a museum or local college to speak about dinosaurs.

10. Go on a field trip to a fossil site or local museum.

11. Create a "Dinosaur Book of World Records" (largest, smallest, heaviest, smallest brain, most ferocious, etc.).

12. Create dinosaur coloring books to share with other students.

13. Put together a traveling dinosaur museum filled with artifacts, books, pictures, etc. collected and created during this unit. Display it during the "Dinosaur Day" festivities and then have the museum go on tour throughout the school.

SUPPLEMENTAL LITERATURE

Books

Aliki. (1985). *Dinosaurs are different.* New York: Crowell, 1985.
The major differences between dinosaurs are discussed through an examination of their bones and skeletons. A "must" for any dinosaur hunter.

Barton, B. (1990). *Bones, bones, dinosaur bones.* New York: T. Y. Crowell.
An ideal book for very young readers. It offers a glimpse into the

search for dinosaur bones, as well as how dinosaur skeletons are constructed.

Barton, B. (1989). *Dinosaurs, dinosaurs*. New York: Crowell.
All kinds of dinosaurs—from big to small, horned to armored, long necked and long tailed—are detailed in this wonderful introduction to the world of dinosaurs.

Butler, M. C., & Biro, V. (1997). *Archie the ugly dinosaur*. New York: Barrons Juvenile.
Archie is a small and clumsy dinosaur that is often left behind and teased. One day, Archie begins to grow spikes on his body and he runs into a forest where the ferocious Rexes live. When his friends finally find him they receive a big surprise.

Cohen, D. (1998). *Dinosaur discovery: Facts, fossils, and fun*. Illustrated by R. Farrell. New York: Puffin Books.
Complete detailed illustrations of each dinosaur along with information about the origins of dinosaurs, where they lived, and theories about why they became extinct.

Florian, D. (1999). *Laugh-eteria*. San Diego, CA: Harcourt Brace Javanovich.
Contains a selection of playful poetry which includes a variety of interesting topics.

Hennessy B. G. (1993). *The dinosaur who lived in my backyard*. Illustrated Susan Davis. New York: Scholastic.
A story about a little boy who fantasized about what it would be like to have a dinosaur living in his backyard.

Hoff, S. (1998). *Danny and the dinosaur go to camp*. New York: Harper Trophy.
Danny brings his favorite dinosaur to camp, they enjoy boating, hiking, and roasting marshmallows.

Hopkins, L. B. (1987). *Dinosaurs*. San Diego, CA: Harcourt Brace.
Eighteen poems give students some fresh perspectives and delightful insights into the world of dinosaurs.

Lauber, P. (1997). *Dinosaurs walked here: And other stories fossils tell*. New York: Bradbury.
Everything the young scientist would want to know about fossils can be found in this enlightening book.

Lee, D. (1999). *Dinosaur dinner*. New York: Random House.
Rib-tickling collection of poems.

Metzger, S. (1996). *Dinofours: It's time for school*! Illustrated by Hans Wilhelm. New York: Scholastic.
On his first day at preschool, Albert the dinosaur misses his mother, until he makes some new friends and discovers that school is fun.

Most, B. (1978). *If the dinosaurs came back*. San Diego, CA: Harcourt Brace.
An imaginative look at life today if the dinosaurs returned.

Most, B. (1991). *A dinosaur named after me*. San Diego, CA: Harcourt Brace.
This book draws a parallel between the physical characteristics and

capabilities of particular dinosaurs and specific children. It also incorporates the name of each child into that of the dinosaur.

Most, B. (1993). *Where to look for a dinosaur*. New York: Harcourt Brace.
This book describes different types of dinosaurs and where fossils have been found around the world.

Peters, D. (1989). *A gallery of dinosaurs and other early reptiles*. New York: Knopf.
The emphasis in this book is on size, with a wonderful collection of colorful illustrations and gatefold pages to describe the enormity of these giants.

Pfister, M. (1994). *Dazzle the dinosaur*. New York: North-South Books.
Dazzle, the dinosaur, helps his friend Maria and her mother get their home back from the nasty Dragonsaurus.

Prelutsky, J. (1988). *Tyrannosaurus was a beast*. Illustrated by A. Lobel. New York: Mulberry Brown.
Poems about dinosaurs—from Ankylosaurus to Seismosuras, and more!

Robinson, H. (1984). *Ranger Rick's dinosaur book*. Washington, D.C.: National Wildlife Federation.
Filled with lots of colorful illustrations and photos, this book offers young scientists a wealth of data about all kinds of dinosaurs.

Schwartz, H. (1992). *Albert goes Hollywood*. New York: Orchard Books.
Liz gets to keep her pet dinosaur Albert when she finds him a job in the movies.

Strickland, H., & Strickland, P. (1994). *Dinosaur roars*. New York: Scholastic.
An easy to read book with a variety of dinosaur sounds, sizes, speed along with large colorful illustrations.

Whayne, S. S. (1995). *The big dinosaur book*. Illustrated by James Spence. New York: Troll Associates.
This fascinating book gives readers a look at the world of dinosaurs by providing clear facts about dinosaurs, describing how they lived and dominated the Earth.

Where to Look for Additional Information About Dinosaurs

Boulder, Colorado—University of Natural History Museums
Jensen, Utah—Dinosaur National Monument
Washington, DC—National Museum of Natural History, Smithsonian Institute

Internet Connections

Web - University of California, Museum of Paleontology, HTTP://WWW/ BERKELEY.EDU

MINI-THEMES

Why Dinosaurs Became Extinct

There are many different reasons offered to explain the extinction of the dinosaurs. Some of the more popular ones include: a sudden change in the earth's climate, a loss of food, and the collision of an enormous meteor with the earth. Although scientists disagree as to the reason for the disappearance of dinosaurs, students will enjoy reading about these theories and offering their own explanations for this phenomena.

Activities

1. Have students correspond with another class in another state (addresses can be obtained from current issues of *Learning Magazine* and *Teaching K–8 Magazine)*. Ask students to explain why they believe the dinosaurs became extinct and have them ask their pen pals to respond to this theory.

2. Have each student select a dinosaur and, as this creature, write a letter explaining why he/she would or would not like to live in today's world.

3. Contact the debate team or club at your local high school or college to determine if their students would be willing to debate the theories related to the disappearance of the dinosaurs. Make a videotape of the debate to share with other classes.

4. Invite a local paleontologist from a nearby college to visit your classroom and share his/her theory to explain the disappearance of the dinosaurs. Have students prepare questions they would like the guest speaker to address.

References

Branley, F. (1982). *Dinosaurs, asteroids, and superstars: Why the dinosaurs disappeared.* New York: Crowell.

Branley, F. (1989). *What happened to the dinosaurs?* New York: Crowell.

Cobb, V. (1983). *The monsters who died: A mystery about dinosaurs.* New York: Coward-McCann.

Coleman, G. (1995). *Countdown to dinosaur doom!* New York: Barrons Juveniles.

Mullins, P. (1997). *V for vanishing: An alphabet of endangered animals.* New York: Harper Collins.

O'Neill, M. (1989). *Dinosaur mysteries.* Illustrated by John Bindon. Mahwah, NJ: Troll Associates.

Silver, D. M. (1995). *Extinction is forever.* Illustrated by Patricia Wynne. New York: Julian Messmer.

Simon, S. (1990). *New questions and answers about dinosaurs.* New York: Morrow.

The Time of the Dinosaurs

During the time of the dinosaurs, the earth looked much different than it does today. Land bridges between continents, massive inland seas, and strange plant life dominated the landscape. Students will enjoy looking at the world as it was during the time of the dinosaurs.

Activities

1. Provide students with empty shoe boxes, various pieces of colored construction paper, glue, scissors, and other art materials. Ask students (individually or in small groups) to design dioramas of selected prehistoric scenes.

2. Have each student take on the role of a selected dinosaur. Invite each student to record a day in the life of this dinosaur. What do they eat? What do they do all day? What surprises do they encounter?

3. Read *Dinosaurs and Their Young* by Russell Freedman (New York: Holiday, 1983), to the entire class. This book discusses the family life of hadrosaurus and describes some of their enemies. After the reading, involve students in a discussion that focuses on comparisons between the family life of dinosaurs and that of other wild and/or domesticated animals.

4. Obtain a copy of the sound filmstrip series, "Plants and Animals of Long Ago" (Catalog No. C30165, National Geographic Society, Washington, DC 20036; telephone: 1-800-368-2728). Have students discuss some of the most interesting, and what they consider important, information presented in the filmstrip.

References

Arnold, C. (1989). *Dinosaur mountain: Graveyard of the past.* New York: Clarion.

Carroll, S. (1986). *How big is a Brachiosaurus?* New York: Plait and Munk.

Freedman, R. (1983). *Dinosaurs and their young.* New York: Holiday.

Gohier, F. (1995). *165 million years of dinosaurs.* Parsippany, NJ: Silver Burdett.

Herman, G. (1998) *Time for school, little dinosaur.* Illustrated by Norman Gorbaty. New York: Random Library.

Manning, L. (1995). *Dinosaur days.* Mahwah, NJ: Troll Associate.

Milton, J. (1985). *Dinosaur days.* New York: Random House.

Nolan, D. (1990). *Dinosaur dream.* New York: Macmillan.

Sattler, H. (1981). *Dinosaurs of North America.* New York: Lothrop.

Sattler, H. (1989). *Tyrannosaurus Rex and its kin: The Mesozoic monsters.* New York: Lothrop

Discovering Dinosaurs

New discoveries about dinosaurs are being made every day. Paleontologists and other scientists are digging up dinosaurs and other ancient creatures around the world—many of these discoveries are making the front page of our local newspapers. The careers involved in dinosaur discoveries and how these scientists work are covered in this mini-theme.

Activities

1. Contact your district's high school and ask to borrow any fossils they may have for display. Show these to students and help them create their own fossils. Provide each student with modeling clay and a variety of leaves. Have students flatten out their clay and place a selected leaf into the clay. Have them carefully remove the leaves from the clay and discuss the impressions made in the clay. Discuss how these are similar to, or different from, the impressions made by living things of ancient times.

2. Have students create several big books. The front and back covers of each can be cut from stiff cardboard into the shape of a selected dinosaur. Sheets of paper can also be cut into the same pattern as the cover and stapled between the cardboard. Each book can be a record of important data about the selected dinosaur. The completed books can eventually be donated to the school library, or be part of a visiting book collection that goes to various classrooms.

3. Have students brainstorm all the adjectives they can think of to describe dinosaurs and list these on the board. Next, have students offer an antonym for each adjective listed. Have them select several adjectives and their antonyms and create an "Attribute Chart" (see below). Have student select several dinosaurs and "rate" each according to how it "measures up" on the chart.

Tyrannosaurus Rex		
Huge .... X .... Small		
Meat-eater .... X .... Plant-eater		
Sharp Teeth .... X .... No Teeth		
Ferocious .... X .... Gentle		

4. Obtain a copy of the video, "Dinosaurs: Puzzles from the Past" (Catalog No C51016, National Geographic Society, Washington, DC 20036; telephone: 1-800-368-2728). Discuss with students how information in the film is similar to or different from that discovered in the selected books.

References

Adler, D. A. (1981). *Cam Jansen and the mystery of the dinosaur bones novel study*. New York: Viking Press.

Aliki. (1988). *Digging up dinosaurs*. New York: Harper Trophy.

Aliki. (1988). *Dinosaur bones*. New York: Crowell.

Aliki. (1990). *Fossils tell of long ago*. New York: HarperCollins.

Barton, B. (1990). *Bones, bones, dinosaur bones*. New York: Ty Crowell Co.

Carrick, C. (1989). *Big old bones: A dinosaur tale*. New York: Clarion Books.

Day, M. (1992). *Dragon in the rocks: A story based on the childhood of early paleontologist, Mary Anning*. Toronto: Greey de Peucier Books.

Gilbert, J. (1981). *Dinosaurs discovered*. New York: Larousse.

Glossup, J. (1997). Velociraptor (the tiny perfect dinosaur book, bones, egg, and poster hit series, no. 6). Illustrated by Ely Kish. New York: Andrews & McNeel.

Lasky, K. (1990). *Dinosaur dig.* New York: Morrow.

Lauber, P. (1987). *Dinosaurs walked here: And other stories fossils tell.* New York: Bradbury.

National Wildlife Federation, (1997). *Digging into dinosaurs.* Blue Ridge Summit, PA: McGraw Hill.

Other Ancient Animals

Dinosaurs certainly weren't the only animals that lived long ago. Mammoths, Mastodons, Pterodactyls and other strange creatures were also part of the history of the earth. Although most appeared after the dinosaurs died out, they are still a source of fascination for many students.

Activities

1. Have students survey teachers, administrators, and other adults about all dinosaurs and other ancient creatures with which they are familiar. What ancient animals are cited most often? The collected data can be arranged in the form of a bar or line graph.

2. Using paper bags and various colors of construction paper, allow each student to construct a prehistoric animal puppet. When the puppets are completed, separate the students into groups of four. In small groups, students can write and design a play using their puppets as the main characters.

3. Many prehistoric animals have features similar to animals of today (for example, the mammoth shares characteristics with the elephant). Have students construct a large bulletin board. On one half of the bulletin board, pictures and illustrations of ancient animals can be posted. The other half of the bulletin board can display illustrations and photos of today's animals. Yarn can be used to link the prehistoric animals with existing animals they most resemble.

4. Have students create Venn diagrams to compare a prehistoric animal with its more current "cousin."

References

Craig, J. (1989). *Discovering prehistoric animals.* Mahwah, NJ: Troll.

Gibbons, G. (1988). *Prehistoric animals.* New York: Holiday House.

Knight, D. C. (1985). *"Dinosaurs" that swam and flew.* New York: Prentice.

Petty, K. (1997). *Dinosaurs laid eggs.* Brookfield, CT: Copper Beech Books.

Sattler, H. (1985). *Pterosaurs, the flying reptiles.* New York: Lothrop.

Schlein, M. (1996). *Before the dinosaurs.* New York: Scholastic.

Selsam, M. (1977). *Sea monsters of long ago.* New York: Four Winds.

Winston, P. O. (1994). *Creatures of long ago: Dinosaurs.* New York: National Geographic Society.

Wright, R. (1991). *Dinosaurs and other prehistoric animals.* New York: Grosset & Dunlap.

Zallinger, P. (1978). *Prehistoric animals.* New York: Random House.

Growing Up

OVERVIEW

Focus

Students will be able recognize that the feelings they have about aging, illness, fear and so forth are all part of growing up. The students will also be able to understand that growing up is individualistic and developmental.

Objectives

On completion of this thematic unit, students will:

1. Explain some changes people go through while growing up.
2. List various issues faced while growing up.
3. Explain feelings experienced while growing up.
4. Understand that growing up is individualistic and developmental.

HOW IT WORKS

Initiating Activity

Ask the children to bring in photographs of themselves when they were babies and at various age intervals up to their current age. Display the pictures. Then discuss the changes that have occurred over the growing years, both physically and mentally, and what changes will occur in the future.

General Activities

1. Have students make their fingerprints by using a stamp pad. Discuss the individuality and uniqueness of each child's fingerprints along with the fact that fingerprints do not change as one grows up.

2. Have the students interview their grandparents to find out what it was like when they were growing up. For example, did they have computers, television, radios, dishwashers, and so forth? What were their schools like? What kinds of transportation did they have? After the students have completed gathering the information, allow time for them to compare and contrast growing up during their grandparents day with growing up today.

3. Ask the students to bring in something that has been or was important to them while they were growing up (i.e. stuffed toy, favorite blanket, bedtime story, etc.). Have the students share these items and explain their personal meaning.

4. Read the poem "Sarah Cynthia Sylvia Stout Would Not Take The Garbage Out" (Shel Silverstein) to the class. Have a discussion with the class on the importance of doing chores, a responsibility of growing up. Have the stu-

dents write a journal entry, in poetry form, about the chore they dislike the most. A sharing time may be optional for students who want to share their poem. (This poem is located in *Where the Sidewalk Ends*, by Shel Silverstein, on pp. 70–71 in the hardback copy.)

5. In the beginning of the year, help the students construct their own height chart by using a yard stick to mark each quarter inch on a two-inch by five foot strip of paper. Students can role the strip up, secure it with a rubber band and keep it in their desks. Have the students measure each other, twice a month, using the strip which can be taped on a wall. Record the date of measurement on the tape at the appropriate height. Continue to record, on the growth charts, until the end of the year, and then send growth chart home to parents as a record of their child's growth during that school year (Bonus—laminate them as a end of the year gift for the children to preserve them).

6. Discuss different cultures and what is important to each culture as their children grow up. For example, the Japanese have students in school almost year-round and for very long school days. This suggests that education is valued as a most important aspect of growing up in Japan. Have the students do some independent or partner research into a certain culture's values in growing up. Have them write a brief report on the culture's values of growing up. Have the students or team present the report to the class. (*Note:* This activity is appropriate for third graders or above.)

7. Discuss with children the importance of self-esteem and growing up. Ask why it is important to feel good about oneself in order to grow up into a healthy, happy person? Have children make a list of positive attributes about themselves. When they are finished with their lists, the children can come up to the front of the room and write on a huge piece of white paper, in different colored markers, one of their positive attributes. As the children write these down on the paper, the class can discuss whether or not they agree with the attributes that are written down. This could be a great way to bring out the positive things about the children in this class.

8. The children can design their own television show about growing up for the class. They can use a cardboard box and cut a television window in the front of the box. Different pictures can be drawn by the children on what it was like to grow up in their house, neighborhood or town. They can put their name on these pictures. Each child can make two pictures. When all of the pictures are finished, they are taped together. At the top of the box, a spool can be connected in which the paper would be turned on. A handle could be placed on either side of the box to turn the spool. As the spool is turned, the pictures will come through the window in the box. As the children's pictures come through the window, they can explain them to the class and take turns being the narrator of the television show.

9. With the permission of the principal, the teacher can invite someone from a pet store to come to the classroom. The pet store person could be asked to bring animals of different sizes and ages. Some may be puppies and kittens and others grown up dogs or cats. Have them talk about the growth

of the animals. How fast do they grow? What is the significance of their years in comparison to human years? Children can learn the likes and differences of growing up for animals as opposed to humans. Having dogs, cats or birds for example, would be significant because many children have these animals for pets. The book, *My First Book About Nature: How Living Things Grow* by Dwight Kuhn would be a good book to share at this time.

10. Children can design a guide book for parents. This would explain to them the important things that they as parents need to know about their child growing up. For example, when I was a baby I needed diapers, a bottle and a rattle. Now that I am seven years old, I need love, food and attention. When I am a teenager I will need . . . The children would include pictures with this guide book. When it is finished, they can show it to their parents either by taking it home or on an open house night when the parents come in to the school.

11. Ask the students, with the help of their parents, to complete the following statements:

    When I was one year old my favorite thing to do was _____.

    When I was two years old my favorite thing to do was _____.

    When I was three years old my favorite thing to do was _____.

    When I was four years old my favorite thing to do was _____.

    When I was five years old my favorite thing to do was _____.

    When I was six years old my favorite thing to do was _____.

    After students have completed this assignment, give each student a code number to put on his/her paper instead of a name. Collect the papers and randomly distribute them to other students. The children will then have to find the person whose interest paper they have by asking questions. When the children are finished, these can be put into a book entitled "Our _____ Grade Class Interest Book."

Discussion Questions

1. What are some things that you like about growing up?
2. What are some things that you do not like about growing up?
3. Do you think everyone grows up in the same way? Explain.
4. Who is your favorite grown-up person, and why?
5. If you could be any age you wanted to be, how old would you be, and why?
6. What do you think are the hardest things about growing up?
7. If you could change places with any living person, who would it be, and why?
8. What do birthdays mean to you? To society?
9. If you were growing up in Japan, Africa, Australia, or another country you know about, how do you think your life might be different? The same?

10. What one thing would you tell children younger than you about growing up?

11. What are some of the similarities between the way you were when you were five years younger then your age and the way that you are now?

LITERATURE RELATED ACTIVITIES

Title: *The Meanest Thing to Say*

Genre: Realistic Fiction

Author: Bill Cosby

Illustrator: Varnette P. Honeywood

Bibliographic Information: Scholastic, Inc., New York, 1997.

Summary: Michael, a new boy in his second grade class, tries to get the other students to play a game that involves saying mean things to one another. One of the boys in the class shows Michael a better way to make friends.

Interest Level: Grades 1–4.

Pre-Reading Activity

Read the title of the book, *The Meanest Things to Say*. Then ask the children to discuss if anyone has ever said anything mean to them or they to someone else. Allow time to share. Discuss how it made them feel. Finally, discuss why anyone would want to say something mean to someone else.

Learning Activities

1. Most of the children will know Bill Cosby, comedian and author of this book. As a group, write Bill Cosby a letter to tell him what they liked about the book. Send the letter to Mr. Cosby, in care of Scholastic, Inc., 555 Broadway, New York, NY 10012.

2. Have a discussion with the children regarding the strategy Little Bill used of saying "So" to everything Michael said that was mean. For example, was it a good strategy? What other strategies might have worked?

3. Collect other books in the Little Bill series written by Bill Cosby and published by Scholastic such as *The Best Way to Play, The Treasure Hunt, Shipwreck Saturday* and *Super-Fine Valentine*. Allow time for the children to read these books and discuss.

4. As a group, decide on a behavior, such as saying mean things to one another, and then write a short story about what strategies should be used for that situation. This may also become an individual activity in which each student decides on an inappropriate behavior and then writes a short story about strategies to deal with the situation. These stories could be put together into a class book.

Discussion Questions

1. Do you agree with the strategy of saying "So" that Little Bill used when Michael said mean things? Why or why not?

2. Why do you think Michael behaved like he did when he first showed up and the boys were playing ball?

3. What might have happened between the children and Michael the next day if Little Bill hadn't gotten the advice from his dad to say "So"?

4. How do you think Michael felt when Little Bill asked him to play basketball the next day?

Title: *Will You Take Care of Me?*

Genre: Picture Book

Author: Margaret Park Bridges

Illustrator: Morrow Junior Books, New York, 1998.

Bibliographic Information: Firefly Books, New York, 1986.

Summary: As a baby kangaroo imagines becoming a tree, a house, a book, a teddy bear, and more, Mama kangaroo tells how she will continue to love and care for her "little one".

Interest Level: Grades 1–3.

Pre-Reading Activity

Children can do a semantic web on the word love and the importance of this word. Ask them to think of anybody or anything they love. For example:

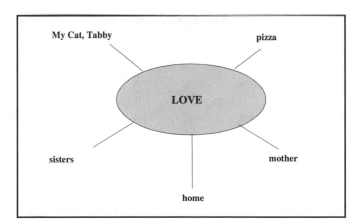

After they have listed all the people or things they love ask them to each think, to themselves, which of these are most important to them and why.

Learning Activities

1. Read the dedications of the book that were written by the author and illustrator. Both dedications were written to their parents. Ask the children to

compose dedications they would do for their parents if they were authors/illustrators.

2. As a group, write a sequel to the book *Will You Take Care of Me?* For example, write a sequel in which the baby kangaroo grows up and has baby kangaroos him/herself.

3. Read the book *Love You Forever* by Robert Munsch, which is a book that shows the enduring love that a parent continues to show her child and how this love crosses generations. Compare and contrast this book with Bridge's *Will You Take Care of Me?*

4. According to the book jacket on the book *Will You Take Care of Me?*, the author Margaret Park Bridges has two daughters. As a group, write a letter to her sharing their sequel story and/or dedications to their parents they created. Then tell her what they liked about the book and ask her about her daughters—ages, names, interests, etc. Her children may even become pen pals with the students in the class.

Discussion Questions

1. Who do you know that you think will always care for you and love you no matter how old you get?

2. Sometimes we forget how important our parents are to us while we are growing up. Was there ever a time when you felt badly about something you might have done or said to one of your parents? What happened?

3. Why do you suppose the mother in the story said that she'll always love the baby, no matter what or who he is?

4. What did you like best about this story? What did you like least?

Title: *Arthur's First Sleepover*

Genre: Picture Book

Author: Marc Brown

Bibliographic Information: Little, Brown & Co., New York, 1994.

Summary: Rumors about sightings of an alien spaceship create excitement when Arthur's friends come to spend the night in his tent.

Interest Level: Grades K–3.

Pre-Reading Activity

Tell the students that this book is about a sleepover at Arthur's, in his tent, with two friends. Arthur's father said that according to the newspaper, a man said he saw a spaceship. One of the boys, Buster, had never spent a night away from home. Even though the boys pretended not to worry about the spaceship, there was concern and they did get scared. Divide the students into small groups and allow time for them to discuss the following questions. Have you ever gotten scared at night? Have you ever spent a night with a friend? If so, what was the first night away from home like? If you haven't spent a night away from home, would you like to? Explain.

Learning Activities

1. Buster brought his baseball card collection to the sleepover at Arthur's. Discuss the different items that people collect—picture postcards, bottlecaps, chewing gum wrappers, rubber stamps, etc. Then ask the children to share collections they may have by providing a space in the classroom and asking them to bring in their collections and displaying them.

2. Play the ABC game in which the first student says, "I'm going to a friends house to stay overnight and I will take _____ (child provides something that begins with a letter "a". For example, an apple, alligator, aspirin, etc. Then the next player must repeat the same line and the "a" word provided and then add a "b" word. The next player adds a "c" word and so forth)."

3. Buster brought his "blankis" along to the sleepover. Most children have something they like to sleep with. Have a sharing day on which all children bring in an item with which they like to sleep. Provide a time for the children, if they want, to tell how they started sleeping with the item.

4. Create a Character Continuum (See Chapter 2, pp. 55–57) by asking the children to brainstorm all the words they can think of that can be used to describe one or more of the characters in *Arthur's First Sleepover*. Record these words in a column on the chalkboard. Invite the children to think of opposites for all the recorded words. Place opposites at end of a continuum. For example:

    Book Title: *Arthur's First Sleepover*

    Character: *D. W.*

    Understanding _____ Not Understanding

    Nice _____ Mean

    Fun _____ Boring

    Friendly _____ Unfriendly

    Kind _____ Cruel

    Sociable _____ Unsociable

    Ask the students to put an "x" on the line to indicate the degree to which an identified character exhibits a particular trait. Allow time for them to discuss their rationale for placing the "x" where they did.

5. Read *Ira Sleeps Over* by Bernard Weber. Then compare and contrast that book with *Arthur's First Sleepover*.

6. Create a class "The First Time I..." book by asking the students to complete the sentence, "The first time I (slept over, rode a bike, went swimming, etc.) this is what happened, _____." Have students illustrate their pages and then compile into a class book.

Discussion Questions

1. Why do you think Arthur's sister, D.W., kept talking about aliens?

2. What were some of the things Arthur did to get ready for the sleepover? (Answers may vary but might include: put up the tent, invite friends, put things in tent to make it cozy, got a flashlight, etc.).

3. How do you think Buster felt when he found out about the alien story? Explain.

4. What do you think will happen next in the story after D.W. saw an alien outside her window?

5. If you were having a sleepover, what would you do? For example, where would you sleep? What would you eat? What would you do?

Title: *Dinofours: It's Time for School*

Genre:	Picture Book
Author:	Steve Metzger
Illustrator:	Hans Wilhelm
Bibliographic Information:	Scholastic, Inc., New York, 1996.
Summary:	On his first day at preschool, Albert the dinosaur misses his mother until he makes some new friends and discovers what school is all about.
Interest Level:	Grades K–3.

Pre-Reading Activity

Albert said he was not ready to go to school and he kept trying to do other things to distract his mother so he didn't have to go. Sometimes we all feel like Albert because there are some things that we don't feel ready to do. What are some things you have felt you weren't ready to do? Things you now feel that you aren't ready to do? Discuss how the students overcame what they weren't ready for and/or how they plan to become ready.

Learning Activities

1. Discuss with the students about how Albert made friends during this first day at school. Make a list of what Albert did and then brainstorm and create a list of additional things you can do to make friends.

2. There are other books available in the Dinofours series. Obtain books such as: *Dinofours: I'm not your friend!*, *Dinofours: I'm Super Dino!*, *Dinofours: It's class trip day!* Compare and contrast these books with *Dinofours: It's Time For School*.

3. Many children, just like Albert the Dinofour, find the first day of school very difficult. Discuss what could be done to help children feel more comfortable about the first day of school.

4. Ask the students to create the "Ideal First Day at School". Include activities to do, ways to make friends, teacher behaviors, etc.

Discussion Questions

1. Do you think Albert's mother should have played at the sand table with him or simply left? Explain.
2. Do you think Albert's mother is a good mother? Why or why not?
3. Do you think Albert behaved the way he should have on his first day at school? Why or why not?
4. Do you think Mrs. Dee is a good teacher? Why or why not?

CULMINATING ACTIVITY

The culminating activity will be a "Growing Up Day." This day could include all or some of the following activities:

1. Have the student's write three brief summaries. One summary should describe important events they remember about growing up during their first five years. These can be happy events or sad events. Second, ask the students to summarize how they feel about growing up now and, third, what they think growing up in the future will be like.

2. Have community speakers come in from a day care center, a retirement home, and a juvenile center. The speaker can be a representative or a person representing the day care center, retirement home and juvenile center. Have them discuss growth. Have the students prepare questions for the speakers prior to their visits.

3. Play charades. Have the student's guess which stage of development their classmate is acting out. For example, infant, adult, elderly, etc.

4. Children can dress up in outfits of people of all ages. For example, one child might have a toddler outfit on. This might include a diaper and shirt. Another child may be dressed as a teenager. He or she might wear a pair of jeans and a t-shirt. The children can design their own outfits and bring the materials to put this outfit together from home. A child dressed as an older man or woman might want to wear a tie or a dressy hat. The children can decide before hand what outfits they are going to wear with an equal distribution of each age bracket. The children can wear these outfits all day. They may want to put on a skit to go along with the outfits they have on.

5. Children could design their own comic strip or book on how to survive birth through whatever grade they are in. This could be a funny comic strip or book on the child's viewpoint of growing up. For example, parents often call 2-year-olds the terrible two's. The children could illustrate and include words to a comic on what they thought they were like during the terrible two years. These comics could be placed altogether on a bulletin board or big piece of oaktag and placed up in front of the room or designed as a book. The children might want to take them home to show their parents.

6. The children could make a video on growing up in their school. They could take a video camera around the school and tape all of the children from kindergarten through fifth or sixth grade depending on what type of

school this is. The children could pretend that they are the interviewers or newscasters and ask the other children the questions. For example, What do you think about being in whatever grade they are in? What grade do you wish you were in? The children could show this video to the whole school when they are finished. All of the children would get to see themselves on the videotape.

SUPPLEMENTAL LITERATURE

Books

Allen, M. N., & Rotner, S. (1991). *Changes*. New York: Macmillan.
The author describes in rhymed text and illustrations, how things in nature change as they grow and develop.

Bown, D. (1995). *Growing up*. New York: DK. Publishing Merchandise.
This book describes what it was like growing up in the 1930's and '40's.

Cleary, B. (1987). *The growing-up feet*. New York: Morrow Books.
Jimmy and Janet are 4-year-old twins whose feet haven't "grown up" enough for new shoes, so they get bright red boots instead.

Cork, B. T. (1989). *Going to school*. New York: Derrydale Books.
This is a story of a little boy named Sam who is going to school for the first time. It tells of his preparation for his first day and then of the exciting adventures when he finally gets to school.

Graves, B. (1998). *No copycats allowed!* Illustrated by Abby Carter. New York: Hyperion.
Wanting desperately to fit in at her new school, Gabrielle tries to be like her classmates, only to learn that the best way to make friends is by being herself.

Graves, B. (1997). *Mystery of the Tooth Gremlin*. Illustrated by Paige Billin-Frye. New York: Hyperion.
As Jesse struggles to recover his stolen first tooth AND to read the requisite books for the class field trip, he discovers the importance of reading and the value of friendship.

Graves, B. (1997). *The whooping crane*. Logan, IA: Perfection Learning.
On an airline flight, Megan learns many interesting facts about the endangered whooping crane when she sits next to a biologist who is transporting a newly hatched whooping crane chick from Texas to Maryland.

Graves, B. (1996) *The best worst day*. Illustrated by Nelle Davis. New York: Hyperion.
When Lucy tries, unsuccessfully, to win Maya's friendship by impressing this exotic new classmate with her artistic talents, she discovers a better way to make friends.

Greenberg, K. E. (1996). *Zack's story: Growing up with same-sex parents*. Minneapolis, MN: Lerner Publishing Co.
An eleven year-old boy describes life as part of a family made up of himself, his mother, and her lesbian partner.

Hazen, B. S. (1992). *Mommy's office*. New York: Atheneum.
    As part of growing up and learning what her mother does at work,
    Emily accompanies her Mommy to her downtown office.

Heide, F. P. (1996). *Oh, grow up!* New York: Orchard Books.
    Poems to help you survive parents, chores, school, and other afflic-
    tions.

Hest, A. (1998). *Gabby growing up*. Illustrated by Amy Schwartz. New York:
    Simon & Schuster.
    Gabby and her grandfather plan to celebrate his birthday by going
    ice-skating. His birthday turns out to be a day full of cake, candles,
    new hair-dos, and other surprises.

Hoberman, M. A. (1992). *Fathers, mothers, sisters, brothers: A collection of
    family poems*. New York: Scholastic.
    Through the collection of poems, readers can identify with growing
    up in all kinds of families—extended, nuclear, foster, fractured, and
    adoptive.

Jukes, M. (1984). *Like Jake and me*. New York: Alfred A. Knopf.
    With the help of a loving family, Alex grows closer to his stepfather.

Kandel, B. (1997). *Trevor's story: Growing up biracial*. Illustrated by Carol
    Halebian. Minneapolis, MN: Lerner Publishing Co.
    A 10-year-old describes his life at home and at school, about what he
    likes and does not like, about being the son of a white mother and a
    black father.

Kuhn, D. (1993). *My first book about nature: How living things grow*. New
    York: Scholastic.
    This book provides an introduction to growth, explaining how it oc-
    curs with such everyday things as dogs, apples, trees, guppies and
    humans. It contains beautiful, realistic photos.

Lebrun, C. (1997). *Little bear is growing up*. Illustrated by Daniele Bour. Chi-
    cago: Children's Press.
    Little Brown Bear takes pride in the things he can do all by himself
    including getting down from his bed in the morning and peeling a
    banana.

London, J. (1995). *Froggy learns to swim*. Illustrated by Frank Remkiewicz.
    New York: Scholastic.
    An inspirational story of how Froggy's parents supported him as he
    overcomes his fear of water and learned to swim.

Moss, T. (1993). *I want to be*. Illustrations by Jerry Pinkney. New York: Dial
    Books.
    A young girl describes, in poetic terms, what kind of a person she
    wants to be when she grows up.

Munch, R. (1986). *Love you forever*. New York: Scholastic.
    A story that describes a young boy as he goes through all the stages
    of childhood and then becomes a man.

Russo, M. (1993). *The trade-in mother*. New York: Greenwillow Books.
A young child gets frustrated with how many times his mother says "no", so at bedtime he expresses his wish to trade-in his mother for a new one.

Silverstein, S. (1974). *Where the sidewalk ends*. New York: Harper & Row.
A collection of humorous poems.

Silverstein, S. (1964). *The giving tree*. New York: Harper & Row.
This is a story of a young boy who loved a tree and the tree loved him. The tree gave and gave to the boy. As the boy grew older, he began to want more and more from the tree. This story is about the gift of giving and acceptance of another's capacity to love in return.

Waters, S. A. (1992). *Growing up*. Illustrated by Teresa O'Brien. New York: Reader's Digest Assoc.
This book is an introduction to creatures in their infancy. It introduces frogs, butterflies, kangaroos, and other animals as they grow from babyhood to maturity.

Weber, B. (1972). *Ira sleeps over*. New York: Houghton Mifflin.
Ira is excited to stay overnight with his friend Reggie but is concerned about spending a night without sleeping with his teddy bear, Tah Tah.

Wyeth, S. (1995). *Always my dad*. Illustrations by Raul Colon. New York: Knopf.
A picture book that will comfort children who are living with one parent because of divorce, separation, or job relocation.

MINI THEMES

Growing Up With Separation and Divorce

Dealing with separation and/or divorce can be very traumatic experience—it creates change in our lives and we must learn how to cope with these changes. Hopefully, by giving children an opportunity to relate to others going through separation/divorce, as well as an opportunity to discuss the changes affecting them and their feelings related to those changes. As a result, the children may be better prepared to accept and adjust to there own situations in a more positive way.

Activities

1. Ask the children to take the position of one of the main characters from a book they have read on divorce and write an autobiography of this character. Tell them to write the autobiography in diary format, documenting the events of the book and how they felt about each.

2. After reading some of the recommended books for this unit, discuss that there is usually one character that feels he/she is the only one hurt and/or inconvenienced by a separation/divorce. As a group, select one of the books and make a list of all of the characters. After you have listed the characters, ask the children what advice they would give to each of them to overcome some of the problems they had or thought they had.

3. Tell the children to pretend they are a main character in one of the books they have read about separation/divorce. As that character, ask them to write a "Dear Ann Landers" or "Dear Abby" letter asking for advice. Next, tell them to give the letter to a friend and ask him/her to write a response and return it to them. When they get their responses, allow time to share the letters and to compare them with what actually happened in the book.

4. Allow time for the children to read some of the recommended books for this unit. Then discuss the similarities and differences among the families in these books. You may want to expand this discussion into similarities and differences among the families in these books and the children's families.

5. Invite an attorney and a psychologist into the classroom. The attorney can discuss the many legal concerns and ramifications of a separation/divorce, such as financial arrangements, custody of the child(ren), living arrangements, etc. The psychologist can discuss some of the emotional problems that are natural to most people who experience a separation/divorce. In addition, ask him/her to suggest how and where to obtain help in solving some of these problems.

6. Discuss with the children that when there is a separation and/or divorce in a family, certain changes do occur. For example, both parents are not living in the same house; new family members—stepmothers, stepfathers, stepbrothers or stepsisters—may become part of the new family; a move to a different house, city and/or state may become necessary; it may become necessary to give up some items of furniture and other belongings; etc. Ask the children to draw three houses and to do the following: In the first house illustrate and/or write about the way you see a family before a separation/divorce. In the second house, illustrate and/or write about the way you see the family after a separation/divorce. In the third house, illustrate and/or write about what they see as perfect or ideal family. The children may use their own family, a fictitious family or one of the families about which they have read.

References

Ballad, R. (1993). *Gracie*. New York: Greenwillow Books.

Boegehold, B. (1985). *Daddy doesn't live here anymore*. Racine, IL: Western.

Christiansen, C. B. (1990). *My mother's house, my father's house*. New York: Puffin Books.

Cole, J. (1998). *My parent's divorce*. Illustrated by O'Neill, C. New York: Cooper Beech Books.

Danzigen, P. (1995). *Amber Brown goes fourth*. Illustrated by T. Ross. New York: Putnam's Sons.

DeVore, C. D. (1993). *Breakfast for dinner; facing divorce*. New York: Abdo & Daughters Publishing.

Drescher, J. (1986). *My mother's getting married*. New York: Dial.

Girard, L. W. (1987). *At daddy's on Saturday*. Chicago: Albert Whitman.

Ives, S., Fassler, D., & Lash, M. (1985). *The divorce workbook: A guide for kids and families*. Burlington, VT: Waterfront Books.

Lash, M., Loughridge, S. I., & Fassler, D. (1990). *My kind of family: A book for kids in single-parent homes*. Burlington, VT: Waterfront Books.

Okimoto, J. D. (1979). *My mother is not married to my father*. New York: G.P. Putnam's Sons.

Parkinson, K. (1998). *Mama and daddy bear's divorce*. Illustrated by C. M. Spelman. Morton Grove, IL: Albert Whitman.

Rogers, F. (1998). *Let's talk about it: Divorce*. Illustrated by J. Judkis. New York: Philomel Books.

Schindel, J. (1995). *Dear daddy*. Illustrated by D. Donohue. Morton Grove, IL: Albert Whitman.

Steel, D. (1989). *Martha's new daddy*. New York: Delacorte Press.

Vigna, J. (1997). *I live with daddy*. Morton Grove, IL: Albert Whitman.

Watson, J. Switzer, R. E., & Hirschberg, J. C. (1988). *Sometimes a family has to split up*. New York: Crown.

Weninger, I. B. (1995). *Good-bye, daddy!* Illustrated by A. Marks. New York: North-South Books.

Winthrop, E. (1998). *As the crow flies*. Illustrated by J. Sandin. New York: Clarion Books.

Wyeth, S. D. (1996). *Ginger Brown: Too many houses*. Illustrated by C. VanWright and Ying-Hwa Hu. New York: Random House.

Vigna, J. (1987). *Mommy and me by ourselves again*. Niles, IL: Albert Whitman.

Death and Dying as Part of Growing Up

Accepting death is naturally one of the most difficult life situations with which we all must deal. In recent years, educators have acknowledged the importance of death education for children. For too long children have been sheltered from death and this has caused them even greater fear and anxiety. Children must be given the opportunity to discuss death and to express their feelings related to death. Writers in the field of death education have noted the importance of this in order to help children put their fears about death into proper perspective. As paradoxical as it may seem, death education leads to a greater appreciation of life.

Activities

1. Tell the students to pretend they have just gotten word that their best friend has an incurable disease and will not live for more than one year. This friend does not need to be in bed or in the hospital at this time. In fact, it is hard to believe that anything is wrong. Ask the children what they would do in this situation? What would they say? Would they act differently toward him/her? Allow time for the children to react and discuss this situation.

2. Plan a field trip to an old graveyard. Allow the students time to "browse" through the graveyard looking at tombstones. Tell them to notice some of the following:

Birthdates and dates of death

Epitaphs

Relationships

Symbols and designs engraved on the tombstones

Names of people

Provide the children with a sheet of paper and ask them to design a tombstone.

3. Invite a funeral director to come to the class to answer the children's questions about funerals. Prior to his/her visit, have the students write questions for him/her on index cards.

4. Assign the children to work in pairs or small groups to research the customs related to death in a particular culture (Native Americans, Mexican Americans, Black Americans, Cubans, Jews, etc). Allow time for each group to share their findings with the class.

5. Make available some newspapers that contain "Death Notices." Here you will find obituaries that highlights pertinent information about a person who has died. Read at least three of these obituaries to the class, pointing out the kind of information that is provided. Discuss that close friends or relatives are often asked to write the obituaries for the person who has died. Ask the children to work in small groups and to select a person (living or dead) and to pretend they have been asked to write his/her obituary. Tell them to use the newspaper obituaries, as a guide, and to write an obituary.

References

Brown, M. W. (1997). *The dead bird*. New York: Young Scott Books.

Buscaglia, L. (1982). *The fall of Freddy the leaf*. New York: Holt Rinehart & Winston.

Carter, D. (1998). *Bye, mis'lela*. Illustrated by H. Stevenson. New York: Farrar Straus-Giroux.

Cave, A. G. (1998). *Balloons for Trevor: Understanding death*. Illustrated by J. Shivington. St Louis, MO: Concordia Publishing House.

DePaola, T. (1973). *Nana upstairs, Nana downstairs*. New York: Puffin Books.

Douglas, E. (1990). *Rachel and the upside down heart*. Los Angeles: Price Stern Sloan.

Fowler, S. G. (1998). *Beautiful*. Illustrated by J. Fowler. New York: Greenwillow.

Grindley, S. (1998). *A flag for grandma*. Illustrated by J. Cockcroft. Morton Grove, IL: Albert Whitman.

Moyer, B. A., & Moyer, A. M. (1998). *Angel Stacy: Earth angel to guardian angel*. Illustrated by A. M. Moyer. New York: Two Bee-A-Twin Bee Publishing.

Spelman, C. (1996). *After Charlotte's mom died*. Illustrated by J. Friedman. Morton Grove, IL: Albert Whitman.

Viost, J. (1971). *The tenth good thing about Barney*. New York: Atheneum Publishing, Inc.

Whelan, G. (1992). *Bringing the farmhouse home*. Illustrations by Joda Rowland. New York: Simon & Schuster.

Holidays and Celebrations

OVERVIEW

Focus

Students will expand their knowledge about holidays.

Objectives

On completion of this thematic unit, students will:

1. Understand the meaning and significance of each holiday/celebration studied.

2. Explain the origin of each holiday/celebration studied.

3. Express insights into how holiday/celebration traditions have changed over the years.

4. Contrast and compare how different cultures celebrate the same holidays.

Note To Teachers: The holidays and celebrations selected for this unit were chosen because they are not based on any specific religious beliefs and can therefore be used in most classroom settings. This unit will need to be implemented at different times throughout the year rather than completed within a specific time frame. The General Activities include generic activities that can be used or adapted for use with any holiday/celebration, as well as activities that are specific to the following holidays: Halloween, April Fool's Day, New Year's and Valentine's Day. The Literature-Related Activities provide activities and discussion questions related to specific books, which include:

> *This is the Pumpkin* by Abby Levine (1997)
>
> *Arthur's April Fool* by Marc Brown (1999)
>
> *Happy New Year Pooh* by Kathleen Zoehfeld (1997)
>
> *Valentine's Day* by Miriam Nerlove (1994)

The Supplemental Literature provides an annotated bibliography of General Holidays/Celebrations, Halloween, April Fool's Day, New Year's Day, and Valentine's Day books. In addition, the Mini-Themes include activities and references for birthdays and Martin Luther King Day. Inform your special subjects teachers about the holiday units so that they can integrate art, music, and physical education activities into their curricula to reinforce the holiday being studied.

HOW IT WORKS

Initiating Activity

With students, create a semantic web of holidays and the symbols that are associated with them. For example:

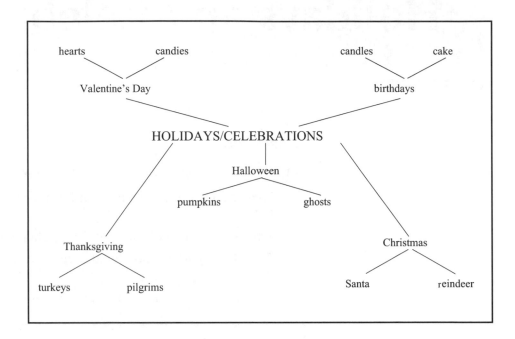

Then have students choose a holiday and write a short excerpt about why they selected their holidays and how they think their specific holidays originated. Save these to compare as origins of holidays are discussed at a later date.

General Activities

1. Have the students select a song from one holiday and put it to lyrics representing another. For example, using the melody from "Jingle Bells," sing the following lyrics about Halloween:

   Halloween, Halloween

   Halloween all the day,

   Oh what fun it is to have

   A Halloween day surprise.

2. Select a particular holiday and ask that each student bring in a recipe for a favorite dish for that holiday. Compile these recipes into a booklet and duplicate for each student. Discuss the nutritional value of each recipe. If possible, find out the country from which each recipe originated. Finally, select one of the recipes and prepare it as a class project. This could be done for several different holidays.

3. Discuss plants and animals that symbolize a particular holiday (reindeers-Christmas, pumpkins-Halloween). Help the students find out why these symbols have meaning for that holiday and discuss the meanings. Then create a bulletin board with pictures of the representative symbols.

4. Have students think about the different seasons in which each holiday falls. Have each student think of a holiday and then, with eyes closed, picture what that holiday would be like if it were in a different season. Have students create a shoe box of the image. Display the scenes on a table or windowsill.

5. Read poems about selected holidays. Some good books for holiday poems are: *Celebrations* by Myra Cohn Livingston, *Where the Sidewalk Ends* and *A Light in the Attic* both by Shel Silverstein, *More Poetry for Holidays* selected by Nancy Larrick, and *The Random House Book of Poetry* by Jack Prelutsky.

6. Have a class discussion on the different ways people celebrate different holidays. Explain what "family custom" or "tradition" is and ask the students to share some of their family traditions for a selected holiday. For example, some families open Christmas gifts on Christmas Eve while others wait until Christmas morning; families may or may not have big celebrations for birthdays; on Valentine's Day, some families send roses or flowers to people they love while others do not. If possible, invite people from other countries to come into your classroom and talk about the holiday traditions and customs of their countries for the selected holiday. Allow time to compare and contrast these customs and traditions.

7. Collect two sets of pictures of holiday symbols for the selected holiday such as hearts, candy, cupid, arrow, flowers, cards, etc. to represent Valentine's Day. Pictures can be found in magazines, coloring books, sticker books and so forth. Adhere one set of pictures to a piece of tagboard that has been divided into squares. Use the other set of pictures to make matching cards. Have students match the pictures.

8. Have a class discussion on memorable moments the students have had on the selected holiday. Then have each student create a poem, story, illustration, etc. that depicts what was so special about the holiday. Allow time to share.

9. Ask the students to create holidays and/or celebrations to break the day to day routine. For example, plan a "Relative Day" where everyone brings in a picture of his/her favorite relative and tells why that relative is the favorite. Create a "Memory Day" where the students tell their best memory about growing up. This may include bringing in pictures, letters, and other memorabilia. If possible, obtain the *52 Special Traditions for Family and Friends* published by Chronicle Books. It is a set of 52 cards that provides ideas for creative holidays or celebrations.

Activities Specific to Halloween

1. Ask the students to create scary music using different instruments and noisemakers. Record the sound. Then, play the tape while the students write spooky stories. Give each of the students two pieces of 12" x 18" black construction paper. Instruct the students to draw a haunted house on one of the pieces of paper and then cut it out. Next ask them to cut the

house in half. Have each student glue the house by its outer, vertical edges to the second piece of paper so that the two parts of the house open outward. Glue the story inside the house and put it on a bulletin board.

2. Read the poem "Halloween" from the book *Celebrations* by Myra Cohn Livingston. Have each student select an object or symbol that represents Halloween (ghost, pumpkin, and witch) and write a poem about it. Have them design their objects/symbols on large pieces (12" x 18") of construction paper and cut them out. Glue the poems onto their objects/symbols. Using all the objects/symbols, create a mobile with string and dowel rods. Hang the mobile in the corner of the room.

3. Invite a police officer into the classroom to speak about the safety aspects of trick-or-treating. Have the officer explain that children should not go trick-or-treating alone, that their parents should check their candy, that they should not go to houses of people they do not know, that they should carry a flashlight, etc.

4. Seat the children in a circle around a pumpkin. Discuss the shape of the pumpkin. Cut the top off the pumpkin and hollow it out. Wash and dry the pumpkin seeds for planting, baking or dyeing. Save the meat of the pumpkin for cooking. Allow the students to look at and feel the inside of the pumpkin (discussion of the senses can also be incorporated into this lesson at this time). Give each student a few pumpkin seeds to plant in individual containers—one container for each of the students. Spread the remaining seeds on an ungreased cookie sheet. Bake them in a 350 degrees oven, stirring them occasionally until they are toasted lightly on all sides. Allow the children to taste the seeds. Next, cut out a mouth, eyes, and nose. Discuss the shapes being cut out. Finally, using the meat of the pumpkin, follow a pumpkin pie filling recipe to create pumpkin-pie filling, pour it into small paper cups. Place the cups in an electric frying pan that is filled with one inch of hot water. Cover the cups and bake the filling for approximately 30 minutes or until a knife inserted comes out clean. With this snack, serve glasses or orange juice, with licorice whips in them for straws. *Note:* This activity requires careful supervision by the teacher.

5. Have a Halloween party. Students can dress up as they like. Have the other student's guess one another's costume identities. Ask the students to explain why they chose to dress up as they did. Have students read their scary stories from Activity 1 to the class. Background music can be played from holiday CDs or cassettes.

6. Make jack-o-lantern snacks by slicing off the tops of thick-skinned oranges and scooping out the insides. Mix the insides with other fruits such as bananas, grapes, apples, etc. Provide black markers and ask the students to draw jack-o-lantern faces on the oranges. Finally, fill each jack-o-lantern with fruit salad to eat for snack time.

7. Ask each student to stuff a brown lunch bag with crumpled newspaper, allowing space at the top for twisting to make a stem. Show the students how to twist the top and secure it with a rubber band. Then ask the students to paint the stem green and the rest of the bag orange with poster or

tempera paint. After the "pumpkins" have dried, help the students paint faces on them. Next, make a pumpkin patch in the classroom, connecting the pumpkin bags with thick, green yarn as the vines. Leaves could be made from green construction paper. Explain how pumpkins grow. If possible, take a trip to a farm where pumpkins are raised.

8. Obtain a copy of *Children Just Like Me: Celebrations!* by Barnabas & Anabal Kindersley. Compare and contrast Halloween in the U.S. with Halloween in Canada.

Activities Specific to April Fool's Day

1. Have a lesson on lies. Discuss the difference between lies and jokes. Have a safety lesson teaching that when playing jokes, you need to be careful not to do anything that is physically dangerous or that would hurt someone's feelings.

2. Ask students to write about and illustrate their favorite April Fool's jokes. Compile these to make a class April Fool's joke book.

3. If possible, have students watch a comedy film that shows people playing tricks on each other (The Three Stooges, Roadrunner, Tweety and Sylvester, etc.). Watch the film with sound. Then watch the film without sound—have the students create their own music and sound effects for the film.

4. Play tricks with numbers by having the students turn numbers into figures of animals or people, having them come up with number games and riddles, or having them crack some number codes. Then allow time for them to share their tricks.

5. Have a classroom or school April Fool's Wacky Day by having the students dress in two different shoes, clothes that are mismatched, funny T-shirts, silly hairstyles, backward clothing, etc.

6. April Fool's Day is celebrated on the first day of April. Let the students investigate to find out if there are other holidays on the first day of a month. If so, what are they?

7. Have the class form a circle. Pick out one student to come into the middle of the circle. Have the class look at him or her closely. Take the student outside the room and change his or her appearance (i.e., take off a sock or put on a mitten). Bring the student back into the middle of the circle and see if the rest of the class can tell what has changed.

Activities Specific to New Years Day

1. Play the song "Auld Lang Syne." Discuss how this song is sung on New Year's Eve to say goodbye to the old year. Talk about the words to the song. Ask the students if they know any other sings that say goodbye to something or somebody.

2. At the beginning of each year many people decide on some things they'd like to change about themselves, so they make New Year's resolutions. Help the students think about this concept by creating a Tally Game. To do

this, develop a list of items or behaviors (good and bad) that students may do in the course of a year (wash dishes, make the bed, fight with a brother or sister, etc.). Assign each behavior a number value. For example, washing the dishes would add three points; fighting with a sibling would subtract three points. Have the students start with a score of 20. For one week, have the students go through the list, adding or subtracting what applies to them. See how each student scores. Finally, point out that they may want to make resolutions to change some of the bad behaviors.

3. Different countries celebrate the New Year in different ways. For example, the Chinese New Year is celebrated between mid-January and mid-February and lasts for five days. Read the *Chinese New Year* by Sarah Moyse and/or *Chinese New Year* by Tricia Brown to find out more about the Chinese New Year. One of the beliefs in China is that each year is governed by one of twelve animals (see chart below).

Year of the rat	1972	1984	1996
Year of the ox	1973	1985	1997
Year of the tiger	1974	1986	1998
Year of the hare	1975	1987	1999
Year of the dragon	1976	1988	2000
Year of the snake	1977	1989	2001
Year of the horse	1978	1990	2002
Year of the sheep	1979	1991	2003
Year of the monkey	1980	1992	2004
Year of the cock	1981	1993	2005
Year of the dog	1982	1994	2006
Year of the boar	1983	1995	2007

Activities Specific to Valentine's Day

1. Mix red and white tempera paint together in stages so students can see how various shades of red and pink are made. Place this paint, as well as some bright red paint, at the art table along with different sizes of heart-shaped cookie cutters or heart shapes cut from sponges. Provide large pieces of white construction paper and allow students to make heart prints.

2. Read *101 Valentine Jokes* by Pa Brigandi. Then ask the students to create their own valentine jokes. Allow time to share.

3. Share the book *Crafts for Valentine's Day* by Kathy Ross. Ask the students to work in pairs to create one of the projects presented in this book. Display projects.

Discussion Questions

1. What is a holiday?

2. Which holiday do you like best? Why?

3. Why do we celebrate holidays?

4. How do you think holidays got their beginnings?

5. If you had a choice, what kind of a day would you make into a holiday? What would you use to symbolize your holiday? Why?

6. Do all people celebrate holidays in the same way? Explain.

7. Do people in different countries celebrate all the same holidays as the people in the United States? Explain. Give examples of holidays that are different and of some that are the same.

8. Do you know anyone who celebrates a holiday that you don't celebrate? If so, what is it? Why does this person celebrate this holiday, and why don't you?

9. Do you think holidays are important? Why or why not?

10. If you were told that all holidays had been canceled for this year, how would you feel? Explain.

LITERATURE RELATED ACTIVITIES

Title: *This is the Pumpkin*

Genre:	Fantasy fiction
Author:	Abby Levine
Illustrator:	Billin-Frye
Bibliographic information:	Albert Whitman & Co., New York: 1997.
Summary:	A cumulative rhyme describes the activities of Max, his younger sister, and other children as they celebrate Halloween at school and trick-or-treating.
Interest level:	Grades K–3

Pre-Reading Activity

Read the poem "Day After Halloween" from the book *A Light in the Attic* by Shel Silverstein. Have the class sit in a circle. Designate a student to say "Halloween reminds me of _____" and write the word provided on the chalkboard. The next student says "Halloween reminds me of _____" as you write the word on the board, the class then chorally reads "Halloween reminds me of _____" and says both words written on the chalkboard. Continue around the circle in this manner.

Learning Activity

1. Show the students the illustration in the center of the book, *This Is the Pumpkin* that represents a group of children trick-or-treating. Talk with the students about their experiences with trick-or-treating. Then, give each

of them a 12" x 18" sheet of paper and ask them to illustrate a real or make-believe trick-or-treating experience. Have orange and black tempera paint available. Allow time for them to share their Halloween illustrations.

2. Show the children the illustrations in *This Is the Pumpkin* of the children at the principal's party at the school. Ask the students to plan and then implement a Halloween party for their class, which includes decorations, stories, videos, snacks, games, etc. Then invite the principal, parents, grandparents, and/or a next door classroom to participate in the party.

3. Have a class discussion about why witches, ghosts, pumpkins, skeletons, bats, and other scary things that are associated with Halloween. Include a class discussion on how they think Halloween originated. Finally, ask the students to make a card or decoration that represents Halloween.

Discussion Questions

1. Which of the things that Max did, do you think he liked best? Why?

2. What did Max see as he walked through his neighborhood that reminded him of Halloween? What else might Max see if he walked around your neighborhood on Halloween night?

3. Why do you think the children got into the van to go trick-or-treating?

4. If your school was putting on a Halloween party like Max's school did, what would you want it to be like? Explain.

5. How do you think Max felt about going trick-or-treating? Why?

6. How do you think Max felt when Halloween was over? Explain.

Title: *Arthur's April Fool*

Genre: Picture Book

Author: Marc Brown

Bibliographic information: Little, Brown & Co., Boston: 1999.

Summary: Arthur worries about remembering his magic tricks for the April Fool's Day program and Binky's threats to pulverize him.

Interest level: Grades K–3

Pre-Reading Activity

When the students come into class on April Fool's Day have a joke ready—such as writing on the board: "No School Today." When all the students are buzzing with excitement, get their attention and say "April Fool's Day!" Then have a class discussion on what they know about April Fool's Day and lead them into the writing activity.

Learning Activity

1. Read other April Fool's books such as *April Fool* by Mary Blount Christian (1986), *Mud Flat April Fools* by James Stevensen (1998) or *Lila's*

April Fool by Francine Pascal (1994). Compare and contrast these books with *Arthur's April Fool* by Marc Brown. Ask the students their opinions as to which one of the stories they have read or heard is the most enjoyable? Most informative? Most realistic? Have them explain their choices.

2. Most holidays have symbols that represent them. Tell the students to create a symbol to represent April Fool's Day. Display.

3. Ask the children to think about if they were governor of their state or president of the United States, how would they have their state or country celebrate April Fool's Day. For example, would schools, stores, etc. be closed? Would there be a parade, etc.? Allow time for the students to illustrate what their declaration of April Fool's Day would look like. Allow time to share.

4. As a class, plan an April Fool's Day assembly similar to the one described in *Arthur's April Fool*. Invite the principal, parents, and other classes.

5. Have the students write short stories about April Fool's jokes they have had played on them or have played on others.

Discussion Questions

1. Why was Arthur so worried about telling his joke at the assembly? (He was afraid Binky would pulverize him).

2. What is the difference between a lie and a joke?

3. Do you like April Fool's Day? Why or why not?

4. If you could play a joke on only one person on April Fool's Day, who would it be? Why?

5. Is it more fun to play a trick on someone or to have a trick played on you? Why?

6. April Fool's Day began a long time ago. What reasons would you give for us to continue celebrating it?

7. Who do you think was the smartest, Binky or Arthur? Explain.

8. Do you think Francine played a good April Fool's joke on Arthur? Why or why not?

Title: *Happy New Year, Pooh!*

Genre: Picture Book

Author: Kathleen W. Zoehfeld

Illustrator: Robbin Cuddy

Bibliographic information: Disney Press, New York: 1997.

Summary: Pooh, Tigger, and Piglet become sad when they turned their calendar from December to the next month and there were no more months. They decided to write a poem to say good-bye to the months. As they were doing that, they heard noises from Rabbit's house where a party was going on to welcome in the New Year. Christopher Robin explained there will be a new January, February, etc. and gave everyone a new calendar.

Interest level: Grades K–3

Pre-Reading Activity

Ask the students to share how they celebrate New Year's Eve and New Year's Day. Do they stay up until midnight? Do they watch parades? Do they celebrate with noisemakers and hats? Then read the book *Happy New Year!* By E. Bernhard that tells how other people celebrate New Year's Eve.

Learning Activities

1. New Year's resolutions are very popular. Have the students write at least five things they are pleased with that they did this past year. Have them write at least two things they did this past year that they would like to change. Would these changes be their New Year's resolutions? What other changes would be included? Finally, ask the children to write at least two New Year's resolutions each. *Note:* Compile a list of the resolutions to use in Activity 3 below.

2. New Year's Day is a day of new beginnings—just like being born. Have students bring in baby pictures to display on a bulletin board. Put the caption "Our Beginning" on the bulletin board. Then have the class guess who each baby is.

3. Place the New Year's resolutions written in Activity 1 in an envelope and put them away. In a few weeks, get the resolutions out and discuss how the students are progressing with their goals.

4. Have the children make their own New Year's hats and noisemakers. Noisemakers can be made by putting small stones or gravel in paper tubes, gluing cardboard over the ends, and then decorating with streamers. Also, wax paper can be put over one end of a paper tube for a horn. Discuss how sound vibrates the wax paper to make the noise.

5. Help the children create a poem to either say good-bye to last year's months, as Pooh and friends were doing, or a poem to welcome in the new months.

6. Ask the students to think about a different way to celebrate New Year's. Then have them illustrate their perfect beginning to a New Year and share it with the class.

7. Have the students make up a calendar beginning a new year at a different time. Make up math problems that pertain to this. (e.g., If the new year began in April, then December would be what month? [9th month]).

Discussion Questions

1. What is your favorite way of celebrating New Year's Day?

2. New Year's Day is a new beginning. What are some other new beginnings? (Being born, graduating)

3. What do you think Pooh, Tigger, and Piglet would have done in January if they hadn't found out about the New Year?

4. Rabbit and his friend were making a lot of noise to welcome in the New Year. Why do you think people are so noisy on New Year's Eve?

Title: *Valentines Day*

Genre:	Realistic Fiction
Author/Illustrator:	Miriam Nerlove
Bibliographic information:	Albert Whitman & Co., New York: 1994.
Summary:	A brief history of Valentine's Day is followed by a girl's account of her celebration at preschool and at home.
Interest level:	Grades 1–3

Pre-Reading Activity

Discuss that the purpose of Valentine's Day is to let people know that you love them and care about them. People usually send cards that have words about love on them. Share some Valentine cards with the students. Then make a semantic web with the word "valentine" for which the students think of kind and loving words.

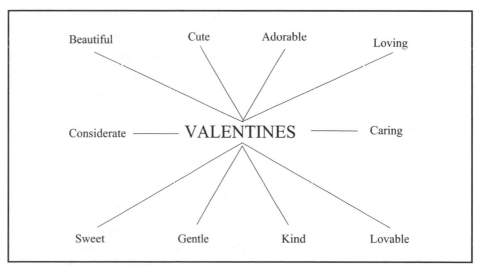

Next, have each student cut out a heart from red construction paper. Have each child write his or her name in the middle of the heart and fold the heart in half. Collect and redistribute the hearts. Have each student write a word that describes the person whose name is on the heart. Words suggested during the webbing may be used. Stress that they are to write only good things about the person. The teacher should check to make sure nothing negative has been said. Then give the hearts back to the students to whom they belong.

Learning Activities

1. Read the poem "Valentine" from Shel Silverstein's *A Light in the Attic*. Have the students think about someone they care about or love. Then have each student write a poem using some of the words generated in the Pre-Reading Activity. Finally, as the young girl did in the story, tell the students to use their poems and to make valentines for others.

2. Read other books related to Valentine's Day such as *The Berenstein Bears Comic Valentine* by S. Berenstein, *Clifford's First Valentine's Day* by N. Bidwell, *Happy Valentine's Day, Miss Hildy* by F. Grambling or *Disney's Winnie the Pooh Valentine* by B. Talkington. Discuss the similarities and differences between these books.

3. Have each student follow this procedure to make a mobile about the book, *Valentine's Day*. First write the title of the book and the author's name on a large, red heart. Cut out three smaller hearts. Draw and write about three events that happened in the story on the hearts. Finally, string the three hearts (in sequence in which they happened in the story) down from the large heart.

Discussion Questions

1. According to the book *Valentine's Day*, how did Valentine's Day get its name?

2. What activities are done in the book, *Valentine's Day*, to celebrate Valentine's Day? Which of these activities would you like to do best? Least? Explain.

3. For whom did the young girl in the story make valentines? Which valentine card that she made, do you think, was liked the most? Why?

4. Describe the valentine the young girl gave to her dog. Why do you think she gave the dog a valentine? Why do you think he chewed on it?

5. If you were having a Valentine Day party, what would you want to do? What would you want for snacks?

6. Could the events in this story really happen? Explain.

7. If you wanted to make your own Valentine cards, what would you need?

CULMINATING ACTIVITY

Invite family members, friends, and other classes to a "Holiday Open House" for a specific holiday. At this open house, allow students to share products/ activities which they completed in this unit.

SUPPLEMENTAL LITERATURE

General Holidays/Celebrations

Angell, C. S. (1996). *Celebrations around the world: A multicultural handbook*. Golden, CO: Fulcrum Publishing.
The book provides information and activities for students based on multicultural holidays.

Goring, R. (1995). *Holidays and celebrations.* Vero Beach, Florida: Rourke Publishing, Inc.
  Introduces readers to the fast growing groups of Latinos and their traditions and cultures.

Kadodwala, D. (1998). *Holi.* Austin, TX: Raintree/Steck-Vaughn.
  Provides information on holidays around the world.

Kindersley, A. (1997). *Children just like me: Celebrations*! Photos by Barnabas Kindersley. New York: Dorling Kindersley Publishing.
  Photographs and illustrations portray children as they celebrate 25 of their favorite holidays and traditions.

Larrick, N. (1973). *More poetry for holidays.* New York: Delacorte Press.
  A collection of holiday poems.

Leunn, N. (1998). *Celebrations of light: A year of holidays around the world.* New York: Atheneum.
  This book takes the reader on a candlelight tour of the world, describing 12 festivals and observances that use light as part of their celebrations.

Livingston, M. C. (1985). *Celebrations.* Photos by Marsha Winborn. Illustrated by Leonard Everett. New York: Holiday House.
  A collection of poems for the holidays of the year.

Markham, L. (1998). *Harvest.* New York: Blackbirch Marketing.
  Presents holidays and ceremonies from around the world.

Prelutsky, J. (1983). *The Random House book of poetry.* New York: Random House.
  Contains a variety of holiday poems.

Silverstein, S. (1974). *Where the sidewalk ends.* New York: Harper & Row.
  Contains outrageously funny narrative poems. Includes the use of rhythm, rhyme, sound patterns, and repetition.

Silverstein, S. (1981). *A light in the attic.* New York: Harper & Row.
  Poems contain improbable characters and situations and includes poems such as Sour Ann, a polar bear in a Frigidaire and so forth.

Sing, R. (1994). *Chinese New Year's Dragon.* Illustrated by Shao Wei Liu. New York: Little Simon Books.
  A young girl's grandmother tells her about dragons on the "Year of the Dragon," and suddenly she finds herself on a dragon's back soaring over ancient China.

Skrepcinski, D., & Stodk, M. (1998). *Silly celebrations: Activities for the strangest holidays you've heard of.* Illustrated by Yayo. New York: Aladdin Paperback.
  A unique activity book that includes information about holidays, celebrations, and regional festivals, plus great ways to enjoy these special days.

Spies, K. (1992). *Our traditional holidays.* Brookfield, CT: Millbrook Press.
  This book examines the history and significance of patriotic holidays that honor famous people, and special American holidays.

Striker, S. (1996). *The anti-coloring book of celebrations*. Illustrated by Sally Schaedler. New York: Henry Holt.
Focuses on the holidays of the year, helping children to stimulate creativity and expression.

Wild, M. (1991). *Let the celebrations begin!* Illustrated by Julie Vivas. New York: Orchard Books.
A child, who remembers life at home before life in a concentration camp, makes toys with the women to give to the other children at the very special party they are going to have when the soldiers arrive to liberate the camp.

Williams, L. E. (1998). *Backwards day*. Illustrated by George Ulrich. New York: Avon.
A child accidentally wearing his shirt backwards to school comes up with the idea to create "A Backwards Day Party" for him and his friends.

Winchester, F. (1996). *African-American holidays*. New York: Capstone.
Discusses special times of the year when African-Americans celebrate, including Black History Month, Mardi Gras, Junteenth, Harambee, Junkanoo, and Kwanzaa.

April Fool's

Brown, M. T. (1999). *Arthur's April fool*. Boston: Little Brown.
Arthur worries about remembering his magic tricks for the April Fool's Day assembly and Binky's threats to pulverize him.

Pascal, F. (1994). *Lila's April fool*. New York: Bantam Books.
Lila invites the entire second-grade class to her April Fool's Day party, but when she tells them it is all a joke, the Wakefield twins and their friends play a prank on Lila.

Stevenson, J. (1998). *Mud Flat April fool*. New York: Greenwillow.
April Fool's Day brings out the jokes in Mud Flat's animal residents: George the fox breaks out his squirting lapel rose, Newt the gator tries the old dollar-on-a-stone trick and a mole produces a note that she claims was left by space aliens.

Waters, K., & Slovenz-Low, M. (1990). *Lion dancer*. Photographs by Martha Cooper. New York: Scholastic.
This book presents a rare look at a Chinese household as they embrace their ancient customs and celebrate their most important holiday—the Chinese New Year.

New Years

Bernhard, E. (1996). *Happy new year!* Illustrated by Durga Bernhard. New York: Lodestar Books.
Describes the origins of New Year traditions and ways in which the coming of the New Year is celebrated around the world.

Brown, T. (1987). *Chinese New Year*. Photographs by Fran Ortiz. New York: Henry Holt.
An informative introduction to Chinese New Year celebrated by Chinese Americans living in San Francisco's Chinatown.

Chinn, K. (1997). *Sam and the lucky money*. Illustrated by Cornelius Van Wright. New York: Lee & Low.
Anticipating spending his gift of Lucky Money on Chinese New Year's Day, Sam accompanies his mother to Chinatown, where he watches a dancing New Year's lion, visits many colorful and good-smelling shops, and learns a special lesson.

Livingston, M. C. (1987). *New Year's poems*. Illustrated by Margot Tomes.
An interesting collection of poems to celebrate New Years.

Low, W. (1997). *Chinatown*. New York: Henry Holt.
A boy and his grandmother wind their way through the streets of Chinatown enjoying all the sights and smells of the Chinese New Year's Day.

Moyse, S. (1998). *Chinese New Year*. New York: Millbrook.
An informative and enjoyable book depicting the customs and traditions of the Chinese New Year.

Rattigan, J. K. (1993). *Dumpling soup*. Illustrated by Lillian Hsu-Flanders. Boston: Little, Brown.
A Korean-American author recalls her youth in Oahu as she tells of a young Hawaiian girl trying to make dumplings for Grandma's special New Year's soup for her culturally diverse family.

Spirn, M. (1998). *New Year (world celebrations and ceremonies)*. New York: Blackbirch Marketing.
This book explores New Year celebrations around the world.

Waters, K., & Slovenz-Low, M. (1990). *Lion dancer: Ernie Wan's Chinese New Year*. Photographs by Martha Cooper. New York: Scholastic.
A rare and intimate look at a Chinese household as they embrace their ancient customs, celebrate their most important holiday, and share a proud moment with Ernie.

Halloween

Bauer, M. D. (1997). *Alison's fierce & ugly Halloween*. Illustrated by Laurie Spencer. New York: Disney Publishing.
Alison dresses as a fierce and ugly pirate for Halloween, but she is disappointed and angry when everyone says she looks cute.

Berenstain, S., & Berenstain, J. (1997). *The Berenstain bears in the spooky fun house: A pop-up book*. New York: Inchworm Publishing.
When the Bear family visits the haunted house, Papa discovers that sometimes it is the biggest bear who gets the biggest scare.

Cushman, D. (1998). *Aunt Eater's mystery Halloween*. New York: HarperCollins Children's Books.

Aunt Eater the anteater finds plenty of mysteries to solve when she attends a Halloween costume party.

Jane, P. (1998). *A-Boo-C: A spooky alphabet story*. Illustrated by Maggie Smith. New York: Grossett & Dunlap.
This book follows angels, dragons, and ghosts through an alphabet of Halloween fun.

Tryon, L. (1998). *Albert's Halloween: The case of the stolen pumpkins*. New York: Atheneum.
Chief Inspector Albert the duck and his three detective assistants follow a series of clues to find the batch of pumpkins stolen from the town pumpkin patch.

Wojciechowski, S. (1998). *The best Halloween of all*. Illustrated by Susan Meddaugh. Cambridge, MA: Candlewick Publishing.
Ben hates the Halloween costumes his parents create for him, so when he is seven, he announces he will design his own.

Yolen, J. (1994). *Beneath the ghost moon: A Halloween tale*. Boston: Little, Brown.
As the farmyard mice are sleeping, with their tiny costumes lying beside each of their beds, the creepy-crawlers prepare to attack.

Valentine's Day

Berenstain, S., & Berenstain, J. (1998). *The Berenstain Bears' comic valentine*. New York: Scholastic, Inc. "Cartwheel Books".
In this charming story, Brother Bear, the star hockey player, receives secret valentines from a secret admirer, Honey Bear. On the day of the championship hockey game, Honey Bear reveals her true identity.

Bidwell, N. (1997). *Clifford's first Valentine's Day*. New York: Cartwheel Books.
So tiny that he can fit into Emily Elizabeth's pocket, the small red puppy Clifford gets into a lot of trouble as he gets covered with Valentine paste, falls into a post office chute, and disappears in a mountain of mail.

Brigandi, P. (1994). *101 Valentine jokes*. Illustrated by Don Orehek. New York: Scholastic Paperbacks.
Children will enjoy this collection of more than one hundred jokes with the theme of Valentine's Day.

Carlson, N. (1985). *Louanne Pig in the mysterious Valentine*. Minneapolis, MN: Carolrhoda Books.
Louanne Pig receive a beautiful valentine, but must find the secret admirer who sent it.

Grambling, L. (1998). *Happy Valentine's Day, Miss Hildy!* Illustrated by Bridget Starr Taylor. New York: Random Library.
Miss Hildy, a detective of sorts, investigates a strange Valentine's that appears on her doorstep.

Scarry, R. (1999). *Be my Valentine*. New York: Simon Spotlights.
Huckly and Lowly chase a runaway Valentine gift through the park when Hilda Hippo's good intentions go awry.

Talkington, B. (1996). *Disney's Winnie the Pooh's valentine*. Illustrated by John Kurtz. New York: Disney Press.
With Valentine's Day fast approaching. Roo is trying to find the perfect way to say "I love you" to Kanga and turns to Pooh and his other friends in the Hundred-Acre Wood for some creative ideas.

Lexair, J. M. (1999). *Don't be my valentine*. New York: Harper-Collins Juvenile Books.
Sam's mean valentine for Amy Lou goes astray at school and almost ruins the day for him and his friends.

Prelutksy, J. (1983). *It's Valentine's Day*. Illustrated by Yossi Abolafia. New York: Greenwillow Books.
This book contains fourteen easy-to-read poems that go straight to the heart—and funnybone—of Valentine's Day and helps children to laugh at themselves.

Ross, K. (1995). *Crafts for Valentine's Day*. Illustrated by Sharon Lane Holm. Brookfield, CT: Millbrook Press.
This book contains easy-to-follow instructions with accessible materials for a variety of special Valentine's Day projects including special valentines and a decorated valentine holder.

MINI–THEMES

Martin Luther King, Jr., Day

Martin Luther King, Jr. had a dream: He wanted the laws of our land applied in the same way to all people. He united blacks and whites in many nonviolent protests and marches. Violence kept Martin Luther King, Jr., from fulfilling his dream of equal rights. He was shot and killed on April 4, 1968. Fifteen years after his death, King's birthday became a legal holiday. It is celebrated on the third Monday of January. On this day, Americans have an opportunity to remember his efforts and honor the goal of equal rights for all citizens.

Activities

1. After reading some of the reference books about Martin Luther King, Jr., tell the students that when someone dies, people send sympathy cards, flowers, contributions to the deceased persons family and/or friends. Ask the students to create a sympathy card for Dr. King and to mail it to Mrs. Coretta King, his wife, at Scholastic, Inc., 730 Broadway, New York, NY 10003. She and Mr. King's son wrote *I Have a Dream* published by Scholastic.

2. Share copies of *My Dream of Martin Luther King, Tar Beach,* and *Aunt Harriet's Underground Railroad in the Sky*, all written by Faith Ringgold. Compare and contrast the illustrations. Ask the students how the illustrations made them feel in each book. Finally, discuss whether or not they think Faith Ringgold's illustrations demonstrate the message she is trying to convey in her books.

3. Each year the Coretta Scott King award is given to an African-American artist who has made an outstanding contribution for illustrations. Read the book *I Have a Dream* by Martin Luther King, III, and Coretta Scott King. This book is illustrated by 15 Coretta Scott King Award and Honor Book Artists. Allow time for the students to discuss and express their opinions about the illustrations. Also, read Dr. Kings "I Have a Dream" speech and discuss its significance with the students.

4. Martin Luther King, Jr. is seen as a hero by many people. Discuss the meaning of "hero". Then create an "Our Heros" bulletin board by illustrating or cutting out pictures to adhere to the bulletin board. Remind the students a person doesn't have to be famous to be a hero, and one person's hero, may not be someone elses hero.

5. Obtain a copy of *Celebrations* by Myra B. Livingston. Read the Martin Luther King Day poems. As a group, create a Martin Luther King, Jr. poem.

References

Hakim, R. (1994). *Martin Luther King, Jr. and the march toward freedom.* Brookfield, CT: Millbrook Publisher Trade.

King, III., M. L., & King, C. S. (1997). *I have a dream.* New York: Scholastic.

Lazo, C. (1994). *Martin Luther King, Jr.* Parsippany, NJ: Silver Burdett Press. Dillon Press.

Marzollo, J. (1995). *Happy birthday, Martin Luther King.* Illustrated by J. Brian Pinkney. New York: Scholastic Trade.

McKissack, P., & Ostendorf, N. (1991). *Martin Luther King, Jr.: Man of peace.* Hillside, NJ: Enslow Publishing, Inc.

Ringgold, F. (1995). *My dream of Martin Luther King.* New York: Crown Publishers.

Roop, P., & Roop, C. (1997). *Dr. Martin Luther King, Jr.* Des Plaines, IL: Heineman Library.

Woodson, J. (1996). *Martin Luther King, Jr. and his birthday.* Illustrated by Floyd Cooper. Englewood Cliff, NJ: Silver Press.

Birthdays

Birthdays began long ago when people believed that on their birthday they could be helped by good spirits or harmed by evil spirits. People had friends and relatives around to protect them and make noise to keep evil spirits away. Today birthday parties are fun with decorations and birthday cakes with candles. There is one candle for each year of life and a silent wish is made by the birthday person and candles are blown out in one big puff.

Activities

1. Ask the students to think of creative ways to have great birthday parties that are different than usual. For example, ask them to create "really silly" or "stupid" birthday party invitations or invite them to create activities for

the party such as asking guests to tell the best and worst birthday present they could imagine. The book *Best Birthday Party Game Book* by Bruce Lansky or *Birthday Happy, Contrary Mary* by Anita Jeram would be an excellent resource for this activity.

2. Read books such as *Birthday* by John Steptoe, *A Birthday Basket for Tia* by Pat Mora, *The Birthday Swap* by Loretta Lopez or *A Farmer Boy Birthday* by Laura Ingalls Wilder.

3. The books *The Case of the Missing Birthday Party* by Joanne Rocklin and *The Baseball Party* by Annabelle Prager both present problems related to mix-ups about birthday party invitations. Select one of the problems but do not give a way it was solved. Then ask the students to problem solve the situation and as a group write a letter to the main character with a solution(s) for solving the problem. Finally, read the solution given in the book. Send the student's solution to the publisher of the book.

4. Read books such as *Alfie & the Birthday Surprise* by Shirley Hughes, *Bow Wow Birthday* by Lee Wardlaw, or *The Birthday Bear* by Antonie Schneider. All three books present unique kinds of birthdays. Ask the students to share the most unique birthday party they have ever had or attended.

5. Read *Alfie & the Birthday Surprise* by Shirley Hughes and then discuss the most unusual gifts the students have ever given or received.

6. Read the birthday poems from the book *Celebrations* by Myra C. Livingston. Then, as a group, create a birthday poem.

References

Brown, M. T. (1998). *Arthur's birthday book and plush toy*. New York: Little Brown.

Enderlain, C. L. (1998). *Celebrating birthdays in Australia*. New York: Grolier Publishing.

Enderlain, C. L. (1998). *Celebrating birthdays in Brazil*. New York: Grolier Publishing.

Enderlain, C. L. (1998). *Celebrating birthdays in China*. New York: Grolier Publishing.

Enderlain, C. L. (1998). *Celebrating birthdays in Russia*. New York: Grolier Publishing.

Gibbons, G. (1986). *Happy birthday*. New York: Holiday House.

Hennessy, B. G. (1997). *Corduroy's birthday: A lift-the-book*. New York: Viking Children's Books.

Hoban, L. (1999). *Arthur's birthday party*. New York: HarperCollins Juvenile Books.

Hughes, S. (1998). *Alfie and the birthday surprise*. New York: Lothrop Lee and Shepard.

Jeram, A. (1998). *Birthday happy, contrary Mary*. New York: Candlewick Publishers.

Lansky, B. (1997). *Best birthday party game book*. New York: Simon Schuster.

Mayer, M. (1996). *Bun Bun's birthday*. New York: Random House.

Mora, P. (1992). *A birthday basket for Tia.* Illustrated by Cecily Lang. New York: Macmillan, Maxwell.

Prager, A. (1995). *The baseball birthday party.* Illustrated by Marilyn Mets. New York: Random House.

Rocklin, J., & Speirs, J. (1997). *The case of the mission birthday party.* Illustrated by Marilyn Burns and Tricia Tusa. New York: Cartwheel Books.

Schneider, A., & Waas, U. (1998). *The birthday bear.* Translated by J. Alison James. New York: North-South Books.

Steptoe, J. (1991). *The Birthday.* New York: Henry Holt.

Wardlaw, L. (1998). *Bow wow birthday.* New York: Boyds Mills Publisher.

Wilder, L. I. (1998). *A farmer boy birthday.* New York: HarperCollins Children's Books.

Folktales from Around the World

OVERVIEW

Focus

Through the reading and discussion of folktales from countries around the world, students will become familiar with a variety of cultures, and gain an appreciation for this literary form.

Objectives

Upon completion of this thematic unit, students will:

1. Retell several folktales that originated in other countries.

2. Recognize that often the folktales of a culture mirror its traditions and values.

3. Relate the differences and the similarities among cultures as reflected in their literature.

4. Create their own folktales to reflect an understanding of the elements of this literary genre.

HOW IT WORKS

Initiating Activity

Decorate a shoe box with words and phrases from the folktale *Rumpelstiltskin* as retold by Paul Zelinski (1986). Inside the box, place objects that are appropriate to the story, such as a small baby doll, a picture of a spinning wheel, pieces of straw, and the like. Show students one object at a time and ask them to try to figure out what folktale is being represented by the items. Once someone has guessed correctly, or when the class is stumped, read the folktale *Rumpelstiltskin.* After the reading, ask students to relate the significance of each object that was in the box. Discuss the story with students, asking such questions as "Which character do you think was the most foolish?"; "Which character do you like most?"; "Which character do you believe is the most cruel?"; and "What does this folktale tell you about the qualities that were admired?" Explain to students that *Rumpelstiltskin* is a folktale that originated in Germany (locate Germany on a class map) and introduce students to folktales.

General Activities

1. Read aloud several folktales. Have students come to a generalized understanding about the way folktales usually begin (once upon a time), how

they usually end (and they lived happily ever after), and when and where folktales usually take place (long ago and far away). Ask them to brainstorm other similarities that many folktales have in common, such as magical happenings, things occurring in threes, talking beasts, good winning over evil, good being rewarded, and so forth.

2. Read aloud several different versions of the same folktale (see "A Comparison of Folktales" chart on p. 182). Ask students why they think there might be so many versions of the same tale. Play the game "Gossip" with students (whisper a short summary of a folktale to one student, have him/her whisper it to the next, until all students have been told the tale). Ask the first student and the last student to repeat the versions they heard and compare them. Again ask students why they think there are so many versions of the same tale. Explain that most folktales were told orally, from generation to generation, and in the process details were changed, reflecting the times and skills of the storyteller.

> Note: Web Sites can also help you locate versions of the same folktale. For example, a list of variations of the Cinderella story can be found on: http://www.acs.ucalgary.ca/~dkbrown/cinderella.html

3. Have students select a favorite folktale from a collection of folktales from around the world (see references at the end of this unit). Have students create a box similar to the one in the initiating activity, and introduce others in the class to the tale. Encourage students to include a variety of objects and materials in their boxes that represent the tale and its country of origin.

4. Divide students into groups. Assign each group several folktales from a specific country (see references at the end of this unit). Have students select their favorite folktale from this country and present it using some type of dramatic interpretation—storytelling, puppet show, flannel board retelling, a short skit, and the like. Have students introduce the tale to the class by identifying the country of origin, pointing out the location of the country on the map and telling five facts about the country.

5. Folktales often reflect a culture's traditions, customs, and values. Read aloud folk tales from various cultures. After each tale is read, discuss what students have learned about the culture and together fill in a chart similar to the one on p. 181. What similarities and what differences can be found? (Several sources can be used to help you locate variations of the same basic tale, such as Margaret Read McDonald's *The Storyteller's Sourcebook: A Subject, Title, and Motif Index to Folklore Collections for Children*. The chart on p. 182 lists just a sample of the versions that exist for a number of favorite folktales.)

Folktale Summary: What We Learned

Title of Folktale				
Country of Origin				
Details about Life				
Values and Attitudes				
Customs				
Other				

6. Create an anthology of favorite folktales with illustrations by the class. The book can be divided into sections based on the folktale's country of origin. Have students illustrate each folktale with art that is appropriate to the country of origin.

7. Many folktales lend themselves to being acted out in a mock trial. For example, Hansel and Gretel can be charged with trespassing, or the wolf in *Lon Po Po* can be charged with impersonating Grandma. Choose a folktale in which the character's motives and final actions can be questioned. Select students for the roles of judge, defendant, plaintiff, attorney for the defense, attorney for the prosecution, witness for the defense, witness for the prosecution, and jury members.

8. Divide students into groups and give each group one or more folktale(s) that originated in different countries. Have students create a board game or floor game based on the tale(s) read.

9. Create mobiles of folktales from all over the world. To do this, have students illustrate a favorite folktale and somewhere on the picture include the name of the folktale and the country from which it originated. Divide the pictures into groups based on the country of origin and attach them to a hanger decorated with the names of the various countries.

10. Review the elements of a folktale. Then, review the "Creative Questioning Paradigm," Figure 2-17, p. 62. Divide students into groups and have each select a favorite folktale. Have them rewrite the tale to create a version that might have originated in modern-day U.S.A., reminding them to use the strategies included in the paradigm to help them adapt their tale. For example, "What would happen if Little Red Riding Hood had gotten lost in New York City?" Remind them that their stories and illustrations should reflect life today (that is, the clothing, forms of transportation, foods, etc.), as well as the values and attitudes of today's culture. For example, "Little Red Baseball Cap" bicycles to her grandmother 's house after hitting the winning home run for her softball team!

| A Comparison of Folktales ||
Folk Tale	Country of Origin
Rapunzel	Germany
Petrosinella	Italy
Rumpelstiltskin	Germany
Tom Tit Tot	England
Duffy and the Devil	England
Sleeping Beauty in the Wood	France
Briar Rose	Germany
The Queen of Tubber Tintye	Ireland
Henny Penny	England
The Hare that Ran Away	India
Johnny Cake	England
The Wee Bannock	Scotland
The Pancake	Norway
Tom Thumb: His Life and Death	England
Little Tom Thumb	Russia
Le Petit Poucet	France
Little One Inch	Japan
Cinderella and the Glass Slipper	France
Little Burnt Face	Milmac Indians
Kari Woodengown	Norway
Yeh-Shen	China
The Brocaded Slipper	Vietnam
Cinderella, or *The Little Glass Slipper*	England
Kongi and Potgi	Korea
Mufaro's Beautiful Daughters	Africa
The Egyptian Cinderella	Egypt
The Maid of the Glass Mountain	Norway
Red Riding Hood	Germany
Lon Po Po	China

Discussion Questions

1. Why are folktales so popular with children and adults alike?

2. What is your favorite folktale? From which country did it originate? What did you learn about the country based on the folktale alone?

3. Why do you think that folktales are often called a "mirror of society"?

4. Why have so many versions of the same basic tale originated in so many diverse countries? (Some believe that the stories came from one prehistoric group that migrated to other countries, taking their folklore with them. Others believe that the stories were independently created and came from the needs and hopes of ALL humans.)

5. How would you define a folktale?

LITERATURE RELATED ACTIVITIES

Title: *East of the Sun and West of the Moon*

Genre: Traditional Literature—Folktale

Author: Scandinavian Folktale, retold by Kathleen and Michael Hague

Illustrator: Michael Hague

Bibliographic Information: Harcourt Brace Jovanovich, San Diego, 1980.

Summary: A handsome prince, the victim of wicked enchantment, lives as a bear by day. He must return to his castle, which lies east of the sun and west of the moon, and only true love can save him from a terrible fate.

Interest Level: Grades 1–6

Pre-Reading Activity

Share the title of this folktale with students. Ask each to create an imaginary land that lies "East of the sun and west of the moon."

Learning Activities

1. After reading the folktale, *East of the Sun and West of the Moon* have students create a semantic web (see Chapter 2, pp. 39–40) in which they generate words to describe their impressions of Scandinavia. Involve students in an activity to compare their impressions with factual information about the area. First, aid students in locating the area of Scandinavia on a map. Divide the class into three groups to represent the three Scandinavian countries (Norway, Sweden, Denmark). Have each group discover five interesting facts about the country they've been assigned and present the information in a creative way. (For example, they can dress up as Vikings and tell about their homeland; they may play the music associated with Scandinavia while showing pictures they've found or created that tell about their land.)

2. While the evil characters in many folktales are wicked witches and fiery dragons, the folktales of Scandinavia often include trolls. Have students create their own trolls with clay and various other materials. Encourage students to be creative and make their trolls humorous. For example, they may wish to create a troll on skis or a troll bride with white veil and bouquet!

3. Have students create a folktale based on one (or more) of the trolls created in Activity 2 above.

4. After reading students this version of *East of the Sun and West of the Moon,* share Mercer Mayer's version (1980). Involve students in creating Venn Diagrams that illustrate the similarities and differences between the two stories.

Discussion Questions

1. From the story *East of the Sun and West of the Moon,* what did you learn about the landscape/climate/geography of Scandinavia? (a cold area, surrounded by water, large areas of dense forests).

2. What message does the tale give the reader about being too curious?

3. If you were the young girl in this tale, what might you have done differently?

4. In what ways is *East of the Sun and West of the Moon* similar to most of the folktales you have read/heard? (It includes magical happenings, talking beasts, things occurring in threes, good triumphing over evil, and so forth.)

5. If you were to retell this tale, what changes would you make?

Title: *One Fine Day*

Genre:	Traditional Literature—Folktale
Author:	An Armenian tale, retold by Nonny Hogrogian
Illustrator:	Nonny Hogrogian
Bibliographic Information:	Macmillan, New York, 1971.
Summary:	This retelling of a favorite Armenian folktale was awarded the Caldecott Medal. The story, a cumulative tale, focuses on a red fox that stole milk from an old farm woman who, in turn, cut off his tail. In order to regain his tail, the fox spends the day bargaining with a variety of characters.
Interest Level:	Grades K–3

Pre-Reading Activity

Involve students in a game in which each student must relate the responses of the students before him/her and then add his/her own response. For example, you may begin the game with the line, "I went on a picnic and brought . . ." The first student lists an object beginning with "A," such as "apple." The next student responds by saying, "I went on a picnic and brought an apple and a banana (B)." The game continues until each student has had the opportunity to respond. Explain that, in a way, this is similar to a cumulative tale, in which items or events are added to previous items or events and keep repeating throughout the story. Introduce *One Fine Day,* telling students that this is an example of a cumulative tale.

Learning Activities

1. Read the story to children and have them retell the events. Put these events on a chart, cut them apart and scramble them. Have students take turns placing the events in the proper order. Story sequencing can also be done using a flannel board and cut-outs of the various characters, with a piece of felt attached to the back of each picture. Students can retell the story as they place the characters on the board and move the fox from character to character.

2. Once students are quite familiar with the tale, assign them different roles: the fox, the old woman, the cow, the field, the stream, the maiden, the peddler, the hen, and the miller. Reread the story, encouraging students to take the parts of the character assigned, and create a dialogue for him/her.

3. Ask students what might happen if the story were to take place in the city instead of in the country? For example, have them imagine that a cat stole milk from a local store. What might happen next? Record their responses to this, or to a similar scenario. Next, place each event students suggest on a different piece of large, unlined chart paper, being sure to include the events that preceded it. Allow students to illustrate one of the pages to create a cumulative tale—*One Fine Day . . . In the City.*

4. Help students locate Armenia on a map. Ask each child to find one piece of information about Armenia that they find interesting. As each child shares the information, add it to a class chart. However, encourage each child to repeat the facts listed on the chart before adding his/her own, thereby creating a cumulative verse.

5. Have students imagine that the fox did not get his tail back. Have each one take on the role of the fox and explain to his friends what happened to his tail. Encourage creativity!

Discussion Questions

1. Do you think the fox's punishment fit the crime? Why or why not?
2. If you had been the woman, how would you punish the fox?
3. When people think of a fox, what words come to mind? How does the fox in the story compare with the idea of foxes that most people have?
4. What do you think the fox learned from his experience? What did you learn?
5. Does the title of the story seem to fit? Why or why not? What title would you give this folktale?

Title: *The Seven Chinese Brothers*

Genre:	Traditional Literature—Folktale
Author:	A Chinese folktale, retold by Margaret Mahy
Illustrator:	Jean and Mou-sien Tseng
Bibliographic Information:	Scholastic, New York, 1990.
Summary:	Seven brothers, each with an amazing power, combine their talents to fool Ch'in Shih Huang, a cruel emperor of China who was responsible for initiating the construction of the Great Wall of China.
Interest Level:	Grades 2+

Pre-Reading Activity

Guide students in locating China on a map. Create a cluster of words about China by encouraging students to generate words that reflect their knowledge and understanding of the country.

Learning Activities

1. In groups, have students research the Great Wall of China. Have each group create a model of the Great Wall using items such as Legos, blocks, etc. Also, have each group write one paragraph that summarizes the information they found most interesting about the Great Wall and its creation. Display models/summaries.

2. Create a Reader's Theatre script for *Seven Chinese Brothers*. Assign students different parts and have them create a cover for their scripts that reflects the story in some way.

3. Have students create an eighth Chinese brother. What would his power be? How could he use it? Have students create a sequel to the story that will incorporate the eighth brother and his amazing ability. Have students share their sequel through storytelling or in written form.

4. Have students create a large class collage of China. They may wish to locate pictures to represent many of the words they generated in the pre-reading activity. Encourage students to include any materials and patterns that reflect the tale of *The Seven Chinese Brothers,* other folktales of China, and the country of China in general. For example, their collage might include pieces of brocaded cloth and a wallpaper border of flowers.

Discussion Questions

1. What does the story tell you about the Chinese attitude toward family? (Family unity is extremely important and each member is highly respected.)

2. What other values of the Chinese people does this tale reflect?

3. Of all the powers displayed by the seven brothers, which do you feel was most important? Why?

4. If you could have any one power, which would you like to have? Explain.

Title: *Saint George and the Dragon*

Genre:	Traditional Literature—Folktale
Author:	An English folktale, retold by Margaret Hodges
Illustrator:	Trina Schart Hyman
Bibliographic Information:	Little, Brown and Company, Boston, 1984.
Summary:	In fourth-century England, Saint George battles the monstrous dragon that has been destroying the land of princess Una.
Interest Level:	Grades 2+

Pre-Reading Activity

Ask students, "What is a dragon?" Have them create several lists in which they describe a dragon, compare it (with another creature), associate it (with other creatures or things), and list its parts. Have students share their lists.

Learning Activities

1. Draw children's attention to the decorated borders of the pages in this book. Among these pictures is agrimony or the fairy wand, which was used as a charm against serpents. As St. George lies wounded in the stream, the borders depict mandrake, which was considered to be an anesthetic. You can request the "Saint George and The Dragon's Guide to Flowers and Herbs," which explains the borders of the book, from Little, Brown and Co., Children's Marketing Dept., 34 Beacon St., Boston, MA. 02108. Involve students in studying the borders, making hypotheses as to the reasons why certain items are included, and in locating information to prove or disprove their hypotheses.

2. Read aloud the description of the dragon on page 15. Have students create their own illustration of the dragon based solely on the description. Mount their pictures on construction paper and cover them with contact paper to create individual place mats.

3. Have students create a folktale based on the dragon's point of view. Have them illustrate their story with borders that are appropriate to the tale.

4. Read other folktales involving dragons (see general references). Have students compare the way stories that originated in Europe differ from those from Asia (for example, *The Dragon's Robe* [Lattimore, 1990.]) in their treatment and attitude toward the dragon.

5. Involve students in reading other tales dealing with dragons. Have the class create a large dragon costume into which many children can fit. Allow one child at a time to come out from under the costume and give a summary or "booktalk" about a dragon story he or she read.

6. Saint George is the patron saint of England. He was a real person—a highly respected soldier during the crusades. Introduce students to the life and

times of Saint George, who lived during the time of the crusades and knighthood. Have students create a diorama that reflects an event in the story and/or an event in his life.

7. The illustrations in the story are quite powerful. Have each student select one illustration from the book that he/she thinks best captures the mood and meaning of the story. Tell students they must convince a team of judges (classmates) to agree with their choices.

Discussion Questions

1. Saint George was the patron saint of England. What is meant by the term "patron saint?" (The protector of the land)

2. Why do you think George was selected as the patron saint of England? What qualities did George possess that were respected by the people?

3. This version of *Saint George and the Dragon,* illustrated by Trina Schart Hyman, won the Caldecott Medal as the most outstanding picture book of 1984. What was so special about the illustrations that the book earned the Caldecott Medal?

4. What does the tale tell you about the England of long ago? (People used plants and herbs for medicinal purposes; courage and bravery were respected over all else; it was a time of knights and the belief that good triumphs over evil; and so forth.)

CULMINATING ACTIVITY

Involve students in a "fractured folktale" festival as they create new versions of folktales from around the world. In a fractured folktale, one or more elements of the story are changed. Read students the folktale "The Three Little Pigs." Then, read them the fractured version, *The True Story of the 3 Little Pigs!* by Jon Scieszka. Next, involve them in a Reader's Theatre of "The Really, Really, *Really,* True Story of the Three Little Pigs," pp. 188–192, (from *Frantic Frogs and Other Frankly Fractured Folktales for Readers Theatre* by Anthony D. Fredericks, Teacher Ideas Press, 1993), in which the story has been "slightly" transformed. Have students (in groups) create a fractured version of a favorite folktale they became familiar with through this unit and present it as a readers theatre. To introduce their readers theatre, each group should create a sign with the name of the folktale, its country of origin, and decorated with items and pictures representative of the story and the culture from which it came. Combine all the scripts for a class version of *Frankly Fractured Folktales for Readers Theatre* and keep it in your class library for future reference.

The Really, Really *Really* True Story of the Three Little Pigs

Staging

The narrator is at a lectern or podium near the front of the staging area. The three pigs are on stools or chairs. The wolf is standing and moves back and forth among the other characters.

Very Smart Pig	Average Pig	Not Too Bright Pig
X	X	X
	Mean and Grouchy Wolf	
	X	
Narrator		
X		

Narrator: A long time ago, when fairy tales used to be inhabited by animals who could talk and think, there lived these three pigs. Yeah, yeah, yeah, I know what you're saying—each of them built a house and along came this mean old wolf with incredibly bad breath who blows down the first two houses because they weren't built according to the local zoning laws and then tries to blow down the third house, which is, incidentally, made of reinforced concrete, not bricks, and he eventually falls into a big pot of boiling water and the three pigs live happily ever after, at least until their mother finds out what they've been doing and sends them to bed without their dinner. Well, that's probably the story you heard when you were a tiny tyke, but that's not the really real story. Actually, your parents couldn't tell you the really real story 'cause it was filled with all kinds of violence and a couple of bad words. Well, now that you're all grown up and very mature, we're going to tell you the really, really, *really* true story of the Three Little Pigs—but, of course, we're going to have to leave out all those bad words.

So anyway, one day these three brothers who, as you know by now, were pigs—and, as you also know, they were talking pigs—were sitting in the living room of their mother's four-bedroom condominium reading some of the latest issues of *Better Pigs and Gardens* and the *New Porker.* And that's where the really, really, *really* true story of the Three Little Pigs begins.

Very Smart Pig: Hey, brothers, you know it's about time we moved out of Mom's house. We're grown up now and ready to go out into the world to seek our fortune. And besides, Mom's getting on in years and won't be able to support us much longer. In fact, pretty soon we're going to have to think about putting her in the Old Porker's Home.

Average Pig:	You know, brother, you've got a point there. Besides, we wouldn't have much of a story if all we did was sit around Mom's living room discussing the color of her drapes or "500 Uses for Bacon Bits."
Not Too Bright Pig:	Yeah! It sure is getting crowded in here, too. You know, because we're pigs we don't clean up after ourselves, so we track mud all over the place, and we make funny grunting noises for most of the day. I think the neighbors are beginning to wonder what we really do. We better move out while we still can.
Narrator:	And so it was that the three brothers decided to move out of Mom's house and buy some property in the country. The real estate agent assured them that the land was ideal—rolling hills, lots of space, and no strange or weird animals in the nearby forest.
Mean and Grouchy Wolf:	*(insulted)* Hey, wait a minute! Aren't I supposed to have a place in this story, too?
Narrator:	*(forcefully)* Hey, keep your shirt on! We'll sneak you over from the Red Riding Hood story, and no one will be the wiser. In fact, if you play your cards right, you can finish this story and get back to Grandma's house in time to hop back into her pajamas and wait for that naive Riding Hood girl to come along.
Mean and Grouchy Wolf:	Okay, okay. But make it quick, buster. You know what the wolf's union says about me doing double time.
Narrator:	Anyway, as I was saying, the three pigs began to build their dream houses along the country road that ran through their property.
Not too Bright Pig:	You know, I'm not very smart, so I think I'll build my house out of straw. So, who cares if it blows down in the first windstorm of the season or leaks like a sieve in the winter.
Mean and Grouchy Wolf:	*(insulted)* Hey, now hold on a minute! Do you honestly think I would want to waste my time with that little porker? You know, I've got far better things to do with my time than wait until that not too bright pig builds his weak, little house of straw for me to come prancing down the lane to huff and puff and blow it down. That's got to be an absolute waste of my finely tuned acting talents!
Narrator:	Well then, what if we move this story along and see what Average Pig does.
Mean and Grouchy Wolf:	Well, okay, but this better be a lot more interesting than that little ham bone with the pile of hay in his backyard.

Narrator:	Settle down! Don't have a coronary! Just let me see what I can do with this part of the story. It's all yours, Average Pig.
Average Pig:	Thanks. While you guys were talking I was walking around my property gathering some sticks and branches and tree limbs. I think I'll build my house out of this stuff. It may not be too sturdy, but at least it won't fall down the fist time I slam the front door. Of course, the local fire marshal may have a thing or two to say about it.
Mean and Grouchy Wolf:	*(angrily)* Now just a gosh darn minute here! You want me to believe that this walking pile of pork chops is really going to build a house of sticks so that I can come along and blow it down just like I was supposed to do with his brother's house? Come on, get real! I mean, what a waste! Why would I even want to take the time to huff and puff my way around this stupid little structure? You know, you guys are really starting to tick me off. All I can say is, this story better get a lot better and real fast, too!
Narrator:	Boy, you sure do get pushy. You know, this is supposed to be a story about the Three Little Pigs, not about some wolf with an attitude.
Mean and Grouchy Wolf:	Look, wise guy, how'd you like me to nibble on your face? If I want to take the lead role in this story, then I'm going to. After all, just look what my brothers and I have been putting up with in all those other stories.
Narrator:	*(indignantly)* Now, just hold on. We still have to see what Very Smart Pig does with this part in the story.
Very Smart Pig:	You know, they don't call me Very Smart Pig for nothin'. In fact, I'm the guy they call on to bring home the bacon . . . get it? Bring home the bacon! So, while this hotshot wolf was thinking about huffing and puffing down some flimsy houses built by my two less than brilliant brothers, I was constructing a house completely out of bricks and steel and reinforced cement. Ain't nobody going to blow this baby down! I mean this beauty is built!!! And any wolf who has any kind of smarts would do well to just keep his distance. I mean we're talkie' SOLID here!
Mean and Grouchy Wolf:	*(very angrily)* Look, I'm not takin' any gruff from some lard-faced pig. I'll huff and puff my way across the whole county if I want to. I'll blow down, damage, and destroy as many houses as I want.

Very Smart Pig:	*(angrily)* Yeah, you and whose army?
Mean and Grouchy Wolf:	*(angrily)* Hey, watch it, pork breath. How would you like me to turn you into a pile of ham sandwiches.
Very Smart Pig:	(very *angrily)* Yeah, just go ahead and try it.
Mean and Grouchy Wolf:	*(extremely angry)* Just watch me.
Narrator:	All day long Very Smart Pig and Mean and Grouchy Wolf argued about who was the strongest and who was the smartest. In fact, Wolf and Pig went far into the night with their argument, and for all we know they're still arguing away. But, of course, that would never make for an exciting story for the kiddies. So a long time ago a bunch of fairy tale writers got together and decided to spice up the story a bit and turn the wolf into a door-to-door salesperson with an asthma problem. The rest, as they say, is history. And now, you know the really, really, *really* true story of the Three Little Pigs.

Source: Fredericks, A. (1993). *Frantic frogs and other frankly fractured folk tales for readers theatre.* Englewood, CO: Teacher Ideas Press. 1-800-237-6124. Used by permission.

SUPPLEMENTAL LITERATURE

Note: For single-title books, the country of origin is indicated to facilitate your lessons.

Books

Collections

Booss, C., ed. (1984). *Scandinavian legends and folk tales.* New York: Crown.

Clarkson, A., & Cross, G., compilers. (1980). *World folktales.* New York: Scribner's.
In addition to folktales from around the world, this collection includes notes, comments, and lists of parallel stories.

Cole, J., compiler. (1982). *Best-loved folktales of the world.* Illustrated by J. K. Schwarz. New York: Doubleday.
A collection of 200 folktales, divided by geographical location and indexed by category.

Colum, P. (1964). *The Arabian nights: Tales of wonder and magnificence.* Illustrated by L. Ward. New York: Macmillan.

Crossley, H., Ed. (1998*). The young Oxford book of folktales.* Oxford, England: Oxford University Press.

Grimm, J., & Grimm, W. (1987). *Grimm's fairy tales.* Translated by J. Zipes. Illustrated by J. B. Gruelle. New York: Bantam.
Includes 210 famous original folktales, plus forty tales never before published in English.

Impey, R. (1992). *Read me a fairy tale: A child's book of classic fairy tales.* Illustrated by I. Berk. New York: Scholastic.
Fourteen best-loved tales, including "Jack and the Beanstalk," "The Frog Prince," and "Rumpelstiltskin".

Massignon, G., ed. (1968). *Folktales of France.* Chicago: University of Chicago Press.
One in the *Folktales of the World* series.

Mayhew, J. (1993). *Koshka's Tales: Stories from Russia.* Illustrated by J. Mayhew. New York: Kingfisher Books.

Mayo, M. (1993). *Magical tales from many lands.* Illustrated by J. Ray. New York: Dutton.
Includes tales from around the world, representing a variety of traditions, including stories from Turkey, Japan, Africa, Scotland, France, China, and Russia.

McCaughrean, G. (1982). *One hundred and one Arabian nights.* Illustrated by S. Lavis. Oxford, England: Oxford University Press.
A collection of stories told to the king by his queen, Shahrezad.

Ozaki, Y. T., compiler. (1970). *The Japanese fairy book.* Illustrated by Y. Kurosaki. Rutland, VT: Charles Tuttle Co.

Passes, D. (1993). *Dragons: Truth, myth, and legend.* Illustrated by W. Anderson. Racine, WI: Western Publishing.
Eleven dragon stories from around the world are included.

Perrault, C. (1989). *Cinderella and other tales from Perrault.* Illustrated by M. Hague. New York: Holt.

Perrault, C. (1993). *The complete fairy tales of Charles Perrault.* Illustrated by S. Holmes. New York: Clarion.

Sadler, C. adapter. (1982). *Treasure mountain: Folktales from Southern China.* Illustrated by C. Mung Yun. New York: Atheneum.
Six Chinese tales illustrated with pencil drawings.

Philiip, N. (1995*). The illustrated book of myths, tales and legends of the world.* Illustrated by N. Mistry. New York: DK Publishers.

Singer, I. B. (1966). *Zlateh the goat.* Illustrated by M. Sendak. New York: Harper. [Poland]
Seven tales based on middle-European Jewish stories.

Walker, P. R. (1997). *Little folk: Stories from around the world.* Ill by J. Bernardin. San Diego, CA: Harcourt.
Collection of folktales about little folk such as fairies, leprechauns, and brownies.

Wyndham, L. (Comp.) (1970). *Tales the people tell in Russia.* Ill. by A. Antal. New York: Messner.

Yep, L. (1989). *The rainbow people.* Illustrated by David Wiesner. New York: Harper.
Twenty tales from China are adapted from oral narratives transcribed in Oakland's Chinatown.

Single Titles

Aardema, V. (1975). *Why mosquitoes buzz in people's ears.* Illustrated by L. and D. Dillon. New York: Dial. [Africa]
The tale of a mosquito whose tall tales led to many problems in the jungle and resulted in the mosquito buzz we hear today.

Beck, I. (1995). *Peter and the wolf.* New York: Atheneum. [Russia]
A beautifully illustrated version of the classic tale.

Chin, C. (1993). *China's bravest girl.* Illustrated by T. Arai. Emeryville, CA: Children's Book Press. [China]
The legend of Hua Mu Lan, who took her father's place as a soldier and became a general.

Climo, S. (1989). *The Egyptian Cinderella.* Illustrated by R. Heller. New York: Harper. [Egypt]
This tale of Rhodopis and the rose-red slippers is one of the world's oldest Cinderella stories.

Czernecki, S. (1997). *The cricket's cage.* New York: Hyperion. [China]
A traditional Chinese folk tale about the construction of four watchtowers surrounding the Forbidden City.

d'Aulaire, I., & d'Aulaire, E. (1972). *Trolls.* New York: Dell. [Scandinavia]

Davol, M. (1997). *The paper dragon.* Ill. by R. Subuda. New York: Atheneum. [China]
Emphasizes four concepts: courage, loyalty, love, and sincerity.

de Beaumont, Mme. (1988). *Beauty and the beast.* Illustrated by M. Hague. New York: Holt. [France]
The tale of a young girl who sees the beauty beneath the skin of a prince who has been transformed into an ugly beast

de Beaumont, Mme. (1989). *Beauty and the beast.* Illustrated by J. Brett. Boston: Houghton Mifflin. [France]

de Beaumont, Mme. (1989). *Beauty and the beast.* Retold and illustrated by M. Gerstein. New York: Dutton. [France]

Grahame, K. (1938). *The reluctant dragon.* Illustrated by E. Shepard. New York: Holiday. [England]
In this reversal of the tale of Saint George, a pacifist dragon wants to help the townspeople.

Grimm, J., & Grimm, W. (1990). *Hansel and Gretel.* Retold and ill. by J. Marshall. New York: Dial. [Germany]
Two young children get lost in the woods and discover a house made of candies and cakes.

Grimm, J., & Grimm, W. (1982). *Hansel and Gretel.* Illustrated by P. Galdone. New York: McGraw-Hill. [Germany]

Grimm, J., & Grimm, W. (1983). *Little Red Cap.* Illustrated by L. Zwerger. New York: Morrow. [Germany]
A version of *Little Red Riding Hood.*

Grimm, J., & Grimm, W. (1987). *Red Riding Hood.* Retold and illustrated by J. Marshall. New York: Dial. [Germany]

A young girl on the way to her grandmother's house encounters a wolf.

Grimm, J., & Grimm, W. (1983). *Little Red Riding Hood.* Illustrated by T. Hyman. New York: Holiday. [Germany]

Grimm, J., & Grimm, W. (1993). *Iron Hans.* Illustrated by M. Heyer. New York: Viking. [Germany]
A mysterious wild man sends a boy out to find his way in the world.

Grimm, J., & Grimm, W. (1982). *Rapunzel.* Illustrated by Maja Dusikova. New York: North South. [Germany]
The tale of a girl in a tower whose lover climbs her rope of hair.

Grimm, J., & Grimm, W. (1991). *Rumpelstiltskin.* Retold and Illustrated by J. Langley. New York: Harper. [Germany]
A miller's daughter spins straw into gold with the help of a strange man. She must learn his name or lose her first-born child to him.

Grimm, J., & Grimm, W. (1986). *Rumplestiltskin.* Retold and illustrated by P. Zelinski. New York: Dutton. [Germany]

Grimm, J., & Grimm, W. (1972). *Snow-White and the Seven Dwarfs.* Translated by R. Jarrell. Ill. by N.E. Brukert. New York: Farrar, Straus and Giroux. [Germany]

Han, O. S., & Plunkett, S. H. (1996). *Kongi and Potgi: A Cinderella story from Korea.* New York: Dial.[Korea]
Korean customs illustrate this version of a traditional tale.

Hogrogian, N. (1988). *The cat who loved to sing.* New York: Knopf. [Russia]
A cumulative tale of a cat who starts trading a thorn in its foot for a needle.

Ketteman, H. (1997). *Bubba the cowboy prince: A fractured Texas tale.* Ill. by J. Warhola. New York: Scholastic. [American West]
A Cinderella variation—Texas style.

Kimmel, E. (1988). *Anansi and the moss-covered rock.* Illustrated by J. Stevens. New York: Holiday House. [Africa]
Anansi, the spider, uses the power of a magic rock to steal the food of other animals.

Kimmel, E. (1991). *Baba Yaga.* Illustrated by M. Lloyd. New York: Holiday House. [Russia]
A Russian tale with elements of Cinderella, and Hansel and Gretel.

Lang, A. adapter. (1981). *Aladdin and the wonderful lamp.* Illustrated by E. LeCain. New York: Viking. [Arabia]
The story of a poor boy whose life is changed when he discovers a genie in a magical lamp.

Lattimore, D. (1990). *The dragon's robe.* New York: Harper. [China]
A poor weaver saves her people when she weaves a robe for the rain dragon.

Lawson, J. (1993). *The dragon's pearl.* Paintings by P. Morin. New York: Clarion.[China]
Xiao finds a shimmering pearl that forever changes his destiny.

Leaf, M. (1987). *Eyes of the dragon*. Illustrated by E. Young. New York: Lothrop. [China]
A Chinese painter agrees to paint a portrait of the Dragon King who controls thunder, lightning, and rain.

Louis, Al-Ling. (1982). *Yeh-Shen: A Cinderella story from China*. Illustrated by Ed Young. New York: Philomel. [China]
A version of Cinderella from China.

Lowell, S. (1997). *The bootmaker and the elves*. Ill. by T. Curry. New York: Orchard. [American West]
A fractured fairy tale based on *The Shoemaker and the Elves*.

McCoy, K. (1993). *A tale of two tengu*. Niles, IL: Whitman and Co. [Japan]
Two Japanese goblins, called Tengu, argue constantly, each trying to better the other.

McDermott, G. (1975). *The stonecutter: A Japanese folktale*. New York: Penguin. [Japan]
A lowly stonecutter was happy with his work until a princess passed his way in a magnificent procession. Then he wished for wealth and his wish was heard by the spirit who lives in the mountain.

Mayer, M. (1989). *The twelve dancing princesses*. Illustrated by K. Y. Craft. New York: Morrow. [France]
The king's twelve daughters, under an evil spell, wear holes in their dancing slippers and become ill.

Mosel, A., ed. (1968). *Tikki Tikki Tembo*. Illustrated by B. Lent. New York: Holt. [China]
This humorous tale explains why the Chinese have short names.

Ness, E. (1965). *Tom Tit Tot*. New York: Scribner's. [England]
A variation on the tale of Rumplestiltskin.

Pearson, S. (1989) *Jack and the beanstalk*. Illustrated by J. Warhola. New York: Simon and Schuster. [England]
Young Jack climbs a beanstalk and comes face to face with a giant from whom he steals the magic harp and the goose that lays golden eggs.

Perrault, C. (1985). *Cinderella*. Retold by A. Ehrlich. Illustrated by S. Jeffers. New York: Dial. [France]
A young girl, mistreated by her stepmother and stepsisters, goes to the ball with the help of her fairy godmother

Perrault, C. (1973). *Cinderella, or the little glass slipper*. Illustrated. by E. Le Cain. New York: Bradbury. [France]

Price, L. (1990). *Aida*. Illustrated by L. and D. Dillon. San Diego, CA: Harcourt Brace. [Africa]
Aida, the Ethiopian princess, is captured by Egyptian soldiers and forced into slavery. The story is based on the opera by Giuseppe Verdi.

Robbins, R. (1960). *Baboushka and the three kings*. Illustrated by N. Sidjakow. Boston: Parnassus. [Russia].
The tale of a selfish old woman and the Wise Men.

Shute, L. (1988). *Clever Tom and the leprechaun.* New York: Lothrop. [Ireland]
Tom catches a leprechaun and tries to obtain his treasure.

Stanley, D. (1995). *Petrosinella: A Neapolitan Rapunzel.* New York: Dial.
An Italian version of the classic tale. [Italy]

Steptoe, J. adapter. (1987). *Mufaro's beautiful daughters: An African tale.* New York: Lothrop. [Africa]
A version of Cinderella.

Stevents, J. (1987). *The three billy goats gruff.* Illustrated by J. Stevents. San Diego, CA: Harcourt Brace. [Norway]
Three billy goats attempt to cross the bridge over an evil troll.

Vojtech, A., & Sturges, P. (1996). *Marushka and the Month Brothers.* Ill. By Vojteck. New York: North-South. [Czech]
A Czech and Slovak folktale version of Cinderella in that Marushka, a kind, good-hearted girl is given all the work by her jealous stepmother and stepsister.

Wade, G. (1993). *The wonderful bag.* New York: Bedrick/Blackie. [Arabia]
Two men claim to own the same bag and must prove their ownership by identifying the contents.

Yep, L. (1993). *The shell woman and the king.* Illustrated by Y. Ming-Yi. New York: Dial. [China]
A brave woman who has the power to transform herself into large seashells outwits a greedy king in this tale of adventure.

Young, E. (1997). *Mouse match: A Chinese folktale.* San Diego, CA: Harcourt. [China]

Young, E. (1989). *Lon Po Po: A Red Riding Hood story from China.* New York: Philomel. [China]

Zemach, H. (1973). *Duffy and the devil: A Cornish tale.* Retold and illustrated by M. Zemach. New York: Farrar, 1973. [England]
A Cornish version of Rumplestiltskin.

Zelinsky, P. (1997). *Rapunzel.* New York. Dutton. [Germany]
This version of Rapunzel won the 1998 Caldecott Metal.

Vozar, D. Rapunzel: *A happenin' rap.* New York. Doubleday. [Germany]
Gives the story of *Rapunzel* in an urban setting and with a rhythmic beat.

Web Sites

http://falcon.jmu.edu/~ramseyil/tradlit.htm
Information related to traditional literature and folklore for K–12.

http://virtual.park.uga.edu/~clandrum/folklore.html
Descriptions of where folklore originated and what determines its tales.

MINI-THEMES

The mini-themes selected focus specifically on the folktales of two groups of Americans: the Native Americans who were already here and the African-Americans who originally were brought to this land as slaves. Their tales reflect their experiences and their cultures, telling of their hopes, their tragedies, and the triumph of the human spirit.

Folktales of Native Americans

More than 400 years ago, millions of Indians, comprising thousands of tribes and clans, were spread across North and South America. These diverse populations, known today as Native Americans, had their own cultures and traditions as reflected in their folklore that was handed down from generation to generation. Many of the folktales of the Native-Americans resemble creation myths—stories that explain the origin of man and beast. Each tribe had its own stories to help them make sense of the world around them.

Activities

1. As their folktales indicate, the Native Americans had a tremendous respect for nature. Read aloud several folktales and, whenever possible, give children the opportunity to experience the setting (for example, a tree, a pond, etc.) firsthand. Have students select their favorite folktale and use objects from nature—a leaf, a stone, a piece of wood, etc.—to create a collage or design that in some way reflects the folktale selected.

2. The Native Americans had a special relationship with the animals that shared their lands. In many Native American tales the animals created the people. Often their tales refer to animals as their relatives and teachers. Have students select one of the animals that played an important part in the folktales of the American Indian and have students create a mini-book that relates factual information about this animal.

3. Have students retell one of the folktales involving the animal selected in Activity 2 and retell the tale using the factual information known about the animal and how it really acts. Students can create an illustration to accompany their storytelling.

4. Discuss the origins of many things in our world as reflected in the folktales of Native Americans. Using one or more of the characters included in their folktales, have students create their own folktale to explain the origin of any natural phenomena, such as the Grand Canyon, waterfalls, rivers, and so forth.

5. The Native Americans sang songs to honor the animals from which they received so many gifts. After reading several folktales of Native Americans, have students make a list of all the gifts we receive from the animal and insect kingdoms even today. Take students on a nature walk and record the voices of the birds, insects and other wildlife. Have students use these sounds to create an "Ode to Nature" and use various materials to create musical accompaniment. Students may also wish to create a dance to accompany the music.

6. As students read various folktales of Native Americans, have them add to a chart that is divided into five areas: clothing, food, shelter, customs, and crafts. Divide students into one of these five groups (or groups based on other areas you and the students would like to investigate) and involve them in the following activities, based on the knowledge and insights gained through the reading of Native American folktales. The work of each group can be combined to create a day to honor our Native Americans.

Group 1—*Clothing:* Students may dress up in the traditional garments worn by several of the many Native American tribes. Divide the entire class into various tribes and suggest appropriate clothing for each group.

Group 2—*Food:* Students may wish to bring in foods made with corn (corn chips, popcorn, corn bread, etc.), as well as other foods representative of Native American diets.

Group 3—*Shelter:* Students may wish to create models of the various types of housing in which Native Americans lived, such as pueblos, longhouses, and teepees.

Group 4—*Customs*: Students may create a reader's theatre, story theatre, puppet show, or other dramatic form to retell a folktale that includes the customs/beliefs of various tribes.

Groups 5—*Crafts:* Students can coordinate the efforts of the class to make one or more of the crafts popular with Native Americans.

7. As a class, create a totem pole that gives tribute to the many aspects of nature that the Native Americans honored.

References

Bierhorst, J. (1987). *Doctor Coyote: A Native American Aesop's fables.* Illustrated by W. Watson. New York: Macmillan.

Bruchac, J. (1997*). Lasting echos: An oral history of Native American people.* Ill. by P. Morin. San Diego, CA: Harcourt.

Bruchac, J. (1993). *The first strawberries: A Cherokee story.* Illustrated by A. Vojtech. New York: Dial.

Bruchac, J. (1993). *Flying with the eagle, racing the great bear.* Illustrated by M. Jacob. New York: Troll.

Caduto, M., & Bruchac, J. (1991). *Native American stories* (from keepers of the earth). Illustrated by J. K. Fadden. Golden, CO: Fulcrum.

Caduto, M., & Bruchac, J. (1991). *Native American animal stories* (from keepers of the animals). Illustrated by J. K. Fadden. Golden, CO: Fulcrum.

dePaola, T. (1988). *The legend of the Indian paintbrush.* New York: Putnam's Songs.

Esbensen, B. J. (1989). *Ladder to the sky.* Illustrated by H. Davis. Boston: Little, Brown.

Goble, P. (1978). *The girl who loved wild horses.* New York: Bradbury.

Goble, P. (1983). *Star boy.* New York: Bradbury.

Harris, C. (1979). *Once more upon a totem.* Illustrated by D. Tait. New York: Atheneum.

McDermott, G. (1984). *Arrow to the sun.* New York: Viking.

Robe, R. Y. (1979). *Tonweya and the eagles and other Lakota tales.* Illustrated by J. Pinkney. New York: Dial.

Root, P. (1993). *Coyote and the magic words.* Illustrated by S. Speidel. New York: Lothrop, Lee and Shepard.

Roth, S. (1990). *The stony of light.* New York: Morrow.

Schoolcraft, H. R. (1970). *The ring in the prairie: A Shawnee legend.* Illustrated by L. Dillon and D. Dillon. New York: Dial.

Taylor, H. P. (1993). *Coyote places the stars.* New York: Bradbury.

Troughton, J. (1986). *How rabbit stole the fire.* New York: Bedrick/Blackie.

Van loan, N. (1993). *Buffalo dance.* Illustrated by B. Vidal. Boston: Little, Brown and Co.

Yolen, J. (1990). *Sky dogs.* Illustrated by B. Moser. San Diego, CA: Harcourt Brace.

Wood, M. (1992). *Spirits, heroes, and hunters* (from North American Indian mythology). Illustrated by J. Sibbick. New York: Peter Bedrick Books.

Young, E. (1993). *Moon mother.* New York: Harper.

African-American Folktales

When the slaves of Africa were first brought to this country they continued to tell the tales of their youth, tales of talking beasts that metaphorically offered hope and expressed the sorrow, loneliness, and fear of a people. In *The People Could Fly,* for example, Virginia Hamilton has collected the tales that "represent the main body of black folktales . . ." (p. xi)—stories that tell of a rich heritage and of the strength and perseverance of a people. In *Her Stories*, Hamilton has compiled African American Folktales, Fairy Tales, and True Tales that is dedicated "to our mothers and grandmothers, aunts and great-aunts, to all the women who stood before us, telling us about where they came from, what they saw, did, and imagined . . . " The activities suggested will give students an understanding of the beauty, humor, and spirit of the African-Americans as reflected in their tales.

Activities

1. Many of the folktales of African-Americans include animals that took on characteristics of the people they found on the plantation where they were originally brought as slaves. The rabbit known as Brer Rabbit, for example, was small and helpless compared to the strong bear and sly fox, but the rabbit's intelligence and creativity enabled him to often outwit the other animals and survive. On a class chart, similar to the one on p. 201, have students list the animal characters, their main qualities, and the person(s) they think the animal was supposed to represent. Next, have each student select one of the animals and create a simile in which the animal is compared to another animal or object with similar qualities: _____ (animal character from folktale) is like a _____ because _____. Have students illustrate their simile with a picture of the animal character from the folktale and the object it was compared with.

Animal Characteristic Comparison Chart

Animal	Qualities	Person/Group the Animal Represents
Brer Rabbit	Smart, clever	Slaves
Bear	Powerful, greedy	Slave owners

2. Stories of John the Conqueror John de Conquer) were popular among slaves. After the Civil War, the character of John often took the place of Brer Rabbit in tales (see Activity 1 above). John was a slave but spent most of his time tricking his master. Read several tales of John the Conqueror (see Sanfield, 1989, and Hamilton, 1985). Have each student create a one-page conversation between himself/ herself and John, and bind these together into a book, *John and Me.*

3. "Juneteenth" is the day on which descendants of slaves in the South remember the Emancipation, which gave them their freedom from slavery. Hold a Juneteenth day and have each student (or group of students) retell a favorite African-American tale. Encourage students to use a variety of storytelling techniques, such as Reader's Theater and Story Theater.

4. Have students locate Africa on the map and involve students in learning about the history of slavery in the United States. Explain the underground railroad, the complex system through which many slaves escaped to freedom, by reading aloud such books as *Aunt Harriet's Underground Railroad in the* Sky by Faith Ringgold (Crown, 1992).

5. Ask students to locate a favorite illustration of a favorite African-American folktale. Have them recreate this picture and add a caption that either tells about the tale or about the event in the picture. Have students share their pictures and summarize the folktale from which it came.

6. After reading various selections from *Her Stories* (Hamilton, 1995), have students select a favorite and group students by choices. Have them present a type of fashion show, but instead of having the narrator describe a fashion, have him/her describe a lesson learned from one of the stories while others in the group walk down the "run-way" in costumes appropriate to the tale.

References

Bang, M. (1976). *Wiley and the hairy man.* New York: Macmillan.

Ceni, A. (1998). *African American folktales.* Ill. by Lorena Chiupp. New York: Barnes and Nobles.

Hamilton, V. (1997). *A ring of tricksters: Animal tales from America, the West Indies, and Africa.* Ill. by B. Moser. New York: Scholastic.

Hamilton, V. (1995). *Her stories: African American folktales, fairy tales, and true tales.* Illustrated by L. Dillon and D. Dillon. New York: Blue Sky Press.

Hamilton, V. (1993). *Many thousand gone.* Illustrated by L. Dillon and D. Dillon. New York: Knopf.

Hamilton, V. (1985). *The people could fly: American black folktales.* Illustrated by L. Dillon and D. Dillon. New York: Knopf.

Harris, J. C. (1986). *Jump! The adventures of Brer* Rabbit. Adapted by V. D. Parks and M. Jones. Illustrated by B. Moser. San Diego, CA: Harcourt Brace.

Harris, J.C. (1987). *Jump again! More adventures of Brer Rabbit.* Adapted by V. D. Parks. Illustrated by B. Moser. San Diego, CA: Harcourt Brace.

Harris, J. C. (1989). *Jump on over! The adventures of Brer Rabbit and his family.* Adapted by V. D. Parks. Illustrated by B. Moser. San Diego, CA: Harcourt Brace.

Keats, E. (1965). *John Henry: An American Legend.* New York: Pantheon.

Kantor, S. (1998). *101 African-American read aloud stories.* New York: Black Dog and Leventhal.

Lester, J. (1972). *The knee-high man and other tales.* Illustrated by R. Pinto. New York: Dial.

Lester, J. (1988). *More tales of Uncle Remus: Further adventures of Brer Rabbit, his friends, enemies, and others.* Illustrated by J. Pickney. New York: Dial.

Lester, J. (1987). *The tales of Uncle Remus: The adventures of Brer Rabbit.* Illustrated by J. Pickney. New York: Dial.

Rees, E. (1967). *Brer Rabbit's tricks.* Illustrated by E. Corey. W.R. Scott.

San Souci, R. (1989). *The talking eggs.* Illustrated by J. Pinkney. New York: Dial.

Sanfield, S. (1989). *The adventures of High John the Conqueror.* Illustrated by J. Ward. New York: Orchard.

Theme

The Caldecott Award

OVERVIEW

Focus

Students will become aware of the diversity of artistic media used to illustrate children's books and become familiar with those illustrators whose books have been awarded the Caldecott Award for the most distinguished picture book published in the United States.

Objectives

Upon completion of this thematic unit, students will be able to:

1. Recognize the work of well-known award-winning illustrators of picture books.
2. Identify various artistic media used to illustrate picture books.
3. Evaluate picture books based upon certain criteria.
4. Use various artistic media to create their own illustrations.

HOW IT WORKS

Initiating Activity

Show students the covers of several books that have been awarded the Caldecott for outstanding illustrations. Ask students to study the covers to see what they have in common. (The answer is the Caldecott Medal.) Explain that each of these books was awarded the Caldecott Medal, which is presented each year by a special awards committee to the most distinguished picture book for children published in America. After discussing the logo on the actual medal, provide students with materials and ribbon to design their own Caldecott Medal. They will have the opportunity to bestow their creations on their selection for the Caldecott Award (see Culminating Activity on p. 211).

Also, discuss with students the importance of illustration in children's picture books. Explain that the words and pictures must supplement each other in telling the story. If the picture book has no text, then naturally, it's the pictures that carry the story.

General Activities

1. Read aloud several Caldecott Medal or Honor books whose illustrations are created using a similar media, such as collage, woodcuts, watercolors, pen and ink, chalk, and so forth. Ask your school's art teacher or a local artist to demonstrate this same technique to your students and give them the opportunity to experiment with the selected media.

203

2. Read aloud several Caldecott Medal or Honor books that were illustrated by the same artist. Create a classroom display that includes a picture of the illustrator and a selection of books he or she illustrated. Help students identify the artistic techniques used in the different books.

3. Share a Caldecott Medal book with children by having them interpret the story from the pictures alone. Record their predictions and then, after reading the story, compare their versions to the actual text. Discuss how the illustrations of a picture book alone should be able to tell the story as well as create a mood.

4. Allow children to select a favorite Caldecott Medal or Honor book. Rewrite the text on large chart paper and give each group of students a different page to illustrate. Bind the pages together to form a big book that can be part of the class library.

5. Have students create a large collage mural, "CELEBRATING THE CALDECOTTS." For each Caldecott Medal and Honor book they have read, have students add pictures and objects to the mural that represents the book in some way.

6. After students have been involved in reading many of the books that have been awarded the Caldecott Medal, poll the class and select a favorite illustrator. Have students decorate the class door with student-made book jackets for the various children's books this person has illustrated.

7. Have students select their favorite Caldecott Medal or Honor book and recreate one of the pictures in the book (using the same media whenever possible). Create a classroom art gallery in which each picture is signed and matted and labeled with the name of the Caldecott book, author, and illustrator that inspired the student's picture.

8. Share the work of a Caldecott-winning illustrator. With students, brainstorm a list of adjectives that describes the artist's work. Divide students into groups and have each group select a Caldecott-winning illustrator and create a similar list. Have students use their list to create a commercial to promote one or more of this artist's picture book(s). Have them present their commercials in other classrooms to familiarize children with the artist and his or her work.

9. Select a Caldecott Medal or Honor book, read it aloud to students without showing the pictures, and have them imagine the illustrations. Next, reread the book and share the illustrations. Ask students, "How did the pictures in your mind compare with the pictures in the story?" "In what ways did the illustrations add to your enjoyment of the story?"

10. Introduce students to the work of famous artists of the past (for example, Degas, Rembrandt, Picasso, or Renoir) through series such as those published by HarperCollins and Rizzioli's *Weekend with the Artist* Series. In pairs, ask students to select a famous artist of the past whose work reminds them in some way of the work of one of the Caldecott illustrators. Have them create a conversation between the two artists in which they talk about their work. Ask students to present the conversation to the rest of the class and share examples of their work.

11. Have students create a slide show of Caldecott winners by scanning them into the computer or by taking pictures of the covers of each book and having them developed into slides. Each pair of students can be assigned one of the books and write a brief script telling a little about the book and its illustrations. Arrange the slides in chronological order (by the year the Caldecott was won) and have students record their scripts in the same order. You may also halve students select background music for their recording.

Discussion Questions

1. Why was the Caldecott Award established? (To honor the work of outstanding illustrators of children's books.)
2. Who was the Caldecott Award named for? (Randolph Caldecott, a prominent English illustrator of children's books, who lived from 1846 to 1886.)
3. What, in your opinion, is the most important thing illustrations for children's books must do?
4. Who is your favorite Caldecott-winning illustrator? Why?
5. Of the different media used to create the illustrations of picture books, which is your favorite? Why?

Note: Each of the Caldecott Award-winning books included in this section represents different forms of artistic media.

LITERATURE RELATED ACTIVITIES

Title: *Smoky Night*

Genre: Picture Book—realistic fiction

Author: Eve Bunting

Illustrator: David Diaz (acrylics—the backgrounds were composed and photographed by the illustrator)

Bibliographic Information: Harcourt Brace & Company, San Diego, CA, 1994.

Summary: The story of "cats—and people—who couldn't get along until a night of rioting brings them all together." Winner of the 1995 Caldecott Medal.

Interest Level: Grades 1–3.

Pre-Reading Activity

Involve students in a discussion of what they do when they are angry and frustrated. Are there other alternatives to the behaviors they describe? Explain that this book is about the way some adults behave when they too are angry and frustrated. Use some of the ideas listed in "Asking Divergent Questions," p. 51, to help students see the problem from different perspective.

Learning Activities

1. Allow time for students to study the cover and to think about the title. Have them create a picture that could accompany the title, *Smoky Night.*

2. Before reading the book, select one of the pictures. (Select one that allows for predictions, such as the picture of the families going down the stairs to escape the fire.) Create a chart with three columns. In the first column, have students describe what they see. In the next column ask them to think of all the words they can to explain what happened "before," and in the third column ask them to predict what might happen next. Read the story aloud, and see how close some of the predictions were.

3. Ask students to think about a situation that might cause them to become angry or frustrated. Select several of the scenarios and have students role play them. Encourage different groups to act out the same scenario using different ways of coping with the situation. Discuss which solution students found to be the most effective and why.

4. Invite a local firefighter to class to discuss safety precautions to help prevent accidental fires and measures families can take in the event of fire. Later, divide students into groups and give each group a different safety tip to illustrate in order to create a brochure on fire safety. If students can write the text, allow them to do so, otherwise insert the text before duplicating.

5. Eve Bunting, the author of *Smoky Night,* dedicated the book to the peacekeepers. Discuss the question, "Who are the peacekeepers?" Can each students be a peacekeeper? How? Create a bulletin board that reflects and honors the peacekeepers of the world—including each of them!

6. The art form in *Smoky Night* uses acrylics and the backgrounds were created and then photographed by the illustrator. Have them each create a background for a picture, using various objects and use the copy machine to make flat copies of this background. Then allow students to create a picture on their backgrounds. Students may use acrylics, tempera paint, or crayons to duplicate the vivid colors of the original illustrations. Discuss illustrations and their effects.

Discussion Questions

1. Imagine that you are the young child in this book. Of all the things that happened during that smoky night, which do you think was: most frightening, happiest, saddest?

2. Mr. Ramirez described the rioters as "hooligans." What do you think this means? What type of things did these "hooligans" do?

3. At first, Jasmine and Mrs. Kim's cat fought all the time. What caused them to stop fighting? Imagine you are Jasmine, how would you describe what happened between you and Mrs. Kim's cat?

4. What lessons about getting along with others did Daniel and his mother learn during the smoky night?

5. Which illustration was your favorite? Why? How did it influence your understanding of the story?

Title: *Grandfather's Journey*

Genre: Picture Book—Biography

Author: Allen Say

Illustrator: Allen Say

Bibliographic Information: Houghton Mifflin Company, Boston, 1993.

Summary: The moving account of the author's family's love for both the country of their birth and the country to which they emigrated. Winner of the 1994 Caldecott Medal.

Interest Level: Grades 1–3.

Pre-Reading Activity

Involve students in a discussion of the word "journey." Where have they journeyed? What have they discovered on their journeys (about the people, the places, themselves)?

Learning Activities

1. After reading this story, write the story events on sentence strips. Have students, in groups, sequence the strips and read their versions aloud.

2. Have students create an accordion book to retell the tale. Each group of students should be responsible for reproducing one of the pages of the tale for placement in the accordion book.

An Accordion Book

Directions: Make an accordian folding book by folding a roll of shelf paper accordion-style to make pages. To make a cover, paste or staple cardboard to the first and last pages. Punch holes in the sides of the covers and fasten with ribbon to close the book.

3. What places in the United States are pictured in the book? Encourage groups to select one of the pictures and try to identify the area and learn as much as possible about it. Have them set up a "Journey Across America" exhibit in which each group displays pictures and information about the subject of the original picture.

4. Interview one or more grandparents to learn about their lives, their childhood, and where they have lived. Create an oral history by taping the interview. During the taping, having them share photographs of themselves at different times and places in their lives. If any of them have lived in a different country, have them also share recollections of their lives in this country and compare it to life in the U.S.

5. Origami is the ancient art of paper folding. An origami boat is pictured on the title page and on back cover. Invite an art teacher to demonstrate the art of origami. Involve the class in using this art form to create various objects.

6. Have students create a moving exhibit that highlights other books written and/or illustrated by Allen Say. These include such titles as: *El Chino, The Lost Lake, A River Dream, The Bicycle Man* (ALA Notable Children's Book), and *Tree of Cranes* (ALA Notable Children's Trade Book in the field of social studies), *The Boy of the Three-Year Nap* (written by Dianne Snyder and the winner of the 1988 Caldecott Honor Medal), and *How My Parents Learned to Eat* (written by Ina Friedman and selected as a Reading Rainbow Review Book).

Discussion Questions

1. Take a close look at the pictures and how they illustrate the cultures of both Japan and the United States. What differences can you discover between life in the U.S. and Japan in terms of clothing and the way people live? What similarities do you see in the two cultures?

2. Discuss the quote on the last page: "The funny thing is, the moment I am in one country, I am homesick for the other." Have you ever felt this way?

3. What are some things you would miss if you had to leave your home and country?

4. Why do you think this book was selected to receive the Caldecott Medal? Do you agree or disagree with the choice?

Title: *Black and White*

Genre: Picture Book

Author: David Macaulay

Illustrator: David Macaulay

Bibliographic Information: Houghton Mifflin, Boston, 1990.

Summary: *Black and White* is actually four stories in one, each created using a different media including watercolors, torn paper, sepia, and pen and ink. The book is like a puzzle and readers must interpret each of the stories and seek a connection among them. Winner of the 1991 Caldecott Medal.

Interest Level: Grades 2–6.

Pre-Reading Activity

Read the warning that appears on the title page of the book. Discuss their interpretations of the warning.

Learning Activities

1. Have students divide a large piece of poster paper into four squares. In each square, have them write the name of one of the stories in *Black and White*. Next, have them write a brief summary of the story and draw an illustration to represent it.

2. Divide the class into groups of four or five. Have each group create their own interpretation of *Black and White* by combining the four stories into one. Have each group present their interpretation in the form of a dramatic skit, using masks, puppetry, flannel board characters, or other artistic forms.

3. Many have compared *Black and White* to a jigsaw puzzle. Have students create a jigsaw puzzle representing one of the illustrations in *Black and White*. This can be done using the following steps:

   a.   Have students select a favorite illustration and create his or her own version of it. Somewhere on the picture, ask students to write the name of the story from which the picture came.

   b.   Glue the picture to a thin piece of cardboard and laminate.

   c.   Have students draw puzzle piece designs over the puzzle and cut it out accordingly.

   d.   Allow time for students to put each others' puzzles together.

4. Encourage students to create their own books modeled after *Black and White*. Students, in groups of six, can brainstorm three different scenarios that can be combined in some way. Pairs can work together on one of the scenarios, being certain to include clues and pictures from the other stories. When the pages are completed, laminate and bind them.

5. Encourage students to read other books by David Macaulay (all published by Houghton Mifflin) such as *The Way Things Work* (1988); *Why the Chicken Crossed the Road* (1987); *Castle* (1977); *Cathedral: The Story of its Construction* (1974); *Mill* (1983), *Pyramid* (1975); and *Underground* (1976).

6. Involve students in developing an interesting and creative activity based on one book by David Macaulay.

Discussion Questions

1. Why do you believe Macaulay gave the book the title, *Black and White?* Of all the reasons you can think of, which do you think is the most probable?

2. *Black and White is* quite different from other picture books. Explain the ways in which it differs. (Most picture books are read from left to right; most books describe a story in sequence; most books have the dedication at the front of the book; the pictures in most books are done in the same style and use the same media throughout the book; and so forth.)

3. Of the four stories included in the book, which is your favorite? Why? Which is your least favorite? Explain.

4. Some people have compared reading *Black and White* to flipping television stations. Do you agree or disagree? What other comparison can you make?

5. Do you believe *Black and White* is really four separate stories or are they simply one story told in an unusual way? Explain.

Title: *Tuesday*

Genre: Picture Book—fantasy

Author: David Wiesner

Illustrator: David Wiesner (watercolors)

Bibliographic Information: Clarion, New York, 1991.

Summary: The incredible adventures of a group of frogs, one Tuesday evening, somewhere in the U.S.A. Winner of the 1992 Caldecott Medal.

Interest Level: Grades K–6.

Pre-Reading Activity

Explain to students that the idea for writing *Tuesday* came to Wiesner from a cover he created for the March 1989 issue of *Cricket Magazine.* In the issue (locate and share the issue, if possible) there were many stories and pictures about frogs. For inspiration, he looked through some *National Geographic* magazines for pictures of frogs. Have students begin a frog collection by bringing in as many pictures of frogs as they can find. Have them create huge lily pads and cover them with pictures from the frog collection and with words and phrases that they would use to describe frogs.

Learning Activities

1. Encourage groups of children to create words to accompany this wordless picture book. Have them tape their version on a cassette and use a specific sound to cue the reader to turn the page.

2. Have students create a mural sequel to the book, entitled *Next Tuesday,* in which pigs fly. Ask each student to imagine an adventure for the pigs and recreate it using watercolors, the same media used in *Tuesday.*

3. Have students create a special news broadcast in which they tell about the incredible events of Tuesday as if they were actually happening. Encourage them to be creative—they can even interview several of the frogs and other characters from the story.

4. Have students research frogs and find five facts about them. Have them create an informational book about frogs using illustrations from the book (photocopy or have students recreate pages such as the one showing the frogs leaping, diving, and sitting on the lily pads) to accompany the facts they have written.

Discussion Questions

1. What did Wiesner do to make the events in the story seem almost believable? (He gave the precise times of the frogs' adventure and used pictures that seemed almost like photographs.)

2. Imagine that you were the inspector in the story who was trying to figure out what had happened. What clues did he find? What other possible solutions could you come up with?

3. Which illustrations show frogs doing things that frogs are generally expected to do?

4. Which picture in the book is your favorite? Explain why.

CULMINATING ACTIVITY

"The One That Got Away"

Students have been spending a good deal of time involved with books that have been named Caldecott winners or Honor books. With students, create a list of criteria that they think illustrations must meet to be considered outstanding. (Be sure their criteria includes that of the Association for Library Service to Children, a division of the American Library Association, which selects the winner each year. This criteria includes: craftsmanship, consistency, coherence with text, and appeal to children up to the age of 14.) Provide students with recently published picture books that have not been awarded the Caldecott. Ask each student to select a book that he or she feels should have been awarded the Caldecott, and have each nominate the book by filling in the form on p. 212. Based on the information they listed on the nomination form, have each create and present a short persuasive speech explaining to classmates the reasons the book deserves special recognition for its illustrations. Have each student award the book the medal that he or she created in the Initiating Activity and display the books, nomination forms, and awards for several days. At the end of a specific period of time, have the class vote for the most outstanding picture book from those nominated. Involve the class in writing a letter to the illustrator (in care of the publisher) to tell him or her of the class's interest in and enthusiasm for the book.

Caldecott Nomination Form

Title: _____

Illustrator: _____

Author: _____

Publisher: _____ Date of Publication: _____

In 20 words or less, explain why you believe this book should win an award for its illustrations.

_____

_____

_____

_____

_____

_____

_____

In one word or phrase, describe the illustrations. _____

_____

Student's Name _____

Date _____

SUPPLEMENTAL LITERATURE

Books

The following include a comprehensive list of all those books that have been named Caldecott Medal Winners and Caldecott Honor Books, from the establishment of the Caldecott Award in 1938 until 1999.

Year	Winner	Honors
1938	*Animals of the Bible* by Helen Dean Fish, illustrated by Dorothy P. Lathrop, Lippincott.	*Seven Simeons* by Boris Artzybasheff, Viking; *Four and Twenty Blackbirds* by Helen Dean Fish, illustrated by Robert Lawson, Stokes.
1939	*Mei Li* by Thomas Handforth, Doubleday.	*The Forest Pool* by Laura Adams Armer, Longmans; *Wee Gillis* by Munro Leaf, illustrated by Robert Lawson, Viking; *Snow White and the Seven Dwarfs* by Wanda Gag, Coward; *Barkis* by Clare Newbery, Harper; *Andy and the Lion* by James Daugherty, Viking.
1940	*Abraham Lincoln* by Ingri and Edgar Parin D'Aulaire, Doubleday.	*Cock-A-Doodle Doo . . .* by Berta and Elmer Hader, Macmillan; *Madeline* by Ludwig Bemelmans, Viking; *The Ageless Story* illustrated by Lauren Ford, Dodd.
1941	*They Were Strong and Good* by Robert Lawson, Viking.	*April's Kittens* by Clare Newberry, Harper.
1942	*Make Way for Ducklings* by Robert McCloskey, Viking.	*An American ABC* by Maud and Miska Petersham, Macmillan; *In My Mother's House* by Ann Nolan Clark, illustrated by Velino Herrera, Viking; *Paddle-to-the-Sea* by Holling C. Holling, Houghton; *Nothing at All* by Wanda Gag, Coward.
1943	*The Little House* by Virginia Lee Burton, Houghton.	*Dash and Dart* by Mary and Conrad Buff, Viking; *Marshmallow* by Clare Newbery, Harper.
1944	*Many Moons* by James Thurber, illustrated by Louis Slobodkin, Harcourt.	*Small Rain: Verses from the Bible* selected by Jessie Orton Jones, illustrated by Elizabeth Orton Jones, Viking; *Pierre Pigeon* by Lee Kingman, illustrated by Arnold E. Bare, Houghton; *The Mighty Hunter* by Berta and Elmer Hader, Macmillan; *A Child's Good Night Book* by Margaret Wise Brown, illustrated by Jean Chariot, W. R Scott; *Good Luck Horse* by Chih-Yi Chan, illustrated by Plao Chan, Whittlesey.
1945	*Prayer for a Child* by Rachel Field, illustrated by Elizabeth Orton Jones, Macmillan.	*Mother Goose* Illustrated by Tasha Tudor, Walck; *In the Forest* by Marie Hall Ets, Viking; *Yonie Wondernose* by Marguerite do Angeli, Doubleday; *The Christians Anna Angel* by Ruth Sawyer, illustrated by Kate Seredy, Viking.
1946	*The Rooster Crows . . .* (traditional Mother Goose) illustrated by Maud and Miska Petersham, Macmillan.	*Little Lost Lamb* by Golden MacDonald, illustrated by Leonard Weisgard, Doubleday; *Sing: Mother Goose* by Opal Wheeler, illustrated by Marjorie Torrey, Dutton; *My Mother Is the Most Beautiful Wonton in the World* by Becky Reyher, illustrated by Ruth Gannett, Lothrop; *You Can Write Chinese* by Kurt Wiese, Viking.
1947	*The Little Island* by Golden MacDonald, illustrated by Leonard Weisgard, Doubleday.	*Rain Drop Splash* by Alvin Tresselt, illustrated by Leonard Weisgard, Lothrop; *Boats on the River* by Marjorie Flack, illustrated by Jay Hyde Barnum, Viking; *Timothy Turtle* by Al Graham, illustrated by Tony Palazzo, Viking; *Pedro, The Angel of Olvera Street* by Leo Politi, Scribner's; *Sing in Praise: A Collection of the Best Loved Hymns* by Opal Wheeler, illustrated by Marjorie Torrey, Dutton.

Year	Winner	Honors
1948	*White Snow, Bright Snow* by Alvin Tresselt, illustrated by Roger Duvoisin, Lothrop.	*Stone Soup* by Marcia Brown, Scribner's; *McElligot's Pool* by Dr. Seuss, Random; *Bambino the Clown* by George Schreiber, Viking; *Roger and the Fox* by Lavinia Davis, illustrated by Hildegard Woodward, Doubleday; *Song of Robin Hood* edited by Anne Malcolmson, illustrated by Virginia Lee Burton, Houghton.
1949	*The Big Snow* by Berta and Elmer Hader, Macmillan.	*Blueberries for Sal* by Robert McCloskey, Viking; *All Around the Town* by Phyllis McGinley, illustrated by Helen Stone, Lippincott; *Juanita* by Leo Politi, Scribner's; *Fish in the Air* by Kurt Wiese, Viking.
1950	*Song of the Swallows* by Leo Politi, Scribner's.	*America's Ethan Allen* by Stewart Holbrook, illustrated by Lynd Ward, Houghton; *The Wild Birthday Cake* by Lavinia Davis, illustrated by Hildegard Woodward, Doubleday; *The Happy Day* by Ruth Krauss, illustrated by Marc Simont, Harper; *Bartholomew and the Oobleck* by Dr. Seuss, Random; *Henry Fisherman* by Marcia Brown, Scribner's.
1951	*The Egg Tree* by Katherine Milhous, Scribner's.	*Dick Whittington and His Cat* by Marcia Brown, Scribner's; *The Two Reds* by William Lipkind, illustrated by Nicholas Mordvinoff, Harcourt; *If I Ran the Zoo* by Dr. Seuss, Random; *The Most Wonderful Doll in the World* by Phyllis McGinley, illustrated by Helen Stone, Lippincott; *T-Bone, the Baby Sitter* by Clare Newberry, Harper.
1952	*Finders Keepers* by William Lipkind, illustrated by Nicholas Mordvinoff, Harcourt.	*Mr. T. W. Anthony Woo* by Marie Hall Ets, Viking; *Skipper John's Cook* by Marcia Brown, Scribner's; *All Falling Down* by Gene Zion, illustrated by Margaret Bloy Graham, Harper; *Bear Party* by William Pene du Bois, Viking; *Feather Mountain* by Elizabeth Olds, Houghton.
1953	*The Biggest Bear* by Lynd Ward, Houghton.	*Puss in Boots* by Charles Perrault, illustrated and translated by Marcia Brown, Scribner's; *One Morning in Maine* by Robert McCloskey, *Viking; Ape in a Cape* by Fritz Eichenberg, Harcourt; *The Storm Book* by Charlotte Zolotow, illustrated by Margaret Bloy Graham, Harper; *Five Little Monkeys* by Juliet Kepes, Houghton.
1954	*Madeline's Rescue* by Ludwig Bemelmans, Viking.	*Journey Cake, Ho!* by Ruth Sawyer, illustrated by Robert McCloskey, Viking; *When Will the World Be Mine?* by Miriam Schlein, illustrated by Jean Charlot, W. R Scott; *The Steadfast Tin Soldier* by Hans Christian Andersen, illustrated by Marcia Brown, Scribner's; *A Very Special House* by Ruth Krauss, illustrated by Maurice Sendak, Harper; *Green Eyes* by A. Birnbaum, Capitol.

Year	Winner	Honors
1955	*Cinderella, or the Little Glass Slipper* by Charles Perrault, translated and illustrated by Marcia Brown, Scribner's.	*Books of Nursery and Mother Goose Rhymes,* illustrated by Marguerite de Angeli, Doubleday; *Wheel on the Chimney* by Margaret Wise Brown, illustrated by Tibor Gergely, Lippincott; *The Thanksgiving Story* by Alice Dalgliesh, illustrated by Helen Sewell, Scribner's.
1956	*Frog Went A-Courtin',* edited by John Langstaff, illustrated by Feodor Rojankovsky, Harcourt.	*Play with Me* by Marie Hall Ets, Viking; *Crow Boy* by Taro Yashima Viking.
1957	*A Tree Is Nice* by Janice May Udry, illustrated by Marc Simont, Harper.	*Mr. Penny's Race Horse* by Marie Hall Ets, Viking; *1 Is One* by Tasha Tudor, Walck; *Anatole* by Eve Titus, illustrated by Paul Galdone, McGraw; *Gillespie and the Guards* by Benjamin Elkin, illustrated by James Daugherty, Viking; *Lion* by William Pene du Bois, Viking.
1958	*Time* of *Wonder* by Robert McCloskey, Viking.	*Fly High, Fly Low* by Don Freeman, Viking; *Anatole and the Cat* by Eve Titus, illustrated by Paul Galdone, McGraw.
1959	*Chanticleer and the Fox,* adapted from Chaucer and illustrated by Barbara Mooney, T. Crowell.	*The House That Jack Built* by Antonio Frasconi, Harcourt; *What Do You Say, Dear?* by Sesyle Joslin, illustrated by Maurice Sendak, W. R. Scott; *Umbrella* by Taro Yashima, Viking.
1960	*Nine Days to Christmas* by Marie Hall Ets and Aurora Labastida, illustrated by Marie Fall Ets, Viking.	*Houses from the Sea* by Alice E. Goudoy, illustrated by Adrienne Adams, Scribner's; *The Moon Jumpers* by Janice May Udry, illustrated by Maurice Sendak, Harper.
1961	*Baboushka and the Three Kings* by Ruth Robbins, illustrated by Nicholas Sidjakov, Parnassus.	*Inch by Inch* by Leo Lionni, Obolensky.
1962	*Once a Mouse . . .* by Marcia Brown, Scribner's.	*The Fox Went Out On a Chilly Night* by Peter Spier, Doubleday; *Little Bear's Visit* by Else Holmelund Minarik, illustrated by Maurice Sendak, Harper; *The Day We Saw the Sun Come Up* by Alice E. Goudey, illustrated by Adrienne Adams, Scribner's.
1963	*The Snooty Day* by Ezra Jack Keats, Viking.	*The Sun Is a Golden Earring* by Natalia M. Belting, illustrated by Bernarda Bryson, Holt; *Mr. Rabbit and the Lovely Present* by Charlotte Zolotow, illustrated by Maurice Sendak, Harper.
1964	*Where the Wild Things Are* by Maurice Sendak, Harper & Row.	*All in the Morning Early* by Sorche Nic Leodhas, illustrated by Evaline Ness, Halt, Rinehart & Winston; *Mother Goose and Nursery Rhymes* by Philip Reed, Atheneum; *Swimmy* by Leo Lionni, Pantheon.
1965	*May I Bring a Friend?* by Beatrice Schenk de Regniers, Atheneum.	*A Pocketful of Cricket* by Rebecca Caudill, illustrated by Evaline Ness, Holt, Rinehart & Winston; *Rain Makes Applesauce* by Julian Scheer, illustrated by Marvin Bileck, Holiday; *The Wave* by Margaret Hodges, illustrated by Blair Lent, Houghton Mifflin.

Year	Winner	Honors
1966	*Always Room for One More* by Sorche Nic Leodhas, illustrated by Nonny Hogrogian, Holt, Rinehart & Winston.	*Hide and Seek Fog* by Alvin Tresselt, illustrated by Roger Duvoisin, Lothrop, Lee & Shepard; *Just Me* by Marie Hall Ets, Viking; *Tom Tit Tot* edited by Joseph Jacobs, illustrated by Evaline Ness, Scribner's.
1967	*Sam, Bangs & Moonshine* by Evaline Ness, Holt, Rinehart & Winston.	*One Wide River to Cross* by Barbara Emberley, illustrated by Ed Emberley, Prentice-Hall.
1968	*Drummer Hoff* by Barbara Emberley, illustrated by Ed Emberley, Prentice-Hall.	*Frederick* by Leo Lionni, Pantheon; *Seashore Story* by Taro Yashima, Viking; *The Emperor and the Kite* by Jane Yolen, illustrated by Ed Young, Harcourt Brace Jovanovich.
1969	*The Fool of the World and the Flying Ship* by Arthur Ransome, illustrated by Uri Shulevitz, Farrar, Straus & Giroux.	*Why the Sun and the Moon Live in the Sky: An African Folktale* by Elphinstone Dayrell, illustrated by Blair Lent, Houghton Mifflin.
1970	*Sylvester and the Magic Pebble* by William Steig, Windmill/Simon & Schuster.	*Alexander and the Wind-Up Mouse* by Leo Lionni, Pantheon; *Goggles!* Ezra Jack Keats, Macmillan; *The Judge: An Untrue Tale* by Harve Zemach, illustrated by Margot Zemach, Farrar, Straus & Giroux; *Pop Corn Emma Goodness* by Edna Mitchell Preston, illustrated by Robert Andrew Parker, Viking; *Thy Friend, Obadiah* by Brinton Turkle, Viking.
1971	*A Story, A Story* by Gail E. Haley, Atheneum.	*The Angry Moon* by William Sleaton, illustrated by Blair Lent, Atlantic-Little; *Frog and Toad Are Friends* by Arnold Lobel, Harper & Row; *In the Night Kitchen* by Maurice Sendak, Harper & Row.
1972	*One Fine Day* by Nonny A. Hogrogian, Macmillan.	*Hildilid's Night* by Cheli Duran Ryan, illustrated by Arnold Lobel, Macmillan; *If All the Seas Were One Sea* by Janina Domanska, Macmillan; *Moja Means One: Swahili Counting Book* by Muriel Feelings, illustrated by Tom Feelings, Dial.
1973	*The Funny Little Woman* by Arlen Mosel, illustrated by Blair Lent, E. P. Dutton	*Hosie's Alphabet* by Hosea, Tobias, and Lisa Baskin, illustrated by Leonard Baskin, Viking; *Snow White and the Seven Dwarfs,* translated by Randall Jarrell from The Brothers Grimm, illustrated by Nancy Ekholm Burkert, Farrar, Straus & Giroux; *When Clay Sings* by Byrd Baylor, illustrated by Tom Bahti, Scribner's.
1974	*Duffy and the Devil* by Harve and Margot Zemach, Farrar, Straus & Giroux.	*Cathedral: The Story of Its Construction* by David Macaulay, Houghton; *The Three Jovial Huntsmen* by Susan Jeffers, Bradbury.
1975	*Arrow to the Sun* by Gerald McDermott, Viking.	*Jumbo Means Hello: A Swahili Alphabet Book* by Muriel Feelings, illustrated by Tom Feelings, Dial.
1976	*Why Mosquitoes Buzz in People's Ears* by Verna Aardema, illustrated by Leo and Diane Dillon, Dial.	*The Desert Is Theirs* by Byrd Baylor, illustrated by Peter Parnall, Scribner's; *Strega Nona* by Tomie de Paola, Prentice-Hall.

Year	Winner	Honors
1977	*Ashanti to Zulu* by Margaret Musgrove, illustrated by Leo and Diane Dillon, Dial.	*The Amazing Bone* by William Steig, Farrar, Straus & Giroux; *The Contest* by Nonny Hogrogian, Greenwillow; *Fish for Supper* by M. B. Goffstein, Dial; *The Golem: A Jewish Legend* by Beverly Brodsky McDermott, Lippincott; *Hawk, I'm Your Brother* by Byrd Baylor, illustrated by Peter Parnall, Scribner's.
1978	*Noah's Ark: The Story of the Flood* by Peter Spier, Doubleday.	*Castle* by David Macaulay, Houghton; *It Could Always Be Worse* by Margot Zemach, Farrar, Straus & Giroux.
1979	*The Girl Who Loved Wild Horses* by Paul Goble, Bradbury.	*Freight Train* by Donald Crews, Greenwillow; *The Way to Start a Day* by Byrd Baylor, illustrated by Peter Parnall, Scribner's.
1980	*Ox-Cart Man* by Donald Hall, illustrated by Barbara Cooney, Viking.	*Ben's Trumpet* by Rachel Isadora, Greenwillow; *The Garden of Abdul Gasazi* by Chris Van Allsburg, Houghton; *The Treasure* by Uri Shulevitz, Farrar, Straus & Giroux.
1981	*Fables* by Arnold Lobel, Harper & Row.	*The Bremen-Town Musicians* by Ilse Plume, Doubleday; *The Grey Lady and the Strawberry Snatcher* by Molly Bang, Four Winds; *Mice Twice* by Joseph Low, Atheneum; *Truck* by Donald Crews, Greenwillow.
1982	*Jumanji* by Chris Van Allsburg, Houghton Mifflin.	*On Market Street* by Arnold Lobel, illustrated by Anita Label, Greenwillow; *Outside Over There* by Maurice Sendak, Harper & Row; *A Visit to Millions Blake's Inn: Poems for Innocent and Experienced Travelers* by Nancy Willard, illustrated by Alice and Martin Provensen, Harcourt; *Where the Buffaloes Begin* by Olaf Baker, illustrated by Stephen Gammell, Warner.
1983	*Shadow* by Blaise Cendrars, translated and illustrated by Marcia Brown, Scribner's.	*A Chair for My Mother* by Vera B. Williams, Greenwillow; *When I Was Young in the Mountains* by Cynthia Rylant, illustrated by Diane Goode, E. P. Dutton.
1984	*The Glorious Flight Across the Channel with Louis Bleriot* by Alice and Martin Provensen, Viking.	*Little Red Riding Hood* by Trina Schart Hyman, Holiday; *Ten, Nine, Eight* by Molly Bang, Greenwillow.
1985	*Saint George and the Dragon* by Margaret Hodges, illustrated by Trina Schart Hyman, Little, Brown.	*Hansel and Gretel* by Rika Lesser, illustrated by Paul O. Zelinsky, Dodd, Mead; *Have You Seen My Duckling?* by Nancy Tafuri, Greenwillow; *The Story of Jumping Mouse* by John Symptom, Lothrop, Lee & Shepard.
1986	*The Polar Express* by Chris Van Allsburg, Houghton Mifflin.	*King Bidgood's in the Bathtub* by Audrey Wood, Harcourt Brace Jovanovich; *The Relatives Came* by Cynthia Rylant, Bradbury.
1987	*Hey, Al* by Arthur Yorinks, illustrated by Richard Egielski, Farrar, Straus & Giroux.	*Alphabetics* by Suse MacDonald, Bradbury; *Rumplestiltskin* by Paul O. Zelinsky, E. P. Dutton; *The Village of Round and Square Houses* by Anne Grifalconi, Little, Brown.
1988	*Owl Moon* by Jane Yolen, illustrated by John Schoenherr, Philomel.	*Mufaro's Beautiful Daughter: An African Tale* by John Steptoe, Morrow.

Year	Winner	Honors
1989	*Song and Dance Man* by Karen Ackerman, illustrated by Stephen Gammell Knopf.	*The Boy of the Three Year Nap* by Dianne Snyder, illustrated TV Allen Say, Houghton Mifflin; *Free Fall* by David Wiesner, Lothrop, Lee, & Shepard; *Goldilocks and the Three Bears* by James Marshall, Dial; *Mirandy and Brother Wind* by Patricia C. McKissack, illustrated by Jerry Pinkney, Knopf.
1990	*Lon Po Po!: A Red Riding Hood Story from China* by Ed Young, Putnam.	*Bill Peet: An Autobiography,* written and illustrated by Bill Peet, Houghton Mifflin; *Color Zoo,* written and illustrated by Lois Ehlert, Harper & Row; *Hershel and the Hanukkah Goblins* by Eric A. Kimmel, illustrated by Trina Schart Hyman, Holiday; *The Talking Eggs* by Robert San Souci, illustrated by Jerry Pinkney, Doubleday.
1991	*Black & White by* David Macaulay, Houghton Mifflin.	*Puss in Boots* by Fred Marcellino, de Capua/Farrar; *"More, More, More" Said the Baby: 3 Love Stories* by Vera B. Williams, Greenwillow.
1992	*Tuesday* by David Wiesner, Clarion Books.	*Tar Beach* by Faith Ringgold, Crown Publishing.
1993	*Seven Blind Mice* by Ed Young, Philomel Books.	*The Stinky Cheese Man and Other Fairly Stupid Tales* by Lane Smith, Viking; *Working Cotton* by Sherley Anne Williams, illustrated by Carole Byard, Harcourt Brace Jovanovich.
1994	*Grandfather's Journey* by Allen Say, Houghton.	*Peppe the Lamplighter*, by Elisa Bartone, illustrated by Ted Lewin, Lothrop; *In the Small, Small Pond* by Denise Fleming, Holt; *Raven: A Trickster Tale from the Pacific Northwest* by Gerald McDermott, Harcott; *Owen* by Kevin Henkes, Greenwillow; *Yo! Yes?* text edited by Richard Jackson, illustrated by Chris Raschka, Orchard.
1995	*Smoky Night* by Eve Bunting, illustrated by David Diaz, Harcourt.	*John Henry* by Julius Lester, illustrated by Jerry Pinkney, Dial; *Swamp Angel,* by Anne Issacs, illustrated by Paul O. Zelinsky, Dutton; *Time Flies* by Eric Rohmann, Crown.
1996	*Officer Buckle and Gloria* by Peggy Rathmann, Putnam.	*Alphabet City* by Stephen T. Johnson, Viking; *Zin! Zin! Zin! a Violin,* by Lloyd Moss, illustrated by Marjorie Priceman, Simon and Schuster; *The Faithful Friend* by Robert D. San Souci, illustrated by Brian Pickney.
1997	*Golem* by David Wisniewski, Clarion.	*Hush: A Thai Lullaby by Minfong Ho,* illustrated by Holly eade, Orchard Books; *The Graphic Alphabet* by David Pelletier, Orchard; *The Paperboy* by Dav Pilkey, Orchard Books; *Starry Messenger* by Peter Sis, Farrar Straus Giroux.
1998	*Rapunzel* by Paul O. Zelinsky, Dutton.	*The Gardener* by Sarah Stewart, illustrated by David Small; *Harlem* by Walter Dean Myers, illustrated by Christopher Myers, Scholastic; *There Was an Old Lady Who Swallowed a Fly* by Simms Talback, Viking.
1999	*Snowflake Bentley* by Jacqueline Briggs Martin, illustrated by Mary Azarian, Houghton Mifflin.	*Duke Ellington* by Andrea Davis Pickney, illustrated by David Pickney, Disney Press; *No, David!* by David Shannon, Scholastic; *Snow* by Uri Shulevitz, Farrar, Straus & Giroux; *Tibet: Through the Red Box* by Peter Sis, Farrar, Straus & Giroux.

Web Sites

Children's Literature: Authors and Illustrators: http://www.users.interport.net/
~fairrosa/cl.authors.html
Internet Public Library Youth Division: http://www.ipl.org/youth
Children's Literature Web Guide (excellent source for award winning literature): http: www.acs.ucalgary.ca/~dkbrown

MINI-THEMES

The following mini-themes focus on two outstanding illustrators of children's
books, each of whom has been recognized for his or her achievements by being
awarded the Caldecott Medal. Their styles are unique and distinctive and their
efforts have created unforgettable characters that will remain with children long
after one of their books has been read.

* indicates that the book was a Caldecott Medal Winner.

† indicates that the book was a Caldecott Honor Book.

Ed Young

Born in Tientsin, China, Ed Young grew up in Shanghai and his heritage is
beautifully reflected in his art. Young's versatility is evident in the variety of
artistic media he uses, including Oriental papercut technique, rich pastels, and
pencil drawings.

Activities

1. Many of the books that Ed Young has illustrated are folktales. Of these,
   many are versions of some of the most popular tales children have grown
   up with, such as *Cinderella* and *Little Red Riding Hood*. Share various
   versions of these two tales, along with the versions illustrated by Ed Young.
   Involve students in a discussion of the two stories and the way the illustrations reflect the culture from which the story came. Have students select a
   favorite folktale and have them brainstorm ways they could transform it
   into a folktale from China. Encourage them to use their ideas to create a
   new version of the story.

2. Ed Young was born in Tientsin, China, and grew up in Shanghai. Have
   students locate Tientsin and Shanghai on a map and research China to
   learn a little about Young's heritage. Have them create a mini-book (see
   directions on p. 220) about China. On each of the eight pages, have students list one fact about China and illustrate the borders with pictures
   representative of the country and its rich culture.

3. *The Other Bone* is a wordless picture book by Young. In groups, have
   students create a text for the story. Have each group select a different form
   of creative expression to tell their story (for example, puppetry, storytelling,
   story theater, flannel board, rap-song, etc.), and present it to the class.

4. From the various books Young has written and/or illustrated, students will
   form impressions about the Asian culture. Involve students in learning

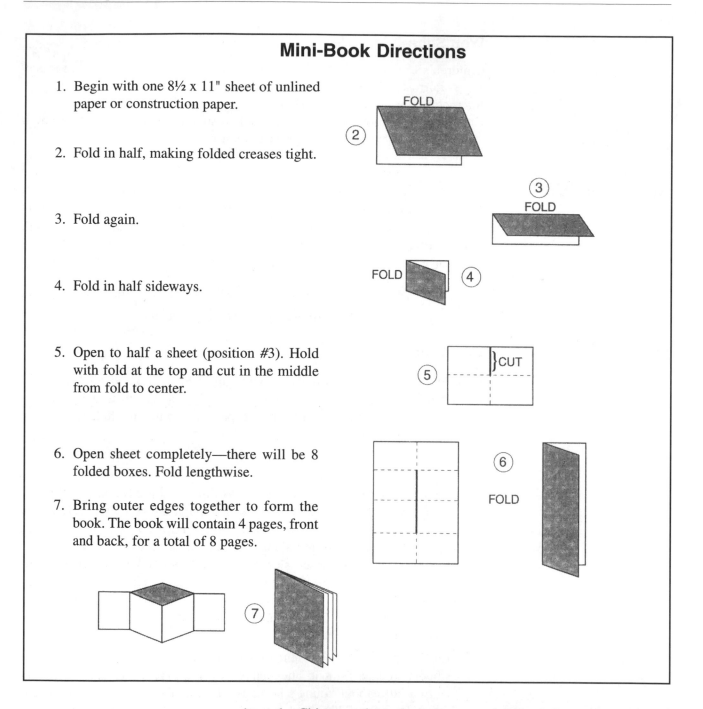

Mini-Book Directions

1. Begin with one 8½ x 11" sheet of unlined paper or construction paper.

2. Fold in half, making folded creases tight.

3. Fold again.

4. Fold in half sideways.

5. Open to half a sheet (position #3). Hold with fold at the top and cut in the middle from fold to center.

6. Open sheet completely—there will be 8 folded boxes. Fold lengthwise.

7. Bring outer edges together to form the book. The book will contain 4 pages, front and back, for a total of 8 pages.

about the Chinese culture through many of their crafts, such as origami (the art of paper folding) and calligraphy (included in Young's illustrations for *Chinese Mother Goose Rhyme)*. Invite guest speakers to demonstrate these art forms to students and have them experiment with them.

5. In *The Girl Who Loved the Wind,* the wind speaks verses to Danina, telling her about life outside the palace walls. Copy the various verses, writing each verse on a different sheet of large chart paper or onto pages of a blank big book. Make each group of students responsible for illustrating one page/verse with pictures, pieces of cloth, and wallpaper, etc. that reflect

the story and its setting. Students should also be encouraged to create a verse of their own as the last page of the newly formed big book.

References

Coerr, E. (1993). *Sadako and the thousand paper cranes.* Illustrated by E. Young. NY: Putnam.

Collodi, C. (1996). *Pinocchio.* NY Philomel.

Hearne, L. (1989). *The voice of the great bell.* Adapted by M. Hodges. Illustrated by E. Young. Boston: Little, Brown.

Larrick, N. (1988). *Cats and Cats.* Illustrated by E. Young. New York: Philomel.

Louis, A. (1982). *Yeh-Shen: A Cinderella story from China.* Illustrated by E. Young. New York: Philomel.

Pollock, P. (1996). *The turkey girl: A Zuni Cinderella.* Illustrated by E. Young. Boston: Little, Brown.

Wolkstein, D. (1972). *8,000 stories: A Chinese folktale.* Illustrated by E. Young. New York: Doubleday.

Wolkstein, D. (1979). *White Wave: A Chinese tale.* Illustrated by E. Young. New York: Crowell.

Wyndham, R., compiler (1968). *Chinese Mother Goose rhymes.* Illustrated by E. Young. San Diego, CA: Harcourt Brace Jovanovich.

† Yolen, J. (1967). *The emperor and the kite.* Illustrated by E. Young. San Diego, CA: Harcourt Brace Jovanovich.

Young, E. (1995). *Cat and rat: The legend of the Chinese zodiac.* New York: Holt.

Yolen, J. (1972). *The girl who loved the wind.* Illustrated by E. Young. New York: Crowell. Young, E. (1997). *Genesis.* New York: HarperCollins

*Young, E. (1989). *Lon Po Po: A Red Riding Hood story from China.* New York: Philomel.

Young, E. (1998). *The Lost Horse.* Silver Whistle.

Young, E. (1997). *Mouse match: A Chinese folktale.* San Diego, CA: Harcourt Brace.

*Young, E. (1992). *Three blind mice.* New York: Philomel.

Young, E. (1984). *The other bone.* New York: Harper.

Leo and Diane Dillon

The collaboration of these two artists results in a finished product created by what they term "the third artist." And, in their words, this artist, "comes up with things neither of us would have done." Coming from very different backgrounds, these two incredibly talented people met at the Parsons School of Design and were immediately captivated by each other's art.

Activities

1. The Dillons employ a variety of techniques and media in the different books they illustrate. Have students read a variety of books the Dillons have illustrated and select their favorite book, based on illustrations alone. Have students create a book jacket for the book, trying to reproduce one of

the illustrations. On the jacket flaps, encourage them to tell a little bit about the story but mainly concentrate on writing about their impressions of the illustrations. Display the book jackets on a special bulletin board honoring the Dillons and their work.

2. Leo and Diane Dillon have worked on every illustration for their children's books together. In their words, "We each have our distinct styles and particular strengths. But . . . after a work is finished, not even we can be certain who did what. The third artist is a combination of the two of us and is different than either of us individually. . . . It comes up with things neither of us would have done." *(Something About the Author,* Vol. 51, page 53.) Have students experiment with collaborating with another student on a picture, first discussing media, subject, and style, and then passing the picture back and forth, with each student adding to it each time they receive it. Once the pictures have been completed, mat them and display.

3. Leo and Diane Dillon are the first, and so far only, artists to have won the Caldecott Medal in two consecutive years—in 1976 for *Why Mosquitoes Buzz in People's Ears* and in 1977 for *Ashanti to Zulu: African Traditions.* Read *Why Mosquitoes Buzz in People's Ears* and have students create a skit to retell the story. For their animal character, allow students to create a mask. Those students who do not have a speaking part can create a jungle mural that will act as background scenery.

4. Read *Ashanti to Zulu: African Traditions.* Have students create their own ABC book which retells traditions from the variety of groups that make up the United States. For example, the "P" page can tell about the Spanish piñata, while the "C" page could describe the chopsticks used by those who emigrated from Asia.

5. Encourage students to write a class letter to the Dillons (in care of their publisher), expressing their feelings about their illustrations and asking questions about their art and their method of working together.

References

* Aardema, V. (1975). *Why mosquitoes buzz in people's ears.* Illustrated by L. and D. Dillon New York: Dial.

Aardema, V (1973) *Behind the brick of the mountain: Black folktales from Southern Africa.* Illustrated by L. and D. Dillon New York: Dial.

Dillon, L., & Dillon, D. (1998). *To everything there is a season.* New York: Scholastic.

Hamilton, V. (1995). *Her stories.* Illustrated by L. and D. Dillon. New York: Blue Sky Press.

Hamilton, V. (1985). *The people could fly.* Illustrated by L. and D. Dillon. New York: Knopf.

Mathis, S. B. (1976). *The hundred-penny box.* Illustrated by L and D. Dillon New York: Viking.

Murphy. S. (1999). W*ind child.* New York. HarperCollins.

* Musgrove, M. (1976). *Ashanti to Zulu.* Illustrated by L. and D. Dillon. New York: Dial.

Price, L. (1990). *Aida.* Illustrated by L. and D. Dillon. San Diego, CA: Harcourt.

Theme

Counting and Computations

OVERVIEW

Focus

Students will develop an intuitive feeling for numbers and their various uses and interpretations.

Objectives

On completion of this thematic unit, students will be able to:

1. Understand the numeration system and how it relates to counting.
2. Be able to do simple mathematical calculations.
3. Understand relative sizes of numbers.
4. Be able to use ordinal and cardinal numbers correctly.
5. Be familiar with small amounts of money.

HOW IT WORKS

Initiating Activity

Have the students brainstorm and then create a web of all the situations in which they use numbers. For example:

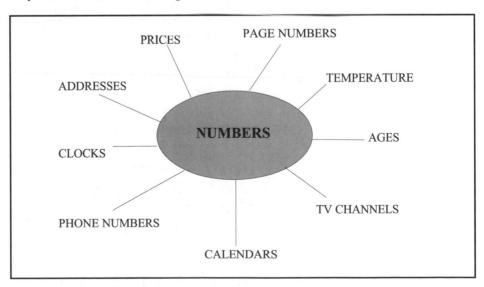

Discuss how their lives would be different if there were no numbers. If possible, share the book *The Day the Numbers Disappeared* by Leonard Simon and Jeanne Bendick.

General Activities

1. Provide a selection of counting books for the children to peruse using the book titles provided in the supplemental literature. Ask the children to work in cooperative learning groups to create their own counting books by using these books provided as models. Allow time to share books.

2. Ask the children to think of ways to keep track of things without using numbers. Allow time to share and discuss their ideas.

3. Ask the children to research how numerals are written in other cultures. Allow time to share different ways of writing the same numeral. *Number Act* by Leonard Fisher would be a helpful resource for this activity.

4. Ask the children to brainstorm songs, movies, sayings, phrases, and the like that uses numbers—for example, "Tea for Two," "Walking on Cloud Nine," "Three Musketeers." Make a list of these and discuss what they mean.

5. Have the children help to create a math learning center that includes counting and other math-related children's books, assorted manipulatives, activity sheets, puzzles, etc. Prepare a "Math Solving Box" and then ask each child to write a story problem related to one of the children's books to put in the box. For example, if the book *One Watermelon Seed* by Celia Baker Lottridge was selected, the child could provide an ear of corn at the center and then submit the following problem:

   > Count the number of kernals there are on the ear of corn. If Max and Josephine picked 100 ears of corn about how many kernels of corn would they have? (Use calculators if necessary).

   Be sure each child puts the name of the book and his or her name on the problem submitted.

6. Make available a copy of *Anno's Math Games II* by Mitsumasa Anno. Assign the children to work in pairs as they select and figure out some of the puzzles, games, and activities. This could be an on-going activity over a period of a week or two. Allow time for each pair to select one of the puzzles, games, or activities to share, explain, or ask questions about.

7. Read the book *How Many Snails?* by Paul Giganti. Then assign different groups of children to investigate some of the questions presented in this book. Or, you and the children could generate your own "How many" questions. For example, how many clouds are in the sky? How many trees are in a nearby park or forest? How many birds are flying in the sky?

Discussion Questions

1. Who was born first in your family? Second? Third?

2. What is the largest amount of money you have ever had? What did you do with it?

3. How far can you count by one's, by two's, by five's, by ten's?

4. Why is being able to count important?

5. How would things be different if there were no numbers?

LITERATURE RELATED ACTIVITIES

Title: *The Doorbell Rang*

Genre:	Picture Book
Author:	Pat Huchins
Bibliographic Information:	William Morrow and Company, New York 1989.
Summary:	Ma bakes twelve cookies for Sam and Victoria (6 each). But just as they are about to eat the cookies, the doorbell rings and friends arrive. Each time a new set of friends arrive, Sam and Victoria divide the cookies so everyone will have some. Finally, there are twelve children around the table with one cookie each and then the doorbell rings again. It is Grandma with a whole tray of cookies.
Interest Level:	Grades K–2.

Pre-Reading Activity

Show the children the illustration and read the text on the first page. Using one of your favorite simple cookie recipes, have the children help you measure the ingredients as you make a batch of cookies. Make the cookies as small as possible and then help the children divide the cookies among the group.

Learning Activities

1. Ask the children to estimate how many cookies were on Grandma's tray when she arrived. Then, ask them to pretend that they had to divide these cookies among the class. Help them to figure out how many cookies each child would get. Discuss the concept of division and that what is left over is the remainder. Ask the children to each write a brief paragraph and/or illustrate what they would do with the remainder of the cookies.

2. The children left their cookies on the table; however, the cat was sitting in the middle of the table. Ask the children to write story problems (on strip of paper) about the cat eating some of the cookies and how many would be left. (For example, there were 12 cookies on the table. The cat ate three cookies. How many cookies are left?) Put the story problems in a box and allow time for the children to select a problem, write it on the chalkboard, and provide an answer.

3. Ask the children to pretend they are Victoria or Sam and that they can invite whomever they want to share the twelve cookies. Tell the children to make a list of who they would invite and to tell how many cookies each person would get.

4. Discuss party invitations and what information should be included in them. Then tell the children to create an invitation to send to the children they

are inviting to their cookie party as described in Activity 3. Allow time to share invitations.

Discussion Questions

1. Do you think *The Doorbell Rang* is a good title for this book? Why or why not?

2. How many children came to visit Victoria and Sam? (12) Why do you think they came?

3. How do you think Victoria and Sam felt when children kept coming to the door and they had to share more and more of their cookies?

4. What would have happened if there had been more children at the door instead of Grandma with the cookies?

Title: *Numbers at Play: A Counting Book*

Genre:	Informational
Author:	Charles Sullivan
Bibliographic Information:	Rizzoli International Publishing, Inc., New York, 1992.
Summary:	This book combines counting with poetry, art, and photography. It involves the children in counting objects in beautiful pictures by such artists as Gauguin and Renoir. Short biographies of each artist are also provided.
Interest Level:	Grades K–4.

Pre-Reading Activity

Obtain a photograph or painting that has a specific number of objects that can be counted, such as those provided in this book. Then ask the children to count the objects. Explain that this is the approach used by the author, Charles Sullivan, to illustrate the numbers one through ten. Then read the poems in the book and allow the children to count the objects in each picture.

Learning Activities

1. As a class project, create a "Numbers at Play" by dividing the class into 10 groups. Assign each group a number (1 to 10) or, depending on grade level of the children, assign higher numbers. Tell each group to create an illustration that would include the number of objects that would represent their assigned number. Then, over a period of time, ask the entire class to assist in writing a poem to go along with the illustrations, as was done by Mr. Sullivan in *Numbers at Play*. When all the illustrations and poems have been completed, put them together in a booklet.

2. In the author's note at the end of the book, Mr. Sullivan, the author, said he likes to get letters from readers of his books telling him what they liked or

disliked. As a group, write a letter to Mr. Sullivan telling him what they thought about his *Numbers at Play* book, and also suggest some other photographs/paintings that he could use to illustrate the numbers 1 to 10 or higher.

3. Ask the children to look at each illustration to find other objects that could represent a number other than the objects pointed out by the author. For example, in William Henry Johnson's illustration entitled "Soapbox Racing," you could count the wheels (3) and make a poem about them, instead of counting the children (6).

4. Ask the children to look at pictures around the school, at home, in magazines, and so forth, and try to find objects in the pictures to count. A game could then be played by having the children bring in pictures to show the class and saying, "What do I see five of in this picture?" Allow time for the children to share their pictures and count objects.

Discussion Questions

1. Which painting/photograph do you think best represents the number it is intended to represent?

2. Do you like this kind of counting book? Why or why not?

3. If you were writing a counting book, how would you do it?

4. In which painting/photograph was it the most difficult to find the number of objects you were looking for?

Title: *The Right Number of Elephants*

Genre: Picture Book

Author: Jeff Sheppard

Illustrator: Felicia Bond

Bibliographic Information: Scholastic, Inc., New York, 1992.

Summary: This is a cleverly written book that counts backwards from 10 to 1 using elephants as the main characters.

Interest Level: Grades K–2.

Pre-Reading Activity

Ask the children the questions on the back of the book—How many elephants would you need to pull a train out of a tunnel and save everyone on board? To paint a ceiling? To escape a summer storm? Write their answers on the chalkboard and then compare them with what the book says.

Learning Activities

1. As a group, write a continuation of *The Right Number of Elephants* story using numerals 11 to 20. Assign groups to illustrate each of the numbers. Then compile the pages into a book for the class to read.

2. Make available other counting backwards books, such as *Ten, Nine, Eight* by Molly Bang or *10 Bears in My Bed* by Stan Mack. Allow time for the children to compare and contrast the book(s) with *The Right Number of Elephants.*

3. Make available the words to the song "The Twelve Days of Christmas." If possible, make one or more of the following books available as an aid: *The Twelve Days of Christmas* by June Williams; *The Twelve Days of Christmas* by Brian Wildsmith; *The Twelve Days of Christmas* by Jack Kent. Sing the song and then discuss the concept of counting backwards as a count down for a special event.

4. As a follow-up to Activity 3 use the concept of counting down from a number (10 to 1) to count down for a special event such as a holiday, class party, or field trip. For example, if the class is having a party, you could plan the party by days. (For example, on the tenth day before the party we make invitations, on the ninth day we send invitations, on the eighth day we plan the food we will have, on the seventh day we decide who will bring what, and so on.)

Discussion Questions

1. Did you like this story? Why or why not?

2. Which of the tasks that the elephants did do you think could really happen?

3. Which of the tasks that the elephants did do you think couldn't really happen?

4. What is something some elephants might help you to do? How many elephants would you need?

Title: *Stay In Line*

Genre: Picture Book

Author: Teddy Slater

Illustrator: Gioia Fiammenghi

Bibliographic Information: Scholastic Inc., New York, 1996.

Summary: Twelve children on a class trip to the zoo have fun grouping themselves into lines of different sizes.

Interest Level: Preschool-Grade K–2.

Pre-Reading Activity

Ask twelve children to form one straight line. Then ask the children how else they may line up. For example, six rows of two children. Allow time for them to demonstrate other ways of lining up (4 rows of 3; 1 row of 9, and 1 row of 3, etc).

Learning Activities

1. Provide the children with kernels of corn, beans, or pieces of macaroni. Tell them to divide the pieces into piles of 12. Ask them to show how many different ways two children could divide 12 between them. Using the twelve cookies as an example, Victoria could have had eight cookies and Sam four, or Sam could have had 11 cookies and Victoria one. Tell them to lay out the different combinations of 12 pieces of corn, beans, or macaroni and then write the number problem it represents, that is, $8 + 4 = 12$, $11 + 1 = 12$.

2. Discuss that twelve objects are often referred to as a dozen. Challenge the students to find objects for which there is one dozen—pack of sodas, eggs, girls or boys in the class, letters in their names, etc. Tell them for one week to record all items for which they see or have a dozen of. Allow time to share lists. If there are more than a dozen in a set of things, tell them to record the dozen with number left over—e.g. 1 dozen plus 6 dinner forks.

3. In this book, different ways of grouping 12 children was presented. For example, three rows of four, six rows of two, and so forth. Provide the children with twelve objects each and then ask them to divide them evenly into groups. Allow time to share the different ways the children grouped their objects.

4. *Stay In Line* by Teddy Slater is one of the *Hello math reader series*. Obtain other books in this series to help your students learn math skills in a fun way.

Discussion Questions

1. The title of the book we just read is *Stay In Line*. What different lines have you been in? For example, at the movies, grocery, bank, cafeteria, and so forth.

2. Why is it usually important that people stay in a straight line when lining up?

3. What is the best part of being in a line? Worst part?

4. Most lines are one person behind the next person and so on. When might people line up by twos, threes, fours, etc?

CULMINATING ACTIVITY

The culminating activity will consist of a variety of activities that involve using numbers. The children may do all or some of the following activities based on their level of ability.

1. Have the children spend an entire day without using numbers. For example, cover the clocks, remove watches, do not refer to page numbers for assignments, etc. Discuss how they felt the day went.

2. Play as many games as possible that require counting and/or using numbers—for example, "Mother, May I," where they have to take three steps forward, or six hops backward, etc.

3. Give directions using ordinal positions instead of names—for example, "Will the third person in the row open the door?"

4. Ask the children to write the largest number they can write and read correctly on a slip of paper, put their names on it, fold it and put it in a designated box. Pull each slip of paper from the box and call on the person who wrote the slip to read it. The child with the largest correct number can win a prize.

5. Ask the children to select a number to use as the focus of an illustration. For example, an 8 could become a snowman. Allow time to share.

SUPPLEMENTAL LITERATURE

Books

Aker, S. (1980). *What comes in 2's, 3's, and 4's?* Illustrated by Bernie Karlin. New York: Scholastic.
A simple, delightful book that shows what comes in 2's—2 eyes, 2 ears. What comes in 3's—3 meals a day, 3 sizes—small, medium, large. What comes in 4's—wheels on a wagon, 4 legs on a table.

Allbright, V. (1985). *Ten* go *hopping.* London: Faber and Faber.
One little boy goes hopping and he is followed in turn by a grasshopper, a mouse, a frog, a rabbit, a cat, a dog, a monkey, a kangaroo, and an elephant.

Anno, M. (1982). *Anno's math games II.* New York: Philomel Books.
Anno uses simple activities, picture puzzles, and games to introduce the mathematical concepts of multiplication, sequence, measurement, ordinal numbering, and direction.

Anno, M. (1995). *Anno's magic seed.* New York: Philomel Books.
The reader of this book is asked to perform a series of mathematical operations integrated into the story of a lazy man who plants magic seeds and reaps an abundant harvest.

Atherlay, S. (1996). *Math in the bath.* Illustrated by Megan Halsey.
This book encourages children to look for math and math elements in the most unexpected places.

Bohdal, S. (1997). *1,2,3 what do you see: An animal counting book.* New York: North-South Books.
This is a counting book in which a freckle-faced girl gives whimsical gifts to groups of animals, from one elephant to ten butterflies.

Brimner, L .D. (1997). *How many ants?* New York: Children Press.
Ants increase by multiples of ten as they march up the hill toward a tall cake.

Calino. (1997). *123 caterpillar.* New York: Abbeville Publishing.
This is a fold-out picture book that features an ever-growing caterpillar on one side—and cars of a train on the other side. It teaches children how to count from one to ten.

Falwell, C. (1993). *Feast for 10.* New York: Clarion.
>   Numbers 1 to 10 are used to show how members of a family shop and work together to prepare a meal.

Fisher, L. E. (1982). *Number act.* New York: Four Winds Press.
>   Portrays how numerals have looked in the past and how they look in other cultures.

Giganti, P. (1988). *How many snails: a counting book.* New York: Greenwillow Books.
>   The author takes walks to various places, such as the lake, the beach, the garden, and so forth. Each time he gets to a different place, he wonders about the things he sees in each place and their different characteristics.

Helman, A. (1996). *123 moose: A pacific northwest counting book.* New York: Scholastic.
>   This book introduces the numbers one through twenty against a background of photographs and brief text describing animal and plant life in the Pacific Northwest.

Hoban, T. (1987). *26 letters and 99 cents.* New York: Greenwillow Books.
>   Color photographs of letters, numbers, coins, and common objects introduce the alphabet, coinage, and counting systems.

Lottridge, C. B. (1986). *One watermelon seed.* Toronto, Canada: Oxford University Press.
>   Two children plant a garden with several seeds and plants. They water and weed and finally end up with many fruits and vegetables to pick. This book provides an opportunity for children to count from 1 to 10, as well as 10 to 100.

Maestro, B., & Maestro, G. (1989). *Harriet goes to the circus.* New York: Crown.
>   Harriet tries to be first in line to get into the circus. One-by-one her animal friends line up behind her. However, the entrance to the circus tent is at the other end of the line. Everyone turns around and now Harriet is last in line. This book provides a good introduction to ordinal numbers.

Medaris, A. S. (1996). *The 100th day of school.* Illustrated by Joan Holub. New York: Cartwheel Books.
>   This book is designed to help build reading and counting skills. It contains one hundred spelling words and punch-out flash cards.

Merriam, E. (1993). *12 ways to get to 11.* Illustrated by Bernie Karlin. New York: Simon & Schuster.
>   This book presents twelve humorous double spreads that depict dozens of objects and take young readers on an adventure-filled counting trip.

Pinczes, E. (1998). *Arctic fives arrive.* New York: Scholastic Publication, Inc.
>   This book uses a variety of Arctic animals to count by fives—forward and backward.

Pinczes, E. (1993). *One hundred hungry arts.* Illustrated by Bonnie MacKain. Boston: Houghton Mifflin.

One hundred hungry ants start out for a picnic but stop to change their line formation, which shows different divisions of 100. However, they lose both time and food in the end.

Simon, L., & Bendick, J. (1963). *The day the numbers disappeared.* New York: Whittlesey.

This book, which is appropriate for grades K–6, allows the reader to sense the importance of the number system to our everyday lives.

MINI-THEMES

Addition and Subtraction

One of the first steps children need to take prior to actually doing the operations of adding and subtracting is learning the basic facts. By using the facts, plus an understanding of place value and mathematical properties, children will be able to successfully perform addition or subtraction problems. Create an environment of stimulating and interesting math activities and related books such as those provided in this unit.

Activities

1. Assign the children a number such as 10 and ask them to write out as many combinations as possible that add up to 10 (i.e. $4 + 6 = 10$, $2 + 8 = 10$, etc.). Allow time to share their equations. Continue this process using other numbers.

2. Collect as many of the recommended books for this unit as possible. Ask the children to select one of the books, such as *Counting Wildflowers* by Bruce McMillan, *Each Orange Had 8 Slices* by Paul Giganti, Jr., or *The Great Take-Away* by Louise Mathews, and to create at least one addition or subtraction story problem that relates to the book. For example, a problem for *The Great Take Away* might be the following: There were 10 ladies wearing necklaces at the masquerade party. After the robber pig left, only two ladies had necklaces. How many necklaces did the pig steal? Allow time to share books and problems.

3. As a group, write a story that involves giving away (subtracting) something (toys, pets, etc.). For example, it could be a story about a little old man who has 15 cats. He gives 2 cats to one neighbor. Now he has 13 cats. Next, his grandchild comes for a visit and she takes a cat. Now he has 12 cats. Continue the story until there are no cats.

References

Barner, B. (1995). *Too many dinosaurs.* New York: Bantam Doubleday Dell Publications.

Brenner, B. (1989). *Annie's pet.* New York: Byron Preiss Visual Productions.

de Paola, T. (1989). *Too many hopkins.* New York: G. P. Putnam's & Son.

Dunbar, J. (1990). *Ten little mice.* Illustrated by Maria Majewska. San Diego, CA: Harcourt Brace Jovanovich.

Giganti, P., Jr. (1992). *Each orange had 8 slices: A counting book.* Illustrated by Donald Crews. New York: Greenwillow Books.

Gisler, D. (1991). *Addition Annie.* Illustrated by Tom Dunnington. Chicago: Children's Press.

Hulme, J. N. (1996). *Sea sums.* Illustrated by C. Swartz. New York: Hyperion Books for Children.

Long, L. (1998). *Dealing with addition.* New York: Charlesbridge Publications.

Mathews, L. (1980). *The great take-away.* New York: Dodd, Mead.

McMillan, B. (1986). *Counting wildflowers.* New York: Lothrop, Lee, and Shepard.

Murphy, S .J. (1997). *Elevator magic.* Illustrated by G. Brian Karas. New York: HarperCollins.

Samton, S. W. (1997). *Ten tiny monsters: A superbly scary story of subtraction.* Brown Publishing.

Schade, S., & Butler, J. (1991). *Hello! Hello!* New York: Simon & Schuster.

Sturges, P. (1995). *Ten flashing fireflies.* New York: North-South Books, Inc.

Toft, K. M. (1998). *One less fish.* Illustrated by Allan Sheather. New York: Charlesbridge Publishing.

Walsh, E. S. (1991). *Mouse count.* New York: Harcourt Brace Jovanovich.

Money

Children often become involved with money prior to coming to school, although they do not recognize or understand the value of it. It is through a variety of experiences that children will learn to value money and use it correctly. Provide the children with as many real-life situations as possible in which money is used.

Activities

1. Many communities have a recycling program in which you get paid for recycling bottles, cans, newspapers, etc. As a group, investigate to find out what is available and then begin a class collection. Project how much money your class could make in a month and what you could buy with that amount.

2. Ask the children to identify something they would really like to have but do not have enough money to buy it. Next, tell them to find out exactly how much it would cost and to devise a plan for earning enough money to buy what they want. Finally, have the children implement their plan and keep a record of their progress. To initiate this activity, read *Dollars and Cents for Harriet* by Betsy and Giulio Maestro.

3. Provide children with some mail order catalogs or grocery ads from the newspapers. Divide the children into groups and tell them they have $50 to spend. Ask each group to make a list of things they would buy that will add up to no more than $50.

4. Set up a pretend restaurant or grocery store in which pretend money is used. Children can play different roles—waiter, waitress, customer, cashier, etc. A book such as Tana Hoban's *26 Letters and 99 Cents* could provide a useful resource for understanding different combinations of money.

References

Barabos, K. (1997). *Let's find out about money.* New York: Scholastic Publishing.

Brisson, P. (1995). *Benny's pennies.* Illustrated by Bob Barner. New York: Books for Young Readers.

Butler, D. H. (1997). *The great tooth fairy rip-off.* Illustrated by Jack Lindstrom. Minneapolis, MN: Fairview Press.

Godfrey, N. S. (1995). *Here's the scoop. Follow an ice-cream cone around the world.* New York: Silver Press.

Hoban, T. (1987). *26 letters and 99 cents.* New York: Greenwillow Books.

Kimmel, E. A. (1989). *Four dollars and fifty cents.* New York: Holiday House.

Maestro, B., & Maestro, G. (1988). *Dollars and cents for Harriet.* New York: Crown.

Schwartz, D. M. (1989). *If you made a million.* New York: Lothrop, Lee, & Shepard.

Shields, C. D. (1995) *Lunch money and other poems about school.* Illustrated by Paul Meisel. New York: Dutton's Children's Books.

Smith, M. (1994). *Argo you lucky dog.* New York: Lothrop Lee & Shepard.

Trapani, I. (1997). *How much is the doggie in the window?* New York: Whiserping Coyote Publishing.

Wells, R. (1997). *Bunny money.* New York: Dial Books for Young Children.

Measurement and Sizes

OVERVIEW

Focus

Student will become familiar with the various aspects of measurement and how it relates to mathematics.

Objectives

On completion of this thematic unit, students will:

1. Recognize that measurement is important in their everyday life.
2. Be aware that measurement can be used in all aspects of life.
3. Learn about a variety of measurement tools (rulers, clocks, thermometers, scales, etc.).
4. Learn how measurement tools are used.

HOW IT WORKS

Initiating Activity

Brainstorm, with the children, vocabulary that relates to size such as, enormous, huge, tiny, etc. List these words on the chalkboard. Then discuss different kinds of measurement that helps determine size, i.e. weight, height, length, etc. Create a "Measurement Center" and provide the children with an opportunity to experiment with different types of measurement tools by providing a scales, tape measure/yard stick, etc.

General Activities

1. Divide the children into groups. Give each group the same size object, i.e. a piece of paper, a chalkboard eraser, a pencil, etc., or allow each group to select their own object. Then ask the group to find five objects that are larger than their selected object and five objects that are smaller. Make a display of each groups collections and discuss.

2. Using the objects collected in Activity 1, ask each group to put their objects in order from smallest to largest according to the same criteria such as height, weight, thickness, etc.

3. Provide the children with large sheets of paper and then ask them to draw a picture of their families in the order of their sizes. Allow time to share.

4. Read books from the Supplemental Literature list such as *Big Gus and Little Gus* by Lee Lorenz or *Revenge of the Small Small* by Jean Little. Then have the children discuss advantages and disadvantages of being small and/or big.

5. Explain that people originally used their body parts to measure things. Have the children create their own measurement tools by tracing around their foot or hand and cutting it out. Tell the children to use their "body part" measuring tool to measure the width of their desk, height of a friend, length of an arm, etc. Prior to measuring, ask the children to estimate the height, width, length, etc. of what they are measuring. You may want to have the children record their different measurements as follows:

OBJECT	ESTIMATE	ACTUAL MEASUREMENT

6. Provide the children with a metric and non-metric ruler. Allow them to measure objects, using both rulers. Discuss the difference between the two rulers and the reason for having two measuring systems.

7. Provide the children with at least four containers of different sizes, i.e., tall and thin, short and fat. Ask them which container holds the most, which holds the least and so on. After they have made their estimates, allow time for them to fill the container they think holds the most with water, rice, sand, etc. Then tell them to test their other estimates by pouring the water, rice, or sand into the other containers.

8. Using the vocabulary words related to size that were generated in the Initiating Activity, brainstorm things that are enormous, huge, tiny, etc. You might want to divide the class into groups and assign each group to brainstorm among themselves and complete and illustrate the following statement: "Enormous is . . ." Their responses could be put together to make a class book.

9. Provide a balance scale and ask the children to put an object on one side of the scale, i.e. a small rock. Tell the children to find another object they feel would weigh about the same as the small rock, put it on the scale to check if they were correct or not. Continue this activity with children finding balancing objects. Discuss the concept that size may not be a factor in whether the scale balances or not, i.e. a big ball of cotton or pile of feathers compared to a smaller rock.

10. Provide a copy of the most recently published *Guiness Book of World Records*. Ask the children to find out such things as the heaviest and lightest animal, tallest building, shortest person, etc. Allow time to share their findings.

Discussion Questions

1. What is the biggest object you have ever seen? Describe it.

2. What is the smallest object you have ever seen? Describe it.

3. Over the years, many tools have been developed to measure various things—time, weight, etc. What are some of these tools? Which of these tools is most important to you?

4. When you hear the word measure, what do you think about?

LITERATURE RELATED ACTIVITIES

Title: *Tiny for a Day*

Genre: Picture Book

Author: Dick Gackenbach

Bibliographic Information: Clarion Books, New York, 1993.

Summary: Sidney has a new invention that he uses to shrink things. He shrinks the dog, his sister, and finally himself.

Interest Level: Grades K–3

Pre-Reading Activity

Read the title of the book and show the children the cover. Discuss the concept of tiny. Ask the children to name things that are tiny as you list them on the board. Remind them that tiny can be relative to what it is being compared to. For example, a fish may not be tiny but when compared to a whale, it is tiny. Ask the children to fold a piece of paper in half and on each half draw something tiny (fish) and something large (whale).

Learning Activities

1. Sidney shrank his sister, his dog, as well as himself. He came out of his machine being only three inches tall. Use a ruler to identify other things that are three inches tall and compare them to the height of Sidney.

2. Discuss with the children the advantages and disadvantages of being tall. Of being short. Make a list of these and then ask the children to write a story about either being short or being tall. Allow time to share stories.

3. Sidney was only three inches tall after he shrank himself. Provide a yard stick and allow time to measure the height of all children in the class. Record the children's height on a growth chart. Measure children each month and compare heights from previous months.

4. Help the children make a tiny book by cutting 3" x 3" pieces of paper for the pages. Ask the children to draw something tiny on their piece of paper and write the sentence, "This is a tiny _____." Compile the pages into a class booklet titled, "Our Tiny Book." Share the book with other classes.

Discussion Questions

1. What events of this story could really happen? Which events are make-believe?

2. What are some things Sidney could do when he was short that he couldn't do when he was taller?

3. What would your mother say if you did things like Sidney did?

4. Would you like to be Sidney's friend? Why or why not?

5. Do you think Sidney liked being small?

Title: *Little Grunt and the Big Egg*

Genre:	Fairy Tale
Author:	Tomie de Paola
Bibliographic Information:	Holiday House, New York, 1990.
Summary:	Little Grunt, the smallest member of the Grunt Tribe is sent out to gather eggs. He finds a very large egg and brings it home. Later that night, the egg hatches and out comes a dinosaur. Mama and Papa Grunt allows Little Grunt to keep the dinosaur as a pet until it grows too big for the cave.
Interest Level:	Grades K–3

Pre-Reading Activity

Read the title of the book, *Little Grunt and the Big Egg*, and show the children the cover of the book. Ask the children to predict what they think the book will be about. Write the predictions on the chalkboard and then compare the predictions with what actually happened in the story.

Learning Activities

1. At the beginning of the story there is a picture of all the members of the Grunt Tribe. Ask the children to draw a picture of the grunt tribe in which they are put in order from largest to smallest. Tell them to label the pictures, Unca Grunt, Ant Grunt, Granny Grunt, Mama Grunt, Papa Grunt, Chief Rockhead Grunt and Little Grunt.

2. In this story the Grunts called George a Tyrannosauros Rex which was a huge dinosaur that lived during the prehistoric times. Tell the children to look through a dinosaur book such as, *Dinosaurs, Dinosaurs* by Byron Barton (New York: Crowell, 1989) to determine the size of some of the largest and smallest dinosaurs. Two dinosaur books, *The Smallest Dinosaurs* by Seymour Simon and *A Gallery of Dinosaurs and Other Early Reptiles* by D. Peters are also listed in the supplemental literature.

3. There were many very large dinosaurs that lived during prehistoric times. Ask the children to name some animals that are living today that they

consider to be large animals, i.e. elephants, hippopotamus, giraffes, etc. Next, categorize these animals by those that are the heaviest, tallest, biggest, etc.

4. Little Grunt went hunting for eggs and found a large dinosaur egg. It was too big for him to carry so he wove a mat, put the egg on it, and pulled it home. As a group, brainstorm some other ways in which Little Grunt could have gotten the egg home.

Discussion Questions

1. How do you think Little Grunt felt about being the smallest of the Grunt Tribe?

2. The older Grunts kept saying that "a nice little cockroach" would make a good pet. Why did they say this?

3. What would have happened to the Grunt Tribe if George, the dinosaur, hadn't rescued them from the volcano?

4. What do you think the Grunts will do with all the baby dinosaurs?

Title: *The Best Bug Parade*

Genre: Informational Book

Author: Stuart J. Murphy

Illustrator: Holly Keller

Bibliographic Information: HarperCollins Publishing, New York, 1996.

Summary: The author introduces the reader to the relativity of size. The concept of big and bigger, of small and smaller, introduced by using examples to show how these words make sense only when two or more objects are compared.

Interest Level: Grades K–3

Pre-Reading Activity

Discuss the concept of big and small. Ask the children to name some things that are big. List these on the chalkboard. Then ask them to name some things that are small. List these on the chalkboard. Ask them how they know that the things they said are big are big and the things they said are small are small. Read the book and then review this activity to see if they still agree with what they said.

Learning Activities

1. Provide a large sheet of paper for the children to draw some bugs. Ask them to cut out their bugs and then arrange them in order of size from small to big.

2. Write the words long, longer, longest, short, shorter, shortest on 3 x 5 index cards. Then provide a beanbag for children to toss. Using the index cards, ask the children to place cards where the beanbags landed as long,

longer, longest, short, shorter, and shortest. As a group, discuss if everyone agrees with where cards are placed.

3. There are advantages and disadvantages to being a big person, as well as being a small person. Put the statements, "I would like to be big because . . ." and "I would like to be small because . . ." on the chalkboard. As a group, brainstorm and make two lists on the chalkboard in response to these two statements.

4. Tell the children to fold a sheet of paper in half four times to make four boxes. Tell them to draw something that is long in the first box, short in the second box, big in the third box, and small in the fourth box. Allow time to share.

Discussion Questions

1. How can you tell if something is big? (by comparing it to something else) How can you tell if something is small? (by comparing it to something else)

2. What advantage do you think a short bug has to a long bug? A long bug to a short bug?

3. What is the smallest living animal you have ever seen?

4. What is the largest living animal you have ever seen?

Title: *Paul Bunyan*

Genre:	Legend
Author:	Steven Kellogg
Bibliographic Information:	William Morrow & Co., New York, 1984.
Summary:	This story tells about a lumberjack, Paul Bunyan, whose unusual size and strength brought him many fantastic adventures. He and his big, blue ox, Babe, did many extraordinary things such as, fought the wild Gumberoos in the Appalachians, dug out the Great Lakes and St. Lawrence River, gouged a trench we call the Grand Canyon and so forth.
Interest Level:	Grades K–4

Pre-Reading Activity

Read the first page and show the illustrations to the children. It says "Paul was the largest, smartest, and strongest baby ever born in the state of Maine." Brainstorm, with the children, other vocabulary words that mean the same as large. For example, huge, big, giant, etc. List these on the chalkboard. Ask the children to share one thing that they think is large.

Learning Activities

1. Paul Bunyan was very large and strong. Brainstorm with the children about other stories in which a character is very large and strong. For example, the giant in Jack and the Beanstalk. List all of these characters on the chalkboard. Then ask the children to select one of these characters that they liked best and to tell why they selected that character.

2. Tell the children to look closely at the signs that are posted throughout the illustrations. Have the children pretend that Paul Bunyan is coming to their community. Ask them to create a sign for his visit. Display signs. Discuss what changes would need to be made to accommodate his size.

3. Paul Bunyan and his men traveled from Maine to California. Using a United States map, help the children trace a route they may have followed. Remember that they went through the Appalachian Mountains, the Great Plains, Rocky Mountains, Texas, and Arizona. Once they have traced the imaginary route, discuss the different time zones they would have gone through. Discuss what forms of transportation would be available for someone the size of Paul Bunyan.

4. Ask the children to write a short story about all the things they would be able to do if they were large and strong like Paul Bunyan.

5. Duplicate and distribute a copy of Literature Log II (Chapter 2, p. 61) and ask the children to complete it. After they have completed the log, allow them to get together in pairs or small groups to discuss them.

Discussion Questions

1. Why did Paul's parents move to the backwoods? (Answers may vary but might include because too many people complained about Paul and life would be more peaceful).

2. What were some of the problems Paul encountered on his trip west? (Answers may vary but might include being ambushed by a gang of Gumberoos, being able to make enough flapjacks to feed his crew, a great blizzard, etc).

3. Would you have liked to travel with Paul? Why or why not? (Answers may vary).

4. What is the most extraordinary or unusual thing Paul did? (Answers may vary).

CULMINATING ACTIVITY

Divide the children into groups of 4 or 5. Tell them they are going on a "Measuring Scavenger Hunt." Give them a copy of the following and allow two or three days for them to collect the information as a team. Allow time to share, compare and defend their findings. The children with the most accurate answers are the winners.

1. Height of tallest building in your community _____.
2. Height of tallest building in the United States _____.

3. Number of miles to the nearest grocery store from your school _____.
4. Number of miles to the nearest beach from your school _____.
5. The person who weighs the most in the United States _____.
6. The person who weighs the least in the United States _____.
7. The person who is the tallest in the United States _____.
8. The person who is the shortest in the United States _____.
9. The amount of time it takes for the earth to revolve around the sun _____.
10. The coldest temperature it has ever been in your community _____.
11. The hottest temperature it has ever been in your community _____.
12. The day of the week on which the President was born _____.
13. The season that most people in your class like best _____.
14. The time of the day that the first space ship was launched _____.
15. The month when most people in your class were born _____.

SUPPLEMENTAL LITERATURE

Books

Baker, Alan. (1990). *Two tiny mice*. New York: Dial Books.
Two small mice explore their environment, observing many different sized animals before finally going home to sleep in their tiny nest.

Barton, B. (1998). *Dinosaurs, dinosaurs*. New York: Crowell.
All kinds of dinosaurs—from big to small, horned to armored, long necked, and long tailed are detailed in this wonderful introduction to the world of dinosaurs.

Bennett, J. (1986). *Teeny tiny*. Illustrated by Tomie de Paola. New York: Putnam.
Retells the tale of the teeny-tiny woman who finds a teeny-tiny bone in a churchyard and puts it away in her cupboard before she goes to sleep.

Challoner, J. (1996). *Big and small*. New York: Raintree/Steck Vaughn.
Provides an introduction to the concept of size. The book describes how sizes are measured and compares sizes of such things plants, buildings and so forth.

Cremins, R. (1997) *African animal giants: A national geographic action book*. Illustrated by James M. Dietz. New York: National Geographic Society.
Young readers can enjoy a richly illustrated pop-up safari to observe the large animals and other huge animals.

Cuyler, M. (1998). *The biggest, best snowman*. Illustrated by Will Hillenbrand. New York: Scholastic Trade.
Little Nell feels intimidated by her family of big people and feels she is too small to do anything, until, with the help of her friends. She builds a great big snowman.

Damjan, M. (1998). *The big squirrel and the little rhinoceros*. Illustrated by Hans Debeer. New York: North South Book.

Three big animals—the rhinoceros, lion, and crocodile—make life difficult for three little animals—the squirrel, mouse, and frog. One morning the little animals' dreams come true—they become big while they are small. They all learn a lesson and learn to live together peacefully.

Henkes, K. (1995). *The biggest boy*. Illustrated by Nancy Tafuri. New York: Greenwillow.

Encouraged by his parent's statements that he is a big boy and getting bigger everyday, Billy lets his imagination run free and is transformed into the biggest boy in the world.

Jenkins, S. (1998). *Big and little*. Boston, MA: Houghton Mifflin Co.

This book illustrates the concept of size by comparing different animals, from the smallest animals to the largest.

Little, J. (1992). *Revenge of the Small Small*. Illustrated by Janet Wilson. New York: Penguin Group.

Patsy Small, the youngest in her family, tells about the perils of being the smallest in the family. At the end, however, the bigger Smalls apologize and repent.

Lorenz, L. (1982). *Big Gus and little Gus*. Englewood Cliffs, NJ: Prentice-Hall, Inc.

Two friends, one big and one little, go out to explore the world and to seek their fortunes. Big Gus is rewarded despite his foolishness.

Mangan, A. (1998). *The smallest bear*. Illustrated by Joanne Moss. New York: Crocodile Books.

Browny, a bear, is unable to do some of the things his bigger friends can do and feels rejected. But with the help of another small friend, Browny discovers a new opportunity and realizes that it is OK to be just as he is.

Mollel, T. M. (1995). *Big boy*. Illustrated by E. B. Lewis. New York: Clarion Books.

Little Oli wants to be big enough to go bird hunting with his brother but has to take a nap instead.

Peters, D. (1989). *A gallery of dinosaurs and other early reptiles*. New York: Knopf.

The emphasis in this book is on size.

Samton, S. W. (1997). *Ten tiny monsters: A superbly scary story of subtraction*. New York: Crown Publishing.

Ten tiny monsters try to make the Master Monster's team by finding something tinier then they are and making that animal scream with fright.

Simon, S. (1982). *The smallest dinosaurs*. New York: Brown.

This book presents seven small members of the Coelursauria, or hollow, lizard family.

Sweat, L. (1993). *The smallest stegosaurus*. Illustrated by Louis Phillips. New York: Viking.

Although he is small and sometimes afraid of the other bigger dinosaurs, a young Stegosaurus finds a way to help his family.

MINI-THEMES

Time

Time of occurrence and length of duration are two attributes of events that can be measured. To describe time of occurrence, you can give a time span such as, "it happened last night" or "it happened in September." For this, the children need to become familiar with the vocabulary and concept of days, months, seasons, etc. which are presented in two of the mini units in this section.

Length of duration can be described by discussing such things as, "How long did it take you to walk to school?" or "Which is longer, the hours you sleep at night or the time you are in school?" This mini unit is intended to help children become more familiar with telling time, the concept of time which leads to being able to measure length of duration.

Activities

1. Often people say, "I'll be ready in a minute" or "It will only take a minute." Tell the children to think about how long a minute is and what are some things they could do in a minute. Using a minute hand, time a minute. Then ask the children to tell you all the things they could *and* could not do in a minute. Make a list of these and then, as a class, write a story about "I could do _____ in a minute, but I couldn't do _____ in a minute." Illustrate the pages. This would be a good time to read the book, *Just a Minute!* by Anita Harper.

2. Read the book, *Bat Time* by Ruth Horowitz. In this book, Leila and her father like the night time because Leila likes to watch for the fluttering bats as they come to have their insect feast. Discuss with the children things they like to do at night time, morning time, etc.

3. Discuss that, as time goes by, people and things get older. Also, as time goes by, people are able to do different things. Read books such as *Old Bear* by Jane Hissey or *The Man Who Wanted to Live Forever* by Selina Hastings. Decide on different ages—2 years old, 6 years old, 16 years old, etc.—and then brainstorm things people of these ages can do and can't do. Finally, have the children identify a time in life they would most like to be in and to explain why.

4. Read the book, *Around the Clock with Harriet* by Betsy and Giulio Maestro which tells what Harriet does from the time she gets up (8:00 a.m.) until she goes to bed (8:00 p.m.). Tell the children to draw a clock showing the time of day for each activity they do and describe what they do. See sample clock on p. 245.

5. Directions for making a model clock can be found in *Projects with Time* by John Williams on page 5. Help children construct clocks and then do numerous activities with setting the clock at designated times.

Sample Clock for
Activity 4

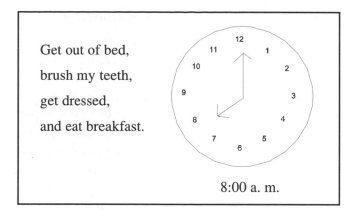

Get out of bed,

brush my teeth,

get dressed,

and eat breakfast.

8:00 a. m.

References

Conboym, F. (1997). *Forgetful Ted.* Illustrated by Jonathan Lambert. New York: Barrons Juvenile.

Fleischman, P. (1991). *Time train.* Illustrations by Claire Ewart. New York: Charlotte Zolotow Book.

Harper, A. (1987). *Just a minute.* Illustrations by Susan Hellard. New York: G. P. Putnam's Sons.

Harper, D. (1998). *Telling time with big mama cat.* Illustrated by Barry & Cara Moser. San Diego, CA: Harcourt Brace.

Hastings, S. (1988). *The man who wanted to live forever.* Illustrations by Reg Cartwright. New York: Henry Holt.

Hissey, J. (1986). *Old bear.* New York: Philomel Books.

Horowitz, R. (1991). *Bat time.* Illustrations by Susan Avishai. New York: Macmillan Publishing Co.

Hutchins, P. (1994). *Clocks & more clocks.* New York: MacMillan.

Jennings, T. (1988). *Junior science time.* New York: Gloucester Press.

Maestro, B., & G. (1984). *Around the clock with Harriet.* New York: Crown Publishing.

Milne, A. A. (1998). *Pooh's first clock.* Illustrated by Ernest H. Shepard. New York: Dutton Books.

Mueller, V. (1997). *Monster goes to school.* Illustrated by Lynn Munsinger. Morton Grove, IL: Albert Whitman & Co.

Paine, P. C. (1990). *Time for Horatio.* Santa Barbara, CA: Advocacy Press.

Scarry, R., & Deesing, J. (1997). *Richard Scarry's pop-up time.* New York: Little Simon.

Taber, A. (1993). *The boy who stopped time.* New York: Macmillan Publishing.

Williams, J. (1992). *Projects with time.* Illustrations by Malcom Walker. Milwaukee, WI: Gareth Stevens Children's Books.

Months and Seasons

A month is a way of recording a specific number of days. Months also relate to seasons—fall, winter, spring, and summer. Children will enjoy learning more about the months of the year and the seasons through reading the recommended books and participating in the activities designed for this mini unit.

Activities

1. Read some of the recommended books for this unit to the children. Then ask the children to select their favorite season of the year, estimate the time and length of the season, and write a brief story explaining that they like about the season they selected. Tell the children to make an illustration to accompany their story. Compile stories into a class book.

2. Read *Clementine's Winter Wardrobe* by Kate Spohn. Discuss the different types of clothes Clementine selected for her winter wardrobe. Then divide the children into three groups—a spring group, a summer group, and a fall group. Then tell each group to create a "Clementine's *(assigned season)* Wardrobe Story. Allow time to share.

3. Introduce the book, *Then and Now* by Stan Ockenga. This book puts together an array of real and literary characters and events for each month. As a group, create a similar type book about members of your class and community, as well as popular people, objects, and events the children want to include. Share the completed book with other classes and the community.

4. Help the children write a rhyming verse for the month you are currently in. To motivate them for this activity, read *Alligator and Others All Year Long* by Crescent Dragonwagon. The author of this book writes a rhyme for each month. After the children have written the rhyme for the current month, divide them into eleven groups and assign each group a remaining month for which to write a rhyme. Allow time to share.

5. Make a birthday chart by charting the children's birthdays for each month of the year.

6. Ask the children to select their favorite month and explain why it is their favorite.

References

Baxter, N. (1996). *Autumn*. Illustrated by Kim Wooley. New York: Children's Press.

Berenstain, S., & Berenstain, J. (1996). *The Berenstain bears four seasons*. New York: Random House.

Bowen, B. (1995). *Antler, bear, canoe: A northwoods alphabet year*. Boston, MA: Little Brown & Co.

Branley, F. M. (1985). *Sunshine makes the seasons*. Illustrations by Guilio Maestro. New York: Thomas Crowell.

Carle, E. (1998). *Stories for all seasons: Rooster's off to see the world, a house for hermit crab, the tiny seed*. New York: Simon & Schuster.

Dragonwagon, C. (1993). *Alligators and others all year long: A book of months*. Illustrations by Jose Aruega and Ariana Dewey. New York: Macmillan Publishing.

Fuchs, D. M. (1995). *A bear for all seasons*. Illustrated by Kathryn Brown. New York: Henry Holt & Co.

Gerstein, M. (1993). *The story of May*. New York: HarperCollins Publishing.

Good, E. W. (1987). *That's what happens when it's spring.* Illustrations by Susie Shenk. Intercourse, PA: Good Books.

Hirschi, R. (1990). *Winter.* Illustrations by D. Mangelsen. New York: Cobblehill Books.

Hirschi, R. (1990). *Spring.* Illustrations by D. Mangelsen. New York: Cobblehill Books.

Hirschi, R. (1990). *Summer.* Illustrations by D. Mangelsen. New York: Cobblehill Books.

Lotz, K. E. (1993). *Can't sit still.* Illustrated by Colleen Browning. New York: Dutton Children's Press.

Maass, R. (1990). *When autumn comes.* New York: Henry Holt and Company.

Ockenga, S. (1990). *Then and now: A book of days.* Boston, MA: Houghton Mifflin.

Richardson, J. (1992). *The seasons.* New York: Franklin Watts, Inc.

Rose, K. (1998). *Crafts to make in the fall* (crafts for all seasons). Illustrated by Vicky Enright. Brookfield, CT: Millbrook Publishing.

Schweninger, A. (1993). *Springtime.* New York: Viking.

Schweninger, A. (1990). *Wintertime.* New York: Viking.

Schweninger, A. (1992). *Summertime.* New York: Viking.

Spohn, K. (1989). *Clementine's winter wardrobe.* New York: Orchard Books.

Steward, S. (1991). *The money tree.* Illustrations by David Small. New York: Farrar, Staraus, Giroux.

Intermediate Thematic Units:
Themes and Mini-Themes

Unit	Focus	Mini-Themes
I. Oceans (Science)	Students will examine and explore the oceans of the world—studying their diverse life forms and how oceans are an endangered ecosystem.	Whales Sharks
II. Space: The Final Frontier (Science)	Students will journey through our Solar System and share in many discoveries that are the results of human's quest for knowledge of our world and our universe.	Space Technology Third Rock from the Sun: The Earth
III. Becoming a Nation (Social Studies)	Students will analyze the conditions in the thirteen British colonies that contributed to the outbreak of the Revolutionary War.	The Constitution and the Bill of Rights: An In-Depth Look The Revolutionaries
IV. The Wild, Wild West (Social Studies)	The Wild West comes alive as students travel through time to one of the most colorful and romanticized periods of American history	The Native Americans of the Wild West Today's Cowboys
V. Poetry: The Words and the Music (Language Arts)	To create in children a delight for poetry and an understanding of the elements that make poetry so appealing to the senses	Curricular Connections Poems of Everyday Life
VI. Biography: Making a Difference (Language Arts)	Students will become aware of the fact that each individual can make a difference in the world. Students will learn about the heroes and heroines of yesterday and today and hopefully be inspired to see themselves as the dreamers and doers of tomorrow.	Women of the World Freedom Fighters
VII. Meet the Newberys (Language Arts)	Students will become involved with Newbery Award-winning literature and the authors whose works have inspired and excited the imaginations of readers.	Introducing the Classics Censorship and Children's Literature
VIII. Fractions (Math)	Students will learn how fractions are an important part of our daily lives.	Decimals Cooking and Eating
IX. Geometry (Math)	Students will develop an understanding of the usefulness of geometry in their daily lives.	Architecture Lines and Angles
X. Art (can be used with both primary and intermediate levels)	Students will develop an awareness and appreciation for artists and their works.	Impressionist Movement Renaissance Movement

Oceans

OVERVIEW

Focus

Students will examine and explore the oceans of the world—studying their diverse life forms and how oceans are an endangered ecosystem.

Objectives

Upon completion of this unit, students will:

1. Understand the richness and diversity of the oceans of the world.
2. Explore the amazing variety of flora and fauna in the ocean.
3. Examine the interdependencies of humans and oceans.
4. Assess the impact of pollution in the world's oceans

HOW IT WORKS

Initiating Activity

Provide students with a list of oceanic occupations similar to the one on p. 252. Invite them to conduct some library research on one or more chosen occupations with specific reference to job requirements, training and education, amount of time spent at sea, and occupational dangers. Provide opportunities for students to share their research with others.

Encourage students to report their findings to others or prepare a short report entitled "A Week in the Life of a _____."

Students may wish to contact any one of the following organizations or obtain any of the listed publications to learn more about marine science careers:

American Association of Zoo Keepers
635 SW Gage Blvd.
Topeka, KS 66606

American Zoo and Aquarium Association
Oglebay Park
Wheeling, WV 26003

Environmental Opportunities
P. O. Box 1437
Keene, NH 03431

Harold Goodwin's
"Today's Youth in Tomorrow's Seas."
Oregon State University
School of Oceanography
Corvallis, OR 97331.

International Marine Animal Trainers Association
1720 South Shores Rd.
San Diego, CA 92109

International Wildlife Rehabilitation Council
4437 Central Place, B-4
Suison, CA 94585

Oceanic Occupations	
Commercial Fishermen	Catch ocean creatures to sell to markets
Marine Geologists	Study rocks and the formation of the ocean floor
Marine Biologists	Study the animals and plants of the ocean
Divers	Assist in finding sunken treasures, repairing underwater equipment, gathering information for research, etc
Oceanographers	Study and explore the ocean
Offshore Drillers	Explore beneath the ocean floor for deposits of petroleum and natural gas to be used for various forms of energy
Mariculturists	Raise farm fish and other sea life for food and/or restocking the ocean
Marine Ichthyologists	Study fish, their habitats, the food they eat, their relationship to their environment
Marine Ecologists	Study the relationships between sea creatures and their environment
Captain/Crew of Ship	Work on a commercial boat or cruise ship
Navigators	Use directions to determine a ship's course at sea

Marine Careers (Videotape)
University of Delaware
Marine Communications Office
Newark, DE 19716
(302) 831-8083

National Marine Educators Association
P. O. Box 5215
Pacific Grove, CA 93950

Sea Grant
For information on regional offices
contact:
Sea Grant National Office
NOAA, Sea Grant
R-ORI, SSMB-1 Room 5214
1335 E-W Highway
Silver Spring, MD 20910-3226

Any college or university with a marine science program will be able to provide students with important and valuable information on careers in marine science.

General Activities

1. Invite youngsters to keep a watch on the local news or local newspaper for reports of ocean pollution from around the world. While they may wish to focus on events related to grounded tankers, other types of pollution can be tracked as well. Invite students to hang up a large wall map of the world. For each incidence of ocean pollution, invite youngsters to write a brief summary (date, nature of occurrence, place, resolution, etc.) on a 3" x 5" index card. Post each card around the wall map and connect the

card with the actual location on the map using a length of yarn (the yarn can be taped or pinned to the wall).

2. Invite students to visit a local grocery store and take along a list similar to the one below. This list represents several varieties of fish that are commonly found in most supermarkets throughout North America and that are sold as food. Encourage students to check off each type of fish as it is located in the store. They may want to visit the fresh fish department, the frozen fish section, and the canned food section.

Fish Commonly Found in Supermarkets

☐	herring	☐	salmon
☐	shrimp	☐	tuna
☐	orange roughy	☐	crab
☐	lobster	☐	scallops
☐	catfish	☐	cod
☐	haddock	☐	flounder
☐	perch	☐	clams
☐	whiting	☐	halibut
☐	monkfish	☐	grouper
☐	scrod	☐	oysters
☐	anchovies	☐	sardines
☐	whitefish	☐	mussels
☐	mackerel	☐	octopus
☐	pollock		

---

3. Here's an activity which will give students an opportunity to create a "homemade" ocean in a bottle.

Materials

An empty one-liter soda bottle (with a screw-on top), salad oil water, blue food coloring

Directions

1. Fill an empty one-liter soda bottle 1/3 of the way up with salad oil.

2. Fill the rest of the bottle (all the way to the brim) with water dyed with a few drops of blue food coloring.

3. Put the top on securely and lay the bottle on its side.

4. Slowly and gently tip the bottle back and forth.

The oil in the bottle will begin to roll and move just like the waves in the ocean. Students will have created a miniature ocean in a bottle.

---

4. Invite students to contact several of the following groups and ask for information on the work they do and the types of printed materials they have available for students:

American Littoral Society
Sandy Hook
Highlands, NJ 07732
201-291-0055

American Oceans Campaign
725 Arizona Ave., Suite 102
Santa Monica, CA 90401
310-576-6162

Center for Marine Conservation
1725 DeSales St., NW, Suite 500
Washington, DC 20036
202-429-5609

Cetacean Society International
P.O. Box 953
Georgetown, CT 06829
203-544-8617

Coastal Conservation Association
4801 Woodway, Suite 220 West
Houston, TX 77056
713-626-4222

The Coral Reef Alliance
809 Delaware St.
Berkeley, CA 94710
510-528-2492

International Marine Mammal
Project
Earth Island Institute
300 Broadway, Suite 28
San Francisco, CA 94133
1-800-DOLPHIN

International Oceanographic
Foundation
4600 Rickenbacker Causeway
Virginia Key, Miami, FL 33149
305-361-4888

International Wildlife Coalition
(IWC) and The Whale Adoption Project
70 E. Falmouth Highway
E. Falmouth, MA 02536
508-548-8328

Marine Environmental Research
Institute
772 W. End Ave.
New York, NY 10025
212-864-6285

Marine Technology Center
1828 L St., NW, Suite 906
Washington, DC 20036-5104
202-775-5966

National Coalition for Marine
Conservation
3 W. Market St.
Leesburg, VA 20176
703-777-0037

National Wildlife Federation
8925 Leesburg Pike
Vienna, VA 22184-0001
703-790-4000

Ocean Voice International
P.O. Box 37026
3332 McCarthy Rd.
Ottawa, Ontario,
Canada K1V 0W0
613-990-8819

Discussion Questions

1. Why are oceans considered to be an important natural resource?
2. Why should we be concerned about the amount of pollution that gets discharged into the ocean?
3. What single question would you like to ask an oceanographer?
4. If you could learn more about one aspect of the world's oceans, what would you like to discover?
5. What are some of the resources we get from oceans? What are some of the resources we get EXCLUSIVELY from oceans?

LITERATURE RELATED ACTIVITIES

Title: *One Small Square: Seashore*

Genre: Non-fiction

Author: Donald M. Silver

Illustrator: Patricia Wynne

Bibliographic Information:New York: W. H. Freeman and Co., 1993.

Summary: In this book, readers meet a dazzling collection of creatures, watch how they interact with each other and with other elements of their environment including plants, rocks, soil, and the weather. There is a lot to discover at the seashore and this book offer young adventurers an array of incredible information.

Interest Level: Grades 4–6

Pre-Reading Activity

The following activity will alert children to the speed at which a seaside community can become fouled by oil. Provide students with four sealable sandwich bags. Label the bags "A," "B," "C," and "D." Fill each bag 1/3 full with distilled water and 1/3 full with used motor oil. Invite students to place a hard-boiled egg in each bag. Seal the bags. Invite students to remove the eggs from each of the bags (they should wear kitchen gloves or some sort of disposable gloves) according to the following schedule:

From Bag "A" - After 15 minutes

From Bag "B" - After 30 minutes

From Bag "C" - After 60 minutes

From Bag "D" - After 120 minutes

Encourage students to peel each of the hard-boiled eggs and note the amount of pollution which has seeped through the shell and onto the actual egg. Which egg has the most pollution? How rapidly did the pollution seep into each egg? Provide time afterwards to discuss the rapidity with which these eggs became polluted and the implications for spilled oil polluting a beach or shoreline.

Learning Activities

1. Waves constantly pound on the shoreline. This is a process that has been going on for millions of years. As a result, rocks are broken down through continual wave action. Here's a fun activity that demonstrates this process.

Materials
White glue, playground sand, water, small coffee can (with lid), cookie sheet

Directions
1. Mix together six tablespoons of white glue with six tablespoons of sand in a bowl.

2. Using the tablespoon, place small lumps of the mixture on a cookie sheet.

3. Place the cookie sheet in a slow oven (250^0 F) and "bake" them for three to four hours.

4. Remove the "rocks" and allow them to cool.

5. Put three or four "rocks" into a coffee can with some water and place the lid securely on top.

6. Shake for four to five minutes and remove the lid.

The rocks will begin to wear down. Some of the "rocks" will be worn down into sand. The action of the "waves" inside the coffee can causes the "rocks" to wear against each other. As a result, they break down into smaller and smaller pieces. On a beach or shoreline this process takes many years, but the result is the same. Rocks become smaller by being tossed against each other by the action of the waves. Over time rocks wear down into sand-like particles which eventually become part of the beach or shoreline.

---

2. Students can build a three-dimensional model of a shoreline or tidal area with the following activity.

Materials
Deep baking pan (a bread loaf pan is ideal), non-stick vegetable spray (Pam®), 4 cups flour, 1 cup salt, 1½ cups of warm water, acrylic or tempera paints

Directions
1. Knead the flour, salt, and warm water together in a large bowl for about 10 minutes (the mixture should be stiff, but pliable).
2. Spray the baking pan with vegetable spray.
3. Spread the mixture into the pan, forming it into various landforms (beach, rocky shore, sand dunes, outcroppings, cliffs). If necessary, make some more of the mixture using the same recipe.   (continued on next page)

> 4. Bake in an oven set at 325⁰ for about one hour or more, depending on size and thickness.
> 5. Test the sculpture for "doneness" by sticking a toothpick into various spots (the sculpture should be firm to hard). If necessary, place the sculpture back in the oven to bake some more.
> 6. Remove the sculpture from the oven and allow to cool.
> 7. Carefully slide the sculpture from the baking pan (this should be done by an adult).
> 8. Paint the sculpture with different colors of acrylic or tempera paints (available at any art, craft, or hobby store).
>
> OPTIONAL: When the paint is dry, spray the sculpture with a clear varnish to preserve it.

Discussion Questions

1. Describe what you might expect to discover on a visit to the seashore?
2. Of all the information in this book, what surprised you the most?
3. How did this book stimulate your interest in oceanography?
4. Compare the life on a seashore with the flora and fauna in your backyard.

Title: *A Swim Through the Sea*

Genre: Fiction and Informational

Author: Kristen Joy Pratt

Illustrator: Kristen Joy Pratt

Bibliographic Information: Nevada City, CA: Dawn Publications, 1994.

Summary: Seamore the Seahorse explores the fascinating plants and animals of the undersea world. His alphabetic journey takes him past a flashlight fish, manatees, a porcupine fish, and a wise and wondrous whale, among others. This journey through the undersea world is a beautiful environmental awareness book full of interesting facts and colorful illustrations.

Interest Level: Grades 2–4

Pre-Reading Activity

Here's a great activity that will help students learn about fish physiology. In fact, this activity has been practiced in Japan for more than 100 years.

> **Materials**
>
> One whole fish (can be obtained from the fish department of any large supermarket), newspaper, paper towels, newsprint (available from any art store or hobby store), water soluble paint

(liquid tempera paint or artist's acrylic paint are both available from hobby, craft, or art stores), artist's paint brushes, masking tape

Directions

1. Wash the fish thoroughly with soap and water to remove any mucus.

2. Lay the fish on a sheet of newspaper.

3. Paint one side of the fish with the paint (any color will do). If necessary, thin the paint with a few drops of water. Stroke the fish from tail to head (this allows ink to catch under the edges of scales and spines and will improve the print—especially if you use a thin coat of paint).

4. Paint the fins and tail last, since they tend to dry out quickly. Do not paint the eye. If the newspaper under the fish becomes wet with ink during the painting process, move the fish to a clean sheet of newspaper before printing. Otherwise, the print will pick up leftover splotches of color.

5. Carefully and slowly lay a sheet of newsprint over the fish. Taking care not to move the paper, use hands and fingers to gently press the paper over the fish. Press the paper gently over the fins and tail. Be careful not to wrinkle the paper or a blurred or double image will result.

6. Slowly and carefully peel the paper off.

7. Paint in the eye with a small brush.

8. Tape the print to a wall and allow to dry.

This activity is a traditional Japanese practice and is called **gyotaku** (pronounced ghio-ta-koo). It comes from two Japanese words (gyo = fish, taku = rubbing). This is a way Japanese record their catches and it has evolved into an art form throughout the world.

Students may want to experiment with different types of paper for this activity. Thinner paper (tissue paper, rice paper) will provide a print that shows more details of the fish, but they tend to wrinkle much easier when wet. Thicker paper (construction paper) is easier to handle, but does not provide a detailed print.

Note: Students may need to practice this activity several times to get the technique down. Encourage them to be patient and they will discover that the more they practice, the more intricate their fish prints will become.

Learning Activities

1. Just like trees, fish have rings on their scales. Here's how students can use these rings to determine the age of a fish:

> **Materials**
> A fish, dark construction paper, hand lens or magnifying glass
>
> **Directions**
> 1. Remove four of five scales from the fish (you may want to assist students by using a fish scaler or use a pair of pliers to gently pull off selected scales).
> 2. Place the scales on the dark construction paper.
> 3. Use the hand lens to examine each scale. Note the bands, or rings, on each scale.
>
> As fish grow they develop bands, or rings, on their scales. As students look at a fish scale they'll probably notice (depending on the species) that a scale has both wide bands and thin bands. The wide bands represent summer growth when there is a lot of food for the fish to eat. The thin bands represent growth during the winter months. Also, students might notice that the wide bands are lighter in color than the thin bands. Because fish grow slower during the winter months the bands are darker and thinner.
>
> Since a year is made up of both summer and winter months, a full year's growth (for a fish) consists of one wide band plus one thin band (or one dark band + one light band). In order to determine how old the fish was students can simply count the total number of wide bands, or rings, on a scale.

2. Provide each student with two paper plates. Invite each student to cut out a circular section from one plate and glue blue cellophane over the inside of the hole to create a water effect. Encourage students to draw illustrations of kelp, various sea creatures from the book, and other underwater items on the face of the uncut plate. They may wish to glue birdseed on the "ocean floor" to simulate sand and/or fish crackers to provide a 3-D effect. Invite students to staple or glue the two plates together (face to face) to create an imaginary porthole.

Discussion Questions

1. If you could write a letter to the author of this book, what would you like to say?
2. What was the most incredible animal in the book? What else would you like to learn about that animal?
3. What are some other animals the author could have included in this book?
4. In what ways did this book change your perceptions about life in the ocean?

Title: *Exploring the Oceans: Science Activities for Kids*

Genre: Informational

Author: Anthony D. Fredericks

Illustrator: Shawn Shea

Bibliographic Information: Golden, CO: Fulcrum Publishing, 1998.

Summary: This book provides readers with a delightful and intriguing collection of "hands-on" activities, experiments, and projects designed to alert them to the mysteries and marvels of ocean life. Packed with information and filled with amazing assortment of data, readers will find this book an ideal addition to any ocean study.

Interest Level: Grades 4+

Pre-Reading Activity

Students are often amazed at the incredible variety of food harvested from the world's oceans. You and your students may wish to put together an "Ocean Picnic" using ocean-related recipes (see below) or others collected from family cookbooks. This feast can be part of an "Oceans Celebration". Plan to discuss the various types of food harvested from the ocean and provide students with library resources for learning more about those food items.

Ocean in a Cup

2 lg. pkg. blueberry jello, 4-5 small gummy fish, Graham cracker crumbs

Mix jello according to package directions. Pour into clear plastic cups leaving a 1" space at top. Refrigerate until slightly set. Mix gummy fish into each cup. Refrigerate until firm. Put graham cracker crumbs on half of each "ocean" to simulate beach. Insert beverage umbrella into "sand".

Shark Eggs

6 hard-boiled eggs, 4 oz. can drained tuna, mayonnaise, pickle relish, paprika

Slice eggs in half lengthwise. Carefully scoop out yolks and put in mixing bowl. Add tuna, mayonnaise and pickle relish to taste. Stir until blended. Fill egg centers with mixture and sprinkle with paprika.

Sea Mix

1 pkg. mini fish pretzels, 1 pkg. mini fish crackers (cheese), 1 pkg. fish cookies, 1/2 lb. Swedish gummy fish, 1 can nuts, 1 box raisins

Combine all ingredients. Serve in a sand pail.

Learning Activities

1. Several organizations have brochures, leaflets, and guidebooks on ocean pollution and ways to prevent it. Encourage students to write to several of these groups requesting pertinent information. When the resources arrive, plan time to discuss with students methods and procedures in which they can participate to prevent or alleviate this global problem. Invite them to prepare an "Action Plan" for themselves and their friends in which they take a pro-active stance against ocean pollution. The following will get them started:

   - The New York Sea Grant Extension Program (125 Nassau Hall, SUNY, Stony Brook, NY 11794-5002 [516-632-8730]) has a 24-page booklet entitled "Earth Guide: 88 Action Tips for Cleaner Water." Copies are free.

   - A variety of informational brochures are available from the NOAA Marine Debris Information Office, Center for Marine Conservation, 1725 DeSales St., NW, Washington, DC 20036.

   - If students are interested in "adopting" an endangered animal, specifically a whale, they can write for further information to the International Wildlife Coalition, Whale Adoption Project, 634 North Falmouth Highway, Box 388, North Falmouth, MA 02566.

   - To join a coalition of environmentally-friendly youngsters from around the country invite students to write to the Strathmore Legacy's Eco Amigos Club, 333 Park St., West Springfield, MA 01089

   - Invite students to contact Keep America Beautiful (99 Park Ave., New York, NY 10016) and ask for "Pollution Pointers for Elementary Students"—a list of environment improvement activities.

2. The book discussed some of the efforts to contain ocean pollution such as spreading oil. One method uses a boom (a floating line) being placed in the water in an attempt to contain the oil spill. Students can experiment with different devices to contain their own oil spill to determine the best material to use in a boom.

   Place water in a large round pan or pie plate. Invite students to collect several different floating objects which could be used as booms (these may include a rubber band; a length of yarn, string, twine, or cotton batting; a ring of Styrofoam cut from the top of a disposable coffee cup, etc. [invite students to use their creative powers in inventing other types of potential booms]). Place several drops of cooking oil in the middle of the water (students will note that since oil and water do not mix the oil floats on top of the water). Invite students to encircle the oil with one or more different devices to determine which device or which material best prevents the oil from spreading across the surface of the water.

   To further test their devices create small ripples in the water of the pan with your finger. Invite students to note what happens to the oil on the surface. Take time to discuss the difficulties that arise in the ocean when the surf is high or the seas are rough and there is a need to contain any oil on the surface. How do their devices work in containing oil on a choppy "sea?" What are the implications in real-life rescue efforts?

Discussion Questions

1. Which of the activities in the book did you enjoy the most?
2. Would you like to become an oceanographer?
3. Based upon what you learned in this book, what measures do you think should be enacted to prevent or reduce ocean pollution?
4. Which of the world's major oceans would you like to visit most? Can you offer some reasons for your choice?
5. What additional information about oceans did you learn from the numerous web sites listed in the book?

Title: *Ocean*

Genre:	Informational
Author:	Miranda Macquitty
Photographer:	Frank Greenaway
Bibliographic Information:	New York: Knopf, 1995.
Summary:	It's all here! Packed with loads of information and dozens of startling facts, this book is a wonderful overview of ocean life. An incredible resource that covers every aspect of sea life and reasons why it needs to be protected. Part of the *Eyewitness Book* series.
Interest Level:	Grades 4+

Pre-Reading Activity

Here's an activity which will allow students to create their own fresh water using principles identical to those used by scientists around the world.

Materials

Water, table salt, measuring cup, measuring spoons, large bowl, small cup, plastic food wrap, small stone

Directions

1. In the large bowl, mix three teaspoons of salt with two cups of water until it's thoroughly dissolved. Use a spoon to carefully taste a small sample of the salt water.
2. Set the small cup inside the bowl in the middle.
3. Cover the bowl with plastic food wrap.
4. Place a small stone in the center of the plastic wrap (directly over the cup) so that there a small depression in the food wrap.
5. Set this entire apparatus in the sun for several hours.

After some time, beads of water will form on the underside of the plastic food wrap and drip into the small cup.

6. Remove the plastic wrap and carefully taste the water in the cup.

The salt water inside the large bowl will begin to evaporate into the air inside the bowl. It will condense as beads of water on the underside of the plastic wrap. Since the plastic wrap is shaped the way it is, the beads of water will roll down and drip into the small cup.

This activity illustrates the process in nature known as solar distillation. Distillation involves changing a liquid into a gas (evaporation) and then cooling the gas vapor (condensation) so that it can change back into a liquid. The energy from the sun is able to evaporate water, but not salt, because salt is heavier than water. Thus, the salt remains in the bowl. The water can now be used for drinking purposes and the salt can be used for food seasoning purposes. This entire process (often referred to as desalination) is used in many countries in the Middle East to make fresh water from salt water.

Learning Activities

1. Underwater, pressure increases by one atmosphere for every 33 feet of depth. That means that at sea level the water pressure is about 14.7 pounds per square inch. At 33 feet below the surface of the ocean the water pressure is now two atmospheres or twice that at sea level (2 X 14.7 = 29.4 pounds per square inch). At 66 feet below sea level the water pressure is three atmospheres (3 X 14.7 = 44.1 pounds per square inch). This activity demonstrates how water pressure increases the further down into the ocean one goes.

Materials

A medicine dropper; a tall, deep, and clear container; water

Directions

1. Fill the container with water (should select a container made of glass or clear plastic so that students will be able to see through the sides).
2. Push the medicine dropper down into the water, open end down, until it reaches the bottom.
3. Hold it there and invite students to note how some water has entered the medicine dropper.
4. Slowly raise the medicine dropper up in the container. As it rises, encourage students to notice how less and less water appears inside the medicine dropper.

Air takes up space—even inside a medicine dropper. However, as the medicine dropper is pushed deeper into the water, the more the increasing water pressure will compress the air trapped inside the medicine dropper. The further down the dropper goes in the water, the pressure becomes greater and greater and the more air molecules are squished inside the dropper. As a result, more water is able to enter the dropper.

In the ocean, water pressure increases the further down one goes. At sea level, the water pressure at the surface of the water is 14.7 pounds per square inch. At the bottom of the Mariana Trench which is 35,827 feet below sea level the water pressure s 14,622.94 pounds per square inch.

2. Here's another activity which will help students appreciate some of the difficulties that may occur at deeper depths.

Materials

Two medium size balloons, two pieces of flexible tubing (about 6' each)—available at most drug stores or hardware stores, rubber bands and/or waterproof tape, large container of water

Directions

1. Stretch each balloon several times to loosen them.
2. Place a piece of flexible tubing in the neck of each balloon. Use a combination of rubber bands and/or waterproof tape to secure the neck of the balloon to the tubing (no air should escape when blowing up the balloons using the tubing).
3. Label the balloons "A" and "B".
4. Invite one students to blow up balloon "A" by blowing into the end of the flexible tubing. Invite that student to note how easy it was to fill that balloon with air.
5. Place balloon "B" at the bottom of a large, deep container of water (a deep sink, a barrel, a swimming pool). Invite the same student to blow it up by blowing into the end of the flexible tubing. Encourage that student to relate how difficult that is.

Balloon "A" was easier to blow up than balloon "B". In fact, it may have been impossible to blow up balloon "B". The reason is because the water pressure was pressing in on the side of balloon "B" thus preventing air getting into the balloon. The water pressure was greater than the pressure of the air the student was trying to force inside of the balloon.

In the ocean, water pressure increases with depth. Students may want to experiment with balloon "B" at various depths of water to determine the ease or difficulty of filling the balloon with air depending on how deep it is in the water.

Discussion Questions

1. How are some of the life cycles portrayed in this book similar to the life cycles of selected land animals?

2. List five significant facts that you learned from this book.

3. Which of the discoveries made within the last 20 years did you find to be the most amazing? The most significant?

4. What are some of the major impacts that humans have had on the world's oceans?

5. What do you imagine will be some of the products humans will be able to harvest from the world's ocean in the next 100 years?

CULMINATING ACTIVITY

Invite students to assemble an informational book on the facts and information learned throughout this unit. Included in the book can be a collection of articles clipped from various magazines, student's illustrations, favorite experiments and activities selected from different teacher resources, photographs donated by family members, fish prints (see pp. 252–258), or other items that students feel would be representative of the information they learned.

Students may elect to donate their "Ocean Book" to the school library or local public library. A special ceremony involving the librarian might be appropriate.

SUPPLEMENTAL LITERATURE

Books

Primary (Grades 1–3)

Aliki. (1996). *My visit to the aquarium*. New York: HarperCollins.
   A variety of marine habitats are explored in this well-done introduction to an aquarium.

Arnold, C. (1988). *A walk on the great barrier reef*. Minneapolis, MN: Lerner.
   The many forms of life on Australia's Great Barrier Reef are described in this exciting book.

Arnold, C. (1990). *A walk by the seashore*. Englewood Cliffs, NJ: Silver Press.
   A young child and an adult take a walk along the seashore and discover some marvelous treasures and surprises.

Arnosky, J. (1993). *Crinkleroot's 25 fish every child should know*. New York: Macmillan.
   An identification guide to salt and fresh water fishes.

Fowler, A. (1990). *It could still be a fish*. Chicago: Children's Press.
   A great introduction to the world of fish for very young readers. Lots of super photographs.

Gibbons, G. (1991). *Whales*. New York: Holiday House.
   Lots of detailed information highlight this text about some of the most majestic creatures in the oceans. A highly recommended book.

Ling, M. (1991). *Amazing fish*. New York: Knopf.
  Examines the behavior and habitats of a wide variety of ocean fish.

McDonald, M. (1990). *Is this a house for a hermit crab?* New York: Orchard Books.
  A hermit crab seeks shelter in this wonderful story enhanced with delightful and engaging illustrations.

Pallotta, J. (1991). *The underwater alphabet book*. Watertown, MA: Charlesbridge Publishers.
  This book is an alphabetic journey describing common and unusual creatures that inhabit the world's oceans.

Intermediate (Grades 4–6)

Anderson, M. (1990). *Oil spills*. New York: Watts.
  Describes the problem of oil spills, their effect on the environment, and what must be done to clean up after them.

Arnold, C. (1991). *Watch out for sharks*. New York: Clarion.
  A thorough and complete introduction to the world of sharks. Dispels some myths and provides welcome information about these misunderstood creatures.

Arnold, C. (1994). *Killer whale*. New York: Morrow.
  Presents the behavior and characteristics of killer whales. An excellent book by an outstanding writer.

Baker, L. (1990). *Life in the oceans*. New York: Watts.
  Presents readers with a thorough overview of ocean life and some of its most interesting elements.

Bellamy, D. (1998). *Our changing world: The rock pool*. New York: Crown.
  This book tells the story of cleaning up a rock pool in the aftermath of an oil spill and describes the return of life to the area.

Bendick, J. (1994). *Exploring an ocean tide pool*. New York: Holt.
  Examines the ecosystem of a tide pool. Discusses tides, tidal zones, and the plants and animals found in a tide pool.

Carr, T. (1991). *Spill! The story of the Exxon Valdez*. New York: Watts.
  This book introduces the 1989 Alaskan oil spill and its effects on the wildlife, ecosystem, and economy.

Coldrey, J. (1990). *Life in the sea*. New York: Bookwright Press.
  Wonderful photography and lots of clearly presented information highlight this all-inclusive book.

Cole, J. (1994). *The Magic School Bus on the ocean floor*. New York: Scholastic.
  Miss Frizzle and her class take a marvelous journey through the ocean's depth to learn some important information.

Corrigan, P. (1996). *Dolphins for kids*. Minnetonka, MN: NorthWord.
  A young girl discovers some fascinating and interesting information about the lives of dolphins. Great photography and delightful illustrations highlight this book.

Ganeri, A. (1995). *I wonder why the sea is salty and other questions about the ocean*. New York: Kingfisher.
Answers questions about the ocean, marine ecology, and marine life.

Ganeri, A. (1995). *The oceans atlas*. New York: Dorling Kindersley.
Packed full of information about major aspects of ocean life, this book is a "must have" for any serious oceanographer.

Greenaway, F. (1992). *Tide pool*. New York: Dorling Kindersley.
Discusses the different kinds of plants and animals that can be found in tide pools and how they interact with one another.

Hirschi, R. (1992). *Where are my puffins, whales, and seals?* New York: Bantam.
This book describes the multitude of life found in and around the sea and how that life is being endangered by marine pollution.

Hirschi, R. (1990). *Ocean*. New York: Bantam.
Colored drawings and high quality photos compliment this description of a variety of ocean creatures.

Hoff, M., & Rodgers, M. (1991). *Our endangered planet: Oceans*. Minneapolis, MN: Lerner.
Describes the threats posed by our use of the world's oceans.

Kagen, N. (Ed.) (1993*). Do fish drink? First questions and answers about water*. New York: Time-Life.
Lots of questions and lots of answers about oceans and their inhabitants are featured in this book.

Lazier, C. (1991). *Seashore life*. Ossining, NY: Young Discovery Library.
Lots and lots of factual information about the enormous variety of life at the seashore.

Maestro, B. (1990). *A sea full of sharks*. New York: Scholastic.
Everything you would ever want to know about sharks is in this informative and highly entertaining book!

Malnig, A. (1987*). Where the waves break: Life at the edge of the sea*. Minneapolis, MN: Lerner.
Beautiful photographs help introduce the young reader to life at the seashore.

McGovern, A. (1991). *The desert beneath the waves*. New York: Scholastic.
This wonderful book describes some of the unusual sea creatures that live on the ocean bottom.

Miller, C., & Berry, L. (1989*). Coastal rescue: Preserving our seashores*. New York: Atheneum.
Examines different types of coasts, how they are shaped by nature, and ways to use the coast's valuable resources.

Oppenheim, J. (1994). *Oceanarium*. New York: Bantam.
This book takes an imaginative approach to tidal waters and the deep sea.

Parker, S. (1990). *Fish*. New York: Knopf.
Lots of photos and an engaging text highlight some amazing sea creatures.

Parker, S. (1989). *Seashore*. New York: Knopf.
Introduces the various animals and plants of the seashore and discusses the importance of preservation.

Penny, M. (1990). *Let's look at sharks*. New York: Bookwright Press.
Provides the reader with basic information about some of the world's most well-known sharks—their habits and habitats.

Rinard, J. (1990). *Along a rocky shore*. Washington, DC: National Geographic.
Clear and crisp photographs introduce the reader to life along a rocky shore.

Simon, S. (1990). *Oceans*. New York: Morrow.
This richly photographed book provides numerous insights into the major features of the world's oceans.

Simon, S. (1990). *Whales*. New York: Harper.
A richly photographed introduction to the behavior, habits, and habitats of whales.

Souza, D. (1992). *Powerful waves*. Minneapolis, MN: Carolrhoda Books.
This books focuses on the power of tsunamis (tidal waves).

Swanson, D. (1994). *Safari beneath the sea*. San Francisco: Sierra Club Books for Children.
An outstanding presentation with fascinating descriptions of both familiar and unusual aspects of sea life.

Wells, S. (1993). *The illustrated world of oceans*. New York: Simon and Schuster.
An atlas of the earth's oceans with illustrations and information about their history, inhabitants, exploration, and uses.

Wheeler, A. (1988). *Discovering saltwater fish*. New York: Watts.
A guide to some of the more easily recognizable fish in the ocean.

Williams, B. (1989). *Under the sea*. New York: Random House.
An illustrated introduction to the world under the sea and the special diving machines that probe the ocean depths.

Wu, N. (1992). *Beneath the waves: Exploring the hidden world of the kelp forest*. San Francisco: Chronicle Books.
A day in the kelp forest introduces a variety of marine life. Highlighted with excellent photos.

Wu, N. (1990). *Life in the oceans*. New York: Bookwright Press.
Spectacular photographs and lots of interesting information offers the reader a glimpse into selected aspects of ocean life.

Websites

http://vpm.com/cordova/
http://www.turtles.org/
http://www.aboveall.com/bb/BBMAIN.html
http://seaweed.ucg.ie/Seaweed.html
http://www.actwin.com/fish/species.cgi
http://www.oceans.net/preserve.html

http://inspire.ospi.wednet.edu:8001/curric/oceans/
http://www.oceans.net/
http://www.nos.noaa.gov/
http://www.pbs.org/kratts/world/oceans/index.html
http://seawifs.gsfc.nasa.gov/OCEAN_PLANET/HTML/
    resource_data_services.html

MINI-THEMES

Whales

Kids love whales! It may be because they are the largest creatures in the world, they are able to "hold their breath" for long periods of time while diving, or because they have been the "stars" of movies such as *Free Willy*. Whatever the reason, it's important that students know that whales are not fish, but rather air-breathing, warm-blooded mammals (just like they are). Most species of whales are noted for their extremely long migration patterns—often traveling thousands of miles to reach breeding or feeding grounds (depending on the season).

But, several species of whales are also on the endangered species list. A hundred years ago there used to be millions of whales throughout the world. However, because they have been over-hunted for their meat, blubber, hide, and bones many varieties are on the verge of dying out.

Activities

1. Invite students to write to one or more of the following organizations requesting information on how many whales still exist and how they can help save the whales.

   American Cetacean Society   Pacific Whale Foundation
   P.O. Box 2639   101 N. Kihei Road
   San Pedro, CA 90731   Kihei, HI 96753

   The Whale Protection Fund
   1725 DeSales
   Washington, DC 20036

   When the information arrives, invite students to create an "advertising campaign" that would alert other students or the general public about the plight of various species of whales.

2. Divide students into several groups and "assign" a whale to each group. Invite each group to conduct necessary research (library books, encyclopedias, cetacean experts, high school biology teacher, etc.) to create a table top diorama of that species of whale in its natural habitat. Invite students to compose a written description of their whale to accompany the diorama. Provide opportunities for students to share their dioramas with others.

3. Here's a simple activity which will demonstrate how a baleen whale obtains its food.

Materials
A sink filled with cold water, a packet of dry vegetable soup, a kitchen strainer

Directions

1. Fill a kitchen sink with cold clear water.
2. Open and sprinkle the packet of vegetable soup over the surface of the water (students will note that the soup does not sink, but rather floats on the surface).
3. Invite one student to hold the kitchen strainer in one hand and skim it slowly over the surface of the water.
4. Encourage students to note how the vegetable pieces are caught in the strainer and how the water passes through the wire mesh of the strainer.

The strainer is able to "capture" the various vegetable pieces in its "bowl." The pieces are caught and the water passes through. If the strainer is lifted out of the water it will contain a wide variety of "food."

Baleen whales sift their food in much the same way as students did with the strainer. However, their food isn't floating on the surface, but rather swims through the water. The baleen combs allow a whale to swim through its dinner, strain the water from the plant or animal life, and eat what remains on its baleen. This is a very efficient form of eating as long as there is a sufficient quantity of food in the water. For example, one blue whale needs to eat about 4 tons of krill every *day* in order to survive. That's a lot of food to strain from the water!

4. This activity will help students appreciate the lengths of various types of whales throughout the world.

Materials

A ball of yarn, scissors, a yardstick

Directions

1. Measure the height of selected students. Cut pieces of yarn according to those heights. Lay the strings of yarn outside (on the sidewalk, the back yard, or on the driveway.
2. Measure other pieces of yarn according to the lengths of the whales listed below:

Porpoise	8 feet	Humpback whale	50 feet
Dolphin	8 feet	Right whale	60 feet
Pilot whale	22 feet	Sperm whale	60 feet
Killer whale	30 feet	Blue whale	100 feet
Grey whale	45 feet		

3. Lay all the various pieces of yarn side by side. How do various students compare with the lengths of common whales around the world?

References

Arnold, C. (1994). *Killer whale*. New York: Morrow.

Carrick, C. (1993). *Whaling days*. New York: Clarion.

Kraus, S., & Mallory, K. (1993*). The search for the right whale*. New York: Crown.

Parker, S. (1994). *Whales and dolphins*. San Francisco: Sierra Club Books for Children.

Patent, D. (1989). *Humpback whales*. New York: Holiday House.

Sheldon, D. (1990). *The whale's song*. New York: Dial.

Simon, S. (1989). *Whales*. New York: HarperCollins.

Waters, J. (1991). *Watching whales*. New York: Cobblehill.

Wexo, J. (1989). *Whales*. Mankato, MN: Creative Education.

Sharks

Sharks have been the subject of countless books and scores of horrifying movies. They are wrapped in mystery and surrounded by superstition and myth. In fact, many primitive people honor and revere the shark for its power and ferociousness. Indeed, sharks have always been fascinating to humans, even though we know very little about them.

Much of the fear of sharks comes from reports of shark attacks on humans (the great white shark being the most recognizable "villain"). However, statistics show that only about 5 to 10 people per year are killed worldwide by sharks. Also interesting is the fact that of the 350 different species of sharks only 32 species have been known to attack humans. Also, over 80 percent of all shark species are less than 6 feet long, and 50 percent of all sharks are less than 3 feet long.

Activities

1. Invite students to assemble a booklet or pamphlet on "Incredible Shark Facts." Here are several facts students may wish to use in the book:

   a. Almost 70 percent of a shark's brain is used for smell.

   b. Sharks are considered the first living creatures to develop teeth.

   c. Sharks can detect 1 drop of blood in 100,000 gallons of water.

   d. Sharks have a two-chambered heart; humans have a four-chambered heart.

   e. Sharks don't eat very often. In fact, some sharks only eat once a month.

   f. The smallest shark in the world is the dwarf shark, which reaches a total length of 6 inches.

2. Students may wish to get some fascinating and interesting information about sharks from one of the most incredible web sites ever: http:// users.bart.nl/~jkoetze/ (don't miss the accompanying music on this site). After students have "surfed" this site, invite them to create a booklet on "Myths and Realities of Sharks."

3. Provide students with a large sheet of newsprint. Invite them to draw an oversized outline of a shark's body on the newsprint. Encourage them to record relevant data about sharks within the outline, as well as illustrate important body organs. This "poster" can be posted along one wall of the classroom.

4. Many species of sharks are on the endangered species list (or will soon be). Invite students to read several of the books listed below, as well as search selected web sites for data on how and why sharks are endangered. Invite students to write letters to various governmental agencies expressing their concerns about the plight of sharks around the world.

5. Invite students to assemble an "anthology" of myths and legends about sharks that have been handed down through generations or those that are specific to cultures around the world. Do any of these myths have features in common? How have ancient people viewed sharks in relationship to people today? Do people in other countries think of sharks in the same way we do in this country?

References

Berger, M. (1999). *Chomp: A book about sharks.* New York: Scholastic.

Brennan, J. (1996). *The great white shark.* New York: Workman.

Dubowski, C. (1998). *Shark attack.* New York: DK.

MacQuitty, M. (1992). *Shark.* New York: DK.

Markle, S. (1996). *Outside and inside sharks.* New York: Atheneum.

Maynard, C. (1997). *Informania sharks.* Cambridge, MA: Candlewick.

Pipe, J. (1999). *The giant book of sharks and other scary predators.* Brookfield, CT: Copper Beech Books.

Wardlow, L. (1997). *Punia and the king of sharks.* New York: Dial Books.

Space: The Final Frontier

OVERVIEW

Focus

Students will journey through our solar system and share in many important discoveries that are the result of the human quest for knowledge of our world and our universe.

Objectives

Upon completion of this unit, students will:

1. Uncover information about the uniqueness of the planets and other heavenly bodies that comprise our solar system.
2. Explore the only world in outer space ever visited by humans—the moon.
3. Trace the various explorations of the solar system and examine the most important expeditions to *the final frontier.*
4. Assess the impact and future of the space program.

HOW IT WORKS

Initiating Activity

Many of the general activities in this unit will involve exploration of the sun and the planets of our solar system (other than Earth). Therefore, to arouse their curiosity about our solar system, involve students in a **Solar System Scavenger Hunt.** Create index cards—each should include an intriguing fact about each planet/sun without identifying the heavenly body (see examples below). There should be enough index cards so that each student gets one and there should be an equal number of cards for each planet/sun. Make many of the books listed in the reference section available and allow time for students to skim the books to locate the heavenly body that fits the fact on his/her index card. Based upon the heavenly body described on his/her index card, each student should then get into the appropriate planet/sun group and share the information on the index card. Below are some of the facts you might wish to include:

The Sun

1.3 million times the size of the Earth
Uses four million tons of hydrogen every second
Temperature is as high as 27 million degrees (F)
The inner atmosphere is the chromosphere, the outer atmosphere is
  the corona

Mercury

One day on this planet is almost as long as a year

Almost airless planet

During the day the temperature is hot enough to melt lead and at night the temperature is –300° (F)

Covered with craters from meteoroid collisions

Venus

Called the Evening Star or Morning Star

Rotates from east to west, the opposite of most other planets

Sometimes called Earth's sister planet but is very different

The hottest planet of the solar system

Mars

Named for the Roman god of war

Doesn't have canals as once believed

Scientists are still debating whether life forms exist there

Soil contains iron oxide

Jupiter

Has giant windstorm called the Great Red Spot

The Great Red Spot, the planet's giant windstorm, is three times the size of Earth

Four of its moons are big enough to be seen from Earth through binoculars or a small telescope and are called the Galean moons

One of its moons has exploding volcanoes

Saturn

Its rings are made of thousands of smaller rings within rings

Has the most moons of any planet in our solar system

One of its moons is the only moon in the solar system to have an atmosphere

It takes 30 years to orbit the sun

Uranus

The planet is lying on its side in space

Right now the south pole is in the midst of 42 years of constant sunlight

Discovered by William Herschel in 1781

Shines with a greenish-blue color

Neptune

Has the strongest winds ever measured on a planet

Its moon is colder than any other object in our solar system

The planet farthest from the Sun until 1999

Was discovered because of its gravitational pull on Uranus

Pluto

Has an odd, stretched, tilted orbit

Smallest, coldest planet in the solar system

Could have been a moon knocked out of a planet's orbit long ago or an asteroid

One of its moons is Charon, named after the boatman on the river Styx in the underworld

---

General Activities

1. Involve students in an in-depth exploration of their groups' planet/sun. Before beginning the research, suggest that each group become involved in the K-W-L strategy to access their knowledge of the planet/sun and aid them in determining what they would like to learn about the topic (see Chapter 2, pp. 42–44). Since our knowledge of our solar system has expanded greatly in recent years, encourage each group to gather information from recently published books (see Supplemental Literature on p. 283). The information gathered should include: size; location in the Solar System; atmosphere; unique land features; rotation; the possibility of life forms; explorations of the planet; discovery (when and by whom); legends and myths regarding the planet/sun; origin and appropriateness of its name; natural resources; and so forth. Have students create a bulletin board display for the planet assigned.

2. Based on the information gathered in Activity 1, have students create a visual representation of the planet that reflects some of its most significant features (for example, the rings of Saturn, the reddish color of Mars, the volcanoes of Jupiter, etc.).

3. Based on the information gathered in Activity 1, have students create a skit. This skit is based on the premise that the students have been involved in a ten-year mission to the planet and, as returning astronauts, they are ready to tell the world of their findings. The skit should be a mixture of fact and fiction. For example, students returning from Neptune might report on the underground homes of the "Neptunians" because the strong winds and freezing temperatures on the planet make life on the surface impossible. Students can also discuss some of the hardships of their visit and technological innovations that were needed to deal with the realities of the planet/sun. It is possible that not all missions were successful. For example, imagine that the Sun Mission had to be aborted due to the fact that their specially made space suits absorbed too much heat. However, students would still be responsible for sharing information about the sun and about their mission there. Remind students to use the visual (Activity 2) as part of their skit.

4. Involve students in experiments that will help them better understand the solar system and space travel. Books such as Gustafson's *Planets, Moons and Meteors* (1992), Schatz's *The Astronomy Activity Book* (1991), and Van Cleaves's *Astronomy for Every Kid* (1991) contain exciting experiments for budding astronomers.

5. Play many of the popular songs that deal with the theme of space, such as "Aquarius" from the show *Hair,* or the themes from *Star Wars, Star Trek,* or *2001 . . . A Space Odyssey.* Discuss how the music captures the mood of space. Have students either create their own modern dance, inspired by one of the pieces of music, or capture the mood through some type of artistic endeavor.

6. Have students create a "Space . . . The Final Frontier" time line. As students read about the advances in space exploration, have them add events, such as the various manned spaced programs (Mercury, Gemini, Apollo, Apollo-Soyuz, Sky Lab), space shuttles (Columbia, Challenger, Discovery, Atlantis, Endeavor) and unmanned NASA Planetary Exploration Missions (Mariner, Magellan, Pioneer, Viking, Voyager, Pathfinder) to the time line. For each event, have students include the name of the mission, the dates, the astronauts/cosmonauts (if appropriate), the main purpose(s) of the mission, and its most significant contributions. You may wish to have poster paper cut into the desired size for the time line. Ask students to illustrate each of the events they highlight.

7. Have students select and research one of the world's space pioneers to learn about his/her background, contributions, successes, failures, motivations, and any other relevant and interesting information. Following the research, tell each student that they are now members of the SEA (Space Explorers Association) panel of experts. Have each student take on the persona of the space pioneer researched and take part in a panel discussion in which each first relates his/her contributions and then shares his/her views on the importance of the space program and its future. These pioneers include (but are certainly not limited to):

Edward E. (Buzz) Aldrin, Jr.	Mae Jemison
William A. Anders	Johannes Kepler
Neil A. Armstrong	James A. Lovell, Jr.
Guion S. Bluford, Jr.	Sharon (Christa) MacAuliff
Frank Borman	Ronald McNair
Scott M. Carpenter	Sir Isaac Newton
Michael Collins	Sally K. Ride
Gordon Cooper	Alan B. Shepard
Robert L. Crippen	Wally Schirra
Yuri Gagarin	Valentina Tereshkova
John H. Glenn, Jr.	Edward J. White
Robert H. Goddard	Wernher von Braun
Virgil Grissom	James W. Young

8. Invite a local college astronomy professor to class to discuss space exploration. In advance, brainstorm possible questions.

9. Create a bulletin board with the following quote: "Man must rise above the Earth . . . to the top of the atmosphere and beyond, for only thus will he understand the world in which he lives" (Socrates). Have them research and read articles from newspapers and magazines that detail various space

explorations and write a brief explanation of what we have learned as a result. Place these articles and summaries on the bulletin board. For example, what findings did John Glenn's October, 1998, mission help us learn about the aging process?

10. Ask students whether they agree that space is the "final frontier." Have students create a mural entitled "New Frontiers," on which they draw pictures to represent other frontiers that await exploration. Ask each to write a brief essay to explain the frontier they have pictured and display the essays on the mural.

Discussion Questions

1. Of all the planets in the solar system, which holds the greatest possibility for supporting some type of life form? Explain. (Mars—clues from the Mars Pathfinder mission which landed on Mars on July 4, 1997, suggests a wet and warm early history of Mars. From soil samples picked up by Viking landers, many scientists think there is a possibility that the planet may be capable of supporting some type of life. Although none has been discovered there yet, some speculate that it may still exist on some unexplored parts of the planet.)

2. What are the most significant contributions of the manned space missions? (An understanding of the challenges of living in space; carrying out many scientific experiments that will, in turn, improve life on Earth, and so forth.)

3. What are some of the most significant contributions of the unmanned missions into space? (They have given us a close look at the planets of our solar system and have helped us better understand the origins of our universe.)

4. What, in your opinion, is the biggest challenge/danger associated with space exploration?

5. What qualities do you think are most important for an astronaut to possess? Explain.

6. Why is space referred to as "The Final Frontier"? Do you agree with this label? Why or why not?

LITERATURE RELATED ACTIVITIES

Title: *Our Solar System*

Genre:	Non-fiction
Author:	Seymour Simon
Illustrator:	Photographs from manned and unmanned missions into space
Bibliographic Information:	Morrow Junior Books, New York, 1992.
Summary:	This volume contains up-to-date information about the sun and the planets, moons, asteroids, meteoroids, and comets that travel around our sun. The text is accompanied by photographs taken from manned and unmanned space missions.
Interest Level:	Grades 3+

Pre-Reading Activity

Have students identify each of the heavenly bodies on the cover of the book. In groups, have them select one (not the planet they have been assigned during the general activities) and create a small replica (from paper). Involve the entire class in a brainstorming session to discover what they know about each planet and the sun. Attach a list of responses to the appropriate replica.

Learning Activities

1. The front of the book contains a chart with all types of information regarding the planets/sun. Duplicate the chart and have each student create five questions that involve a comparison of the planets/sun.

2. Have students come up with statistical puzzles regarding the planets and the sun. For example: "The sun is how many times bigger than all the planets put together." (Answer: 600 times bigger.) The chart in the book will help students create and solve these puzzles.

3. Involve students in a "Brain Bowl" in which they use the chart to answer the questions created in Learning Activities 1 and 2 above. You may wish to divide students into teams for this competition.

4. Evenly assign each student one of the planets (except Earth) or the sun. Have students come up with a new name for the planet/sun. This name should be significant and be based on the information uncovered about this body. Have students prepare a short persuasive argument for changing the name and present the new names planet by planet. They might also launch a mini-campaign with advertisements outlining the reasons for the name change. After all speeches for one planet have been presented, allow students to vote for one of the names or for keeping the name as it is.

5. Based on the photographs of the planets, involve students in selecting one of the planets/sun and creating a map of its surface. Have students label unique features on the planet.

Discussion Questions

1. Which of the planets did you find most interesting? Why?

2. How have the unmanned missions aided in our understanding of the planets of our solar system? (We've learned about the surfaces of the planets and their moons, about the possibility of life existing, about the weather and temperature conditions, and we've been able to hypothesize about the origins of the planets.)

3. Of all the information uncovered by the unmanned missions, which do you think is the most relevant/important?

4. Of the planets in our solar system, why does it appear that Earth and Earth alone can sustain any type of advanced living forms? (The extreme temperatures and atmospheric gases of the other planets make the existence of life forms there extremely unlikely.

Title: *The Moon Book*

Genre: Non-fiction
Author: Gail Gibbons
Bibliographic Information: Holiday House, New York, 1997.
Interest Level: Grades 3+

Title: *The Moon and You*

Genre: Non-fiction
Author: E. C. Krupp
Illustrator: Robin Rector Krupp
Bibliographic Information: Macmillan, New York, 1993.
Summary: Both books offer fascinating information on the moon and man's exploration of it. Stories and folklore about the moon from around the world are also included.
Interest Level: Grades 3+

Questions and activities listed below can be applied to both books.

Pre-Reading Activity

Have students brainstorm a list of songs, sayings, and phrases about the moon that have been handed down (i.e.: The man in the moon; the moon is made of cheese; once in a blue moon; harvest moon). Involve them in the Reflective Sharing Technique, in which they share and discuss ideas they have related to the topic of the moon (see Chapter 2, pp. 48–50).

Learning Activities

1. *The Moon and You:* Discuss the moon's phases and reasons for it. With students, recreate the demonstration on pages 16–17 in *The Moon and You* to explain the moon's phases.

—OR—

   The Moon Book: Discuss the phenomena of the solar eclipse. With students, recreate the "Solar Eclipse Project."

2. Encourage students to keep a pictorial diary of the phases of the moon. Every three or four days, for a month, have them take pictures of the moon and keep track of the date and time the picture was taken. Have them create a booklet on the moon and accompany each picture with a descriptive simile or metaphor (i.e.: the full moon lights up the sky like a giant firefly).

3. Have students locate, copy, illustrate, and share a favorite poem on the subject of the moon.

4. Have students select a favorite myth/legend concerning the moon and have them create a short skit so that they can retell it to the class.

5. Discuss the first landing on the moon and the famous words of Neil Armstrong as he set foot on the surface, "That's one small step for a man, one giant leap for mankind." Have students imagine that they are the first humans to set foot on the moon. Have them create a diary entry to describe their feelings and what they would say.

6. The first men to set foot on the moon, Neil Armstrong and Buzz Aldrin, left a plaque on the moon that said:

> HERE MEN FROM THE PLANET EARTH
> FIRST SET FOOT UPON THE MOON
> JULY, 1969, A.D.
> WE CAME IN PEACE FOR ALL MANKIND

Have students design a plaque they would leave if they were the first to visit another world in our solar system.

Discussion Questions

1. Why is a calendar month close to 29½ days? (That is the length of time from one new moon to the next.)

2. How does the moon's gravity affect the Earth? (It affects ocean tides.)

3. Describe the moon, its atmosphere, its surface, size, etc. (There is no air; the temperature is freezing during the night and boiling during the day; the moon's sky always looks black; the moon is 2,000 miles across and 6,800 miles around; gravity is much weaker than on Earth; filled with craters caused by meteorites; the moon's core is all rock; there is no water on the moon; and so forth.)

4. Describe the first landing of man on the moon.

5. Considering the fact that there are various theories to explain the origin of our moon, which do you believe? Why?

Title: *The Magic School Bus: Lost in the Solar System*

Genre:	Non-fiction/Fantasy
Author:	Joanna Cole
Illustrator:	Bruce Degen
Bibliographic Information:	Scholastic, New York, 1990.
Summary:	This adventure in the "Magic School Bus" takes the reader through the Solar System. A fantasy adventure is accompanied by many facts related to space and space travel.
Interest Level:	Grades 3+

Pre-Reading Activity

Discuss other books in the "Magic School Bus" series that students have read. Have them make predictions as to where the Magic School Bus will take them in this book. As an alternative, involve the students in using concept cards to tap into their background knowledge of space (see Chapter 2, pp. 41–42).

To supplement the unit, you may wish to obtain the video, *The Magic School Bus, Lost in Space* (Scholastic, 1995) or the software *The Magic School Bus Explores the Solar System* (Microsoft, 1994).

Learning Activities

1. After reading the book, have students compile a "Book of Facts: The Solar System." Have students illustrate their pages and bind them together in book form. As an alternative, students may wish to create an ABC book based on the solar system.

2. Throughout the book, the children on the bus have written short papers describing some aspect of space. Have each student select one of the papers and elaborate on it by researching the subject more fully.

3. Create a travel brochure and map of our solar system to help those who are visiting—or lost!

4. On the last page of the book, the author gives reasons why the reader should not attempt this trip on their own school bus. Ask children to make up their own "Top 10" list of reasons why they should or should not try this same trip. Have students list these reasons on poster board and illustrate. (*Remember:* Humor counts.)

Discussion Questions

1. Of all the information the students in Mrs. Frizzle's class uncovered, what surprised you the most?

2. What are some of the problems astronauts have to overcome in order to explore space? (gravity, or lack of it, lack of oxygen, extreme temperatures, distance from earth, etc.)

3. What career related to space exploration interests you most? Explain.

4. Would you consider this book to be more a book of fiction or of non-fiction? Explain.

Title: *Sweetwater*

Genre: Science fiction

Author: Lawrence Yep

Illustrator: Julia Noonan

Bibliographic Information: Harper and Row, New York, 1973.

Summary: The story of Tyree, whose ancestors came from Earth, and his life in a star colony on the planet Harmony.

Interest Level: Grades 4+

Pre-Reading Activity

Have students look at the cover carefully and discuss the types of life forms in the picture. Explain to students that the story is set on a planet called Harmony. In groups, have them create a scenario of what might happen between the two life forms on a planet called Harmony and present it to the rest of the class.

Learning Activities

1. Many unusual life forms existed on Harmony. Ask students to create another life form which may have existed in Old Sion. Using clay, or other materials, have them make a model of this life form and tell the class about it and how it affected the lives of the people in the star colony. Use enough detail so that Tyree's sister would be able to "see" the creature.

2. Using the Bill of Rights and the Preamble to the Constitution, create a new Preamble and Bill of Rights to help govern Harmony.

3. The colonists in Old Sion split into two groups. In our country, people have split into many groups. Ask students to describe the groups that exist in their community. Involve them in a problem-solving exercise to see how they can bring the various groups together. They may wish to write up the best solutions and send them to the local newspaper in the form of editorials.

4. Discuss the ways in which the colonists who settled on the planet Harmony were similar to the pioneers of the American West. Have students select a favorite song of the Old West to use as a model for a new song that tells about life in a star colony.

Discussion Questions

1. Compare life on Earth with life in the star colony.

2. What did Amadeus mean when he told Tyree that, "The only thing that matters in the changing universe is the song, the eternal song that waits for you"?

3. What can we learn about conflict and resolving conflicts from the different groups living on Harmony?

4. Why were star colonies important to Earth? (They shipped back materials that Earth needed, such as metal and soil.) What do you think of the possibility of this happening in the future? Explain.

5. Why is this book considered science fiction?

CULMINATING ACTIVITY

Have students hold a mini-debate in which they discuss the following issue: Should funding for space exploration and colonization be continued when money is so badly needed to solve social problems such as hunger, crime, and disease on Earth?

SUPPLEMENTAL LITERATURE

(*Note:* Unless otherwise noted, all books included are informational except books of science fiction which are indicated by an *.)

Beasant, P. (1992). *1000 facts about space.* Ill. by P. Bull, G. Smith, and M. Steward. New York: Kingfish Books.
An exciting facts about stars, astronomy, and space discovery.

Berger, M. (1992). *Discovering Mars.* Illustrated by J. Holub. New York: Scholastic.
An exciting look at the red planet.

Branley, F. M. (1994) *Venus: Magellan explores our twin planet.* New York: HarperCollins.
Focuses on what we've learned about the planet Venus.

Campbell, A. (Ill.) (1997). *New York Public Library Amazing space: A book of answers for kids.* New York: John Wiley and Sons.

Couper, H., & Henbest, N. (1998). *Is anybody out there?* New York: DK Publishers.
Considers the question of the likelihood of intelligent life existing in deep space. Answers questions that kids have about the wonders of space

*Danziger, P. (1986). *This planet has no atmosphere.* New York: Delacorte.
The story of a lunar colony.

*Engdahl, S. (1970). *Journey between worlds.* New York: Atheneum.
Explores the prejudice of Terrans against Martian colonists.

Fradin, D. B. (1997). *The planet hunters: The search for other worlds.* New York: Simon & Schuster/McElderry.
Presents a history of planetary discoveries.

George, M. (1992). *The moon.* Mankato, MN: Creative Education.
An aid to understanding the moon.

Gustafson, J. (1992). *Planets, moons and meteors.* New York: Julian Messner.
Tips and activities for stargazing and using a telescope to explore the planets. Also introduces the reader to the planets and their unique features.

Moore, P. (1990). *The universe for beginners.* New York: Press Syndicate of the University of Cambridge.
Takes reader on a journey into the infinite future and back to the beginning of time. Explores theories such as the big bang.

Nicolson, I. (1991). *The illustrated world of space.* New York: Simon and Schuster.
Over 200 full-color illustrations, 40 maps, diagrams and charts concerning the universe.

Rathbun, E. (1989). *Exploring your Solar System.* Washington, DC: National Geographic Society.
Travel to the sun and the nine planets. Includes outstanding photos and original artwork.

Redfern, M. (1998). *The Kingfisher young people's book of space.* New York: Kingfisher.
Explains the changing and sometimes violent universe.

Schatz, D. (1991). *Astronomy activity book.* Illustrated by R. Doty. New York: Simon and Schuster.
All kinds of activities introduce children to the wonders of our solar system.

Scott, E. (1998). *Close encounters: Exploring the universe with the Hubble Space Telescope.* Burbank, CA. Disney Publications.

Simon, S. (1985). *Jupiter.* New York: Mulberry Books.
Introduces the reader to this fascinating planet. The text accompanies photos taken on the Voyager Missions.

Simon, S. (1985). *Saturn.* New York: William Morrow.
An intriguing look at the ringed planet.

Simon, S. (1986). *The sun.* New York: Mulberry Books.
Explores the wonders of the sun, from nuclear explosions at its core to its sea of boiling gases at the surface. Contains over 20 full-color photos.

Simon, S. (1987). *Uranus.* New York: Mulberry Books.
Contains photos and text to help us learn about this planet that is two billion miles from the sun.

Simon, S. (1992). *Venus.* New York: Morrow Jr. Books.
Explores Earth's "sister planet." Full-color photos taken by NASA's Magellan and the Pioneer Venus Orbiter help us learn about Venus.

Simon, S. ed. (1995). *Star walk.* New York: Morrow.
Poetry of the night sky accompanied by photographs of outer space.

Sis, P. (1996). *Starry messenger.* New York: Farrar.
A book depicting the life of a famous scientist, mathematician, astronomer, philosopher, physicist Galileo Galilei.

Van Cleaves, J. (1991). *Astronomy for every kid.* New York: John Wiley and Sons.
Contains 101 easy experiments dealing with astronomy.

The visual dictionary of the universe. (1993). London: Dorling Kindersley.
Gives information on vocabulary associated with astronomy.

*Walsh, J. (1982). *The green book.* Illustrated by L. Bloom. New York: Farrar, Straus.
A group of Britons leave a dying Earth for a new home on another planet.

*Wrightson, P. (1965). *Down to Earth.* Illustrated by M. Horder. San Diego, CA: Harcourt Brace Javonovich.
A humorous story of a visitor from Mars.

Wunsch, S. (1998). *The adventures of Sojourner: The mission to Mars that thrilled the world.* Willowdale, Ontario, Canada: Firefly Books.

Web Sites

The Astronomy Café. http://www2.ari.net/home/odenwald/café.html

Air and Space/Smithsonian. http://www.airspacemag.com/ASM/Home.html

Astronomy Picture of the Day. http://antwrp.gsfc.nasa.gov/apod/astropix.html

Live from Earth and Mars. http://www-k12.atmos.washington.edu/k12/index.html

NASA Homepage. http://www.sni.nasa.gov/

NASA Kennedy Space Center. http://www.kksc.nasa.gov/

MINI-THEMES

Space Technology: Satellites, Shuttles, Space Stations, and Colonization

Since the beginning of the Space Age on October 4, 1957, when the Soviet Union successfully launched Sputnik I, tremendous advances have been made in space technology. Satellites for weather and communication provide all types of services, from helping us predict the weather to bringing us our favorite television programs. Space stations are being developed to serve as a laboratory to conduct research, an observatory, a manufacturing plant, an assembly plant where structures can be put together, a storehouse to keep spare parts, and a garage where other spacecraft can be repaired. The technology of the space age has improved by leaps and bounds and, with continued funding, the sky is no longer the limit.

Activities

1. Have students select and create a model of one of the space satellites in use today. Have them share the satellite by developing a commercial describing its benefits. (You may also wish to have one group concentrate their efforts on the Hubble Telescope.)

2. Have students read about several experiments conducted in the space shuttles. Have them design their own experiments that could be conducted in space and send their ideas to NASA.

3. Have students create their own space shuttles. (For example, they can split open large plastic jugs so that one side is still attached. Cut out cardboard semicircles and glue them inside the jugs to make decks. Cut holes for hatches and make toothpick ladders to go through the hatches. Label the various decks—flight, living, storage, etc.)

4. 1998 can be considered "The Year of the International Space Station." The first American construction crew delivered the second piece of the ISS (international space station) *Freedom* (the first component was sent into space a few weeks earlier by Russia). The project, however, is expected to cost $76 billion to complete with taxpayers picking up $52.7 billion of the tab. Have students research the amount of spending that is allocated for space exploration, the amount of jobs generated, and other pertinent information. They can get this information by writing to their congressional representative or to NASA, Washington, D.C. 20546. Have students research the many ways space exploration has enhanced our own lives. For

example, experts say the ISS will serve as an orbiting platform for environmental observations of Earth and astronomical observations. Furthermore, they say that sustained research in space will lead to breakthroughs in medical science. Have students list their findings on one large classroom chart that includes two columns—one "pro" and one "con" concerning continued space spending. Discuss findings.

5. Encourage students to research the effects of the comet which slammed into Jupiter in July, 1994. Ask the class to imagine that a huge comet will destroy three-quarters of the earth. They must find a way to colonize another planet. In groups, have them choose a planet from our Solar System best suited for colonization, and using what they know about the planet, have them make drawings of what they think a space colony on this planet would look like.

6. Space has become littered with rockets and other "space junk" over the past 30 years. In November, 1993, the space shuttle *Endeavor* had to change its plans or it would have come within six-tenths of a mile of a spent Russian rocket launched in 1965. On Earth we have many ways for eliminating our trash. Read *Junk in Space* (Maurer, 1989). Have students brainstorm ways of eliminating space trash. Have them display their ideas on poster board and illustrate them.

References

Asimov, I. (1990). *Colonizing the planets and stars.* New York: Careth Stevens.

Branley, F. (1986). *From Sputnik to space shuttles: Into the new space age.* New York: Crowell.

Butterfield, M. (1985). *Satellites and space stations.* New York: Usborne.

Clay, R. (1997). *Space travel and exploration.* Breckenridge, CO: Twenty First Century Books.

Dwiggings, D. (1985). *Flying the space shuttles.* New York: Dodd, Mead.

Herbst, Judith. (1993). *Star crossing: How to get around the universe.* New York: Atheneum.

Maurer, R. (1989). *Junk in space.* New York: Simon and Schuster.

Rickard, G. (1989). *Homes in space.* Minneapolis, MN: Lerner Publications.

Ridpath, I. and Muirden, J. (1992). *The world around us—space.* Illustrated by R. Jobson. New York: Kingfisher Books.

Scott, E. (1995). *Adventure in Space: The Flight to Fix the Hubble.* New York: Hyperion.

Scott, E. (1998). *Close encounters: Exploring the universe with the Hubble Space Telescope.* Burbank, CA: Disney Publications.

Smith, H. E. (1987). *Daring the unknown: A history of NASA.* San Diego, CA: Harcourt Brace Javonovich.

Stott, C. (1997). *Space exploration.* New York: Knopf.

Weiss, M. (1984). *Far out factories: Manufacturing in space.* New York: Lodestar Books.

Wunsch, S. (1998*). The adventures of Sojourner: The mission to Mars that thrilled the world.* Willowdale, Ontario, Canada: Firefly Books.

Third Rock from the Sun: The Earth

A study of space and our Solar System would not be complete without a look at our own planet, Earth. Our planet is unique in the Solar System; it is the only one supporting any complex type of life form, as we know it. And yet, with all the technological advancements, with our ability to explore the depths of outer space, we tend to forget the fragility of our own world. This mini-unit explores planet Earth, its unique resources, natural land formations, and the need for each of us to protect and live in harmony with our environment.

Activities

1. In *The Big Book for Our Planet* (Durell, et al., 1993), many well-known authors and illustrators of children's books have pooled their talents to honor the Earth. Read to the children the "Earth Game" by author Pam Conrad who describes a special game in which you can involve your students. Gather students into a circle and tie the end of a ball of twine to your finger. Toss the ball in the air to one of the students, who in turn wraps the string around his/her thumb and tosses it to another student. Have students do this until all are joined in the circle with the twine. Have students imagine that they are the Earth. Each student becomes a different part of the Earth (i.e., the Arctic Ocean, the jungles in Africa, a rain forest in Brazil) and tells one way that this area is being ruined by polluters, hunters, etc. As each student speaks, he/she tugs on the twine so that all students feel the effects. Once all the students have spoken, repeat the process, but have each student tell one thing that can be done to improve his/her part of the Earth. After the game, have students react to what has been said and to the significance of the twine that connected them all.

2. Our Earth has been shaped by various natural phenomena. Group students by such phenomena as earthquakes, rivers and glaciers, erosion, volcanoes, and so forth. Have each group research its phenomenon to create a demonstration that illustrates the ways this phenomenon has shaped the land. Books such as *Land Masses* (Arnold, 1985), *Volcanoes* (Simon, 1988), and *Earthquakes* (Simon, 1991) can help with this.

3. Have students create a large floor map of one of the continents (select a continent that reflects your social studies curriculum). Group students and assign each a different physical feature (mountain, desert, glacier, river, etc.) of the continent. Have each group research its feature, select a specific example of the feature (i.e., the Painted Desert, the Sierra Nevada Mountains, Carlsbad Caverns, etc.) and learn its location and how it was created. Have them create a symbol to represent the physical feature. Ask each group to present a skit that teaches the class about the feature, its location, and its effect on the land and people around it. Students should place the symbols they created in the correct locations on the class map.

4. Read aloud portions of books about various geographical regions. For example, Jean Craighead George has a series of books that deals with various regions, such as *One Day in the Desert* (1983), *One Day in the Alpine Tundra* (1984), *One Day in the Prairie* (1986), and *One Day in the Woods*

(1988). Assign groups of students their own regions and have them create their own *One Day in the* books.

5. Have students create collages that reflect the variety of geographical features on our planet. Using the song "America the Beautiful" as a model, create a song to honor planet Earth.

6. Contact a local environmentalist and ask him/her to speak to the class on the subject of environmental protection. Have students compose several interview questions before the guest arrives.

7. Read various poems and stories from *The Big Book for Our Planet* (Durell, et al., 1993) and discuss students' reactions to each. Many of the entries can be used as models for the students' own work. For example, based on Tana Hoban's contribution, have students create a picture book to promote environmental awareness. Ask each student to submit at least one photo that reflects the beauty of our world (i.e., a butterfly, a tree, the ocean tide, a seashell, a mountain peak, a green plant). As a class, create a text for the book that encourages readers to protect the Earth and all its natural wonders.

8. In *Anthology for the Earth* (Allen, 1998), the writings of many individuals from different places and different eras challenge us and examine our beliefs about Earth's ecology. Have students debate concepts related to earth's ecology by citing specific writings from this volume.

References

Allen, J. ed. (1998). *Anthology for the Earth.* Cambridge, MA: Candlewick Press.

Apt. J. et al. (1996). *Nasa Astronauts photograph the Earth.* Washington, DC: National Geography Society.

Brownstone, D. M., & Franck, I. M. (1989). *Natural wonders of America.* New York: Atheneum.

Beven, F. (1998). *Beneath the Earth: Facts and fables.* New York: Children's Press.

Butterfield, M. (1998). *1000 facts about the Earth.* New York: Kingfisher.

Cole, J. (1987). *The magic school bus inside the Earth.* Illustrated by B. Degen. New York: Scholastic.

Durell, A., et al. (Eds.) (1993). *The big book for our planet.* New York: Dutton.

The Earthwords Group. (1990). *50 simple things kids can do to save the Earth.* Illustrated by M. Montez. Kansas City, KS: University Press.

Ferndon, J. (1992). *How the Earth works: 100 ways parents and kids can share the secrets of the Earth.* Photos by M. Dunning. New York: Readers' Digest Association.

Ganeri, A. (1991). *Explore the world of forces of* nature. Illustrated by M. Saunders. Racine, WI: Western Publishing.

George, J. C. (1984). *One day in the alpine tundra.* New York: Harper and Row.

George, J. C. (1993). *One day in the desert.* New York: Harper and Row.

George, J. C. (1986). *One day in the prairie.* New York: Harper and Row.

George, J. C. (1988). *One day in the woods.* New York: Harper and Row.

Grimshaw, C. et al. (1995). *Earth.* Chicago: World Book, Inc.

Green, J. (1998). *Earth.* Brookfield CT: Copper Beech Books.

Hooper, M., & Coady, C. (1996*) The pebble in my pocket: A history of Earth.* New York: Viking.

Lauber, P. (1986). *Volcano.* New York: Bradbury Press.

McSween, H. Jr. (1997) *Fanfare for Earth: The origin of our planet and life.* New York: St. Martins Press.

Pringle, L. (1987). *Restoring our earth.* Hillside, NJ: Enslow.

Radlauer, E., & Radlauer, R. (1987). *Earthquakes.* New York: Children's Press.

Robin, G. (1984). *Glaciers and ice sheets.* San Diego, CA: Harcourt Brace Javonovich.

Royston, A., & Adams, J. (1997). *The Earth.* Portsmouth, NH: Heinemann.

Simon, E. (1991). *Earthquakes.* New York: Morrow.

Simon, S. (1988). *Volcanoes.* New York: Morrow.

Yolen, J. (1996) *Mother Earth Father Sky.* Honesdale, PA: Boyds Mills Press. [Anthology of nature poems]

Williams, B. (1992). *The living world.* New York: Kingfisher Books.

Williams, B., & Williams, B. (1993). *The Random House book of 1001 questions and answers about planet Earth.* New York: Random House.

Becoming A Nation

OVERVIEW

Focus

Students will analyze the conditions in the thirteen British colonies that contributed to the outbreak of the Revolutionary War. Students will examine significant events of the war as well as the war's outcomes.

Objectives

On completion of this thematic unit, students will:

1. Analyze basic causes and events leading to the Revolutionary War.
2. List the contributions of significant leaders of the Revolution.
3. Relate major events of the Revolutionary War.
4. Explore the Constitution of the United States of America and the ways in which it governs and guides our lives today.

HOW IT WORKS

Initiating Activity

Tell students that as a result of many meetings with the school's entire faculty and administration, new rules have been established for the school. Post these rules in the classroom (do not list parallel events found in parentheses) and discuss each:

1. Students must purchase stamps from the teacher to affix to each home-work assignment and test paper in order for it to be graded. (Stamp Act)
2. Raising hands to answer questions will no longer be tolerated. The teacher will call on students at random. Those who don't know the answer will pay penalties for wasting class time. (Townshend Acts)
3. Students will take turns bringing in lunch for the teacher. (Quartering Act)
4. Students who have dogs will become part of the teacher's Law Enforcement Agency. (If more than 10 students have dogs, select a different type of pet.) Students in the L.E.A. will not have to follow the above rules and will receive special privileges. (Acts of 1763)
5. All students who do not follow these established rules are subject to loss of recess and lunch time and will receive additional work.

Give students several minutes to copy down the rules and to think about them. Then divide students into groups in the following way:

1. Those who are willing to follow the new rules.
2. Those who refuse to follow the rules and are thereby willing to accept the consequences

3. Members of the L.E.A.

Have the first two groups each compose and sign a letter to the teacher, explaining the reasons its members chose that group. Have the students in the L.E.A. write a letter to the teacher explaining why they are the most qualified to carry out the new rules. Those who do not feel they are qualified can join one of the two other groups.

After each group has read its letter aloud, explain to the students that their experiences were simulations modeled after events leading to the American Revolution. Group 1 might be called the Loyalists (those who followed the established rules), Group 2 might be called the Patriots (those who worked to change rules they felt were unjust), and Group 3 might be called the British Army (those who were sent to the colonies to see that British rule was carried out).

Explain that this unit will allow students to study the times and events that led to the Revolutionary War. During the activities, point out events that parallel those in this simulation.

General Activities

1. How might the events leading up to the Revolutionary War have been reported if there had been television in the late 1700's? Divide students into groups, each selecting and researching a different event. Ask each group to create a news script to report its events. Groups may wish to draw or locate pictures to illustrate the news segments. Select two students as anchors and have them write clever introductions to each report event). To enhance the broadcast, have each group of students create and act out a commercial to advertise a product that might have been used during Revolutionary times.

2. Give students a copy of the text of the Declaration of Independence and read the document aloud. Divide students into groups and have each select one of the reasons cited in the Declaration for establishing a new government. Ask each group to research this problem and create a political cartoon to reflect the colonists' position. Bind the cartoons into a book and give it a clever title.

3. Place a red ball, a blue ball, and a white ball in a hat (or box). Have students take turns selecting one of the balls without looking. Those who select the white ball are to take the role of the Loyalists, those who select the blue ball are the Patriots, and those who select the red ball are the British Redcoats. After spending time learning about the conditions in the colonies in the 1770's, have each students deliver a one minute extemporaneous speech to tell other colonists whether or not to revolt, depending upon the role he or she has selected. Those who are Redcoats must give reasons why Britain wants to keep the colonies and how the colonists would benefit from continued British rule.

4. Ask the art teacher or a parent who knows calligraphy to teach students this form of writing. Have students write the Preamble to the Declaration of Independence in calligraphy on parchment paper. Have them design borders around their documents.

5. Allow groups of students to dramatize a favorite event from those that lead the colonists to independence (The Boston Tea Party, the meetings of the Sons of Liberty, the writing/signing of the Declaration of Independence, etc.). Make sure no incident is duplicated.

6. Read aloud "Paul Revere's Ride" by Henry Wadsworth Longfellow. Explain that Revere is one of the best known revolutionaries because of this poem. Actually, the poem is not quite accurate. Students might enjoy doing research to learn the truth about that famous ride.

7. Along with students, locate copies of paintings that tell the story of the Revolutionary War ("Washington Crossing the Delaware"; "The Surrender at Yorktown," etc.) Have each student select a favorite and create his or her own version of the painting. Ask them to write a brief summary of the event depicted to accompany the picture.

8. Read and discuss the Preamble to the Constitution with students. Have them rewrite the Preamble using contemporary language.

9. Discuss the Constitution of the United States. Assign groups different sections and have each summarize its section in a 20 word telegram to the American people, explaining its importance.

10. Have a birthday party for the United States! Divide students into groups of four or five and ask each group to bring in an unfrosted cake along with a can of vanilla icing, tubes of colored icing or food coloring, and any edible materials (M & M's, candy corn, etc.). Have them plan a design for their cake and then decorate it to celebrate America's Independence. After groups share their designs, allow each student to vote for his or her favorite and offer a prize for the winning group. Then, "Let them eat cake."

Discussion Questions

1. What conditions in the colonies led to the revolution?

2. Why did some colonists remain loyal to Britain while other joined the Patriots?

3. Did the Patriots have sufficient cause to revolt? Explain.

4. What do you consider to be the most important event leading to the Patriots' victory during the Revolutionary War?

5. What if the British had won the war?

6. What are the greatest strengths of the Constitution?

7. If the Revolutionary War had never happened, how might our lives be different?

LITERATURE RELATED ACTIVITIES

Title: *The Journal of William Thomas Emerson: A Revolutionary War Patriot*

(Part of the *My Name is America* series)

Genre: Historical Fiction

Author: Barry Denenberg

Bibliographic Information: Scholastic Inc., 1998.

Summary: In 1774, Will, a 12-year old orphan, is befriended by Mr. Wilson, who is secretly working with the patriots to win eventual independence from the British. The book is written as a series of journal entries and gives the reader an accurate picture of life in Boston in the years preceding the writing of the Declaration of Independence.

Interest Level: Grades 4–7

Pre-Reading Activity

Discuss the use of diaries. Why do people keep diaries? What type of information do people usually put into their diaries? Discuss whether any of the students keep a diary. Explain that this book is made up of a series of diary entries written by William Thomas Emerson, a fictitious character who describes pre-Revolutionary life in Boston, Massachusetts, 1774.

Learning Activities

1. Have students create a "Sensory Graphic Organizer." Ask them to draw five columns on a piece of paper and head them: sight, sound, taste, touch, smell. Under each column have them list words/phrases used throughout the book that appeal to the senses. After completing the graphic organizer, ask students to create a written picture of Boston, Massachusetts, 1774, to capture the time and place.

2. Many "Rules of Good Behavior" were offered in the book. During the colonial times, people like Benjamin Franklin wrote books and pamphlets that encouraged people to live by a code and offered various proverbs to help them along the way. Phrases like, "A penny saved is a penny earned," and "Early to bed, early to rise, makes a man healthy, wealthy, and wise," were two such proverbs. Have students interview parents and other adults to identify a favorite proverb. Have them scramble the proverb or write it in code. Ask groups of students to work together to decipher the various proverbs. Discuss the meanings of each. Rewrite the proverbs correctly, illustrate each and decorate the room with these words of wisdom.

3. Encourage students to study the various illustrations that appear in the back of the book. In groups, have students create a coloring book that tells the story of the American Revolution. Coloring books can be photocopied and shared with younger students.

4. Group students into pairs. Have each pair select an issue that was at the forefront in pre-Revolutionary times, such as: the blockade, the Stamp Tax, the Boston Tea Party, etc. Have students write about the issue from the patriots' standpoint and then write about the same issue from the British or loyalists' standpoint.

5. Encourage students to keep a diary. They can make their own journals or buy blank books. Have students keep their diaries for at least one month and record happenings in their lives, their community, the country, and the world. Have them include personal reactions to each. At the end of the month, ask each student to read through their diaries and make some observations about the times in which they live.

Discussion Questions

1. How were criminals such as thieves treated in 1774? Do they agree or disagree with the punishments?

2. What health problems did the colonists of 1774 face?

3. Discuss the ways in which the loyalists and the patriots were portrayed.

4. In the book, the author wrote, " The most important decision a man can make in his whole life is what he is willing to die for." Discuss such decisions that have helped shape the history of our country.

5. What events described in the history section at the end of the book parallel with diary events?

6. The author of this book wrote that he had two purposes in mind when writing, "…to reveal what it was like to live in 1774 in Boston. And to bring the revolution to life by showing how it affected ordinary people and how they affected it." Did he succeed in his goals? Explain.

Title: *Shh! We're Writing the Constitution*

Genre: Historical fiction

Author: Jean Fritz

Bibliographic Information: Scholastic, 1987.

Summary: The story of the writing of the Constitution unfolds as readers learn the problems, issues, and determination involved in designing and ratifying our Constitution.

Interest Level: Grades 4–7

Pre-Reading Activity

Ask students, "If you could talk with Thomas Jefferson, James Madison, Patrick Henry, and the others as they worked to create our Constitution, what questions would you ask?" Write these questions down and refer to them after the book has been completed to see how many questions were answered. Help students research those questions which remained unanswered.

Learning Activities

1. Have students imagine that they were at the Continental Convention in Philadelphia that was scheduled to begin May 14, 1787. Have them write a letter home giving a first hand account of what impressed them most.

2. Have students create a picture book for children that simplifies the story of the writing of the Constitution. Encourage them to illustrate the book with original art.

3. Have students create a special edition of a newspaper that might have been published after the Constitution was ratified. Articles and editorial cartoons should relate the happenings of the Constitutional Convention. Students should include quotes from delegates they "interviewed" at the Convention.

4. Have the class create a graph to show the way each state voted on the ratification of the Constitution. Which state had the highest percentage of votes in favor of ratification. Which state had the lowest?

5. Have students take part in a Constitutional Quiz Bowl. Questions can be created by students from information in the text of the book as well as from their notes from the unit and their copy of the Constitution that appears at the back of *Shh! We're Writing the Constitution.*

Discussion Questions

1. Why did the delegates believe a constitution was necessary? Why weren't the Articles of Confederation sufficient?

2. Why did it take the delegates so long to write the Constitution?

3. What problems did the delegates to the Convention face?

4. Which issues debated by the delegates do you believe were the most important? Explain.

5. Was 'We the People' a fitting beginning for the Preamble? Why or why not?

6. How did the title of the book reflect its content and tone?

Title: *Sarah Bishop*

Genre:	Historical fiction
Author:	Scott O'Dell
Bibliographic Information:	Houghton Mifflin, 1980.
Summary:	Sarah's family is torn apart by the Revolutionary War. Her father is a Tory; her mother is a Patriot. Sarah finds herself alone and pursued by the British. She takes refuge in the wilderness and learns to survive.
Interest Level:	Grades 6+

Pre-Reading Activity

Explain that there have been times in our country's history when family members actually fought against each other over certain issues (Civil War, Revolutionary War). Discuss what might have happened to cause this and what problems would result. Ask students to think of issues and problems today that split families apart.

Learning Activities

1. Have students write a journal entry to explain how their attitudes about the Tories, the British, and/or the Loyalists were influenced by the story of Sarah Bishop.

2. Have each student create a Reader's Theater piece to tell about one of their favorite scenes. An example is on pp. 188–192.

3. Have students create "Wanted" posters for Sarah Bishop.

4. Hold a mock trial in which Mr. Bishop is prosecuted for tearing up the pamphlet *Common Sense,* or students may wish to select a different character to bring to trial.

5. Discuss the dangers Sarah faced in the wilderness. Create a guide to help people survive such dangers (identifying poisonous snakes, staying warm, etc.).

Discussion Questions

1. Did the book have a bias? Were both sides (Tory and Patriot) portrayed fairly? Explain.

2. In what ways is this book's portrayal of the war different from others you have read?

3. Isaac Morton told Sarah that "fear causes hatred." Explain what he meant. Give examples from history and from events today that support this statement.

4. If you lived in revolutionary times, would Sarah Bishop be a person you would trust or choose for a friend? Explain.

Title: *Johnny Tremain*

Genre: Historical fiction

Author: Esther Forbes

Bibliographic Information: Dell, 1943.

Summary: This classic tells the story of Johnny, a young apprentice silversmith, who is caught in the events that lead to the Revolutionary War. Through his adventures, we learn about the Sons of Liberty, the Boston Tea Party, and the spirit of the times.

Interest Level: Grades 4–8

Pre-Reading Activity

Discuss with students the parts they would have liked to play in the Revolutionary War if they had lived during that time period.

Learning Activities

1. In the first chapters of the book, Johnny's life begins to fall apart. Have students write a journal entry as if they were Johnny in which he reflects upon one of the tragedies that has occurred.

2. Have students create a biopoem for Johnny Tremain:

   Line 1:   First name
   Line 2:   Title
   Line 3:   Four words that describe Johnny
   Line 4:   Lover of . . . (three or more things or ideas)
   Line 5:   Who believed . . .(one or more ideals)
   Line 6:   Who wanted . . .(three things or ideas)
   Line 7:   Who used... (three things or methods)
   Line 8:   Who gave... (three things)
   Line 9:   Who said....(select a favorite quote from the book)
   Line 10: Last name

3. Have students recreate the Boston of Johnny Tremain's day. Have them use a variety of materials to capture the sights and sounds so vividly described in the book.

4. Have students look through books on colonial America and create a display of crafts (use pictures and copies of real crafts). Students can describe each craft on index cards and place these cards next to the appropriate items and pictures.

5. Johnny's badly burned hand did not receive proper medical treatment. Ask students to create posters warning students about the dangers of burns and include some first-aid tips.

Discussion Questions

1. What is the role of an apprentice? Do we have apprentices today? Explain.
2. Is this book a good example of historical fiction? Why or why not?
3. Does the book have a bias? Were the issues and beliefs important to both sides discussed? Explain.
4. Throughout the book and at the end the phrase "A man can stand up" is repeated? What does this mean?

CULMINATING ACTIVITY

Remind students of the initiating activity. Ask them to move into their original groups and remind them what each group represented: "Loyalist, Patriot, or British Soldier." Within their groups, they should discuss the rules that had been posted by the teacher and how they related to the happenings that led to the Revolutionary War. Once again, have them analyze their group's positions. Have any students in the group changed their minds? Why? Would each be willing to fight for the position selected? What things are worth fighting for? Have students write position papers to express their feelings and the reasons for any changes in their original ideas. Encourage students to relate their ideas to insights gained from this unit.

SUPPLEMENTAL LITERATURE

Books

Historical Fiction

Avi. (1984). *The fighting ground*. New York: J. M. Lippincott.

Clapp, P. (1968*). I'm Deborah Sampson: A soldier of the revolution*. New York: Lothrop, Lee & Shepard Books.

Collier, J. L., & Collier, C. (1981). *Jump ship to freedom*. New York: Delacorte.

Collier, J. L., & Collier, C. (1974). *My brother Sam is dead*. New York: Four Winds.

Collier, J. L., & Collier, C. (1984). *The winter hero*. New York: Four Winds.

Danenberg, B. (1998). *The journal of William Thomas Emerson: A revolutionary war patriot*. New York Scholastic. (Part of the *Dear America Series*)

Fast, H. (1961). *April morning*. New York: Crown.

Fritz, J. (1973). *And then what happened, Paul Revere?* New York: Coward.

Fritz, J. (1977). *Can't you make them behave, King George?* New York: Coward.

Fritz, J. (1987). *Early thunder*. New York: Viking.

Gregory, K. (1996). *The winter of red snow: The revolutionary war diary of Abigail Jane Stewart*. New York: Scholastic. (Part of the *Dear America Series*.)

McGovern, A. (1987). *The secret soldier: The story of Deborah Sampson*. New York: Four Winds.

Myers, A. (1997). *The keeping room*. New York: Walker.

Non-Fiction

Asimov, I. (1974). *The birth of the United States: 1763–1816*. Boston: Houghton Mifflin.

Brenner, B. (1994). *If you were there in 1776*. New York: Simon and Schuster.

Carter, A. (1988). *The American Revolution: Birth of the republic*. New York: Franklin Watts.

Collier, C. and Collier, J. (1998). *The American revolution*. Benchmark.

Cox, C. (1999*). Come all you brave soldiers: Blacks in the revolutionary war*. New York: Cartwheel Books.

Davis, B. and Brooke, E. (1992). *Black heroes of the American revolution*. San Diego, CA: Harcourt Brace.

Dolan, E. (1995). *The American Revolution: How we fought the war of independence*. Brookfield, CT: Millbrook Press.

Gay, K. and Gay, M. (1995). *Revolutionary war*. New York: Twenty-first Century Books.

Kent, D. (1994*). The American Revolution: 'Give me liberty, or give me death!'* Springfield, NJ: Enslow.

Lukes, B. (1996). *The American revolution.* San Diego, CA: Lucent Books. (World History Series)

Nardo, D. (Ed.) (1998). *The American revolution.* San Diego, CA. Greenhaven. (Offers opposing viewpoints, including prewar disputes, patriot verses loyalist views, etc.)

Marrin, A. (1988). *The war for independence: The story of the American revolution.* New York: Antheneum.

Meltzer, M. (1987). *The American revolutionaries: A history in their own words, 1750–1800.* New York: Thomas Y. Crowell.

Meltzer, M. (1990). *The Bill of Rights: How we got it and what it means.* New York: Thomas Y. Crowell.

Moore, K. (1998). Ill. by D. O'Leary. *If you lived at the time of the American revolution.* New York: Scholastic.

Stein, R. (1997). *The Declaration of Independence.* New York: Children's Press.

Stein, R. (1998). *The Boston tea party.* New York: Children's Press.

Steins, R. (1995). *A nation is born: Rebellion and independence in America 1700–1820.* Merrimac, NH: 21st Century Learning Products.

Tunis, E. (1965). *Colonial craftsmen.* New York: Thomas Y. Crowell.

Web Sites

American Revolutionary War Timeline
http://www.ilt.columbia.edu/k12/history/timeline.html

Benjamin Franklin: Glimpses of the Man
http://sin.fi.edu/franklin/rotten.html

Eighteenth-Century Resources
http://andromeda.rutgers.edu/~jlynch/18th/

Liberty! The American Revolution (the official online companion to the PBS series)
http://www.pbs.org/ktca/liberty/

MINI-THEMES

The Constitution and Bill of Rights: An In-Depth Look

What foresight the framers of our Constitution had; they created a document that has been the cornerstone of democracy for over 200 years! The Constitution has been responsible for the interpretation of law and has helped our country maintain a steady course, despite the many crises and storms we've encountered. While most of us are aware of the existence and importance of the Constitution, few are familiar with its depth and scope. This unit explores the Constitution and the Bill of Rights in depth—an exploration of the words that have powered and empowered a nation.

Activities

1. Use one of the "Cooperative Learning" strategies to help students learn about the various components of the Constitution. (see Chapter 2, pp. 52–55.)

2. Involve students in an Intergalactic Constitutional Convention! Read the following futuristic scenario: "Over the past decades, many nations have

worked together to create a space colony. This colony, the first of many, will be settled by people from each of the countries involved. Since each country has a different form of government, it is vital that a new Constitution be written that will guide the new colony." Divide students into groups and ask each to create a Constitution and Preamble. Encourage them to use our own Constitution as a model.

3. Using the same scenario as Activity 1 above, have students create a Bill of Rights to accompany their Constitution.

4. Have students cut out articles from the newspaper that reflect how each of the amendments under the Bill of Rights affect our lives today. Have students lead discussions based on the articles found.

5. Select an issue that is being debated today based on the Bill of Rights. Hold a mock Supreme Court hearing in which the issue is discussed and a ruling is made based on the justices' interpretation of the Bill of Rights.

6. Discuss the following: "How would our lives be different today if we didn't have a Constitution?" Have students create written or artistic essays to express their answers.

References

Levy, E. (1987). *If you were there when they signed the Constitution*. New York: Scholastic.

Meltzer, M. (1990). *The Bill of Rights: How we got it and what it means*. New York: Thomas Y. Crowell.

Prolman, M. (1995). *The Constitution*. New York: Children's Press.

Stein, R. (1994). *The Bill of Rights*. New York: Children's Press.

The Revolutionaries: A Closer Look

Who were the leaders whose courage and vision toppled the British monarchy and led to the creation of a new nation, "conceived in liberty and dedicated to the proposition that all men are created equal"? What qualities did these revolutionaries have that helped equip them for this unique struggle? What were their hopes, dreams, and visions?

Activities

1. Have students determine the most influential leaders of Revolutionary times. Have individuals or groups select one of the leaders and create a 3-D collage that reflects the person's contributions to the Revolution as well as his/her family, career, etc. Benjamin Franklin, for example, was an author, an inventor, and a statesman.

2. Have students select a famous hero of the revolution and write a verse modeled after Longfellow's poem, "Paul Revere's Ride." Have them read these poems to the class and bind work into a book entitled, "Heroes of the Revolution."

3. Have students write several diary entries as if they were one of the leaders of the Revolution. In their diaries, have them include some of the conflicts

in their lives in respect to their positions and actions during and preceding the war years, as well as their assessment of the various events that are taking place.

4. They say everyone has a twin somewhere. Ask students to pair one revolutionist with a contemporary leader/ hero of today. Have them write an essay that compares and contrasts these two people and include photos if possible.

References

Bruns, R. (1986). *World leaders past and present.* New York: Chelsea House. This is a series which includes books on founding fathers such as Thomas Jefferson.

Meltzer, M. (1987). *The American revolutionaries: A history in their own words, 1750–1800.* New York: Thomas Y. Crowell.

Murphy, J. (1998). *A young patriot: The American revolution as experienced by one boy.* New York: Clarion.
This book tells of a 15-year-old, Joseph Plumb Martin, who enlisted in 1776. Based on Martin's extensive biography. Includes reproductions of period—engravings, paintings, and documents.

Wheeler, R. (Ed.) and Catton, B. (1997). *The voices of 1776: The story of the American Revolution in the words of those who were there.* San Diego, CA: Meridian.

Young, R. (1996*). Revolutionaries: The real patriots of the American revolution.* Parsippany, NJ: Dillon Press

Theme

The Wild, Wild West

OVERVIEW

Focus

The Wild West comes alive as students travel through time to one of the most colorful and romanticized periods of American history.

Objective

Upon completion of this unit, students will:

1. Relate significant historical events that reflect how the West was won—and lost.

2. Describe the reasons for moving west and relate the dangers the pioneers faced.

3. Compare the reality of life in the Wild West with the way it was depicted through legend and lore.

4. Become familiar with the art and music of the Wild West—pictures and songs that capture the courage and spirit of the Wild West.

HOW IT WORKS

Initiating Activity

The opening of the American West and the growth of photography took place during the same time. By the 1850s, frontier photographers were traveling throughout the West, capturing and preserving for posterity the life and times of the pioneers who journeyed to and settled the West. Photocopy many of the photographs that appear in such book as *Children of the Wild West* (Freedman, 1983) and *Cowboys of the Wild West* (Freedman, 1985), and distribute them to students. Group students and ask them to make predictions about all the aspects of life during the time, based solely on what they can hypothesize from the pictures. Have students share their photographs and predictions. At the end of the unit have students re-evaluate their interpretations based on the knowledge and understandings they have gained.

General Activities

1. Have students create their own Wild West character. To do this, divide students into groups and have each group trace one of its members on butcher paper. Students can then staple the front and back of the traced pattern, leaving a temporary opening so that the figure can be stuffed with rolled up pieces of newspaper. Using the information and photographs in the many reference books on life in the West, have students recreate a Wild West character (i.e. cowboy, Native American, teacher, store clerk,

etc.) they find especially interesting. Have students use various clothing and objects to make their figure look authentic and life-like. Allow time for students to share their character and tell the class something about his/her life during the time of the Wild, Wild West.

2. After reading about the Wild West, have students create a large mural in which they depict one aspect of life in the Wild West (i.e. a cowboy roping cattle; branding cattle; a schoolhouse; a general store; panning for gold; hunting for food and fur; keeping law and order; building the railroad to the West; and so forth). The characters created in General Activity 1 can then be placed in an area with the appropriate background scenery.

3. The West inspired its own music. Many of the songs were sung by cowboys around the campfire during the long trail drives. Have each group of students select and learn a favorite song about life in the Wild West and have them teach their song to other groups of students. Many of these songs can be found in books such as *From Sea to Shining Sea* (Cohn, 1993).

4. Read *The Quilt* by Ann Jonas (Greenwillow, 1984) to students. Explain that quilting was a popular craft in the days of the Old West and remains a popular art form today. Since many communities have people involved in quilting, try to locate a local quilt-maker willing to demonstrate the craft. (Ask people in local craft stores or fabric stores to help you locate quilters.) Provide each student with a 12" by 12" piece of fabric. Have students illustrate a scene from the Wild West on their piece of fabric. Combine squares to form a quilt.

5. Group students and have them become one of the states of the West. As "the state" have each group present a brief skit telling about its life during the days of the Wild West, why it became a popular location for settlement, how/when it became a state, as well as containing any anecdotes and stories about famous people associated with the area.

6. Horace Greeley, editor of the *New York Tribune* during the mid 1800s, once penned the words, "Go west, young man, go west and grow up with the country." Ask students to create a poster, using these famous words as a caption to entice people to travel west. Their posters should capture one or more of the compelling reasons (i.e. fur trade, gold rush, opportunity for religious freedom, etc.) that would cause people to uproot themselves and face the dangers associated with travel to the West.

7. The West was settled by many men and women of courage and perseverance. Have students research one of the men/women listed on p. 305 who have had a part in how the West was won—and lost. (Other names can be added.) After their research is completed, have them share their findings with the class in a creative way. For example, they might create a ballad about the person, set to the tune of a song of the Old West, or they might create a monologue that that person would use to describe his/her exploits, and so forth.

Men and Women of the Wild West

Stephen Austin and the Texas Rangers	James Harte
William Becknell	Doc Holiday
James Butler (Wild Bill Hickok)	President Andrew Jackson
Brigham Young	Frank and Jesse James
Martha Jane Cannary (Calamity Jane)	William Clark and Meriwether Lewis
Kit Carson	Henry McCarty (Billy the Kid)
Butch Cassidy	Bill Picket
George Catlin	Annie Oakley
John Chisholm	Frederic Remington
Buffalo Bill Cody	Charles Russell
Wyatt Earp	Susanna Salter
John Fremont	Levi Strauss
James Gadson	John Sutter
Zane Grey	Henry Wells and William Fargo
Horace Greeley	

---

8. Read *The Cowboy and the Black-Eyed Pea* (Johnson, 1993), a parody of *The Princess and the Pea,* with language and details of the Wild West. As a class, create a story frame (see Chapter 2, pp. 63–64) based on this book to help students organize their thoughts about the story and its elements. Have students create and illustrate their own folktales of the Wild West based on their favorite childhood folktale. Bind each story and have students share them with younger children.

9. After reading about actual life in the Wild West, allow students to watch a video of a well-known movie that depicts the West, such as *Dances with Wolves.* Involve students in a discussion of the stereotypes fostered by the movie, the inaccuracies, and so forth.

10. Many artists have captured the spirit of the Wild West. Encourage students to look at pictures of sculptures and other artistic media by such people as Frederic Remington, Charles Lewis, and Ansel Adams. *Wild West,* a bimonthly publication of Empire Press, Inc. (602 S. King Street, Suite 300, Leesburg, VA, 22075), features photos of many such works. Have students select a favorite sculpture, painting, and the like and try to recreate it. Have them accompany their artwork with a brief essay on how the original work captured the feelings of the Wild West.

11. Historian Cathi Luchetti wrote, "Women experienced an autonomy never before dreamed of . . . and 'women's work' soon came to mean whatever had to be done." Locate specific information/photos to support her views. Have students create a "Go west, young woman, go west" collage.

12. Create a "Wild West" time capsule that might have been left by one of the settlers of the Wild West. To do this, divide students into groups based on various disciplines of social studies and science (i.e. anthropology, sociology, politics, economics, geography, history, biology). After explaining each discipline, have the groups bring in and/or make replicas of items

that reflect the Wild West from the perspective of the discipline assigned (i.e. clothing, pictures, crafts, copies of songs and poetry, books). As they place these items in the box, have students describe the item's significance. You may wish to keep this time capsule and use it to introduce the unit on the Wild West next year.

13. Involve students in crafts, recipes, and projects that allow them to experience various facets of life in the Wild West. Books such as *Westward Ho!* (Carlson, 1996) and *The Cowboy's Handbook* (Cody, 1996) include ideas for many such projects.

Discussion Questions

1. Life in the Wild West was often quite different from the legends and lore that surround it. What do you believe is the most important difference between fact and fiction regarding the Wild West?

2. Why do you think the time/place was referred to as "The Wild West"? Do you agree or disagree with this term? What term do you think would be more appropriate?

3. Many people risked their lives to travel to the West. Do you think the advantages outweighed the disadvantages? Explain.

4. Imagine that you lived during the mid-1800s in New York. What would entice you to travel to and settle in the Wild West?

5. Many people have various reasons to explain the end of the era of the Wild West. How would you explain it?

6. What if the first immigrants to this country had settled on the west coast instead of the east coast?

LITERATURE RELATED ACTIVITIES

Title: *Cowboys of the Wild West*

Genre: Informational

Author: Russell Freedman

Illustrator: Photographs from the days of the Wild West

Bibliographic Information: Clarion, New York, 1985.

Summary: Newbery Medalist Russell Freedman provides insight into life in the Wild West of the 1800s. Through text and photographs, the reader can feel the spirit and courage of those who inspired the legends of the old-time, trail-driving cowboy.

Interest Level: Grades 4+

Pre-Reading Activity

Ask students to close their eyes and picture a "cowboy" in their minds. Involve students in a semantic webbing (see Chapter 2, pp. 39–40) of the word "cowboy" based on the images they "see." Share the cover of *Cowboys of the Wild West*. Involve them in a discussion of the ways in which the cowboys pictured differed from the way they imagined they would look.

Learning Activities

1. Have students create a journal entry written by a cowboy at the end of a long day on the trail.

2. Have students create a chart that pictures the different clothing and equipment worn/used by the cowboys. Next to each have them explain how the item was developed to solve a specific problem. Ask students to think of life today and what we could do to make our clothing more functional.

3. Have students select a favorite picture from the book. Ask them to write a descriptive paragraph in such a way that others will see it, feel the emotion, mood, and so forth that the picture evokes.

4. Reprint the map on page 15. Have the students create questions about distances between various cities and routes between cities. Involve them in further research to learn about the terrain that had to be crossed as cowboys moved cattle from one area to another.

5. Have students compile the poems and songs referenced in this book, along with other favorites, to create a *Cowboy Anthology—Poems and Songs of the Wild West.*

Discussion Questions

1. Why was the cowboy's job so important during the days of the Wild West? (As the demand for beef grew, the cattle-raising industry spread from Texas. Cattle had to be moved from Texas to railroad towns to be shipped to meat-packing plants.)

2. Who were the original cowboys? (Cowboys originated over four hundred years ago in Mexico when Spanish settlers brought the first domesticated horses and cattle to North America. Ranchers who looked after the herds were called vaqueros—from "vaca," the Spanish word for cow.)

3. According to the book, only a few cowboys stayed on the job for more than ten years. What do you think was the most difficult thing about being a cowboy—the lifestyle or the physical work? Cite specific references from the book to support your answer.

4. In what ways did this book change your perceptions about cowboys and cowboy life?

5. Discuss the lines on page 79 that are from a Texas song. What do they tell you about the reasons for the end of the cowboy era? (Cattle ranchers were putting up barbed-wire fences that kept livestock from straying. The network of railroad tracks was spreading and by the 1890s reached into central Texas, making long trail drives unnecessary.)

Title: *The Righteous Revenge of Artemis Bonner*

Genre: Fiction

Author: Walter Dean Myers

Bibliographic Information: HarperCollins, New York, 1992.

Summary: Fifteen-year-old Artemis Bonner leaves New York City in 1880 to find his uncle's murderer and to find the gold mine his uncle sketched on a map from memory. The story traces Artemis's journey and adventures through the Old West.

Interest Level: Grades 5+

Pre-Reading Activity

Ask students to discuss the following questions: "What do you think the term *righteous revenge* in the title means?" "How is the term *righteous revenge* an oxymoron?" "Do you believe that there should be such a thing as *righteous revenge*—why or why not?"

Learning Activities

1. Artemis traveled throughout the Wild West. During his journey he said, "If a town could be a bird or an animal, Seattle would be a seagull. It did not as much mind what it was doing as take wings and fly. And just like a sea gull it took its own sweet time about doing anything." Based on the students' knowledge of the Wild West and based on the descriptions Artemis gave, have students create a metaphor similar to the one above for each of the following cities Artemis visited, comparing it to a bird or an animal, and explain the comparison: Tombstone, Arizona; Lincoln, Nebraska; Juarez City, Mexico; Seattle, Washington; and Anchorage, Alaska. Ask each student to select their favorite metaphor, then illustrate and display it.

2. Tall tales grew out of America's dream for freedom and the vastness of the wide-open spaces of the Wild West. Many feats told through tall tales were based on fact but were exaggerated into legendary proportions. An example of this would be the story told to Artemis by O'Hara, the prospector who told how he had found the biggest hunk of gold ever found: "It was so big, it took two horses just to drag it around town." Involve students in reading tall tales of the Wild West, such as those about Pecos Bill and Paul Bunyan. Have students discuss what factual information was included about the Wild West and what was exaggerated.

3. The gold rush of 1849 brought many men and women west. Have the students research this era. Research can include the methods used for finding gold; the dangers involved; the numbers of people the gold rush attracted; how the gold rush affected life in the Wild West; and so on. Have students present their findings in a creative way (i.e. become a prospector and tell about your life; become a piece of gold nugget and tell how you were found).

4. In groups, have students create a sequel to the story and present it in some form of creative dramatics. Remind students that details in the sequel should be accurate in terms of time and place.

Discussion Questions

1. How did the book portray the Wild West? Based on your knowledge of the Wild West, how accurate was this portrayal?

2. What other ways might Artemis and Cat Fish have solved their differences other than resorting to violence?

3. Explain the irony of the statement, "Moby might have been honorable in the killing department, but I did not know that much about him, or even if he had come from a decent home." (p. 81)

4. Artemis believed that the Wild West was settled by cutthroats, heathens, and foreigners. Agree or disagree with him, citing specific references from this book and others.

Title: *Across America on an Emigrant Train*

Genre: Informational

Author: Jim Murphy

Illustrator: Illustrated with Photographs and Prints

Bibliographic Information: Clarion, New York, 1993.

Summary: Follow the journey made in 1879 by writer Robert Louis Stevenson, when he set out from Scotland headed for California. He and his fellow travelers crossed the Atlantic and then undertook a three-thousand-mile train ride to settle in the American West. Through Stevenson's eyes, we meet the people and visit what has been referred to as the Wild West.

Interest Level: Grades 5+

Pre-Reading Activity

Ask students if they know who Robert Louis Stevenson was. See which of his writings they are familiar with (i.e. *Treasure Island, A Child's Garden of Verses, The Strange Case of Dr. Jekyll and Mr. Hyde, Kidnapped*). Also, discuss the difference between immigration and emigration. Ask them, "Why do you think the book was called *Across America on an Emigrant Train* rather than on an *Immigrant Train?*" (Generally, to emigrate is to leave from a country or place. To immigrate is to enter or arrive in a country or place. As the book explains, Stevenson's traveling companions, though they were in America, had not yet arrived at their final destinations. Stevenson believed, therefore, that they were still in the process of emigrating.)

Learning Activities

1. Read aloud Jacqueline Geis's book *Where the Buffalo Roam* (1992), in which she expands a popular song of the West to describe the vegetation of America's Southwest. Based on Stevenson's descriptions of the West, have students create their own verses to add to the song. Have them illustrate their verses and compile them into *A Song Book of the West*.

2. Based on the information related in the book, have students create the "Top Ten Reasons to Immigrate to America's West." The list can be humorous but it should be based on fact.

3. States competed with one another for immigrants. To lure people west and especially to their state, advertisements and pamphlets were written and distributed. Have students form groups (one per state, west of the Mississippi) and have them create an advertisement similar to those pictured in the book (p. 3). Their advertisement should include factual information about the territory and what it offers the immigrant.

4. Many settlers to the Wild West wrote to their relatives telling them about their lives and asking them to journey west. Write a letter to a relative describing your life in the Wild West and explaining why he/she should join you.

5. Brainstorm a list of countries from which a large number of people immigrated to the Wild West. Divide students into groups based on the list of countries and involve them in research to learn why so many decided to leave their homes, the type of work they did in the West, and where in the West they mainly settled. Have students create a poster to display their findings, along with a graph to indicate appropriate information.

Discussion Questions

1. Why were the government, individual states, and the railroad so eager to attract immigrants? (The government needed people to work the land and harvest the natural resources of the West. The states wanted the money immigrants brought with them, the railroads needed people to lay tracks, and so forth.)

2. List five things that surprised you most about Stevenson's journey across America.

3. The Sioux chief, White Cloud, said, "Wherever the whites are established the red hunter must die of hunger." To what was he referring? (The white settlers were killing all the bison and other game that the Indians relied on for survival. Much of the time the killing was for sport.)

4. Discuss Stevenson's feelings about the treatment of the Native Americans. How do his beliefs coincide/disagree with yours?

5. Looking at life in the West as it is depicted in the photographs, would you have liked living during the days of the Wild West? Why or why not?

Title: *Calamity Jane—Her Life and Her Legend*

Genre:	Biography
Author:	Doris Faber
Illustrator:	Illustrated with photographs
Bibliographic Information:	Houghton Mifflin, Boston, 1992.
Summary:	Who was Calamity Jane? Was she really a sharp-shooter as legend claims? Was she married to Wild Bill Hickok? Was she a scout for General Custer? This biography attempts to separate fact from fiction as it explores the life of Martha Jane Cannary—Calamity Jane.
Interest Level:	Grades 5+

Pre-Reading Activity

Discuss the fact that often actual people were transformed into legendary figures. Some of these include Johnny Appleseed, Buffalo Bill Cody, and Calamity Jane. Have students study the picture of Calamity Jane on the cover. Ask them why they think Calamity might have become a legend. Does the picture offer any clues?

Learning Activities

1. Calamity Jane seemed to create much of the legend that surrounded her. Have students select one of Calamity Jane's adventures and use it as a basis for a tall tale. Have them present it in storytelling form.

2. Have students create a picture postcard depicting one of Calamity Jane's feats. On the other side of the card have them write a brief message describing Calamity Jane to a friend.

3. From the photographs in the books have students create a diorama to depict a scene common to the Wild West.

4. Create a monument to Calamity Jane or to any other person who immigrated to the West. (See the monument built to honor Wild Bill Hickok on p. 30.)

5. Many legendary heroes/heroines of the wild West had nicknames, such as Wild Bill, Buffalo Bill, Calamity Jane. Ask students to give themselves a nickname and create a story about themselves as a hero of the Wild West. Have students write their stories in the style of those written by Ned Wheeler for the dime novels (see pp. 37 and 39) and remind them to keep the details authentic in terms of character, setting, and the like. Compile class stories into a Wild West paper.

Discussion Questions

1. How was Calamity Jane's life like the Wild West? (untamed, free, larger than life, daring, and so forth.) How did Calamity Jane differ from "The

Spirit of the Frontier" pictured on page 3? (Women were supposed to inspire men, not seek out adventures of their own.)

2. How was Calamity Jane different from most of the women of her time? (She dressed like a man, spent all her time with men, drank whiskey, pretended to be a boy to get more exciting jobs, and so forth.)

3. The legend of Calamity Jane seems like an inter-weaving of fact and fiction. How do you account for this phenomena?

4. Of Calamity Jane, one western historian wrote, "She was most certainly somebody." Defend this statement.

CULMINATING ACTIVITY

Hold a Wild West Extravaganza with Buffalo Bill Cody as host! Have students dress up in the costumes of the time, share their songs, art, and stories of the Wild West around a simulated campfire! Have students prepare foods associated with the Wild West. Group students and involve them in a role-playing activity in which they act out one of the following situations as if they lived during the mid and late 1800s:

1. You and your family are recent immigrants to America. You've been living on the East Coast but see little hope for business opportunities. Some members of your family do not want to venture West, others do.

2. You are on a wagon train heading west during the last weeks of Fall. There are two routes to follow—a shorter, more dangerous one by water; a much longer but safer one by land. Your supplies are running low and your oxen are near exhaustion. The members of your wagon train are divided as to what to do.

3. You and your companions have found a gold deposit but are afraid that one of your group will stake the claim before the rest of you have the opportunity.

4. You live in a small western town. A young Indian has been accused of shooting and killing one of the town's citizens. The youth admits to the killing but says it was in self-defense. The crowd wants him hung and the judge isn't expected for several months.

5. You are members of the Texas Rangers. You learn that a very prominent citizen has been rustling cattle and branding it as his own.

6. Create and act out a problem situation that was common in the days of the Wild West.

SUPPLEMENTAL LITERATURE

Books

Note: Unless otherwise noted, the books listed are informational.

Brink, C. (1936). *Caddie Woodlawn.* New York: Macmillan.
[Historical Fiction] An account of the life of Caddie Woodlawn and her family as they live and survive the many dangers of life in the West.

Carmer, C. (1942). *America sings.* New York: Knopf.
  Includes poems that celebrate every aspect of American history.

Carlson, L. (1996). *Westward ho! An activity guide to the wild west.* Chicago: Chicago Review Press.
  Includes a brief history of North America, the westward movement and introduces over 50 activities and projects (crafts, recipes, songs and games such as panning for gold and hooking a rug).

Cohn, A. L. (1993). *From sea to shining sea.* Illustrated by 15 Caldecott Medal/Honor Book Artists. New York. Scholastic.
  This volume contains over 140 American folktales, folk songs, poems, and essays, with a large section devoted to the pioneers who settled the American West.

Cody, T. (1996). *The cowboy's handbook: How to become a hero of the Wild West.* New York: Cobblehill.
  Written by a descendent of Buffalo Bill Cody, this book includes information, recipes, and a code of conduct to help students become heroes of the West.

Freeman, R. (1983). *Children of the wild west.* Illustrated with photographs. New York: Clarion.
  A history, in words and photographs, of the lives of the children who traveled west in wagon trains and settled on the frontier.

Freeman, R. (1985). *Cowboys of the wild west.* Illustrated with photographs. New York: Clarion.
  A history, in words and photographs, of the lives of the cowboys who inspired the legends of the Wild West.

Gels, J. (1992). *Where the buffalo roam.* Nashville, TN: Ideals.
  Pictures depicting the West accompany Geis' own adaptation of the song "Home on the Range."

Hammer, T. (1986). *The advancing frontier.* New York: Franklin Watts.
  Emphasizes the settlement of the West and the role of women and blacks. Also discusses the "dark side" of western expansion—the discrimination against minorities and the treatment of Native Americans.

Henry. M. (1992). *Mustang: Wild spirit of the West.* New York: Aladdin.
  [Historical Fiction] Based on the true tale of Wild Horse Annie who helped save the herds of wild mustangs from extinction.

Ingoglia, G. (1991). *The big Golden Book of the wild west.* Illustrated by G. Biggs. New York: Western Publishing.
  Traces the settlement of the West from the first settlers to the Old West as it is today.

Katz, W. (1995). *Black women of the old west.* New York: Antheneum.
  Information presented regarding the role of black women in settling the West.

King. D. (1998). *Wild West days: Discover the past with fun projects, games, activities, and recipes.* New York: John Wiley and Sons.

Activity pocket book transports readers to a cattle ranch near Cheyenne in the 1870's and allows them to join Tom as he goes on his first cattle drive.

Lomax, J. A., & Lomax, A., compilers. (1938). *Cowboy songs and other frontier ballads.* New York: Macmillan.
Includes many songs sung by the cowboys.

Metropolitan Museum of Art. (1991). *Songs of the Wild West.* New York: Simon and Schuster.
A collection of tunes created by the cowboys and settlers of the Old West.

Meyer, C. (1992). *Where the broken heart still beats.* San Diego, CA: Harcourt Brace Jovanovich.
[Historical Fiction] The story of a 12-year-old girl who is kidnapped and raised by the Comanches for 25 years before being "rescued" by Texas Rangers.

Moeri, L. (1981). *Save Queen of Sheba.* New York: Dutton.
[Historical Fiction] The story of two children who survive an Indian attack while traveling in a wagon train.

Smith, C. Ed. (1992). *The legendary wild west: A sourcebook on the American west.* Brookfield, CT: Millbrook Press.
Describes and illustrates the American West from 1763 to 1912.

Stotter, M. (1997). *Wild West.* New York: Kingfisher Books.
Visit the untamed American West. See life in a covered wagon, a frontier town, and a cattle ranch.

Wilder, L. I. *The little house series.* New York: Harper and Row.
[Historical Fiction] The life of Laura Ingalls Wilder and her family as they settle in different areas of the American West and face the dangers and triumphs of pioneer life.

Wood, T. (1997). *The wild west.* New York: Viking.
Travel to the days of the West and discover life during its heyday.

Web Sites

American West Heritage Center
http://www.americanwestcenter.org/

Jim Janke's Old West
http://homepages.dsu.edu/jankej/oldwest/oldwest.htm

Old West Links (Compiled by the Old West Living History Foundation)
http://www.oldwest.org/cows/links.html

Oregon Trail
http://www.isu.edu/~trinmich/Oregontrail.html

Gunfighters of the Wild West
http://www.geocities.com/~christianna/gunfighters/WildWest.html

MINI-THEMES

Native Americans of the Wild West

The area known to us as the Wild West belonged to Native Americans. As more and more settlers moved west and the states extended westward, the Native Americans were either forced to accept the government's offers to resettle elsewhere or be driven away by force. As their land was stolen, so too was their way of life.

Activities

1. Have students simulate a "Meeting of Chiefs" in which various leaders of Native American tribes discuss whether to agree to the government's conditions or fight. Before the simulation, students need to be involved in research on the various Indian leaders, take on the persona of one, and determine what that chief's position would be and why.

2. Discuss with students the Indian Removal Act of 1830. (Between 1830 and 1840, 50,000 Native Americans were forced to leave their homes and were moved to Indian Territory, which is now the state of Oklahoma. During this time, over 4,000 Cherokees lost their lives. The journey is now referred to as The Trail of Tears.) Have students create a television documentary recreating this time.

3. Involve students in creating a Native American Museum in which they recreate objects that were of special significance to the various tribes living in the West (for example, the sacred pipe, Indian headdress, the sacred hoop, beads). Have students label each item and briefly explain its importance. If possible, take students on a field trip to a museum to see actual Native American artifacts.

4. Read aloud many of the poems included in *Dancing Teepees,* compiled by Virginia Driving Hawk Sneve (1989). The poems included were generally passed from generation to generation of Native American youths and offer insights into their lives. Ask each student to select a favorite poem and use it as a model for an original poem that reflects an aspect of the life of Native American youth that each finds especially intriguing. Have them create their own illustrations to accompany their poetry.

5. Have students imagine that they are Native Americans living in the West during the mid-1800s. Have them write a journal entry (either as an Indian maiden, a warrior, the tribe's medicine man, etc.) describing their feelings as the settlers move into their territories and the way this immigration is affecting their lives.

References

Brandt, K. (1985). *Indian crafts.* Illustrated by G. Guzzi. New York: Troll.

Brandt, K. (1985). *Indian homes.* Illustrated by G. Guzzi. New York: Troll.

Collier, P. (1973). *When shall they rest: The Cherokee's long struggle with America.* New York: Holt, Rinehart, and Winston.

Doherty, C.A., & Doherty, K. M. (1991). *The Apaches and Navajos.* New York: Franklin Watts. (Part of a series on Native American tribes)

Driving Hawk Sneve, V., compiler. (1989). *Dancing teepees: Poems of American Indian youth.* Illustrated by S. Gammell. New York: Holiday House.

Force, R., & Force, M. (1991). *The American Indians.* New York: Chelsea House.

Green, C., & Sanford, W. (1997). *Sacagawea: Native American hero.* Springfield, NJ: Enslow Publishers.

Gobel, P., & Goble, D. (1969). *Red Hawk's account of Custer's last stand.* New York: Pantheon.

Hook, J. (1989). *Indian warrior chiefs.* Dorset, England: Firebird Books.

Marrin, A. (1984). *War clouds in the West: Indians and cavalrymen 1860–1890.* New York: Atheneum.

Porter, F. III (General Ed.). *Indians of North America.* (A series of books) New York: Chelsea House (a series of books).

Ruoff, A. (1991). *Literature of the American Indians.* New York: Chelsea House.

St. George, J. (1996). *To see with the heart: The life of Sitting Bull.* New York: Putnam.

Sanford, W. (1997). *Native American leaders of the Wild West.* (7 volumes— Chief Joseph: Nez Perce Warrior; Geronimo: Apache Warrier; Osceola,:Seminole Warrior; Quanah Parker: Comanche Warrior; Crazy Horse: Sioux Warrior; Red Cloud: Sioux Warrior; Red Cloud: Sioux Warrior; Sitting Bull: Sioux Warrior) Springfield, NJ. Enslow Publishers, Inc.

Stein, R. C. (1983). *The story of Wounded Knee.* Illustrated by D. J. Catrow III. Chicago: Children's Press.

Today's Cowboy

By the 1890s, the open range roundups and the trail drives faded into history and the life of the cowboy changed forever. But, as long as there is a West, there will be cowboys still singing of their home on the range, still doing many of the same jobs that the cowboys of the past did. But, with some changes.

Activities

1. With the help of a travel agent, try to get the names and addresses of various working ranches in the West. Brainstorm a list of questions students might ask about life on a ranch and have students write letters to the cowboys/cowgirls who work at the ranches to discover the answers.

2. Share the poetry and art included in Charles Sullivan's *Cowboys* (1993). Have students select one of the types of media in the book (photograph, sculpture, painting, poem, and so forth) and use this form to create a tribute to today's cowboy. For example, students may wish to create a life-size sculpture using a variety of materials or write an original ballad.

3. Select a common cowboy song or song of the West. Ask each student to write an original verse honoring today's cowboy/cowgirl and the work he/she does. Put the verses together and make copies so that the class can learn the entire new version.

4. Involve students in a game of mime by asking each student to select one of the many jobs undertaken by today's cowboys/cowgirls and mime it for the rest of the class.

5. Divide students into pairs. One student in each pair should represent the cowboy of the Wild West and one should represent the cowboy of today. Have students plan and present (in costume) a factually based skit in which each tries to better the other by making his/her life sound more exciting, more fulfilling, and so forth.

6. Have students create a traditional cowboy meal. Follow the directions for three-bean vegetarian chili as explained in *The Cowboy's Handbook* (Cody, 1996).

7. In *The Cowboy's Handbook,* Cody (1996) offers a list of cowboy etiquette. After involving students in a discussion of this list, have them brainstorm and create a code of conduct that would help improve their own neighborhood.

References

Cody, T. (1996). *The cowboy's handbook: How to become a hero of the Wild West.* New York: Cobblehill.

Haney, L. (1975). *Ride 'em cowgirl.* New York: G. P. Putnam's Sons.

Johnson, N. (1992). *Jack Creek cowboy.* New York: Dial.

Lomax, J. A., & Lomax, A., compilers. (1938). *Cowboy songs and other frontier ballads.* New York: Macmillan.

Murdock, D. (1993). *Cowboy.* Photographs by G. Brightling. New York: Knopf.

Rounds, G. (1972). *The cowboy trade.* New York: Holiday House.

Scott, A. H. (1993). *A brand is forever.* Illustrated by R. Rimler. New York: Clarion.

Sullivan. (1993) *Cowboys.* New York: Rizzoli.

Taylor, L., & Maar, I. (1983). *The American cowboy.* Washington, DC: Library of Congress.

Tyler, R. (1975). *The cowboy.* New York: William Morrow.

Poetry:
The Words and The Music

OVERVIEW

Focus

To create in children a delight for poetry and an understanding of the elements that make poetry so appealing to the senses.

Objectives

Upon completion of this unit, students will:

1. Gain an appreciation for and enjoyment of poetry.
2. Identify traditional and contemporary poets and their poems.
3. Read and write using a variety of poetic forms.
4. Recognize and experiment with the various devices used in poetry.
5. Use quality poetry as models for their own verses.

HOW IT WORKS

Initiating Activity

Create a cluster or semantic web (see Chapter 2, pp. 39–40) of the word "poetry" on the chalkboard by having students generate as many words as they can to describe poetry. Using the cluster/map as a guide, ask students to write their own definitions of poetry by completing the phrase, "Poetry is _____." Next, group students, asking each group to come up with one single definition by combining the ideas of the individuals in the group. Finally, after each group shares its definition, create a class definition. Copy the definition onto a large piece of butcher paper and display it in the room as a mural. Throughout the unit, encourage students to add to the mural, including verses from favorite poems, their responses to and feelings about poetry, and original illustrations. When appropriate, share the quotes below and on the following page, and discuss them with the children, along with the responses they have added to the mural. At the end of the unit, have students revisit their class definition and discuss what changes they would make.

> Poetry is not a rose, but the scent of the rose . . .
> Not the sea, but the sound of the sea.
> —*Eleanor Farjeon*
> Poetry is a meteor.
> —*Wallace Stevens*

Prose = words in their best order.
Poetry = the best words in their best order.
—Samuel Taylor Coleridge

A poem . . . begins as a lump in the throat, a sense
of wrong, a homesickness, a love sickness . . . It
finds the thought and the thought finds the words . . .
—Robert Frost

But at the core of every good poem, every poem
that touches me, is the language . . . Language that
surprises the reader. Language that lets a good
poem sing.
—Paul Janeczko

General Activities

1. Introduce children, through reading aloud and choral reading, to the poetry of some of the most popular contemporary poets (see p. 323). Have
   the students select the class's favorite poet and plan a special week dedicated to the poet and his/her work. During the week, you may decorate the
   bulletin board and door with copies of poems and student-made illustrations; have students create their own poems modeled after various poems
   written by the poet; involve students in choral readings of favorite poems
   as well as group and individual readings; involve students in researching
   the life of the poet and collectively write a brief biographical sketch; create an anthology of favorite poems by the poet. Once students have become hooked on contemporary poets, repeat this activity based on the work
   of some of the more traditional poets (see p. 323).

2. Encourage students to keep poetry journals (similar to literature logs discussed in Chapter 2, p. 60–61) in which they write reactions to poems they
   have listened to and read. Allow time for students to discuss specific poems with their classmates through small group (literary circles) and class
   discussions. Discussion may focus on their responses to the poems, interpretations, poetic devices and techniques that affect the poem and affect
   their feelings about the poem.

3. Encourage each student to skim through books of poetry to find a poem
   that says something special to him/her. Many of the more contemporary
   poems contain verses that children can readily identify with, poems that
   reflect their experiences, their hopes, their fears, and their dreams. Some
   of these include poems from Eloise Greenfield's *Honey, I Love,* Langston
   Hughes' *The Dream Keeper,* Nancy Larrick's *Bring Me All of Your Dreams,*
   and Judith Viorst's *If I Were in Charge of the World.* Have students research the life of the author of the poem. Have them create original presentations to introduce these poets to the class. Each presentation should
   also include a reading of the poem that initiated the project. Combine the
   poems selected into an illustrated anthology of *Poetry that Speaks to Us:*

Our Classroom Favorites. Students who have selected the work of the same poet might be encouraged to combine their efforts into a group presentation.

> *Note:* To get information about certain contemporary poets, students may wish to consult the following sources:
>
> Copeland, J. (1993). *Speaking of poets: Interviews with poets who write for children and young adults.* NCTE.
> Copeland, J. (1994). *Speaking of poets: Interviews with poets who write for children and young adults.* Vol II. NCTE.
> Janeszko, P. (1983). *Poetspeak: In their work, about their work.* New York: Simon and Schuster.

4. Introduce students to the very original style of poetry written by Paul Fleischman in his Newbery Award-winning book, *Joyful Noise: Poems for Two Voices.* To get students accustomed to this type of poetry, divide the class into two groups and have each group choral read one of the two columns in the poem. Once students are comfortable with this type of reading, divide them into groups, giving each group a different poem. Have them practice reading the poem and choreographing movements as suggested by the music of the poetry. You may also wish to follow a similar strategy with Fleischman's *I Am Phoenix: Poems for Two Voices.*

5. Every culture has its own poetry. Read examples of poems from different cultures to the students and discuss how they depict life. For example, the following collections reflect African-American poetry: *The Dream Keeper* by Langston Hughes; *The Poetry of Black America: Anthology of the 20th Century,* edited by Arnold Adoff; *Honey I Love* and *Night on Neighborhood Street* by Eloise Greenfield; and *Sing to the Sun* by Ashley Bryan.

6. Discuss the question, "For what reasons are poems written?" Possible responses include: to tell a story; to offer insight; to create a feeling; to capture a mood or a moment; to entertain. Divide students into groups, one group per purpose. Ask each group to select one favorite contemporary and one favorite traditional poem that seem to be written for the purpose they were assigned. For example, Alfred Noyes' "The Highwayman" tells an incredible story of a highwayman and lost love, whereas Eloise Greenfield's poem, "By Myself" (from *Honey I Love)* offers insights into liking and accepting oneself. Have each group choral read the poem and lead a class discussion of the poem's purpose.

7. An understanding of the devices poets use—such as rhythm, alliteration, blank or free verse, rhyme, figurative language (simile, metaphor, personification), repetition, and onomatopoeia, to name a few—helps students better understand, appreciate, and write their own poetry. Periodically, select and read aloud/choral read poems that use one or more of these devices. For example, a study of alliteration might include "Sea Fever" by John Masefield, and "Fireflies" by Paul Fleischman (from *Joyful Noises).* A study of personification might include "Silver" by Walter De la Mare,

or "The Cherries' Garden Gala" (from *The New Kid on the Block)* by Jack Prelutsky. A study of free verse might include many of the poems found in the two collections by Arnold Adoff, *Eats Poems* and *Chocolate Dreams.*

8. After reading several poems that reflect one or more poetic devices (see Activity 7), have students use the poem as a model and write their own poems, experimenting with using the same poetic device(s).

9. Poetry is an ideal form of literature for dramatic activity. Encourage students to add physical movement to rhythmical poems. Story poems are perfect for dramatic interpretation as well. Students can become involved in such activities as story theater.

10. A favorite type of poetry, the haiku, originated in Japan hundreds of years ago. Have students explore this poetic form through the following activities:

    a. Divide students into groups and give each group a book of haiku poetry, such as *The Moment of Wonder* (Lewis, 1964); *Cricket Songs* (Behn, 1964); and *In a Spring Garden* (Lewis, 1964).

    b. Ask each group to list five characteristics of the haiku. The list might include the following: a haiku is often based on nature; it has three lines; usually the first line has five syllables, the second has seven and the third has five (this may vary in some poems because of the difficulty of translating Japanese into English); it evokes an image or emotion; every words counts. Make a class list of the characteristics of the haiku.

    c. Show a picture of some aspect of nature—a waterfall, a lagoon, a mountain, an animal. As a class, select one of the pictures. Create a cluster or semantic map (p. 39), based on the picture to generate a quantity of words that could be used in a haiku.

    d. Divide students into groups, and tell each group to write a haiku based on the picture and cluster. Share poems.

    e. Give students magazines and allow each student to select a picture related to nature. *(Natural Geographic* has incredible photographs.) Have them create a haiku based on the picture.

    f. Have students affix their poems and pictures to paper and bind the poems into book form.

Discussion Questions

1. What is poetry?

2. How does poetry differ from prose? (Poetry invites the reader to go beyond literal interpretation. Poetry helps us see life from different perspectives. Poetry appeals to the senses, to thoughts and feelings. Poetry evokes strong images and emotional responses, and so forth.)

3. Who are your favorite poets (both traditional and contemporary)? What is there about their poetry that appeals to you?

4. What are some of the elements or devices of poetry? (rhythm, rhyme, blank verse, alliteration, figurative language [simile, metaphor, personification], repetition, onomatopoeia, etc.)

5. How does the use of figurative language appeal to our senses?

6. It has been said that good poetry draws the reader back again and again. Explain this phenomena.

Poets of the Past and Present	
Traditional Poets Body of Work Written Prior to 1960s	**Contemporary Poets** Body of work written 1960 to the Present
Rosemary and Stephen Binet	Arnold Adoff
Lewis Carroll	Maya Angelou
Elizabeth Coatsworth	N. M. Bodecker
Samuel Taylor Coleridge	Beatrice Schenck De Regniers
e.e. cummings	Barbara Juster Esbensen
Walter De la Mare	Norma Farber
Emily Dickinson	Aileen Fisher
T. S. Eliot	Paul Fleischman
Ralph Waldo Emerson	Nikki Giovanni
Eleanor Farjeon	Eloise Greenfield
Eugene Field	Lee Bennett Hopkins
Robert Frost	Paul Janeczko
Oliver Wendell Holmes	X. J. Kennedy
Langston Hughes	Denise Lee
Rudyard Kipling	Myra Cohn Livingston
Emma Lazarus	David McCord
Edward Lear	Eve Merriam
Vachel Lindsay	Lillian Moore
Henry Wadsworth Longfellow	Lillian Morrison
John Masefield	Toni Morrison
Edna St. Vincent Millay	Jack Prelutsky
A. A. Milne	Joanne Ryder
Ogden Nash	Cynthia Rylant
Alfred Noyes	Diane Siebert
Edgar Allan Poe	Shel Silverstein
James Whitcomb Riley	Judith Viorst
Christina Rossetti	Nancy Willard
Carl Sandburg	Valerie Worth
Robert Louis Stevenson	Jane Yolen
Sara Teasdale	
Alfred Lord Tennyson	
Ernest L. Thayer	
Walt Whitman	

LITERATURE RELATED ACTIVITIES

Note to teachers: The four story poems included here were selected to provide a balance between traditional and contemporary poetry, between poems that are nonsensical and those that are more serious in nature. They were selected to provide children with poetry written for a variety of purposes, poetry that uses a variety of devices, poetry that is imaginative and offers insights into meaningful ideas. And, they were selected to involve students in poetry that draws the reader back again and again.

Title: *Jabberwocky*

Genre: Poetry

Author: Louis Carroll

Illustrator: Graeme Base

Bibliographic Information: Harry N. Abrams, Inc., New York, 1989.

Summary: Carroll's poem, "The Jabberwocky," is imaginatively illustrated by Graeme Base, creator of *Animalia, The Eleventh Hour,* and *The Sign of the Seahorse.* The poem, written with nonsense words, tells of a boy who ignores his father's warning about the dangers of encountering the vicious Jabberwocky.

Interest Level: Grades 5+

Pre-Reading Activity

Ask students, "What would a Jabberwocky look like"? Have students create their own artistic renderings of this creature and then compare them with Graeme Base's image. Involve them in discussing other divergent questions that require a diversity of responses, as outlined in Chapter 2, pp. 51–52.

Learning Activities

1. Read the poem, *Jabberwocky,* several times. Involve students in a choral reading. You might wish to rewrite the verses on a large chart or on a transparency for use with an overhead projector.

2. *Jabberwocky* is made up of nonsense verses composed of portmanteau words, that is, words that combine the meaning and parts of two other words to create a new one. For example "Brillig" could be a combination of the words brilliant and light. Discuss what words were possibly combined to create the word Jabberwocky. Have each student select four portmanteau words from the poem and experiment with finding the words that might have been combined to create them. Ask students to come up with their own definition for these words and combine them into a *Jabberwocky Dictionary.* Multiple definitions can be included in case more than one student selected the same word.

3. Assign each group of students a different verse of the poem. Ask students to rewrite their verse by substituting known words for the nonsense words.

Encourage them to use a thesaurus to select words that sound right and that create a special image. Have students illustrate their verses to create a new version of *Jabberwocky*.

4. Compare this version of *Jabberwocky* with others such as that illustrated with pictures from the Disney Archives (Disney Press, New York, 1992) or with the original illustrations by John Tenniel (Macmillan, 1963). Engage students in a discussion focusing on which version they prefer and why.

5. Involve students in research into the life of Charles Lutwidge Dodgson (Lewis Carroll), whose work, even though it is over 100 years old, still appeals to children and adults alike.

Discussion Questions

1. What do you believe accounts for the incredible popularity of *Jabberwocky*? What do you find most remarkable about the poem?

2. In what ways do the illustrations in the book affect the poem and its impact on the reader?

3. What do you think is going through the young boy's mind as he stands at the top of the castle and leans against the "tumtum tree"?

4. What type of threat do you think the beast posed to the village and its people?

5. Look closely at the last illustration in the book, in which the king is congratulating his son. What item(s) seem out of place? (The telephone doesn't seem to fit the mood or setting.) Why do you think Graeme Base drew the picture this way? Can you find any other such examples elsewhere in the book? (i.e. an alarm clock is sitting on the grass in the forest, a crushed can of Coke is under a tree, various automobile symbols are affixed to the son's horse, and so on.)

Title: *Casey at the Bat*

Genre:	Poetry
Author:	Ernest Lawrence Thayer
Illustrator:	Jim Hull
Bibliographic Information:	Dover Publishers, New York, 1977.
Summary:	One of American's best-loved poems, the classic baseball saga tells of mighty Casey who is expected to save the day for his team and instead strikes out.
Interest Level:	Grades 3+

Pre-Reading Activity

Discuss sports that students are involved with. Have them relate some of their triumphs and (if they will) defeats.

Learning Activities

1. After reading the poem, *Casey at the Bat,* several times, involve students in a story theater. While one or several students read the narrative, others dramatize the action.

2. *Casey at the Bat* has been the stimulus for a song, two silent movies, two animated cartoons, and an opera. Involve students in selecting an art form to retell the story. For example, students could create a sight-and-sound show using "Power Point" or by making slides from photographs of the book's illustrations (or their own original renditions) and creating a cassette version on which the poem is read to accompany the slides.

3. Many poems have been dedicated to the sport of baseball, such as those that appear in *Extra Innings* (Hopkins, 1993). They capture the hope, drama, and joy of America's favorite pastime. Share several poems that reflect the theme of baseball and have students compare these poems with their reactions to "Casey at the Bat."

4. Many have tried to explain the popularity of *Casey at the Bat.* In his introduction to the book, Martin Gardner (p. viii) wrote, "It is precisely the blend of the absurd and the tragic that lies at the heart of Thayer's remarkable poem." Hold a discussion with students in which they discuss this quote. What about the poem seems absurd? What is tragic? Is Casey, as Gardner suggests, both a pathetic and a comic figure?

5. Have students look at various baseball cards. What type of information is included? As a class, list the members of Casey's team (students will have to make up several names to accompany Flynn, Blake, Cooney, Burrows, and Casey). Divide students into groups and have each create a baseball card for one of the members of the Mudville team or for a favorite poet (this would require a great deal of creative thought). When the cards are completed, compare statistics and other relevant data, and display the cards.

Discussion Questions

1. How would you describe Casey?

2. What did Thayer mean when he said, ". . . The rest clung to the hope which springs eternal in the human breast . . ." Tell about a time during a sporting event when you clung to hope despite the odds.

3. When you first heard the last lines of the poem, what was your reaction?

4. What lessons for life does *Casey at the Bat* suggest?

Title: *Stopping by Woods on a Snowy Evening*

Genre: Poetry

Author: Robert Frost

Illustrator: Susan Jeffers

Bibliographic Information: Dutton, New York, 1978.

Summary: The poem gives the reader a memorable picture of the delights of winter and of a person with "promises to keep."

Interest Level: Grades 4+

Pre-Reading Activity

Involve students in a discussion of snow. What does it look like, feel like, taste like, smell like? Have them "become snow" and imagine how they would move during a blizzard, during a light snow-fall, and so forth.

Learning Activities

1. Read the poem to the class several times and encourage students to join in. Allow the mood of the poetry to permeate the room. Ask students to share the mood the poem evoked—in one word, in one phrase or sentence. Have them create large snowflakes and affix their word or phrase/sentence to it. Display these on a "Snowy Evening" bulletin board.

2. Robert Frost once explained that, "Every poem is a new metaphor inside or it is nothing." Poetry helps develop new insights and new ways of seeing the world. Involve students in a literary circle in which they discuss insights gained from the poem and how the poem offered new perspectives.

3. Ask students to tell about a time when they had to put off doing something they really wanted to do because of certain responsibilities. Using the poem as a model, ask students to write an original poem that describes their experience.

4. Robert Frost's poetry speaks to children in a special way. Read Frost's poem, "The Road Not Taken." Discuss with children the metaphor inside, by asking, "What might the two roads represent?" Have students write and deliver a brief talk that tells about a time when they had to make an important choice.

Discussion Questions

1. Of all your senses, which one does the poem most heighten? Explain.

2. Why do you think Frost repeated the last line? How does this add to the mysterious element of the poem?

3. Why do you think the illustrator, Susan Jeffers, chose to create most of the images in black and white, using color very sparingly? What effects did this have?

4. Imagine that you were the person in this poem, telling about your experiences in the woods. Describe your feelings as you spend time in the woods and how you feel about having to leave.

Title: *Life Doesn't Frighten Me*

Genre: Poetry

Author: Maya Angelou

Illustrator: Jean-Michel Basquiat

Bibliographic Information: Stewart, Tabori and Chang, New York, 1993.

Summary: The poem speaks of those things in our lives that frighten us and celebrates the courage to face whatever we fear.

Interest Level: Grades 3+

Pre-Reading Activity

Share the title and cover with students. Have each of them create a picture that represents something in their lives that frightens them. Ask them to share their pictures. Collect the pictures and hold them for Learning Activity 3.

Learning Activities

1. After reading the poem aloud and sharing the pictures, discuss the words and images that they contained. What mood does the poem create? How is this mood achieved?

2. Together, compile a list of things that seem to frighten the author and things that seem to frighten the illustrator. Discuss how each of these fears affect students in the class.

3. Write several of the verses on a chart board or on a transparency for use with an overhead projector. Using these verses as a model, group the children, and have them combine the ideas represented by their own illustrations (Pre-Reading Activity) into new verses for the poem. Encourage them to refine their drawings and then put the verses and drawings of each group together to form a sequel—"Life Doesn't Frighten Me, Part II."

4. From the verses in the book alone, how would you describe Maya Angelou's life? How would you describe Jean-Michel Basquiat's life? Compare your analysis with the biographies of these creative individuals that is found at the end of the book.

5. Encourage the students to react to the information in the poem/illustrations/biographies in their poetry or writing journals. Allow time for the students to share their entries.

6. Invite a counselor or local psychologist to discuss fears and ways of overcoming those fears that negatively affect our lives. Prior to the talk, encourage each student to write several questions on the topic of "fear" that he/she would like to have discussed.

Discussion Questions

1. If you could meet Maya Angelou, what would you like to ask her regarding "Life Doesn't Frighten Me?" What is one thing you'd like to tell her

about the book and how it affected you? (You may wish to send these questions and comments to Ms. Angelou, c/o the publisher.)

2. When is it healthy to fear?

3. When can fears be considered unhealthy or even dangerous?

4. What is something you especially fear? Is it a healthy fear? If not, what might be one effective way of overcoming this fear?

5. Did the poem in anyway change the way certain fears affect you? Explain.

CULMINATING ACTIVITY

Plan and hold a Poetry Festival in which students are involved in the following:

1. Create invitations (written in rhyme or free verse) and send them to school staff, the children's families and the local media (newspapers, television, radio).

2. Poetry Readings—of published poems and students' original poetry.

3. Dramatic and Artistic Interpretations—of specific poems, traditional and contemporary.

4. Poetry Picnic: Students and their families enjoy a picnic lunch together and read favorite poems to one another.

5. Featured Speakers: Invite local poets to discuss and read their work as well as discuss the creative process.

6. Storytelling: Invite a local storyteller to retell several narrative poems.

7. Decorate the area with many of the displays and products students created during the unit.

8. Involve the audience in choral readings of specially selected favorites.

Many of the activities can involve the whole group, while others can be run concurrently to allow guests to make choices as to what they would like to take part in.

SUPPLEMENTAL LITERATURE

Single-Story Poems

Note: Many of these single-story poems are superbly illustrated versions of classic poems that will delight students.

Blake, William. (1993). *The tyger.* Illustrated by N. Waldman. San Diego, CA: Harcourt.

Hesse. K. (1997) *Out of the dust: A novel.* New York: Scholastic. (1997 Newbery Medal)

Longfellow, H. W. (1983). *Hiawatha.* Illustrated by J. Jerrers. New York: Dial.

Myers, W. (1997*). Harlem.* New York: Scholastic (1997 Caldecott Honor Book and 1998 Coretta Scott King Illustrator Honor Book.)

Noyes, A. (1983). *The highwayman.* Illustrated C. Mikolaycak. New York: Lothrop, Lee & Shepard.

Siebert, D. (1989). *Heartland.* Paintings by W. Minor. New York: HarperCollins.

Willard, N. (1981). *A visit to William Blake's inn.* Illustrated by Alice and Martin Provensen. San Diego, CA: Harcourt.

Collections

Note: Each of these collections contains poems generally appropriate to a wide variety of ages.

Adoff, A. (Ed.) (1973). *The poetry of black America: Anthology of the 20th Century.* New York: HarperCollins.

Adoff, A. (1979). *Eats poems.* New York: Lothrop.
An entertaining collection of poems for children that celebrates food.

Adoff, A. (1989). *Chocolate dreams.* New York: Lothrop.
A collection of poems that reflects the author's love for sweets.

Adoff, A. (1997). *Love letters.* Ill. L. Desimini. New York: Blue Sky.
20 school, family, and pet love poems are illustrated by collage, oil, photographs, and mixed-media computer graphics.

Adoff, A. (Ed.) (1997). *I am the darker brother: An anthology of modern poems by African Americans.* New York: Simon & Schuster.
A reissue of the outstanding anthology first published in 1968. This edition includes new selections from 19 poets as well thematic sections.

Behn, H. (Ed.) (1964). *Cricket songs.* New York: Harcourt, Brace, and World.
A collection of haikus.

Blishen, E., compiler. (1963). *Oxford book of poetry for children.* Illustrated by B. Wildsmith. New York: Watts.
Comprehensive anthology with a rich collection of work by traditional poets.

Bryan, A. (1992). *Sing to the sun.* New York: HarperCollins.
First collection of poetry for children to be written by an African-American male. Contains 23 poems that deal with life as seen through the poet's eyes.

Carroll, J. A., & E. Wilson (Ed.) (1997). *Lunch poems to read aloud.* Spring, TX: Absey & Co.
Read aloud poems that cover a wide range of emotions, moods, and subjects.

Cole, J., (Ed.) (1984). *A new treasury of children's poetry: Old favorites and new discoveries.* Garden City, NY: Doubleday.
Comprehensive collection of over 200 poems that range from nonsensical to serious.

de Paola, T., (Ed.) (1988). *Tomie de Paola's book of poems.* New York: Putnam.
An anthology of eighty-six poems including classical and contemporary poems. Some of the poems are in Spanish.

de Regniers, B. S., et al., (Eds.) (1988). *Sing a song of popcorn.* New York: Scholastic.

Illustrated by nine Caldecott Medal artists in full color, the book contains over 125 poems, arranged thematically, that will captivate children. The work of both classical and contemporary poets is included.

Fleischman, P. (1985). *I am phoenix: Poems for two voices.* New York: Harper and Row.
A collection of poems for two readers (or two groups of readers) that capture the world of birds.

Fleischman, P. (1988). *Joyful noise: Poems for two voices.* New York: Harper and Row.
A collection of poems for two readers (or two groups of readers) that capture the music of the insect world.

Frost, R. (1988). *Birches.* Illustrated by E. Young. New York: Henry Holt.

Frost, R. (1949). *Complete poems of Robert* Frost. New York: Holt.
A collection of poems written by Frost.

Greenfleld, E. (1978). *Honey I love and other love poems.* Illustrated by Diane and Leo Dillon. New York: HarperCollins.
The sixteen poems included elicit a new appreciation of everyday life, offering new insights and accompanied by beautiful drawings.

Greenfield, E. (1991). *Night on neighborhood street.* New York: Dial.
Poems depicting contemporary children and their world.

Hopkins, L. B., (Ed.) (1993). *Extra innings.* Illustrated by S. Medlock. San Diego, CA: Harcourt, Brace Jovanovich.
A collection of poems that capture the excitement, hope, drama, and joy of America's favorite pastime—baseball.

Hopkins, L. B., (Ed.) (1988). *Voyages: Poems by Walt Whitman.* San Diego, CA: Harcourt Brace Javonovich.
A collection of the poetry of Walt Whitman.

Hughes, L. (1995). *The block.* New York: Metropolitan Museum of Art and Viking.
Hughes's poems are matched with the six panel collage tribute to Harlem by Romare Bearden.

Hughes, L. (1994). *The dream keeper and other poems.* Ill. by Brian Pinkney. New York: Knopf.
Poems depicting the African-American experience.

Janeczko, P. B., compiler. (1990). *The place my words are looking for.* New York: Bradbury Press.
Includes the poems of approximately 40 poets, as well as photographs of the poets and brief commentaries they've written concerning the writing of poetry and the creative process.

Johnston, T. (1996). *My Mexico—Mexico mio.* Ill. F. J. Sierra. New York: Putnam.
A bilingual poetry collection. Each two-pages features one poem written in Spanish and English with illustrations of Mexican scenes to highlight the culture of Mexico.

Larrick, N., (Ed.) (1980). *Bring me all of your dreams.* New York: M. Evans.
Contains poems by well-known contemporary poets that help children discover who they are and address many of the concerns of childhood.

Larrick, N., (Ed.) (1968). *Piping down the valleys wild.* Illustrated by E. Raskin. New York: Delacorte.
A collection of over 250 poems ranging from poems from the traditional to the contemporary.

Lear, E. (1946). *The complete nonsense book.* New York: Dodd, Mead.
A collection of poems that could only have been written by Lear!

Lewis, R., (Ed.) (1964). *In a spring garden.* Illustrated by E. Keats. New York: Dial.
Collection of haiku poetry.

Lewis, R., (Ed.) (1964). *The moment of wonder.* New York: Dial.
Collection of haiku poetry.

Prelutsky, J. *The beauty of the beast: Poems from the animal kingdom.* New York: Knopf/Random House.
A collection of poems that celebrate all creatures of the earth.

Prelutsky, J. (1984). *The new kid on the* block. Illustrated by J. Stevenson. New York: Scholastic.
106 poems that take a humorous look at life.

Prelutsky, J., (Ed.) (1983). *The Random House book of poetry for children.* New York: Random House.
Contains over 500 poems by contemporary and traditional poets.

Robb, L. (Ed.) (1997). *Music and drum: Voices of war and peace, hope and dreams.* New York: Philomel.
Contains the poetry of child survivors of war as well as the poetry of Carl Sandburg and Langston Hughes. The poems focus on hope and peace.

Rylant, C. (1994). *Something permanent.* Orlando, FL: Harcourt.
Contains poems that were written to accompany the black-and-white photographs of Walker Evans taking to document the Great Depression.

Silverstein, S. (1996). *Falling up.* New York: HarperCollins.
A collection of humorous verse.

Silverstein, S. (1981). *A light in the attic.* New York: Harper and Row.
A collection of poems that continue in the tradition of those included in *Where the Sidewalk Ends.* The poems are often humorous, often tender, always entertaining and wondrous.

Silverstein, S. (1974). *Where the sidewalk ends.* New York: Harper and Row.
A collection of poems that are both funny and profound.

Slier, D., (Ed.) (1991). *Make a joyful sound: Poems for children by African-American poets.* New York: Checkerboard Press.
A collection of poems written by some of the best-loved African-American poets.

Sneve, V. D. H., (Ed.) (1989). *Dancing teepees: Poems of American Indian youth.* New York: Holiday House.

A weaving of poems that have been handed down from generation to generation of American Indians and poems written by Indian youths today. The poems describe the traditions and life of this great culture.

Viorst, J. (1981). *If I were in charge of the world and other worries.* Illustrated by L. Cherry. New York: Macmillan.

The poems in this collection capture the dreams, hopes, and fears of childhood.

Web Sites

The Academy of American Poets
    http://www.poets.org. (includes ideas for celebrating National Poetry Month)

ISLMC Poetry for Children
    http://falcon.jmu.edu/ramseyil/poechild.htm

Poetry Daily
    http://www.cs.cmu.edu/~doughb/rhyme.html (an anthology of contemporary poetry

Wordsmiths: Teen Voices @ Teen Link
    http://www.nypl.org/branch/teen/vox.html (Gives older students 12+ an opportunity to publish their poetry on the internet)

International Library of Poetry Contest information
    http://www.poems.com/

MINI-THEMES

Curricular Connections

Poetry touches children in a very special way and offers them insights not generally found in prose. It is important, therefore, to include poetry whenever possible to augment a theme or topic under study, giving students the opportunity to gain additional perspectives. Many poems, both contemporary and classic, can be found to supplement the topics being taught throughout the curriculum. Many anthologies have been published in which the selection of poems is based on a specific subject, such as the seasons, weather, Indian life, nature, animals, insects, and so forth. Other anthologies are based on the work of a specific poet, while still others are a collection of poetry that the compiler found meaningful and appealing. Single-story poems are also available to supplement a specific theme or topic. The poetry below is just a sampling of the myriad of choices available and the activities that follow will help you integrate poetry into your curricular plans.

Activities

1. With the tremendous scope of poetry available, both traditional and contemporary, poems can be found on virtually every topic. Allow students to

help compile poetry anthologies for the various units or topics you are studying. Criteria for the anthologies need to be established by the entire class, for example, it is meaningful, relates to subject; entertaining; gives new perspectives; reflects contemporary and traditional poetry; and so forth. For example, an anthology on the Revolutionary War can include "The Midnight Ride of Paul Revere" (Longfellow), one on the Civil War might include "O Captain! My Captain!" (Whitman), and one on immigration might include "The New Colossus" by Emma Lazarus. For each anthology, a different student or pair of students can act as editor(s). Each student in the class should submit a poem related to the subject. Once the poem has been approved by the editors, the person who has submitted it can type it and either illustrate it or find photographs to accompany the poem. Anthologies can be then be duplicated for each class member. During the unit, poems from the anthology can be used to introduce or supplement the lesson and other literature. Poems can be read chorally, dramatized, used to model original poetry, and discussed.

2. Many poems add new dimensions to the way we see things. Some poems, especially those that are more narrative, lend themselves well to creative dramatics and story theater. Others lend themselves to artistic responses. As they do with various works of literature, students should have the opportunity to respond to poetry in a variety of ways (speaking, writing, drama, art, music, etc.) and activities can be developed to tie the poem to a specific content area being taught. During a study of insects, for example, you may wish to use Paul Fleischman's *Joyful Noise: Poems for Two Voices*. Divide students into different groups, giving each a different insect poem. Have students read the poem (in two voices) and put it together with interpretive movement. After the presentation of one of the poems, involve students in a discussion of the way the words captured the sound of the insect and its movements.

   To connect the poem with a science lesson, have students determine what other insect(s) they would like to learn more about. If possible, have them collect several specimens of the insect (in jars with ventilation, food, and water). Have students observe the insect and after several days have them create a cluster of words that recreate the way the insect sounds and moves. Aid students in using these words to create their own poem for two voices. Be sure students return the insects to their original environment.

3. Involve students in creating a poetry calendar based on a specific topic, such as the seasons, environment, space, animals, or friendship. Students can all work on the same topic or you may wish to allow them to select other topics that have been, or will be, studied that appeal to them most. Have students select 12 poems, one for each month of the year. Have students affix each poem to a piece of paper and illustrate it, attaching pictures and poems that correspond to each month on facing pages. (You may wish to make up a generic calendar form on which students insert the months and days.)

4. Depending upon the topic being studied, match poetry with trade books to enhance the lesson and provide additional insights. For example, if stu-

dents have been studying about Christopher Columbus in such books as *I Discover Columbus* by Robert Lawson (1941, Little, Brown), or *Where do you think you're going, Christopher Columbus?* by Jean Fritz (1980, G. P. Putnam's Sons), have them read "Columbus" from *America Forever New* (Brewton and Brewton, 1968). Allow students to discuss such questions as "What ideas did the poem present that seemed unique?" "What images of Columbus did the poem introduce that the books did not?"

5. Depending upon the topic being studied, have students create a poetry bulletin board that contains various poems related to the subject. Different students can be in charge of the poetry board each month. In addition to poems, pictures and biographies of the poets and accompanying illustrations can be displayed. Instead of a bulletin board, students can create three-dimensional objects related to what is being studied and display the poems on these objects. For example, during a study of the environment, students can create a poetry tree.

6. Have students create recordings of favorite poems that extend specific lessons. Have them select music (orchestration only—no lyrics) that fits the subject to accompany the recording of the poem.

References

Brewton, S., & Brewton, J., compilers. (1976). *American forever new.* New York: Crowell. (Americana)

Eliot, T. S. (1991). *Mr. Mistoffelees with Mugojerrie and Rumpelteazer.* Illustrated by E. LeCain. San Diego, CA: Harcourt. (Cats)

Fleischman, P. (1985). *I am phoenix: Poems for two voices.* New York: Harper and Row. (Birds)

Fleischman, P. (1988). *Joyful noise: Poems for two voices.* New York: Harper and Row. (Insects)

Hopkins, L. B., (Ed.) (1986). *The sea is calling me.* Illustrated By W. Gaffney-Kessell. San Diego, CA: Harcourt. (Ocean life)

Hopkins, L. B., (Ed.) (1987). *Dinosaurs.* Illustrated by M. Tinkelman. San Diego, CA: Harcourt. (Dinosaurs)

Larrick, N., (Ed.) (1991). *To the moon and back.* Illustrated by C. O'Neill. New York: Delacorte. (Contains many poems on Native-Americans and Eskimos.)

Lewis, J. P. (1991). *Earth verse and water rhymes.* Illustrated by R. Sabuda. New York: Atheneum. (Nature)

Livingston, M. C. (1988). *Space songs.* Illustrated by L. E. Fisher. New York: Holiday. (Space)

Livingston, M. (1984). *Sky songs.* New York: Holiday. (Space)

Longfellow, H. W. (1983). *Hiawatha.* Illustrated by J. Jerrers. New York: Dial. (Native Americans)

Longfellow, H. W. (1990). *Paul Revere's ride.* Illustrated by T. Rand. New York: Dutton. (Revolutionary War)

Siebert, D. (1989). *Heartland.* Illustrated by W. Minor. New York: Crowell. (Environment)

Siebert, D. (1991). *Sierra.* Illustrated by W. Minor. New York: HarperCollins. (Environment)

Simon, S. (Ed.) (1995). *Star walk.* New York: Morrow. (Space)

Sneve, V. D. H., (Ed.) (1989). *Dancing teepees: Poems of American Indian youth.* New York: Holiday House. (Native Americans)

Sullivan, C. (1993). *Cowboys.* New York: Rizzoli. (The West)

Volavkova, H., (Ed.) (1978). *I never saw another butterfly: Children's drawings and poems from Terezin Concentration Camp, 1942–1944.* New York: Schocken. (The Holocaust)

Yolen, J. (1990). *Birdwatch.* Illustrated by T. Lewin. New York: Philomel. (Nature/Birds)

Wood, N. (1998). *Sacred fire: Poetry and prose of Nancy Wood.* New York: Doubleday. (Pueblo Indians—history, legends, philosophy)

Poems of Everyday Life

Poetry reflects life, both the good and bad aspects of it. It reflects our hopes, our dreams, our ideas. It reflects our fears, our doubts, our concerns. Poetry helps us see the remarkable in the unremarkable, the "beauty in a grain of sand." Poetry has been written on subjects ranging from the most common human experiences to the most profound social issues. Poetry intensifies our experiences, heightens our senses, and provides new ways in which to view our world. The poetry listed in this mini-lesson varies in scope, yet each provides us with a look at life through images that are fresh and thought provoking.

Activities

1. Have the class create a mural that depicts various experiences from their childhood. Scenes might include: snowball fights; playing with a pet; moving to a new city; eating spinach; playing baseball; facing a bully; peer pressure; and so forth. (Students may wish to use some of their own photographs as well.) Involve students in finding several poems that speak to the same experiences that they created on the mural. Have them copy their favorite poem and place it next to the appropriate scene. Allow time for students to talk about the experience, share the poem, and discuss how the poem reflected their childhood experience and how it made them see it differently.

2. Read the title poem from Judith Viorst's *If I Were in Charge of the World.* Have students brainstorm all the things they would do if they were in charge of the world. Ask each to create a verse for the poem, using the original as a model. Have them create a book of their verses and illustrations.

3. Share many verses of poetry that deal with things children love, (for example, "Honey, I Love," Greenfield, 1978); things they dislike ("Sarah Cynthia Sylvia Stout Would Not Take the Garbage Out," Silverstein, 1974); things that worry them ("Fifteen, Maybe Sixteen, Things to Worry About," Viorst, 1981); and things that make them laugh ("The New Kid on the Block," Prelutsky, 1984). Involve students in a survey to find out what things cause other students to love, hate, fear, and laugh (or any other

emotion they choose). Divide students into groups—one per emotion—and have them create an anthology of poems that speaks to that emotion. Create a classroom environment reminiscent of the 1950s during which poets sat on stools in dimly lit coffee houses and read to their audience. Ask each group to put together a poetry reading in which they read several of the poems they collected in their anthologies.

4. Many poems address social issues, problems with which our society and we as individuals, must deal. Have students research both traditional and contemporary poetry to discover what social issues were addressed. Divide students into groups and have them research one of these social issues. Encourage them to read newspaper and magazine articles that deal with the subject. After each group has completed its research, have it present a creative oral report on the social issue and include a reading of several of the poems that deal with the subject. Allow time for class discussion of the issue, how it affects them, how the poems changed or enhanced their understanding of the problem, and ways that the issue can be resolved.

5. Poems are often set to music. For example, Shel Silverstein's "The Unicorn" (1974) was also a very popular musical recording. Have students select a favorite poem. It can be one that reminds them of a childhood experience, one that reflects their attitude toward life or one that speaks to them in a very personal way. Have them put this poem to music, using either an original piece or using the music of another song that seems to fit the poem. Have students teach a group of students the new version and allow them to share it with the rest of the class.

6. Poetry is a wonderful way to help students gain insight and perspective into the realities of other cultures or regions of the U.S. Involve students in reading the poetry found in books such as *The Palm of My Heart: Poetry by African American Children* (Adedjouma,1996), *My Mexico—Mexico Mio* (Johnston, 1996*), Stories I Ain't Told Nobody Yet: Selections from the People Pieces* (Carson, 1989*), or Confetti: Poems for Children* (Mora, 1996). Have students create an artifact box with pictures, artifacts, recipes, and poems to celebrate the rich and varied cultures that are part of us all.

References

Adedjouma. D. (Ed.) (1996). *The palm of my heart: Poetry by African American children*. Ill. G. Christie. New York: Lee and Low.

Bryan, A. (1992). *Sing to the sun*. New York: HarperCollins.

Carson, J. (1989). *Stories I ain't told nobody yet: Selections from the People Pieces*. New York: Orchard. (poems based on conversations with people from the Appalachian region.)

Dakos, K. (1990) *If you're not here, please raise your hand*. New York: Four Winds.

Esbensen, B. (1992). *Who shrank my grandmother's house? Poems of discovery*. Illustrated by E. Bellows. New York: HarperCollins.

Greenfield, E. (1978). *Honey I love and other love* poems. Illustrated by Diane and Leo Dillon. New York: HarperCollins.

Greenfield, E. (1991). *Night on Neighborhood Street.* Illustrated by J. Spivey Gilchrist. New York: Dial.

Hopkins, L. B. (1992). *Through our eyes: Poems and pictures about growing up.* Photography by J. Dunn. New York: Little, Brown.

Hughes, L. (1932). *The dream keeper and other poems.* New York: Knopf.

Johnston, T. (1996). *My Mexico—Mexico mio.* Ill. F. J. Sierra. New York: Putnam.

Larrick, N., (Ed.) (1980). *Bring me all of your dreams.* New York: M. Evans.

Livingston, M., ed. (1987). *1 like you if you like me: Poems of friendship.* New York: McElderry.

Mora, P. (1996). *Confetti: Poems for children.* Ill. E.O. Sanchez. New York: Lee & Low.

Morrison, L. (1995). *Slam dunk: Basketball poems.* New York: Hyperion.

Prelutsky, J. (1984). *The new kid on the block.* Illustrated by J. Stevenson. New York: Scholastic.

Rylant, C. (1984). *Waiting to waltz: A childhood.* Illustrated by S. Gammell. New York: Bradbury.

Silverstein, S. (1974). *Where the sidewalk ends.* New York: Harper and Row.

Viorst, J. (1981). *If I were in charge of the world and other worries.* Illustrated by L. Cherry. New York: Macmillan.

Yolen, J. Compiler. (1996). *Sky scrape/city scope: Poems of city life.* Honesdale, PA: Wordsong/Boyd Mills.

Biography: Making a Difference

OVERVIEW

Focus

Students will become aware of the fact that each individual can make a difference in the world. Despite hardships and obstacles, each individual has the potential to make positive contributions. This unit will involve students in learning about the heroes and heroines of yesterday and today; those who have earned a place in history because of their dedication and determination. As students read the inspirational stories of others, it is hoped that they will become the dreamers and doers of tomorrow.

Objectives

On completion of this thematic unit, students will:

1. Identify many of the men and women in our history, in various fields of endeavor, who have made a difference.
2. Describe the debt we owe to those throughout history who have dedicated their lives to helping others.
3. Analyze the way in which obstacles are often overcome to create change.
4. Explore the various ways in which individuals have affected positive change.
5. Envision themselves as leaders of tomorrow.

HOW IT WORKS

Initiating Activity

Involve students in creating a calendar that covers the entire school year and title it, "Those Who Have Made a Difference." Place pictures of each student in the box of the appropriate month and day to reflect their birthdays. Throughout this unit, as various men and women are studied, have their pictures added to the calendar to indicate their birthdays. Also, add a brief caption identifying the names and contributions of these individuals who have made a difference in our world.

General Activities

1. Have students create various semantic webs (see p. 39) with the names of those who have made a difference. Each web should reflect a different field of endeavor such as science, the humanities, medicine, exploration, entertainment, sports, mathematics, politics, law, etc.
2. Have students select one of the men/women from the web (General Activity 1 above), and read a biography based on that individual's life. Select

339

one of the following forums for sharing information gained about this person:

a. Create a "Hall of Fame" which includes a short summary of the person's life along with a picture of the person.

b. Create and present a speech that includes the following: strengths, weaknesses, influences, contributions, the time when he/she lived, the places he/she lived, obstacles faced, ways in which they were overcome, etc.

c. Write and present a monologue that reflects a significant moment, achievement, decision, etc. in the person's life.

d. Develop a model or toy that in some way reflects the person's life/contributions. i.e. The Teddy Bear for Theodore Roosevelt).

e. Create a series of stamps that illustrates major contributions and achievements.

f. Create a cover for *Time* magazine's "Person of the Year" and write an accompanying cover story.

g. Create a picture book based on the biography read so that a child in grades K–3 could learn about this person's life.

h. Create a "Scrabble" game in which aspects of the person's life are revealed by building on different words.

3. Provide a wide assortment of magazines and newspapers. Have the students cut out words and pictures to illustrate those who have made a difference. Have groups work together to create their own displays (each group might wish to focus on a specific field of endeavor).

4. Have students brainstorm a list of public places (i.e. roads, bridges, buildings) in their community that have been named for specific individuals. Have them research the contributions of those individuals with whom they are not familiar.

5. Have students Create a "Top 10"—it can be related to a specific time period, a specific field of endeavor, or it can be generic. Students brainstorm nominees for this prestigious list. Students then select one name and become an advocate for this person's inclusion in the list. Students can mount campaigns to see that the person selected gets included in the Top 10 list by making posters, buttons, bumper stickers, etc.

6. Discuss the fact that there are many people who make a positive difference in the lives of others who are not generally know to the public. Have students interview a family member or community leader who has made a difference and write a narrative to summarize the information elicited.

7. Have students visualize themselves in the future. What contributions do they hope to make to society? Have students write a futuristic autobiography that includes what is known about their lives and what they hope will happen in the future. Encourage students to include photographs.

8. Invite a community leader to school. Have students prepare questions that will help them understand what influenced this person and what obstacles

he/she has had to overcome to achieve what they have. Videotape the interview and share them with the rest of the school.

9. Arrange a visit to a local cemetery. Have students read the epitaphs on the headstones and try to determine something about the person's life. Which would they consider to be heroes/heroines? Why? Ask students to write an epitaph for themselves that reflects what they hope to accomplish in life.

10. As a class, determine one question to which you would like famous people in various fields to respond (i.e. "Was there one moment in your life that was most significant in terms of what you have accomplished?" "What is the most important ingredient for success?" etc.) Write letters to selected individuals posing this question. Bind the responses into a book that can be kept in the library for all to share.

Discussion Questions

1. What do you think leads a person to achieve success and make a difference in the world?

2. What are some similarities between present-day leaders and those from the past?

3. Are all people who have made a significant positive difference in the world famous? Which is most important, fame or achievement?

4. Based on the biographies read, how does childhood affect a person's adulthood?

5. How would the world be different if _____ (insert name of one of the people studied) had not lived?

LITERATURE RELATED ACTIVITIES

Title: *Eleanor Roosevelt: A Life of Discovery*

Genre: Biography

Author: Russell Freedman

Bibliographic Information: Clarion Books, New York, 1993.

Summary: The life of this remarkable first lady, Eleanor Roosevelt, unfolds in pictures and prose. Eleanor Roosevelt began life as—in her own words—an "ugly duckling," yet emerged as "First Lady of the World." Her work on human rights has earned her a place in the hearts of people across the globe.

Interest Level: Grades 4+

Pre-Reading Activity

Eleanor Roosevelt said, "You gain strength, courage, and confidence by every experience in which you really stop to look fear in the face . . . You must do the thing you think you cannot do." Share this quote, which appears just before Chapter 1 and have students write a journal entry that discusses what the quote means. Ask them to also write about a time in life when each did something he/she didn't think they could do. Have students share their journal entries and discuss whether or not Roosevelt was right, do experiences such as these help us gain "strength, courage, and confidence"?

Learning Activities

1. Have students select a favorite quote attributed to Eleanor Roosevelt. Ask them to copy the quote and draw a picture that illustrates its meaning. Bind these together and display.

2. Ask students to select a favorite illustration from the book. Have them make as many inferences as they can about the subject and times based on the details in the photograph. Next, have them select 2 or 3 of their inferences and research them to see how accurate they were.

3. Eleanor Roosevelt was actively involved in human rights. Under her leadership, the United Nations Human Rights Commission wrote the Universal Declaration of Human Rights which defined the basic rights of people all over the world. Have students locate a copy of this bill of rights or compile their own list of human rights. Next, ask students to bring in articles from the newspaper/magazines that describe situations in which people in the U.S. and all over the world are still not enjoying the basic rights they listed.

4. Based on Activity 3 above, have students select one of the situations in which rights were being denied and involve them in a problem solving exercise to find a solution that they can implement.

5. Ask students to select one of their favorite stories about Eleanor Roosevelt. Have them write and deliver a monologue as Mrs. Roosevelt describing the event.

6. Have students use the internet to discover additional information about Eleanor Roosevelt and her life.

Discussion Questions

1. After reading about the life of Eleanor Roosevelt, would you describe her as "an ugly duckling" or as a swan. Explain.

2. Of all the contributions Ms. Roosevelt made, which do you think is most significant? Why?

3. If you could meet Ms. Roosevelt, what would you ask her? How do you think she might answer this question?

4. What if Eleanor Roosevelt had been president instead of her husband?

5. A political cartoon appears on page 163 in which a child points to the Statue of Liberty and says, "Of course I know—It's Mrs. Roosevelt." Discuss the cartoon and its implications.

6. In what ways is Mrs. Roosevelt similar to and different from our present first lady?

7. Based on your readings, and based on what Eleanor Roosevelt said about the key to happiness (p. 77), do you believe she was truly happy? Explain.

Title: *Lincoln: A Photobiography*

Genre:	Biography
Author:	Russell Freedman
Illustrator:	Illustrated with Photographs and Prints
Bibliographic Information:	Clarion, New York, 1987.
Summary:	The life and times of Abraham Lincoln as told through photographs, prints, and Russell Freedman's fascinating text.
Interest Level:	Grades 4–7.

Pre-Reading Activity

What do students know about Abraham Lincoln? Ask students to individually list all the facts they know about Lincoln. Have them select the fact they believe is most interesting and create a picture to illustrate it. Have students use their illustrations to cover a large box—the Lincoln Artifact Box—which will be the focus of Learning Activity 1.

Learning Activities

1. As students learn additional information about Lincoln, have each select a new fact or new impression about him they think is significant. Have the students create an object or locate some type of visual that represents this newly acquired fact or idea and place this in the artifact box created in the Pre-Reading Activity. At the conclusion of their study of *Lincoln: A Photobiography,* involve students in a discussion of the artifacts and the way in which each reflects Lincoln—his life and times.

2. Have students create a Photoautobiography in which they tell about their lives through pictures and text.

3. Based on the insights they have gained about Lincoln, have groups of students create large collage caricatures of Lincoln that reflect Lincoln's personality and characteristics.

4. It is often said that "a picture is worth a thousand words." Select a picture from the book that you believe especially supports this statement and write a brief essay that explains the photograph's impact. In small groups, have students discuss the pictures selected.

5. Throughout the text, Freedman includes many of Lincoln's quotes. Have students select a favorite quotation, illustrate it (with original art or with pictures and cartoons), and combine their work into a book of sayings by Lincoln.

6. At the back of the book is a list of other books about Lincoln. Have students read one more of these books and compare the insights and under-

standings about Lincoln that they gained from the book with those they gained from *Lincoln: A Photobiography.* Ask students: "Which book gave you the deepest understanding of Lincoln and his times?" "How was this accomplished?"

Discussion Questions

1. How did the book reinforce or change your opinions and ideas about Abraham Lincoln?
2. How did the photographs included in this book affect you?
3. What did you learn about Abraham Lincoln that surprised you most?
4. From your knowledge of Lincoln and his times, what do you think was the most difficult thing Abraham Lincoln had to face? Explain.
5. Imagine that you are a children's literary critic. How would you rate *Lincoln: A Photobiography?* Explain your opinion.

Title: *Amistad: A Long Road to Freedom*

Author: Walter Dean Myers

Genre: Biography/Informational

Bibliographic Information: Dutton Children's Books, New York, 1998.

Summary: This book powerfully relates the long struggle for freedom fought by the captives of the *Amistad.* In 1839, the slave ship *Amistad* set sail for Havana, Cuba. The ship carried slaves, and along the way the captives, led by Sengbe Pieh, took control of the ship. They tried to sail back to Africa but instead landed in the United States where they were put on trial. After lengthy trials, the case was ultimately heard by the U.S. Supreme Court, which ruled that the captives of the *Amistad* were free. The captives returned to their homeland nearly three years after their capture.

Interest Level: Grades 4+

Pre-Reading Activity

Involve students in a K-W-L [see Chapter 2, pp. 42–44] based on the topic of the slave trade. Using a map, trace the voyage of the *Tecora* and later the *Amistad* from Sierra Leone to the United States. Also, have students make inferences about Sengbe Pieh based solely on the portrait on the cover of the book. Keep a list of their reactions and after reading the book, compare their inferences with the facts learned.

Learning Activities

1. After students have read the book, discuss the time line that precedes the account of the *Amistad*. Divide students into groups and have each group select one event that they feel is most significant (be sure that each group has selected a different event). On a piece of poster board, have them list the date at the top and then create an illustration that depicts the event. On the bottom of the poster board have them add an explanation of the event.

2. Involve students in research of the slave trade and slave ships. Using this information along with the descriptions included in this book, have them create several "daily logs" that Sebgbe Pieh might have written that reflects his journey to America and the treatment of the slaves.

3. Roger Baldwin and John Quincy Adams pleaded for the captives in front of the Supreme Court. Baldwin argued the legal issues while Adams addressed the moral issues. Have students imagine that they were defending the *Amistad* captives. Ask them to write and deliver a speech as if they were to address the Supreme Court.

4. Create a classroom newspaper. In groups, have students create a newspaper that would have appeared in the U.S. in 1839. Encourage students to include factual articles concerning the *Amistad* captives as well as advertisements, editorials, editorial cartoons, etc. that would be appropriate to the times.

5. Conduct a debate in which students discuss whether or not the *Amistad* captives were entitled to rebel because they had a natural right to freedom (see p. 57 for an explanation of natural law).

Discussion Questions

1. According to the author, it was in the captives that "America first saw the greatness of Africa's people." Discuss what he might have meant by this.

2. What is your definition of courage? Of the people described in this account, whom do you feel best exemplifies your definition of courage? Explain.

3. How could a nation like the U.S. fight a war for independence, write the Declaration of Independence, that begins with: "We hold these truths to be self-evident, that all men are created equal, that they are endowed by their Creator with certain unalienable Rights, that among these are Life, Liberty, and the pursuit of Happiness, "and yet keep men, women, and children enslaved?

4. What is meant by the term abolitionist? What dangers did an abolitionist face during the days of slavery in the U.S.? Why would people take these risks—what does it tell you about their character?

5. Discuss the questions that appeared in the New York *Commercial Advertiser,* (see pp. 42–44). What other issues were at the forefront?

6. Discuss the letter to John Quincy Adams written by 10 year old Kali. What points did Kali make that you believe are most important? What did he say that touched you on a more emotional level?

7. Justice Story, in expressing the Supreme Court's decision said the Africans had the "ultimate right of all human beings in extreme cases to resist oppression, and to apply force against ruinous injustice." What does this mean?

8. What problems did the Africans face once they were "freed" and taken to Farmington?

9. Why was the outcome of the trial and events surrounding the *Amistad* and its captives so significant to all Americans?

Title: *Jack London*

Genre: Biography

Author: Daniel Dyer

Bibliographic Information: Scholastic Inc. New York.

Summary: Jack London did it all—he was an oyster pirate, a seal hunter, a factory worker, and a sailor, and even a prisoner—all by the time he was nineteen. By the time he was twenty-nine years old, Jack London was one of the most popular writers in the world, captivating his readers with stories that were often based on his own adventures. This book captures the life, spirit, and wonderings of this talented writer, whose words appeal to adults and young adults alike.

Interest Level: Grades 5+

Pre-Reading Activity

Read one of Jack London's books, such as *White Fang* or *The Call of the Wild*. As students read the biography of London, ask them to keep a list of the things in London's life that inspired the book in some way. Compare their lists after completing the biography.

Learning Activities

1. Jack London once wrote a self-portrait in words (see p. 109). Analyze this piece and discuss what they learned about London. Have students create their own self portrait in a similar fashion.

2. Hold a "Jack London Day." Students can dress up as characters from his books and visit other classrooms to give a book talk (a summary of the book aimed at motivating others to read it).

3. Involve students in a discussion of major issues/questions/concepts that they would like to discuss based on one of London's books or on this biography of London. Students need to bring questions they wish to pursue.

4. Each of the chapters in this biography is introduced by a quote from London. Assign groups of students one of the quotes. Have them copy the

years the chapter covers and the quote, then illustrate the quote based on the information learned about London from the chapter. Put several quotes together to form "time-line" mobiles and display them around the room.

5. The Klondike gold rush was significant to London's life. Research this event and prepare a newspaper article based on some aspect of the gold rush: the people who came looking for treasure, conditions in the Klondike, equipment, the trip to the Klondike, prospecting, etc. Put these articles together into a newspaper that might have been written in the Klondike in the late 1890's.

6. London kept a "tramp diary" in which he recorded brief notes about his experiences. Have students create their own diaries and encourage them to keep track not only of their experiences but their reactions and feelings about what has happened.

7. At the end of the unit, have students read over their diaries (see Activity 6 above), and create their own picture book based on one or more of the events recorded.

Discussion Questions

1. What were some of the major events that led to Jack London's accomplishments?

2. London said that the book *Signa*, the true story of an Italian peasant boy who became a famous violinist and composer, had a profound affect on his life. Why do you think the book might have made such a lasting impression upon him? Has any book touched you in a similar way?

3. How did the times in which he lived affect London's writing?

4. What do you think London would say if he were alive today about the books you read?

5. We tend to think that people are often all good or all bad. Jack London was a complex individual, with many positive, as well as negative qualities. Discuss both sides of the man—his strengths and weaknesses.

6. London studied the work of other writers to see why they had succeeded. Why do you think that London succeeded as a writer? (Look at his writings and at his commitment to writing.)

7. Discuss the advice London gave concerning the art of writing. (see p. 110).

CULMINATING ACTIVITY

Students will create traveling museum carts to honor the contributions of people in various fields of endeavor. To accomplish this, have each student (pair/group) select an individual to honor. Have them research this individual, reading a variety of biographies and non-fiction writings. Students need to decorate it so that it can be easily moved from classroom to classroom. The museum cart can include:

1. An audio tape to introduce people to the contributions of the individual.

2. Pictures from childhood through adulthood (labeled).

3. Artifacts (labeled) that represent various aspects of the person and his/her life.

4. A timeline reflecting main events in the person's life.

5. Any of the materials developed in the "General Activities" for this unit.

6. A bibliography of resources they could seek to learn more about the person.

SUPPLEMENTAL LITERATURE

Note: The tremendous list of titles is overwhelming. Biographies and autobiographies can be found on almost any individual who has helped to shape our world in significant way. Therefore, the resource list below lists a variety of biography series to help facilitate your search.

Series

Art for Children Series. New York: HarperCollins.
   Presents the lives of 16 of the world's most recognized artists, including Michelangelo. Picasso, and Matisse.

American Women of Achievement. New York: Chelsea House Pub.
   Includes the lives of 50 women from Abigail Adams, a woman's right advocate, to Babe Didrikson Zaharias, a champion athlete.

Black Americans of Achievement Series: New York: Chelsea House.

Extraordinary People Series, New York: Children's Press.
   Extraordinary American Indians
   Extraordinary Asian Pacific Americans
   Extraordinary Black Americans
   Extraordinary Hispanic Americans
   Extraordinary Jewish Americans
   Extraordinary People with Disabilities
   Extraordinary Woman Journalists
   Extraordinary Women of Medicine
   Extraordinary Women Scientists
   Extraordinary Young People

Great Lives Series: New York: Atheneum.
   American Government
   American Literature
   Exploration
   Human Culture
   Invention
   Medicine
   Technology
   Theater

Childhoods of Famous Americans Series. New York: Aladdin Paperbacks.
   Subjects represent all areas of endeavor

Meet the Author Series. New York: Richard Owens

Profiles in Science for Young People. Hauppauge, New York: Barrons.
  Includes books on famous people such as Albert Einstein, Thomas
  Edison, Charles Darwin, Marie Curie.

Watts Impact Biography Series. New York: Watts.
  Includes biographies of individuals who are synonymous with the
  music makers of the blues, soul, and jazz, such as Louis Armstrong,
  Miles Davis, Aretha Franklin, Duke Ellington, and Ella Fitzgerald.

Web Sites

Use search engines to locate sites of individuals you want to research.

MINI-THEMES

Women of the World

Historically, in most societies, women were seen as the caretakers, assigned to
tend to the family and the home. For centuries their role as the "weaker" sex
was accepted and women had few choices and fewer chances of making a difference outside of the home. However, since the beginning of time, there have
been women who challenged society, and have against all odd, made their way
in a male dominated world to make a difference. This unit honors these women
and their accomplishments, and explores the ways in which each sought to create their own destinies.

Activities

1. Using sources such as *Great Women Through the Ages* (Hazell, 1996),
   have students explore the contributions of women throughout the course
   of history and the various obstacles they have had to overcome in terms of
   gender. Students can create a visual map of the changing times by illustrating each woman's contributions and the dates.

2. Have students access one of the following web sites or others they find
   related to women who have made a difference. Have them create a display
   that reflects some of their most important findings:
       http://www.netsrq.com/~dbois/index.html
   This is a biographical dictionary of notable women past and present.
       http://www.gale.com/cwh/cwhset.html
   Celebrates women's history with bios of more than 60 women, past and
   present. Also includes a timeline of significant events in women's history,
   activities, and more.

3. Create a show such as "This is Your Life" based on a specific woman who
   has made a difference.

4. Create lists of areas of endeavor such as: sports, science, medicine, art,
   literature, music, environmental protection, space, business, government,
   etc. Have students add names to the list of women who have made a significant contribution to a particular field and write one or two sentences to
   describe the person's accomplishments. Use the information from these

lists to prepare brief "Women's Notes" that can be read over closed-circuit TV during "Women's History Month" in March.

5. Explore the ways in which boys and girls are treated equally or differently in school—i.e. academics, sports, government, etc. What changes need to be made. How can these changes be affected?

6. Discuss the amendment to the Constitution that gave women the right to vote. Have students research the events that led to this landmark amendment.

7. After reading books such as *The Hundred Most Influential Women of All Time* (Felder, 1996), or Rolka and Rolka's *100 Women Who Shaped World History* (1994), have students compile their own list of this country's most influential women.

8. Involve students in research concerning women's rights around the world. For example, a ruling in a recent case (Magaya vs. Magaya) in Zimbabwe (March, 1999) stripped women of almost all the rights they had gained since the nation broke free of colonial rule 20 years ago.

Resources

Behrens, J. (1990). *Barbara Bush: First lady of literacy*. New York: Children's Press.

Felder, D. (1996). *The hundred most influential women of all times: A ranking of past and present*. Secaucus, NJ: Citadel Press.

Fritz, J. (1995). *You want women to vote, Lizzie Stanton?* New York: Putnam's Sons.

Hazell, R. (1996). *Great women through the ages*. New York: Abbeville Publishing Group.

Hanson, J. (1998). *Women of hope: African American women who made a difference*. New York: Scholastic.

Hines, S. (1994). *I remember Laura Ingalls Wilder*. Nashville, TN: Thomas Nelson Pub.

Hurwitz, J. (1988). *Anne Frank: A life in hiding*. New York: Beech Tree.

Hurwitz, J., & Hurwitz, S. (1989). *Sally Ride*. Columbine, NY: Fawcett.

Lauber, P. (1988). *Lost star: The story of Amelia Earhart*. New York: Scholastic.

Lowry, L. (1998). *Looking back: A book of memories*. Boston: Houghton Mifflin.

Morpurgo, M. (1999). *Joan of Arc*. Illustrated by M. Foreman. San Diego, CA: Harcourt Brace.

Pettit, J. (1996). *Maya Angelou: Journey of the Heart*. New York: Puffin.

Rolka, G., & Rolka, B. (1994). *100 women who shaped history*. San Francisco, CA: Bluewood Books.

Sills, L. (1989). *Inspirations: Stories about women artists*. Morton Grove, IL: Whitman. Stanley, D. and Vennema, P. (1990). *Good Queen Bess: The story of Elizabeth I of England*. New York: Four Winds.

Series

American Women of Achievement, New York: Chelsea House Pub.
    Series includes the lives of 50 women from Abigail Adams, a woman's right advocate, to Babe Didrikson Zaharias, a champion athlete.)

Advocates for Women's Freedom Series. New York: Aladdin.

Freedom Fighters

In every age a hero/heroine has emerged to fight injustice. These are the unique individuals whose courage, determination, and innate sense of right and wrong pitted them against the dictates of time, the prejudice of generations, and the policies of governments. They are the individuals who fought for freedom on a variety of fronts—the David's who challenged Goliath.

Activities

1. Have students locate Martin Luther King, Jr.'s "I Have a Dream" speech (Lambert, 1993). Have them rewrite the speech in their own words.

2. Involve students in research concerning the Civil Rights Movement of the 1960's (King and Osborne, 1997). Have each group of students select one event that they believe was the most significant of the time and have them prepare a persuasive speech to support their choice.

3. After reading biographies of those who have risked their lives to help others, involve students in creating a "courage to care" quilt in which they honor the strength and heroism of these individuals. Using fabric markers and attaching other accessories, students can each create one quilt square based on the biography read. Squares can then be sewed together.

4. Involve student in Kamishibai storytelling (from "kami" meaning "paper" and "shibai" meaning "drama"). To do this, students use large cards with illustrations on one side and text printed on the back. (For more information on Kamishibai contact:

    Kamishibai for Kids, P.O. Box 20069, Park West Station, N.Y., N.Y. 10025-1510, [212-663-2471].

    Have them present the story of one of the freedom fighters.

5. Have students compare the fight for rights and freedoms that were denied to so many in the books they read.

6. Involve students in a discussion of "What if's" concerning the freedom fighter they read about. For example:

   • What if he/she hadn't been born?

   • What if you could meet this person—what would you say or ask?

   • What if you they were making a movie of this person's life. Who would play the lead? What would the title of the movie be?

Resources

Abdul-Jabbar, K., & Steinberg, A. (1996). *Black profiles in courage.* New York: William Morrow.

Coombs, K. (1997). Jackie Robinson: *Baseball's civil rights legend.* Springfield, NJ: Enslow.

Ferris, J. (1988). *Go free or die: A story about Harriet Tubman.* Minneapolis, MN: Carolrhoda Books.

Fremon, D. (1994). *The trail of tears.* New York: New Discovery.

Jurmain, S. (1998). *Freedom's Song: The true story of the Amistad mutiny.* New York: Lothrop, Lee & Shepard.

King, C., & Osborne, L. B. (1997). *Oh, freedom.* New York: Knopf.

Lambert, K. (1993). *Martin Luther King, Jr.: Civil rights leader.* New York: Chelsea House.

Meltzer, M. (1991). *Rescue: The story of how gentiles saved Jews in the Holocaust.* New York: HarperCollins.

McKissack, P., & McKissack, F. (1996). *Rebels against slavery.* New York: Scholastic.

Parks, R. with Reed, G. (1996*). Dear Mrs. Parks: A dialogue with today's youth.* New York: Lee and Low.

Mochizuki, K. (1997). *Passage to Freedom: The Sugihara story.* Illus. by Dom Lee. New York: Lee and Low.
Relates the heroism of a Japanese consulate in Lithuania during the Holocaust.

Nicholson, M., & Winner, D. (1990). *Raoul Wallenberg.* Ridgefield, CT: Morehouse.

Schulke, F. (Ed.) (1976*). Martin Luther King, Jr.: A documentary, Montgomery to Memphis.* New York: Norton.

Sinnott, S. (1999*). Lorraine Hansberry: Award-winning playwright and civil rights activist.* Berkley, CA: Conari Pr.

Sullivan, G. (1990). *Sadat: The man who changed Mid-East history.* New York: Walker.

Meet The Newberys

OVERVIEW

Focus

Students will become involved with Newbery Award-winning literature and the authors whose works have inspired and excited the imaginations of readers.

Objectives

Upon completion of this thematic unit, students will be able to:

1. Read for enjoyment those books that have been awarded the Newbery Medal.

2. Recognize the authors of literature awarded the Newbery Medal.

3. Gain insight into the writing process and the ways ideas are generated and developed.

4. Identify and apply criteria for evaluating literature.

HOW IT WORKS

Initiating Activity

Discuss the significance of the Newbery Medal with students. The award is given to the author of the most distinguished contribution to literature published in the United States during the preceding year. (The author must be a citizen or resident of the U.S.) Have students suggest books they think should have been selected for the Newbery Award and list them on large chart paper. Then, go through the list of Newbery Award winners and honor books to see which of these have been recognized. At the completion of the unit, have students reassess their list and indicate whether or not they believe the same books should have been honored. Have them support their stand.

General Activities

1. Involve students in reading various books that have been awarded the Newbery Medal. Have students identify the main subjects/topic each book focuses on and collaboratively create an annotated subject index for the Newbery Award winners. As students continue their reading, have them constantly update the index. If possible, include the books that were identified as Newbery Honor books as well. The index can then be used when planning thematic units.

2. Have students create a flag honoring a favorite Newbery Medal winner. Flags can be cut from various pieces of fabric and decorated with assorted materials to reflect something special about the book. Flags should also

include the book's title and author. Encourage students to create individual flag holders so that flags can be displayed around the room.

3. Have students create a monthly newsletter that focuses on several Newbery Medal books each time. The newspaper can contain a variety of articles and features (comic strips, word searches, puzzles, advice columns, advertisements, and so on) related to the books being highlighted. Newsletters could be thematic—tied to the content being studied—and each month could be dedicated to books by a certain author, or based on books of a certain genre.

4. As a class, have students identify the criteria they think should be used to select the Newbery Medal for the most distinguished contribution to literature for children. On a large piece of butcher paper, create a chart, similar to the one below, with a column for titles and columns in which students can evaluate each book based on the criteria established. Assign each group of students a year between 1922, when the Newberys were first awarded, and today. Have the students read the Newbery Medal winner and at least two honor books for their year. Have students evaluate the books based on the class criteria and place their evaluations on the class chart. Would they have selected the same book the American Library Association selected? Have students share their group's findings with the rest of the class, explaining the reasons for their evaluation

Meet The Newberys	
Title	**Evaluation**

5. Have students select a favorite author of a Newbery Medal winner. Have students research this author using such sources as *Something About the Author* (from Gale Publications—a reference found in most libraries). Have students, as a class, prepare an outline for reporting information he/she found most intriguing and then use this outline to create a biographical sketch of the author. Have students illustrate their report with illustrations representing one or more of the author's books. Compile these reports for a *Meet the Newbery Authors* reference book.

6. Have students create T-Shirts that creatively represent their favorite Newbery Award winning book. They can wear their shirts during the Culminating Activity.

7. Divide students into groups and have them each write three interpretive questions based on the book assigned after you have modeled several questions based on a book all of them are familiar with. (Interpretive questions are those for which there is no right or wrong answer. They can focus on a

myriad of ideas such as author purpose, character motivation, effect of the setting, and so on. Responses are based on individual interpretations but should be supported by specific references from the book.) Involve students in Literary Circles in which they each discuss one or more of the questions they developed with others in their group.

8. Each year the *Horn Book* publishes the acceptance speech of that year's Newbery Award-winning author. Involve students in reading the award-winning book and then read aloud the acceptance speech. Discuss the speech and the insights they gained.

9. Create a class poem honoring the Newbery winners. As a class, decide upon the rhyming pattern of the poem and write one verse together, based on one of the Newbery books all of them have read. Then, have students, in groups, create a verse for their assigned book, using the class verse as a model. Have groups illustrate their verses and combine the work into a single poem. Send a copy to *Horn Book* or to magazines that publish student work.

10. Cereal companies are always looking for a new promotional idea to help them sell their cereals. Have students create a campaign that focuses on the heroes/heroines of children's literature. Have each student select a favorite Newbery Award-winning book character as the basis for the picture(s) and text for the front of a cereal box. Send copies of students' designs to one of the cereal companies, suggesting that the company do a series on children's literature.

Discussion Questions

1. For whom was the Newbery Medal named? (John Newbery [1713–1767], the first English publisher of books for children.)

2. For what is the Newbery Medal awarded? (It is awarded to the most distinguished book of literature for children published in the United States during the preceding year.)

3. Do you believe awards such as the Newbery Medal are important? Why or why not?

4. Who is your favorite Newbery Medal author? Explain.

5. Which Newbery Medal award-winning book is your favorite? Explain.

6. What criteria do you believe are most important when evaluating books for the Newbery Award? Which criterion is *the* most important? Why?

LITERATURE RELATED ACTIVITIES

Note: Each of the books in this section was awarded the Newbery Medal for the year following its publication date.

Title: *The Giver*

Genre: Fantasy—Science Fiction

Author: Lois Lowry

Bibliographic Information: Dell, New York, 1993.

Summary: Everything in Jonas's world is perfect. There is no hunger, pain, or war. But in Jonas's world, there are also no choices. Everyone is assigned a specific job when they are twelve years old; Jonas is given the honor of being selected to become the "Receiver of Memories" and begins training with the Giver. As the memories of the past fill Jonah with new feelings, including love and pain, he is compelled to discover his own truths and reality.

Interest Level: Grades 5–7+

Pre-Reading Activity

Discuss the title and its possible meanings. Who might "The Giver" be and what might his role involve? Have students study the illustrations on the cover and make interpretations based on the pictures, colors used, etc.

Learning Activities

1. Select various issues that are reflected in the book and have pairs of students debate each, being sure to cite specific references from the book. Issues can include:

   • Does the government have the right to make laws to protect people from learning about things that might hurt them?

   • Should free choice be limited? Who should set these limits and how?

   • Is "sameness" a valid way of life if it prevents prejudice and discrimination?

   • Is there any possible way to create a utopian way of life?

   • Is "release" humane or inhumane?

2. Have students read Chapters 1–4 carefully. Have them make a list of things that seem unusual and that suggest that Jonas's society is far different from their own. For each item listed, have students consider the implications and make predictions as to what each actually implies.

3. Have students create their own utopian society. To prepare, they need to determine what problems in our current society will be eliminated in their own and how this will be accomplished. Have them create a visual "floor-plan" to illustrate the society and write a Chapter 1 that introduces some of the unique qualities of the society.

4. One of the most important themes of *The Giver* deals with the importance of memory. Have students select one of their most special memories which involves a member (or members) of their family. Ask them to summarize the memory, illustrate it and send it with a card to the family members most responsible for this special time and thank them for the memory.

5. Write a sequel to the story. What happens next to Jonah and Gabriel as they follow the music? Ask students to tape their stories or write them in book form and illustrate.

6. Select one social problem affecting society today. Have students read various news and magazine articles that outline the problem. In groups, have students determine the underlying problem and brainstorm possible solutions. From the solutions generated, have them select the best one (based on pre-determined criteria)and create a plan for implementing the solution.

Discussion Questions

1. What is the role of the Giver? The Receiver?

2. Jonas's community has many laws and rules. Is there one rule or law you believe we should adopt in our own society? Explain.

3. What are your thoughts about the Ceremony of Release?

4. Think of some of the things that Jonas's community banished. For example, only the Giver possesses books. Why is the censorship of books important to the success of Jonas's community? Discuss some of the other items that have been banned from the community and explain why the planners of the community might have "outlawed' them.

5. What do you believe is the most important thing the members of Jonas's community lost in order to create the "perfect" society they created? Do you think it was worth it?

6. What is the importance of past memories to your present life and to your future?

7. Can a "perfect" society exist? Why or why not?

Title: *Walk Two Moons*

Genre:	Realistic Fiction
Author:	Sharon Creech
Bibliographic Information:	HarperCollins, New York, 1994.
Summary:	Salamanca Hiddle drives with her eccentric grandparents from Ohio to Idaho in search of her missing mother who left a year earlier after promising to return. Along the way, she entertains her grandparents with tales of her friend, Phoebe Winterbottom, whose own mother has vanished without explanation.
Interest Level:	Grades 4–8.

Pre-Reading Activity

Discuss the quote, " Don't judge a man until you've walked two moons in his moccasins." Have students write this quote on a piece of construction paper and create an illustration suggesting its meaning. Allow time for students to share their interpretive pieces. Then discuss the book's title and cover and have students offer possible scenarios for the book.

Learning Activities

1. After she first left, Sal's mother sent postcards from various places she visited. Ask students to imagine that they are Sal and write a postcard to Phoebe telling her about one of the places she visited on her trip from Euclid, Ohio, to Lewiston, Idaho, such as the Missouri River.

2. Mr. Birkway assigned his students various 15 second exercises. One of them was to "Draw your soul." Encourage students to try this same exercise.

3. The character of Sal is quite interesting and complex. Have students select five sentences/phrases that capture something special about Sal's personality or character and then explain what each reveals.

4. Sal finally acknowledges to herself that her mother will not be coming back. Along her journey to Idaho she remembers all the good times she and her mother had together and things her mother had taught her. Ask students to imagine that they are Sal and have them create either an epitaph (the inscription on a headstone that often tells something special about the person buried there) or a eulogy (a short speech given during a funeral that reminds everyone about the special qualities/contributions of the person who has died) for her mother.

5. Have students think about their goals for themselves and the things they hope to achieve in life. Have them create an epitaph for themselves. Encourage them to create epitaphs that are not only humorous but that, in some way, suggest their accomplishments.

6. Many themes are suggested by *Walk Two Moons*—friendship, courage, growing up, and dealing with death. Have students select one of these themes and personify it, creating a verbal (essay) or visual (picture/sculpture) portrait of it—how it looks, tastes, feels, affects others, and so on.

Discussion Questions

1. What made Sal's and Phoebe's friendship so special? What things did they seem to have in common? In what ways were they different? Would you choose them for your friends? Why or why not?

2. What was the purpose of the trip to Lewiston, Idaho, from Sal's grandparents' point of view. Did it achieve its purpose?

3. Phoebe Winterbottom's mother received many mysterious messages. Ask students to reflect on each and explain what the message says to each of them personally. Then discuss the messages in terms of what they were trying to say to Phoebe and her family.

4. How would you describe the tone of the story? What feelings did the book evoke? What did the author Sharon Creech do to create a book that was able to elicit so many feelings?

5. *Walk Two Moons* was awarded the Newbery Medal. List five reasons why you think the book was so honored. Discuss your responses and try to reach a class consensus.

Title: *A View from Saturday*

Genre:	Realistic Fiction
Author:	E. L. Konigsburg
Bibliographic Information:	Simon and Schuster, New York, 1996.
Summary:	An unlikely foursome of awkward sixth graders learn about life and friendship. Along the way, they become the champions of the Academic Bowl, beating the best seventh and eight grade teams in the district!
Interest Level:	Grades 4–7.

Pre-Reading Activity

Discuss with students what they know about local, state, and district academic bowls. Allow students who have taken part in such activities to explain the academic bowl—it's purpose and their preparation for it.

Learning Activities

1. In groups, have students research one of the following subjects that helped launch the academic bowl careers of the "The Souls" or have them research an alternative topic that corresponds with what they are learning in one of their subjects
   - The Life and Times of Florida Sea Turtles
   - The Art of Calligraphy
   - The Women's Suffrage Movement

   Ask students to present their findings in a creative way—for example, the presentation on calligraphy can include a demonstration in which students "try their hands" at this ancient form of writing.

2. Create a class Academic Bowl. At the back of the book are fifteen sample questions. Students can use their text books to frame questions. Each question should be accompanied by an answer! You may wish to expand the Academic Bowl to include the entire school.

3. Learn about the various academic competitions sponsored by organizations dealing with specific subjects such as the National Council for the Social Studies (3501 Newark St. NW Washington, DC 20016 [202-966-7840]). The two competitions listed on the next page are also popular with students of all age groups and you may wish to enter a group of students from your class and compete first at the local level . . . who knows where this will lead:

Odyssey of the Mind
P.O. Box 547
Glassboro, NJ 08028
609-881-1603

Future Problem Solving
University of Michigan
318 W. Ann St.
Ann Arbor, Michigan

4. Serve tea and pastries and create your own "View from _____." (You pick the day of the week.) Have students bring in puzzles, logic problems, etc. that students can work on together as a team.

5. Have students create a "family tree" or other visual graphic to show the relationship between and among The Souls.

6. During one of the Saturday teas, Ethan asked The Souls, "If you could live one day of your life all over again, what day would it be? And why?" Have students write a journal entry that addresses these questions.

Discussion Questions

1. Is "The Souls" a good name for the group? Explain. What name would you give them?

2. The name of the school The Souls attend is called Epiphany. Find the definition of "epiphany." Why is this name so appropriate? What epiphanies did the various members of the group (and Mrs. Olinsky) have? What did they discover on their journeys?

3. Mrs. Olinski spoke to Mr. Singh about "a cup of kindness." How could this be shared with people like Hamilton Knapp?

4. Did Mrs. Olinski choose The Souls or did they choose her? Explain.

5. If you were to join the Souls, what qualities could you bring to the group?

6. If you could meet one character from the book, who would it be? What advice would you give him/her?

Title: *Holes*

Genre: Realistic Fiction

Author: Louis Sachar

Bibliographic Information: Farrar, Straus and Giroux, New York, 1998.

Summary: Stanley Yelnats's family has a long history of bad luck which they usually blame on that "no-good-dirty-rotten-pig stealing great-grandfather" of theirs. Stanley isn't surprised when his luck lands him in a juvenile detention center for something he didn't do. At Camp Green Lake, Stanley spends his days digging holes, and at the same time, he digs for truths about himself and his family.

Interest Level: Grades 5–8.

Pre-Reading Activity

Ask students to write a journal entry that relates a time in their lives in which they were blamed for something they didn't do. Share journals and discuss ways to handle situations such as these.

Learning Activities

1. As they are reading *Holes,* have students keep a simulated journal, one in which they write as if they are one of the main characters of the book. Allow time for students to share their journal entries and discuss their feelings/insights.

2. Involve students in a mock trial in which they try Stanley for the theft of the sneakers.

3. Stanley's father was involved in finding ways to recycle sneakers. Group students and ask each group to brainstorm a list of ways that sneakers can be recycled. From this list, have them select one and create a plan to recycle sneakers. If possible, have them put this plan into action to benefit the community.

4. Stanley's mother always looked on the bright side of things. Ask each student to list some of the problems they have had recently. For each, have them discover how they might turn the problem into a positive outcome. Have them put their favorite example on poster board and illustrate. Share with the class.

5. *Holes* relates the legend of Kissin' Kate Barlow. Either individually, or in pairs, have students create another version to explain Kate Barlow's metamorphosis from upstanding citizen to outlaw.

6. At the end of the book, Louis Sachar writes that many changes took place in the 1½ years after Stanley and Hector left Camp Green Lake. He encourages the reader to "fill in the holes." On a large piece of construction paper, draw at least 5 holes. In each hole, predict one event you believe may have happened during this time period to the main characters and/or their families.

7. Have students research life in a local juvenile detention center. What is life typically like for the juveniles sent there? How does the center differ from Camp Green Lake?

Discussion Questions

1. In Chapter 1, what mood was created regarding Camp Green Lake? What words especially helped evoke this feeling?

2. How would you describe life in Camp Green Lake?

3. The philosophy of Camp Green Lake was "If you take a bad boy and make him dig a hole every day in the hot sun it will turn him into a good boy." How do you respond to this belief?

4. Why was Stanley able to get along so well with the boys at Camp Green Lake, yet was victimized in school by boys much smaller and less danger-

ous? What advice do you think he would now give to people who are being bullied to help them handle the situation?

5. What was Stanley's most impressive quality? How and when was this quality demonstrated?

6. Of all the characters in *Holes,* who do you admire least? Who do you admire most? Explain.

7. Was "Caveman" an appropriate nickname for Stanley? If you were to give him a nickname, what would it be? Explain.

8. Why didn't Stanley and Zero get bitten by the lizards? (Hint: Relate this to the story of Sam the Onion Man.)

9. In a review of *Holes, The Horn Book* wrote, "...exceptionally funny and heartrending. Sachar is masterful at bringing his realistic story and tall tale motifs together..." Explain what is meant by this.

CULMINATING ACTIVITY

"Meet the Newberys!" Involve students in a multi-media presentation of the best in children's literature. Each group of 3 to 4 students should select a favorite Newbery Award-winning book and present it to the audience in a creative way using one or more audio-visual materials and one or more dramatic forms (dance, music, art, storytelling, puppetry, etc.). Each presentation should be introduced by a creatively designed sign that includes the name of the book and its author, as well as names of the members of the group.

Invitations to this event should be sent to the school's faculty and classrooms, as well as to participants' parents. Decorate the room with book jackets, anthologies, newsletters, and the like that reflect the work done during this unit. You may have groups prepare food and drink that in some way represent the books being presented.

SUPPLEMENTAL LITERATURE

The following is a list of those books that have been awarded the Newbery Medal or those that have been named Newbery Honor books.

Year	Winner	Honors
1922	*The Story of Mankind* by Hendrik Willem van Loon, Liveright.	*The Great Quest* by Charles Hawes, Little; *Cedric the Forester* by Bernard Marshall, Appleton; *The Old Tobacco Shop* by William Bowen, Macmillan; *The Golden Fleece and the Heroes Who Lived Before Achilles* by Padraic Colum, Macmillan; *Windy Hill* by Cornelia Meigs, Macmillan.
1923	*The Voyages of Doctor Dolittle* by Hugh Lofting, Lippincott.	No record
1924	*The Hark Frigate* by Charles Hawes, Atlantic/Little.	No record
1925	*Tales from Silver Lands* by Charles Finger, Doubleday.	*Nicholas* by Anne Carroll Moore, Putnam; *Dream Coach* by Anne Parrish, Macmillan.
1926	*Shen of the Sea* by Arthur Bowie Chrisman, Dutton.	*Voyagers* by Padraic Colum, Macmillan.
1927	*Smoky, the Cowhorse* by Will James, Scribner's.	No record
1928	*Gayneck, The Story of a Pigeon* by Dhan Gopal Mukerji, Dutton.	*The Wonder Smith and His Son* by Ella Young, Longmans; *Downright Dencey* by Caroline Snedeker, Doubleday.
1929	*The Trumpeter of Krakow* by Eric P. Kelly, Macmillan.	*Pigtail of Ah Lee Ben Loo* by John Bennett; *Longmans; Millions of Cats* by Wanda Gag, Coward; *The Boy Who Was* by Grace Hallock, Dutton; *Clearing Weather* by Cornelia Meigs, Little; *Runaway Papoose* by Grace Moon, Doubleday; *Tod of the Fens* by Elinor Whitney, Macmillan.
1930	*Hitty, Her First Hundred Years* by Rachel Field, Macmillan.	*Daughter of the Seine* by Jeanette Eaton, Harper; *Pran of Albania* by Elizabeth Miller, Doubleday; *Jumping-off Place* by Marian Hurd McNeely, Longmans; *Tangle-Coated Horse and Other Tales* by Ella Young, Longmans; *Vaino* by Julia Davis Adams, Dutton; *Little Blacknose* by Hildegarde Swift, Harcourt.
1931	*The Cat Who Went to Heaven* by Elizabeth Coatsworth, Macmillan.	*Floating Island* by Anne Parrish, Harper; *The Dark Star of Itza* by Alida Malkus, Harcourt; *Queer Person* by Ralph Hubbard, Doubleday; *Mountains Are Free* by Julia Davis Adams, Dutton; *Spice and the Devil's Cave* by Agnes Hewes, Knopf; *Meggy Macintosh* by Elizabeth Janet Gray, Doubleday; *Arrant the Hunter* by Herbert Best, Doubleday; *Ood-Le-Uk the Wanderer* by Alice Lide and Margaret Johansen, Little.
1932	*Waterless Mountain* by Laura Adams Armer, Longmans.	*The Fairy Circles* by Dorothy P. Lathrop, Macmillan; *Calico Blush* by Rachel Field, Macmillan; *Boy of the South Seas* by Eunice Tietjens, Coward; *Oust of the Flame* by Eloise Lownsbery, Longmans; *Jane's Island* by Marjorie Allee, Houghton; *Trance of the Wolf and Other Tales of Old Italy* by Mary Gould Davis, Harcourt.

Year	Winner	Honors
1933	*Young Fu of the Upper Yangtze* by Elizabeth Foreman Lewis, Winston.	*Swift Rivers* by Cornelia Meigs, Little; *The Railroad to Freedom* by Hildegarde Swift, Harcourt; *Children of the Soil* by Nora Burglon, Doubleday.
1934	*Invincible Louisa* by Cornelia Meigs, Little.	*The Forgotten Daughter* by Caroline Snedeker, Doubleday; *Swords of Steel* by Elsie Singmaster, Houghton; *ABC Bunny* by Wanda Gag, Coward; *Winged Girl of Knossos* by Erik Berry, Appleton; *New Land* by Sarah Schmidt, McBride; *Big Tree of Bunlahy* by Padraic Colum, Macmillan; *Glory of the Seas* by Agnes Hewes, Knopf; *Apprentice of Florence* by Anne Kyle, Houghton.
1935	*Dobry* by Monica Shannon, Viking.	*Pageant of Chinese History* by Elizabeth Seeger, Longmans; *Davy Crockett* by Constance Rourke, Harcourt; *Day on Skates* by Hilda Van Stockum, Harper.
1936	*Caddie Woodlawn* by Carol Brink, Macmillan.	*Honk, The Moose* by Phil Stong, Dodd; *The Good Master* by Kate Seredy, Viking; *Young Walter Scott* by Elizabeth Janet Gray, Viking; *All Sail Set* by Armstrong Sperry, Winston.
1937	*Roller Skates* by Ruth Sawyer, Viking.	*Phebe Fairchild: Her Book* by Lois Lenski, Stokes; *Whistler's Van* by Idwal Jones, Viking; *Golden Basket* by Ludwig Bemelmans, Viking; *Winterbound* by Margery Bianco, Viking; *Audubon* by Constance Rourke, Harcourt; *The Codfish Musket* by Agnes Hewes, Doubleday.
1938	*The White Stag* by Kate Seredy, Viking.	*Pecos Bill* by James Cloyd Bowman, Little; *Bright Island* by Mabel Robinson, Random; *On the Banks of Plum Creek* by Laura Ingalls Wilder, Harper.
1939	*Thimble Summer* by Elizabeth Enright, Rinehart.	*Nino* by Valenti Angelo, Viking; *Mr. Popper's Penguins* by Richard and Florence Atwater, Little; *"Hello the Boat!"* by Phyllis Crawford, Holt; *Leader by Destiny: George Washington, Man and Patriot* by Jeanette Eaton, Harcourt; *Penn* by Elizabeth Janet Gray, Viking.
1940	*Daniel Boone* by James Daugherty, Viking.	*The Singing Tree* by Kate Seredy, Viking; *Runner of the Mountain Tops* by Mabel Robinson, Random; *By the Shores of Silver Lake* by Laura Ingalls Wilder, Harper; *Boy with a Pack* by Stephen W. Meader, Harcourt.
1941	*Call It Courage* by Armstrong Sperry, Macmillan.	*Blue Willow* by Doris Gates, Viking; *Young Mac of Fort Vancouver* by Mary Jane Carr, T. Crowell; *The Long Winter* by Laura Ingalls Wilder, Harper; *Nansen* by Anna Gertrude Hall, Viking.
1942	*The Matchlock Gun* by Walter D. Edmonds, Dodd.	*Little Town on the Prairie* by Laura Ingalls Wilder, Harper; *George Washington's World* by Genevieve Foster, Scribner's; *Indian Captive: The Story of Mary Jemison* by Lois Lenski, Lippincott; *Down Ryton Water* by Eva Roe Gaggin, Viking.
1943	*Adam of the Road* by Elizabeth Janet Gray, Viking.	*The Middle Moffat* by Eleanor Estes, Harcourt; *Have You Seen Tom Thumb?* by Mabel Leigh Hunt, Lippincott.

Year	Winner	Honors
1944	*Johnny Tremain* by Esther Forbes, Houghton.	*These Happy Golden Years* by Laura Ingalls Wilder, Harper; *Fog Magic* by Julia Saner, Viking; *Rufus M.* by Eleanor Estes, Harcourt; *Mountain Born* by Elizabeth Yates, Coward.
1945	*Rabbit Hill* by Robert Lawson, Viking.	*The Hundred Dresses* by Eleanor Estes, Harcourt; *The Silver Pencil* by Alice Dalgliesh, Scribner's; *Abraham Lincoln's World* by Genevieve Foster, Scribner's; *Lone Journey: The Life of Roger Williams* by Jeanette Eaton, Harcourt.
1946	*Strawberry Girl* by Lois Lenski, Lippincott.	*Justin Morgan Had a Horse* by Marguerite Henry, Rand; *The Moved-Outers* by Florence Crannell Means, Houghton; *Bhimsa, The Dancing Bear* by Christine Weston, Scribner's; *New Found World* by Katherine Shippen, Viking.
1947	*Miss Hickory* by Carolyn Sherwin Bailey, Viking.	*Wonderful Year* by Nancy Barnes, Messner; *Big Tree* by Mary and Conrad Buff, Viking; *The Heavenly Tenants* by William Maxwell, Harper; *The Avion My Uncle Flew* by Cyrus Fisher, Appleton; *The Hidden Treasure of Glaston* by Eleanore Jewett, Viking.
1948	*The Twenty-one Balloons* by William Pene du Bois, Viking.	*Pancakes-Paris* by Claire Huchet Bishop, Viking; *Li Lun, Lad of Courage* by Carolyn Treffinger, Abingdon; *The Quaint and Curious Quest of Johnny Longfoot* by Catherine Besterman, Bobbs; *The Cow-Tail Switch, and Other West African Stories* by Harold Courlander, Holt; *Misty of Chincoteague* by Marguerite Henry, Rand.
1949	*King of the Wind* by Marguerite Henry, Rand.	*Seabird* by Holling C. Holling, Houghton; *Daughter of the Mountains* by Louise Rankin, Viking; *My Father's Dragon* by Ruth S. Gannett, Random; *Story of the Negro* by Arna Bontemps, Knopf.
1950	*The Door in the Wall* by Marguerite de Angeli, Doubleday.	*Tree of Freedom* by Rebecca Caudill, Viking; *The Blue Cat of Castle Town* by Catherine Coblentz, Longmans; *Kildee House* by Rutherford Montgomery, Doubleday; *George Washington* by Genevieve Foster, Scribner's; *Song of the Pines* by Walter and Marion Havighurst, Winston.
1951	*Amos Fortune, Free Man* by Elizabeth Yates, Aladdin.	*Better Known as Johnny Appleseed* by Mabel Leigh Hunt, Lippincott; *Gandhi, Fighter Without a Sword* by Jeanette Eaton, Morrow; *Abraham Lincoln, Friend of the People* by Clara Ingram Judson, Follett; *The Story of Appleby Capple* by Anne Parrish, Harper.
1952	*Ginger Pye* by Eleanor Estes, Harcourt.	*Americans Before Columbus* by Elizabeth Baity, Viking; *Minn of the Mississippi* by Holling C. Holling, Houghton; *The Defender* by Nicholas Kalashnikoff, Scribner's; *The Light at Tern Rock* by Julia Sauer, Viking; *The Apple and the Arrow* by Mary and Conrad Buff, Houghton.
1953	*Secret of the Andes* by Ann Nolan Clark, Viking.	*Charlotte's Web* by E. B. White, Harper; *Moccasin Trail* by Eloise McGraw, Coward; *Red Sails to Capri* by Ann Well, Viking; *The Bears on Hemlock Mountain* by Alice Dalgliesh, Scribner's; *Birthdays of Freedom*, Vol. 1 by Genevieve Foster, Scribner's.

Year	Winner	Honors
1954	*. . . and now Miguel* by Joseph Krumgold, T. Crowell.	*All Alone* by Claire Huchet Bishop, Viking; *Shadrach* by Meindert DeJong, Harper; *Hurry Home Candy* by Meindert DeJong, Harper; *Theodore Roosevelt, Fighting Patriot* by Clara Ingram Judson, Follett; *Magic Maze* by Mary and Conrad Buff, Houghton.
1955	*The Wheel on the School* by Meindert DeJong, Harper.	*The Courage of Sarah Noble* by Alice Dalgliesh, Scribner's; *Banner in the Sky* by James Ullman, Lippincott.
1956	*Carry on, Mr. Dowditch* by Jean Lee Latham, Houghton.	*The Secret River* by Marjorie Kinan Rawlings, Scribner's; *The Golden Name Day* by Jennie Lindquist, Harper; *Men, Microscopes, and Living Things* by Katherine Shippen, Viking.
1957	*Miracles on Maple Hill* by Virginia Sorensen, Harcourt.	*Old Yeller* by Fred Gipson, Harper; *The House of Sixty Fathers* by Meindert DeJong, Harper; *Mr. Justice Holmes* by Clara Ingram Judson, Follett; *The Corn Grows Ripe* by Dorothy Rhoads, Viking; *Black Fox of Lorne* by Marguerite de Angeli, Doubleday.
1958	*Rifles for Watie* by Harold Keith, T. Crowell.	*The Horsecatcher* by Mari Sandoz, Westminster; *Gone-Away Lake* by Elizabeth Enright, Harcourt; *The Great Wheel* by Robert Lawson, Viking; *Tom Paine, Freedom's Apostle* by Leo Gurko, T. Crowell.
1959	*The Witch of Blackbird Pond* by Elizabeth George Speare, Houghton.	*The Family Under the Bridge* by Natalie S. Carlson, Harper; *Along Came a Dog* by Meindert DeJong, Harper; *Chucaro: Wild Pony of the Pampa* by Francis Kalnay, Harcourt; *The Perilous Road* by William O. Steele, Harcourt.
1960	*Onion John* by Joseph Krumgold, T. Crowell.	*My Side of the Mountain* by Jean George, Dutton; *America Is Born* by Gerald W. Johnson, Morrow; *The Gammage Cup* by Carol Kendall, Harcourt.
1961	*Island of the Blue Dolphins* by Scott O'Dell, Houghton.	*America Moves Forward* by Gerald W. Johnson, Morrow; *Old Ramon* by Jack Schaefer, Houghton; *The Cricket in Times Square* by George Selden, Farrar.
1962	*The Bronze Bow* by Elizabeth George Speare, Houghton.	*Frontier Living* by Edwin Tunis, World; *The Golden Goblet* by Eloise McGraw, Coward; *Belling the Tiger* by Mary Stolz, Harper.
1963	*A Wrinkle in Time* by Madeleine L'Engle, Farrar.	*Thistle and Thyme* by Sorche Nic Leodhas, Holt; *Men of Athens* by Olivia Coolidge, Houghton.
1964	*It's Like This, Cat* by Emily Cheney Neville, Harper.	*Rascal* by Sterling North, Dutton; *The Loner* by Esther Wier, McKay.
1965	*Shadow of a Bull* by Maia Wojciechowska, Atheneum.	*Across Five Aprils* by Irene Hunt, Follett.
1966	*I, Juan de Pareja* by Elizabeth Borten de Trevino, Farrar.	*The Black Cauldron* by Lloyd Alexander, Holt; *The Animal Family* by Randall Jarrell, Pantheon; *The Noonday Friends* by Mary Stolz, Harper.
1967	*Up a Road Slowly* by Irene Hunt, Follett.	*The King's Fifth* by Scott O'Dell, Houghton; *Zlateh the Goat and Other Stories* by Isaac Bashevis Singer, Harper; *The Jazz Man* by Mary H. Weik, Atheneum.

Year	Winner	Honors
1968	*From the Mixed-Up Files of Mrs. Basil E. Frankweiler* by E. L. Konigsburg, Atheneum.	*The Black Pearl* by Scott O'Dell, Houghton Mifflin; *The Egypt Game* by Zilpha Keatley Snyder, Atheneum; *The Fearsome Inn* by Isaac Bashevis Singer, Scribner; *Jennifer, Hecate, Macbeth, William McKinley, and Me, Elizabeth* by E. L. Konigsburg, Atheneum.
1969	*The High King* by Lloyd Alexander, Holt, Rinehart & Winston.	*To Be a Slave* by Julius Lester, Dial; *When Shlemiel Went to Warsaw and Other Stories* by Isaac Bashevis Singer, Farrar, Straus & Giroux.
1970	*Sounder* by William Armstrong, Harper & Row.	*Journey Outside* by Mary Q. Steele, Viking; *Our Eddie* by Sulamith Ish-Kishor, Pantheon; *The Many Ways of Seeing: An Introduction to the Pleasures of Art* by Janet Gaylord Moore, Harcourt Brace Jovanovich.
1971	*The Summer of the Swans* by Betsy Byars, Viking.	*Enchantress from the Stars* by Sylvia Louise Engdahl, Atheneum; *Kneeknock Rose* by Natalie Babbitt, Farrar, Straus & Giroux; *Sing Down the Moon* by Scott O'Dell, Houghton Mifflin.
1972	*Mrs. Frisby and the Rats of Nimh* by Robert C. O'Brien, Atheneum.	*Annie and the Old One* by Miska Miles, Atlantic-Little; *The Headless Cupid* by Zilpha Keatley Snyder, Atheneum; *Incident at Hawk's Hill* by Allan W. Eckert, Little, Brown; *The Planet of Junior Brown* by Virginia Hamilton, Macmillan; *The Tombs of Atuan* by Ursula K. LeGuin, Atheneum.
1973	*Julie of the Wolves* by Jean C. George, Harper & Row.	*Frog and Toad Together* by Arnold Lobel, Harper & Row; *The Upstairs Room* by Johanna Reiss, Crowell; *The Witches of Worn,* by Zilpha Keatley Snyder, Atheneum.
1974	*The Slave Dancer* by Paula Fox, Bradbury.	*The Dark Is Rising* by Susan Cooper, Atheneum.
1975	*M. C. Higgins, the Great* by Virginia Hamilton, Macmillan.	*Figgs and Phantoms* by Ellen Raskin, E. P. Dutton; *My Brother Sam Is Dead* by James Lincoln Collier and Christopher Collier, Four Winds; *The Perilous Gard* by Elizabeth Marie Pope, Houghton Mifflin; *Philip Hall Likes Me, I Reckon Maybe* by Bette Greene, Dial.
1976	*The Grey King* by Susan Cooper, Atheneum.	*Dragonwings* by Laurence Yep, Harper & Row; *The Hundred-Penny Box* by Sharon Bell Mathis, Viking.
1977	*Roll of Thunder, Hear My Cry* by Mildred Taylor, Dial.	*Abel's Island* by William Steig, Farrar, Straus & Giroux; *A String in the Harp* by Nancy Bond, Atheneum.
1978	*Bridge to Terabithia* by Katherine Paterson, Crowell.	*Anpao: An American Indian Odyssey* by Jamake Highwater, Lippincott; *Ramona and Her Father* by Beverly Cleary, Morrow.
1979	*The Westing Game* by Ellen Raskin, Dutton.	*The Great Gilly Hopkins* by Katherine Paterson, Crowell.
1980	A *Gathering of Days: A New England Girl's Journal, 1830–32* by Joan W. Blos, Scribner.	*The Road from Home: The Story of an Armenian Girl* by David Kerdian, Greenwillow.
1981	*Jacob Have I Loved* by Katherine Paterson, Crowell.	*The Fledging* by Jane Langton, Harper & Row; *A Ring of Endless Light* by Madeleine L'Engle, Farrar, Straus & Giroux.

Year	Winner	Honors
1982	*A Visit to William Blake's Inn: Poems for Innocent and Experienced Travelers* by Nancy Willard, Harcourt Brace Jovanovich.	*Ramona Quimby, Age 8* by Beverly Cleary, Morrow; *Upon the Head of the Goat: A Childhood in Hungary, 1939–1944* by Aranka Siegal, Farrar, Straus & Giroux.
1983	*Dicey's Song* by Cynthia Voigt, Atheneum.	*The Blue Sword* by Robin McKinley, Greenwillow; *Doctor DeSoto* by William Steig, Farrar, Straus & Giroux; *Graven Images* by Paul Fleischman, Harper & Row; *Homesick: My Own Story* by Jean Fritz, Putnam; *Sweet Whispers, Brother Rush* by Virginia Hamilton, Philomel.
1984	*Dear Mr. Henshaw* by Beverly Cleary, Morrow.	*The Sign of the Beaver* by Elizabeth George Speare, Houghton Mifflin; *A Solitary Blue* by Cynthia Voigt, Atheneum; *Sugaring Time* by Kathryn Lasky, Macmillan; *The Wish Giver* by Bill Brittain, Harper & Row.
1985	*The Hero and the Crown* by Robin McKinley, Greenwillow.	*Like Jake and Me* by Mavis Jukes, Alfred A. Knopf; *The Moves Make the Man* by Bruce Brooks, Harper & Row; *One-Eyed Cat* by Paula Fox, Bradbury.
1986	*Sarah, Plain and Tall* by Patricia MacLachlan, Harper & Row.	*Commodore Perry in the Land of the Shogun* by Rhoda Blumberg, Lothrop, Lee & Shepard; *Dogsong* by Gary Paulsen, Bradbury.
1987	*The Whipping Boy* by Sid Fleischman, Greenwillow.	*A Fine White Dust* by Cynthia Rylant, Bradbury; *On My Honor* by Marion Dane Bauer, Clarion; *Volcano: The Eruption and Healing of Mount St. Helen's* by Patricia Lauber, Bradbury.
1988	*Lincoln: A Photobiography* by Russell Freedman, Clarion.	*After the Rain* by Norma Fox Mazer, Morrow; *Hatchet* by Gary Paulsen, Bradbury.
1989	*Joyful Noise: Poems for Two Voices* by Paul Fleischman, Harper & Row.	*In the Beginning: Creation Stories from Around the World* by Virginia Hamilton, Harcourt Brace Jovanovich; *Scorpions* by Walter Dean Myers, Harper & Row.
1990	*Number the Stars* by Lois Lowry, Houghton Mifflin.	*Afternoon of the Elves* by Janet Taylor Lifle, *Watts;* *Shabanu: Daughter of the Wind* by Suzanne Fisher Staples, Knopf; *The Winter Room* by Gary Paulsen, Watts.
1991	*Maniac Magee* by Jerry Spinelli, Little, Brown.	*The True Confession of Charlotte Doyle* by Avi, Jackson/Orchard.
1992	*Shiloh* by Phyllis Reynolds Naylor, Atheneum.	*Nothing But the Truth: A Documentation Novel* by Avi, Jackson/Orchard; *The Wright Brothers: How They Invented the Airplane* by Russell Freedman, Holiday House.
1993	*Missing May* by Cynthia Rylant, Jackson/Orchard.	*The Dark-thirty* by Patricia McKissack, Knopf; *Somewhere in the Darkness* by Walter Dean Myers, Scholastic; *What Hearts?* by Bruce Brooks, HarperCollins.
1994	*The Giver,* by Lois Lowry, Houghton Mifflin.	*Crazy Lady!* by Jane Leslie, HarperCollins; Eleanor *Roosevelt: A Life of Discovery* by Russell Freedman, Clarion; *Dragon's Gate* by Laurence Yep, HarperCollins.

Year	Winner	Honors
1995	*Walk Two Moons,* by Sharon Creech, HarperCollins.	*Catherine, Called Birdy,* by Karen Cushman, Clarion; *The Ear, the Eye and thc Arm,* by Nancy Farmer, Jackson/Orchard.
1996	*The Midwife's Apprentice* by Karen Cushman, Clarion.	*What Jamie Saw* by Carolyn Coman, Front Street; *The Watsons Go to Birmingham: 1963* by Christopher Paul Curtis, Delacorte.
1997	*The View from Saturday* by E. L. Konigsburg, Jean Karl/Atheneum.	*A Girl Named Disaster* by Nancy Farmer, Richard Jackson/Orchard Books; *Moorchild* by Eloise McGraw, Margaret McElderry/Simon & Schuster; *The Thief* by Megan Whalen Turner, Greenwillow/Morrow; *Belle Prater's Boy* by Ruth White, Farrar Straus Giroux.
1998	*Out of the Dust* by Karen Hesse, Scholastic.	*Ella Enchanted* by Gail Carson Levine, HarperCollins; *Lily's Crossing* by Patricia Reilly Giff, Delacorte; *Wringe*r by Jerry Spinelli, HarperCollins.
1999	*Holes* by Lois Sachar, Farrar, Straus & Giroux.	*A Long Way from Chicago* by Richard Peck, Dial.

Web Sites

Children's Literature: Authors and Illustrators:
      http://www.users.interport.net/~fairrosa/cl.authors.html
Internet Public Library Youth Division:
      http://www.ipl.org/youth
Children's Literature Web Guide (excellent source for award winning literature):
      http: www.acs.ucalgary.ca/~dkbrown
List of Newbery Winners and other references concerning writers and illustrators of children's books:
      http://www.interactivebooks.com/childrens-newbery.htm

MINI-THEMES

Introducing the Classics

While contemporary children's literature is popular with children today, rarely are they introduced to the classics. It is important that children also be exposed to those books that have withstood the test of time and are still considered outstanding examples of children's literature.

Activities

1. Involve students in a "Meeting of Minds" in which students take on the persona of a favorite author of a favorite classic and become members of a panel in which they discuss their writing.

2. After reading a favorite classic, have groups create a time capsule that includes objects, photographs, and the like that represent the book and its time. Have students share their time capsule with other classes to encourage students to read the classics.

3. After reading a classic, involve students in a discussion of the way in which the development of theme compares with the way in which a similar theme

is dealt with today. Have students create a Venn Diagram (see example below) to depict their findings.

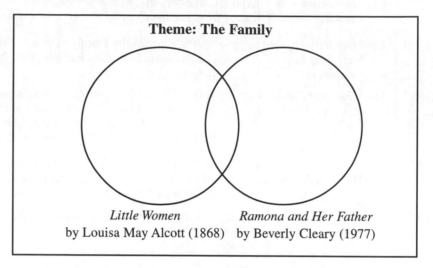

Theme: The Family

Little Women
by Louisa May Alcott (1868)

Ramona and Her Father
by Beverly Cleary (1977)

4. After reading one of the classics, have students select one of the main characters and write a dialogue between this character and a favorite character from a Newbery award-winning book.

5. Select a favorite modern-day children's book and a favorite classic. Imagine that the character in the modern-day book took a quantum leap and found himself/herself in the pages of the classic. Write a brief journal entry that expresses the difference he/she has found.

6. Involve students in a discussion of "What is a classic?" What modern-day books do they think will become tomorrow's classics?

7. Have students create *Something About the Author—the Classics,* a book similar to the one they created in General Activity 5 on p. 354.

8. Many classics were transformed into "Classic Comics." In groups, have students choose a favorite classic and create their own comic book that retells the story. (Share various comic books with students so that they have an understanding of the components of a comic book.)

References

Note: For purposes of this mini-theme, books identified as classics are those originally published before the second half of the twentieth century. The original publishing date is listed after the publisher.)

Alcott, L. M. (1968). *Little women.* Illustrated by J. W. Smith. Boston: Little. (1868).

Barrie, J. M. (1980). *Peter Pan in Kensington Gardens.* Illustrated by A. Rackham. Cutchogue, NY: Buccaneer Books. (1906).

Baum, F. (1980). *The Wizard of Oz.* Illustrated by M. Hague. New York: Halt. (1900).

Brink, C. R. (1970). *Caddie Woodlawn.* New York: Macmillan. (1935).

Burnett, F. H. (1981). *Little Lord Fauntleroy.* Buccaneer. (1886).

Burnett., F. H. (1989). *The secret garden.* Illustrated by S. Hughes. New York: Viking. (1910).

Carroll, L. (1988). *Alice's adventures in Wonderland.* Illustrated by A. Browne. New York: Knopf. (1865).

Collodi, C. (1988). *The adventures of Pinocchio.* Illustrated by R. Innocenti. New York: Knopf. (1891).

Cooper, J. F. (1986). *The Last of the Mohicans.* Illustrated by N.C. Wyeth. New York: Scribner's. (1826).

Dodge, M. M. (1988). *Hans Brinker, Or the silver skates.* New York: Scholastic. (1865).

DuBois, W. P. (1947). *The twenty-one balloons.* New York: Viking.

Estes, E. (1974). *The hundred dresses.* San Diego, CA: Harcourt Brace Javonovich. (1944).

Forbes, E. (1943). *Johnny Tremain.* Illustrated by L. Ward. Boston: Houghton.

Grahame, K. (1983). *The wind in the willows.* Illustrated by J. Burningham. New York: Viking. (1908).

Kipling, R. (1950). *The jungle book.* Illustrated by F. Eichenberg. New York: Grosset. (1894).

Kipling, R. (1991). *Just so stories.* Illustrated by D. Frampton. New York: HarperCollins. (1902).

Lawson, R. (1944). *Rabbit Hill.* New York: Viking.

Milne, A. A. (1988). *Winnie the Pooh.* Illustrated by E. H. Shepard. New York: Mutton. (1926).

Scott, W. (1964). *Ivanhoe.* London, England: Airmont. (1820).

Sewell, A. (1945). *Black Beauty.* New York: Grosset. (1877).

Spyri, J. (1982). *Heidi.* Illustrated by T. Howell. New York: Messner. (1884).

Stevenson, R. L. (1985). *A child's garden of verses.* Illustrated by M. Foreman. New York: Delacorte. (1885).

Stevenson, R. L. (1981). *Treasure Island.* Illustrated by N.C. Wyeth. New York: Scribner's. (1883).

Travers, P. (1934). *Mary Poppins.* San Diego, CA: Harcourt Brace Javonovich.

Twain, M. (1989). *The adventures of Tom Sawyer.* Illustrated by B. Moser. New York: Morrow. (1876).

Verne, J. (1988). *Around the world in eighty days.* Illustrated by B. Moser. New York: Morrow. (1872).

Verne, J. (1986). *Journey to the center of the earth.* New York: Penguin. (1864).

Verne, J. (1964). *Twenty thousand leagues under the sea.* London, England: Airmont. (1869).

Wiggin, K. D. (1986). *Rebecca of Sunnybrook Farm.* New York: Penguin. (1903).

Wyss, D. (1981). *The Swiss Family Robinson.* Sharon. (1814).

Censorship and Children's Literature

In recent years, more and more pressure has been exerted by individuals and groups seeking to influence the content of children's literature. Those who wish to control children's reading choices find the issues, ideas, and language of many books inappropriate for children. Those who oppose censorship of literature are concerned with the principle of intellectual freedom. The reference section on pp. 373–374 cites many popular award-winning books that have been banned for the reasons listed next to the titles. The activities will involve students in becoming aware of the causes and effects of censorship and the way our country works to defend individual rights.

Activities

1. Discuss the term *censorship* with students. Try to obtain a group consensus of the definition.

2. Provide students with copies of the Bill of Rights. Have them write and deliver a persuasive speech to reflect their interpretation of the First Amendment as it applies to censorship of children's literature.

3. Survey students to discover which of the banned books listed in the reference section (pp. 373–374) they have read. Select one of the books that a majority of students have read or are familiar with and have students prepare a mock trial in which the book itself is tried for the reason(s) cited by those who challenged it.

4. Have students look at censorship in a different way by completing the following analogies. Once they have completed the analogies, have them draw their own interpretive illustration of censorship by combining their responses in a creative way.

    Censorship is like (name of a vegetable) because _____.
    Censorship is like (name of an animal) because _____.
    Censorship is like (name of a country) because _____.
    Censorship is like (name of a mineral) because _____.

5. Invite speakers from organizations such as The American Civil Liberties Union to speak to the class or call the American Library Association, Office for Intellectual Freedom (312-280-4223), for more information on censorship of children's books.

6. In 1992, 600 incidents of attempted censorship were reported to the American Library Association. This, however, is only a fraction of the actual attempts. Have students respond to the following question by creating a one-frame comic strip: "What if all books that were challenged were actually banned . . . "

7. The American Library Association's Office for Intellectual Freedom is the only library censorship monitoring group. Each year, for one week in September, the American Library Association sponsors a "Banned Books Week . . . Celebrating the Freedom to Read." Have students plan and take part in a week of activities that brings attention to the issues relating to censorship.

8. Involve students in a discussion of the following questions:

    a.   What types of censorship exist? (moral, military, political, religious, etc.)

    b.   How does censorship affect your life?

c. Why do some people feel censorship is important?

d. Why do some people feel that censorship is never justified?

e. Should book censorship be allowed? If so, in what situations?

f. If book censorship were allowed, who should determine what is and what is not censored?

References

Blume, J. (1970). *Are you there, God? It's me, Margaret.* New York: Bradbury. Challenged because protagonist is allowed to choose her own religion and because book discusses puberty.

Blume, J. (1974). *Blubber.* New York: Bradbury. Challengers said that in the book bad behavior is never punished.

Grimm, J., & Grimm, W. (1988). *Hansel and Gretel.* Illustrated by A. Browne. New York: Knopf. Challenged because it teaches children that it is acceptable to kill witches and depicts witches as child-eating monsters.

Grimm, J., & Grimm, W. (1974). *Snow White.* Illustrated by T. S. Hyman. Boston: Little, Brown. Challenged because of its graphic violence; a hunter kills a wild boar, a wicked witch orders Snow White's heart to be torn out.

Lowry, L. (1979). *Anastasia Krupkik.* Boston: Houghton. Challenged because of its language and the book's occasional reference to underage drinking.

Maruki, T. (1982). *Hiroshima no pike.* New York: Lothrop, Lee and Shepard. Challenged because it shows the devastating effects of war and leaves the reader feeling that war is far from a noble endeavor.

Paterson, K. (1977). *Bridge to Terabithia.* New York: Crowell. Challenged because of its language and reference to witchcraft.

Paterson, K. (1978). *The Great Gilly Hopkins.* New York: Crowell. Challenged because of its language.

Sendak, M. (1970). *In the Night Kitchen.* New York: Harper. Challenged because it "could lay the foundation for future use of pornography."

Shyer, M. (1978). *Welcome home, Jellybean.* New York: Scribner. Challenged because two school board members considered the book depressing.

Silverstein, S. (1981). *A light in the attic.* New York: Harper. Challenged because one of the poems is illustrated with a caricature of a person whose nude behind has been stung by a bee; challenged because the poem "Little Abigail and the Beautiful Pony" is morbid.

Silverstein, S. (1964). *The giving tree.* New York: Harper. Challenge by feminists as condoning sexist stereotypes.

Slepian, J. (1980). *The Alfred summer.* New York: Macmillan. Challenged because of language.

Taylor, T. (1989). *The cay.* New York: Doubleday.
   Challenged because it allegedly maligns African-Americans.

Twain, M. (1989). *Adventures of Tom Sawyer.* Illustrated by B. Moser. New York: Morrow. (1876)
   Challenged because of its inclusion of a degrading, offensive slang word to describe a black person.

Yep, L. (1977). *Dragonwings.* New York: Harper.
   Challenged because of the frequent use of the word "demon" in the book and the belief by some that it might encourage children to commit suicide because they think they can be reincarnated as something or someone else.

Fractions

OVERVIEW

Focus

Students will learn how fractions are an important part of our daily lives.

Objectives

On completion of this thematic unit, students will be able to:

1. Understand the value of fractions in the everyday world.
2. Describe various ways of using fractions.
3. Demonstrate the use of fractions in different situations.
4. Be able to use fractions correctly.

Initiating Activity

Invite students to list all the different ways in which fractions are used in everyday life—for example, in cooking, in weather predictions, in sports scores, and so on. Ask students to create a large wall mural of the various activities and occupations that use fractions on a regular basis. Students may wish to interview other students, parents, or adults about some of the ways in which fractions are used in their lives. Additional ideas or situations can be added to the wall mural throughout the year.

HOW IT WORKS

General Activities

1. Provide students with one or more copies of selected cookbooks (see references on p. 384). Ask students to review several recipes and to note the various ways in which fractions are used. If possible, provide opportunities for students to prepare some of the recipes to share with each other.

2. Invite students to talk about various ways in which fractions are used in different sports (for example, the first half, the last quarter, a quarter-mile race, and so on). Which sport uses fractions the most? Which sports do not use any fractions?

3. Ask students to look through the daily newspaper and note the instances in which fractions are used to report significant news events (for example, "After a 2½-mile chase through city streets, the police were only able to recover 1/3 of the bank money"). Invite students to maintain an ongoing news journal of fraction uses.

4. Invite a mathematician from a local college or university to visit your classroom. Ask that person to discuss the different ways in which frac-

tions are used in everyday life. Have students prepare a list of questions before the visit.

5. Invite students to prepare the following recipe for brownies. Later, challenge them to compute the amount of ingredients for (a) twice as many people, and (b) half as many people:

Ingredients

3 ounces unsweetened chocolate, 6 tablespoons butter, 1 cup sugar, 3 eggs 1 1/2 teaspoons vanilla extract, 1/2 cup cake flour, 1/4 teaspoon baking soda, 3/4 cup walnut halves, 1/2 cup chocolate chips

Directions

1. Preheat oven to 325°.
2. Melt the chocolate and butter over low heat, stirring constantly.
3. Remove from the heat and pour into a large mixing bowl.
4. Beat in the sugar.
5. Add eggs one at a time, beating well after each addition.
6. Stir in vanilla.
7. Fold in flour and baking soda.
8. Pour the batter into a well-greased 8 x 8 inch pan.
9. Sprinkle with nuts and chocolate chips.
10. Bake 25 minutes. Cool one hour before slicing.

---

6. Invite the music teacher to demonstrate to students how fractions are used to write music. Ask him or her to explain 1/2 notes, 1/4 notes, and 1/8 notes. Help students understand that each musical note is a fraction of the whole.

7. Have students work to create a "Fraction Concentration Game." On one card write a fraction (such as "1/2") and on an opposing card its equivalent (for example, "4/8"). Create a pack of 20 to 25 pairs and invite students to play the game with each other.

8. Challenge students to look in textbooks other than their math book for examples of fractions. How are fractions used in their social studies or science texts, for example?

9. Invite students to investigate the average weight of a whale. What objects weigh half as much as a whale? What objects weigh one-tenth as much as a whale? One twentieth as much as a whale?

Discussion Questions

1. Why is it important for people to know about fractions?

2. How are fractions used in everyday life? Do adults use fractions more than children? If so, why?

3. What are some of the ways in which fractions are used around your home? On what types of items or objects would you most likely find fractions?

4. If you could be any fraction, which one would you be? Why?

LITERATURE RELATED ACTIVITIES

1

Title: *If You Made a Million*

Genre: Picture Book

Author: David M. Schwartz

Bibliographic Information: Lothrop, Lee & Shepard, New York, 1989.

Summary: Various monetary values are presented in this intriguing tale of a marvelous magician and the ways in which he explains the concept of equivalence.

Interest Level: Grades 3–6.

Pre-Reading Activity

Ask students to compute the various combinations of coins that will equal $1.00. Can students combine four coins to equal $1.00? Five coins? Seven coins? More than ten coins? Invite students to illustrate the various possible coin combinations that equal $1.00. What fraction of a dollar is a quarter? Is a dime? A penny? A nickel? These can be displayed on a large wall chart.

Learning Activities

1. The author states that $1 million is equivalent to a 360-foot pile of one dollar bills. Ask students to determine the height of $200,000, $50,000, or $150,000. Do they know of any objects that might be equivalent to the height of $1 million?

2. Invite students to divide the $1 million into five piles. How much money would be in each pile? How much money would be in each of 20 piles? How much in each of 50 piles? What fraction of the million dollars would the pile of 20 be? Pile of 50?

3. How much money would each person in the class get if the $1 million was divided equally (including the teacher)?

Discussion Questions

1. How much would each person in your family get if $1 million was divided equally among all family members?

2. What would you do with $1 million?

3. What made this an interesting (or uninteresting) book?

4. What are some of the ways in which fractions could have been used by the author, but were not?

2

Title: *Fraction Action*

Genre: Picture Book

Author: Loreen Leedy

Bibliographic Information: Holiday House, New York, 1994.

Summary: Miss Prime and her animal students explore fractions by finding many examples in the world around them.

Interest Level: Grades 1–4.

Pre-Reading Activity

Invite students to look around the classroom and locate items that have been divided into fractions (for example, the blackboard may be in two equal sections, someone's chocolate bar may be divided into eight equal sections). Have students create an ongoing poster of the items that are divided into fractions. Be sure to share with students the idea that fractions are equal parts of a whole object (each part within the object must be of equal size in order for them to qualify as fractions).

Learning Activities

1. Ask the class to brainstorm various ways in which they can divide themselves into different categories of fractions. For example, what fraction of the students have blue eyes, brown eyes, blond hair, red hair, brunette hair, etc. Have students chart their discoveries on a large mural.

2. Ask students to experiment with Cuisenaire rods and the fractions that can result from their use. For example, ten white pieces is equivalent to one orange rod, thus one white piece can be represented by the fraction Rio. Invite students to create equivalents of other selected fractions.

3. Some of the most "widely used" fractions are 1/2, 1/3, 1/4, and 3/4. Ask students to locate examples of those fractions throughout the classroom and throughout their homes. Which fraction is used the most?

Discussion Questions

1. What made this an easy book to understand?

2. What are some of the ways in which your parents use fractions in the kitchen? In the living room? In the garage?

3. How many ways have you used fractions to describe events in your own life?

4. Do you think fractions provide a good way to express number? Why or why not?

Title: *Eating Fractions*

Genre: Picture Book

Author: Bruce McMillan

Bibliographic Information: Scholastic, New York, 1986.

Summary: This book introduces the mathematical concept of fractions by using a tasty meal that is shared by two youngsters and their dog. It also contains recipes for food used for the meal.

Interest Level: Grades 1–6.

Pre-Reading Activity

Bring in an inexpensive cheese pizza from a local pizza shop. Invite students to determine how the pizza could be cut so that each member of the class would get an equal-sized piece. What would happen if two people in the class decided that they didn't want a piece of pizza? What would happen if two additional people joined the class? Invite students to illustrate their responses.

Learning Activities

1. Arrange with a preschool or primary teacher for your students to assist in a cooking activity. As measuring is being done, encourage the older students to reinforce the fractional measurement being used.

2. Ask students to share ways in which they use fractions everyday. For example, they may eat ½ of a candy bar, walk half the way to school and run the other half, and so forth. Make a list of the ways fractions are used in everyday life.

3. Ask the students to create a text to go with the illustrations in *Eating Fractions*. Then provide an opportunity for them to share their new text with children in grades 1–3 and to also divide some real objects into halves, fourths, and thirds.

4. Invite students to collect recipes from home in which fractions are used. Have students discuss the importance of accurate measurements in the preparation of selected recipes.

Discussion Questions

1. If you were dividing a banana, would you want a whole, half or a fourth of a piece? Why?

2. If you had three friends plus yourself for a pizza and you divided it equally, how much of the whole pizza would each of you get? (one-fourth)

3. What did you enjoy most about this book? Least about the book?

4. How much is one-half and one-half? (a whole)

Title: *Fractions and Decimals*

Genre:	Nonfiction
Author:	Karen Bryant-Mole
Illustrator:	Grahan Round
Bibliographic Information:	EDC Publications, Tulsa, OK 1995.
Summary:	Through the eccentric "Stone Age" world of the Og family, basic and essential skills for understanding fractions and decimals are presented. The reader has fun helping the Og family play their games, solve their problems, and correct their mistakes.
Interest Level:	Grades 3–6.

Pre-Reading Activity

Select and reproduce one of the games/problems from the book *Fractions and Decimals* such as the Ogtown Fair (pp. 8 & 9) or Reptile Road (pp. 12 & 13) to work through as a group. An overhead would work well for this activity.

Learning Activities

1. Divide the students into groups. Provide each group with one of the following:

   • Number of students in their class.
   • Number of students in entire school.
   • Number of residents in their community.
   • Total number of administrators, secretaries, custodians, librarians, teachers in the school.
   • Other totals.

   Next, ask them to use the numbers provided and to determine how many people would there be in each group if the group was divided into 1/2, 1/4, 1/6, 1/8. Ask each group to report their findings and seek agreement with students in other groups.

2. As a group, create a problem or game involving fractions for the Og family to solve.

3. There are other mathematics books similar to *Fractions and Decimals* in the Usborne Series published by EDC Publishing, 10302 East 55 Place, Tulsa, OK 74146. Obtain other titles such as *Adding and Subtraction Puzzles, Multiplying Puzzles,* and *Charts and Graphs.* Allow time for the students to explore these books and work in small groups to solve the problem.

4. Invite students to divide a classroom object, such as a table or desk, into various fractions. Have students divide the object into equal sections using lengths of masking tape. How is this division process similar to or different from the division of a circular object such as pie?

Discussion Questions

1. Aside from food items, what are some other things that sometimes must be divided into equal pieces? (lumber, water pipes, and so on)
2. What did you enjoy most about this book? What did you enjoy least?
3. Does everything shared between two friends always have to "be equal"?
4. What kinds of things do you enjoy sharing with your friends?
5. What is the top number of a fraction called? (a numerator) What is the bottom number of a fraction called? (a denominator)
6. How are numerators and denominators determined? (denominators show the total number of equal pieces, slices, etc. in the whole; the numerator shows the fraction of the piece, slice, etc. that you have once whole has been divided)

7. Which of the Og games/problems did you enjoy most? From which did you learn the most? Explain answers.

8. Did the Og family games and puzzles in *Fractions and Decimals* help you to better understand fractions and decimals. Why or why not?

CULMINATING ACTIVITY

The culminating activity could be a "Fraction Day." Challenge students to use only fractions throughout an entire day. Instead of saying or writing a whole number (such as 14), encourage students to use the fractional representation of that number (28/2, for example). Invite students to use fractions in stories they write, conversations they have with each other, and other classroom events in which numbers are used. At the end of the day, discuss with students some of the challenges they faced in converting all the numbers into fractions.

SUPPLEMENTAL LITERATURE

Books

Adler, D. A. (1996). *Fraction fun.* Illustrated by Nancy Tobin. New York: Holiday House.
  Hands-on activities and colorful illustrations provide an introduction to the concept of math and problem solving by presenting fun and exciting fraction problems.

Atherlay, S. (1995). *Math in the bath and other fun places, too.* Illustrated by Megan Halsey. New York: Scholastic.
  This book encourages children to look for math and math elements in most unexpected places.

Conford, E. (1989). *What's cooking, Jenny Archer?* Boston: Little, Brown.
  Jenny learns (the hard way) about making money and all the expenses that go along with any business enterprise.

Howe, J. (1990). *Harold and Chester in hot fudge.* New York: Morrow.
  Four pets are embroiled in a mystery about some fudge and its chocolate covering.

Hutchins, P. (1986). *The doorbell rang.* New York: Greenwillow.
  Two children discover how a batch of cookies can be divided into several different fractions.

MacCabe, R. (1993). *Fractions.* Illustrated by David Stienecker. Estes Park, CO: Benchmark Books.
  An assortment of activities and illustrations to help in explaining the concept of fractions is presented in this book.

Pomerantz, C. (1984). *The half-birthday party.* New York: Clarion.
  The fraction 1/2 is the centerpiece of this story about a birthday party and things that are divided in half.

MINI-THEMES

Decimals

Decimals are just another way of expressing fractions. We use decimals in many aspects of our lives, and youngsters are often surprised to discover that many of the measurements they take for granted are actually decimals. The collection of books cited in the Reference Section below would all be wonderful additions to the math library of any classroom.

Activities

1. Invite students to investigate the various ways in which decimals are used in everyday transactions. Aside from money, what are some other instances in which decimals are utilized? In which sports are decimals used?

2. Invite students to take individual walking "field trips" throughout the local community, locating different signs and billboards on which there are one or more decimals. How are those decimals represented? Why were decimals used instead of fractions?

3. Have students look through an edition of the local newspaper for examples of decimals. In what section would you expect to discover the most decimals? In what section would you find the least?

4. Ask students to select one of the books on fractions from the reference list. Challenge students to convert all the fractions in the book(s) to decimals. Were there some fractions that could not be converted? What difficulties were encountered?

References

Anno, M. (1984). *Anno's flea market.* New York: Philomel Books.
Brenner, B. (1989). *Annie's pet.* New York: Bantam Books.
Butterworth, N., & Inkpen, M. (1989). *Joist like Jasper!* Boston: Little, Brown.
Caple, K. (1986). *The purse.* Boston: Houghton Mifflin.
Conford, E. (1988). *A job for Jenny Archer.* Boston: Little, Brown.
Day, A. (1989). *Paddy's pay-day.* New York: Viking.
Mole, K. B. (1994). *Fractions and Decimals.* Illustrated by Graham Round. Tulsa, OK: EDC Publishing.
Shaw, N. (1991). *Sheep in a shop.* Boston: Houghton Mifflin.
Van Leeuwen, J. (1983). *Benjy in business.* New York: Dutton.

Cooking and Eating

Kids love to cook! Cooking is one of the most enjoyable learning activities teachers and children can share together. Cooking can not only be used as a forum for studying fractions and decimals, but can also be used to illustrate proper nutritional habits, science concepts, social customs, and a host of other significant events in all curricular areas.

Activities

1. Ask students to prepare one or more of the recipes in the recipe books identified in the reference section. Invite them to "customize" a selected

recipe in terms of the number of people being fed. For example, what measurements (for a cake, pie, or cookie recipe) would have to be used to give everyone in the class an equal portion?

2. Here is a recipe for "Peanut Butter Pie" that students will enjoy:

Ingredients

1 8-ounce package of cream cheese, 1 cup of confectioner's sugar, 1 cup of peanut butter, ½ cup of milk, 1 1/3-ounce package of Cool Whip®, 2 prepared graham cracker crusts

Directions

1. Mix the first four ingredients.
2. Fold in the Cool Whip®
3. Spread the mixture into the graham cracker crusts.

After students have prepared their pies, have them divide the pies into various fractions and photograph them for presentation in a large "Fraction Notebook." Afterwards, the pies can be eaten.

---

3. Ask students to bring in different examples of measuring cups and utensils. What similarities are observed? What significant differences? Discuss with students the importance of accurate measurement during cooking.

4. The following recipe for "Incredible Edible Cookies" makes about 12 dozen cookies. Ask students to rewrite the recipe to serve different groups of people (for example, four dozen people, 36 people, 24 people). Ask students to reduce one of the ingredients (for example, if the chocolate chips were reduced to two ounces, how much would each of the other ingredients need to be reduced?).

Ingredients

1 cup margarine (softened), 2 cups peanut butter, 2 cups sugar, 1 pound brown sugar, 6 eggs, dash of light corn syrup, 8 ounces chocolate chips, 8 ounces M & M's, 4 teaspoons baking soda, 1 teaspoon vanilla, ½ cup chopped nuts, 1 cup raisins, 9 cups uncooked quick oats

Directions

1. Preheat the oven to 350°.
2. Mix together all the ingredients in a very large bowl
3. Add the oats last.
4. Drop a heaping teaspoons onto an ungreased cookie sheet.
5. Bake for 10 to 12 minutes.

References

Blain, D. (1991). *The boxcar children cookbook.* Morton Grove, IL: Albert Whitman.

Darling, J. D. (1989). *Better Homes and Gardens new junior cookbook.* Des Moines, IA: Meredith Corp.

Douglass, B. (1985). *The chocolate chip cookie contest.* New York: Lothrop, Lee Shepard.

Khalsa, D. (1989). *How pizza came to Queens.* New York: Potter.

Levitin, S. (1980). *Nobody stole the pie.* New York: Harcourt Brace Jovanovich.

MacDonald, K. (1985). *The Anne of Green Gables cookbook.* Toronto: Oxford University Press.

McGrath, B. B. (1998). *More M & M's math.* Illustrated by Roger Glass. Watertown, MA: Charlesbridge Publishing.

McMillan, B. (1991). *Eating fractions.* New York: Scholastic.

Powell, J. (1997). *Bread (Everyone eats).* Austin, TX: Raintree/Steck Vaughn.

Watson, N. (1987). *The little pig's first cookbook.* Boston: Little, Brown.

Wilkes, A. (1997). *Children's quick and easy cookbook.* New York: Dorling Kindersley Publishing.

Willard, N. (1990). *The high rise glorious skittle skat roarious sky pie angel food cake.* New York: Harcourt Brace Jovanovich.

OVERVIEW

Focus

Students will develop an understanding of the usefulness of geometry in their daily lives.

Objectives

On completion of this thematic unit, students will:

1. Understand various geometric forms and shapes.
2. Be able to use geometry in everyday pursuits.
3. Understand the role of geometry in selected occupations.
4. Describe and use various shapes.

HOW IT WORKS

Initiating Activity

Invite students to bring in photographs from home—particularly photographs of rooms and spaces in and outside their homes. Divide the class into several ad hoc groups and invite each group to list the various types of geometric shapes (circles, squares, rectangles, etc.) found within each of the photographs. Invite each group to compose a graph of the number of squares, rectangles, etc. found in each photograph as well as the entire assembly of photos. (Students may wish to make predictions as to which geometric shapes will "show up" most often in the collection of photos and then compare their final results with their predictions). Post these around the room.

General Activities

1. Provide students with one or more copies of David Macauley's architectural books (see References on p. 395). Invite students to note the various geometric shapes displayed within each of the books. Ask students to take their own "personal field trips" throughout their neighborhood or community to note similar structures and shapes. What comparisons can they make?
2. Provide students with several examples of Tana Hoban's "shape" books (see Supplemental Literature on p. 392) the bibliographies). Invite students to work together in small groups to construct their own original shape books for younger students in another grade. If possible, provide students with a camera and ask them to photograph items around the school or community which could be combined into a shape book for a grade lower than yours.

3. Provide students with light wire coat hangers and invite them to create some of the more familiar geometric shapes. Ask students to create some new shapes and assign various names to those shapes. Do the names have anything to do with the actual shape? Should the name be functional?

4. Invite a mathematician from a local college or university to visit your class. Ask the invited speaker to discuss some of the geometric shapes represented in the "outside world." Ask the speaker to discuss the importance of geometry in everyday life.

5. Invite students to brainstorm for songs or song titles which contain the names of various geometric shapes. Do they know any songs which use the words "circle," "square," or "rectangle" for example? Which geometric word seems to be used most often?

6. Provide each student group with a box of sugar cubes and some white glue. Invite each group to construct a variety of 3-dimensional geometric models (i.e. cubes, pyramids, etc.) for display in the classroom. Ask students to discuss any difficulties they have in constructing the shapes and whether there is any relationship between the frequency of that shape in the "outside world" and the difficulty people might have in building the shape.

Discussion Questions

1. Why would it be important for architects to have a knowledge of geometry? (structural weight and size)

2. Can you think of any other occupations which need to have a knowledge of geometry? (billiards player, race car driver)

3. How will geometry be useful in your own life?

4. How do your parents or relatives use geometric shapes in their jobs or at home?

5. What are some of the largest geometric figures you can think of? (sphere: planet; pyramid: pyramid) What is the smallest geometric figure you can think of?

LITERATURE RELATED ACTIVITIES

Title: *Bridges Are to Cross*

Genre: Nonfiction

Author: Philemon Sturges

Bibliographic Information: Putnam's, New York, 1998.

Summary: Feast your eyes on these bridges from around the world, all painstakingly created with intricately cut paper. These bridges represent the most simple (a log across a river) to the most complex (the Golden Gate Bridge). But more than ways to get across water, bridges also reflect an intricate variety of geometric forms and patterns.

This book shares the wonders of bridges as symbols, celebrations, and solutions.

Interest Level: Grades 2–6

Pre-Reading Activity

Students may enjoy looking at more bridges from around the world: where they are located, how they were constructed, and their specific dimensions. Here are some wonderful web sites that will provide them with lots of incredible information:

http://hyperion.advanced.org/23378/
http://www.pbs.org/wgbh/nova/bridge/
http://www.xs4all.nl/~hnetten/index.html

Learning Activities

1. Invite students to construct a bulletin board display which presents the various types of bridges profiled in this book. For each bridge profiled, invite students to list the various geometric shapes and forms represented with the structure of that bridge. Do some bridges seem to include a certain geometric shape more than others? What is the most geometrically "perfect" bridge depicted in the book?

2. Invite students to participate in one or more of the following "bridge-building" activities. Be sure to plan sufficient time for students to discuss some of the challenges they faced in constructing their bridges, as well as some of the geometric forms or principles used in the construction process.

   Paper Structures: Invite students to take a sheet of newspaper and begin rolling it from one corner to the opposite diagonal corner (keep the newspaper rolled as tight as possible). At the end, tape the newspaper "roll" together. Encourage students to continue building a series of newspaper "logs." Invite students to construct one or more "bridges" with their "logs." What are some rules of geometry which contribute to the construction process?

   Marshmallow Structures: Provide student teams with a box of wooden toothpicks and a bag of miniature marshmallows. Invite them to construct the following using the toothpicks as beams and the marshmallows as "glue":

   • What is the tallest structure which can be built using nine marshmallows and 15 toothpicks?

   • Build a structure with nine toothpicks and 15 marshmallows? Is it stronger than the first structure? What contributes to its strength?

   • Using 14 marshmallows and 20 toothpicks, create a structure that is strong enough to support a book.

   • Build a "bridge" between two tables (1' apart) which will support a stack of four quarters.

Spaghetti Structures: Provide students with raw spaghetti and masking tape. Invite them to create one or more of the following:

- What is the tallest free-standing structure students can create using only 50 sticks of raw spaghetti?

- What is the strongest structure students can create between two tables using fifty (or less) sticks of spaghetti? The "bridge" must be able to hold a weight for a minimum of six seconds (place a container on top and gradually add sand or clay until the structure collapses; afterwards, weigh the container contents).

- What is the longest unsupported structure students can create with 50 sticks of spaghetti? One end must be secured to the end of a table; the other end must not touch any other object.

3. Invite students to experiment with cut paper collages. Prove them with scissors and sheets of construction paper. Encourage them to create a cut paper replica of something with which they are familiar (i.e. their house, a community building, a store). You may wish to challenge some students to duplicate one of the structures illustrated in the book (or a portion of that structure). This will be a challenging activity for many students—plan to take time to discuss some of the challenges students had, as well as some of the challenges the illustrator must have had in designing the bridges in the book.

4. Invite students to investigate natural bridges—bridges created by nature (such as **Window Rock** in Arizona). Where are some natural bridges located? How are they created? Are there any natural bridges which include various geometric shapes?

Discussion Questions

1. Which of the bridges in this book did you enjoy most?
2. Which of the bridges seemed to be most complex?
3. What are some other man-made structures which use the same geometric shapes and forms as bridges do?
4. Why are there so many different styles of bridges throughout the world?

Title: *Janice VanCleave's Geometry for Every Kid: Easy Activities That Make Learning Geometry Fun*

Genre: Nonfiction

Author: Janice VanCleave

Bibliographic Information: Wiley, New York, 1994.

Summary: This book introduces concepts in geometry through short explanations and hands-on activities. From recognition of lines, shapes, patterns, and angles readers are moved into more complex geometric items. Lots of line drawing and diagrams compliment the text.

Interest Level: Grades 4–6

Pre-Reading Activity

Invite students to brainstorm for a list of man-made items in (a) the classroom, (b) at home, and/or (c) their parents place of employment. Ask students to create lists of the various geometric shapes represented in each of those sites. What two-dimensional shapes seem to predominate? What three-dimensional shapes seem to dominate. Invite students to graph or chart their results.

Learning Activities

1. Ask each student to select a man-made item in the classroom and list all the various shapes it contains. Are there shapes represented in that item for which there is no name? Invite students to share and compare their observations.

2. Ask students to work together in two-person teams. Invite each team to determine the reasons why certain manmade items are shaped as they are. Ask students to discuss the implications if a particular item was in a different shape. How would the new shape affect the function of that item (i.e. If a clock were rectangular instead of circular, how would it function?).

3. After reading the book invite students to look for various geometric patterns in nature. Could a stand of trees represent a series of parallel lines? Could the shape of a flower indicate a series of concentric circles? Could a rainbow represent a curved line? Can students locate triangles or squares in a piece of fruit or a vegetable?

4. Invite students to discuss the importance of geometry in everyone's life. Students may wish to construct a chart or graph which illustrates the role of geometry in everyone's life. Challenge students to describe a job or occupation in which geometry does NOT play a role? Is there a sport or free-time activity in which geometry does not influence the rules or playing of that activity?

Discussion Questions

1. What do you think is the most prevalent three-dimensional shape in nature?

2. What is the least frequent two-dimensional shape in nature?

3. What are some examples of symmetry which occur naturally in the environment around our school?

4. How would a knowledge of shapes help someone become a better architect or pursue an other occupation? (structure, relationships)

Title: *Grandfather Tang's Story*

Genre: Fiction

Author: Ann Tompert

Bibliographic Information: Crown, New York, 1990.

Summary: A boy and his grandfather spend an afternoon making various shapes with their tangrams. The shapes evolve into a story about two fox fairies and the shapes they can assume.

Interest Level: Grades 2–5

Pre-Reading Activity

Invite students to cut various shapes from construction paper (i.e. squares, rectangles, parallelograms, etc.). Ask each student to select two or three shapes, place them on his or her desk, and create a make believe story about the shapes. The shapes can be used as body parts for different characters, props within the setting of the story, or as specific objects. Students may wish to draw faces or other illustrations on the pieces to complete their stories. This activity can be done in small groups or teams, too.

Learning Activities

1. Provide each child with the cross illustrated below. Ask each child to cut out the cross and then to cut along the dotted lines (thus forming five separate pieces). Have children mix the pieces and challenge a friend to put the cross back together again.

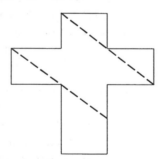

2. Invite students to cut out a series of squares, triangles, and rectangles from pieces of construction paper. Have students assemble a collection of those geometric shapes into various letters of the alphabet (Can the letter "A" be assembled using nothing but triangles?; What is the least number of squares and rectangles necessary to put together the letter "M"?).

3. Invite children to select a folk tale or fairy tale with which they are familiar. Challenge them to retell the story using a variety of tangrams to stand for characters or special items within the story.

4. Students may want to retell the story of Wu Ling and Chou to a lower grade using their own self-created tangrams. These renditions may be videotaped and shared with several classes.

Discussion Questions

1. What was the most distinctive element of this particular story? (answers will vary)

2. What made this story significantly different from or similar to other folk tales or fairy tales with which you are familiar? (answers will vary)

3. What did you enjoy most about Grandfather Tang? How is he similar to or different from your own grandfather? (answers will vary)

4. Do you like this type of story/book? (answers will vary)

Title: *Building*

Genre:	Nonfiction
Author:	Philip Wilkinson
Bibliographic Information:	Knopf, New York, 1995.
Summary:	Take an exciting tour of world architecture and discover how all kinds of structures are built—from African mud huts to Turkish mosques.
Interest Level:	Grades 3–6

Pre-Reading Activity

Invite students to take a photographic journey through their town or neighborhood. Invite them to take photos of various buildings and structures. What types of geometric forms do they discover? Why are building shaped the way they are? Is the shape of a building related to its function (store, house, garage)? What do we know about the architect who designed a building just by looking at it?

Learning Activities

1. If possible, borrow some building blocks from a kindergarten teacher in your school. Invite students to experiment with those blocks to create various structures and buildings. Based on their "experiments" which types of buildings seem to be the most stable, the least stable, the fastest to construct, the one able to support the greatest weight, etc.?

2. Invite a local architect in to address your class. Ask the individual to discuss how he or she uses shapes in the design of various buildings. If possible, have the person bring a set of building blueprints and illustrate for students the different shapes used in the plans for a building.

3. Invite students to illustrate selected buildings in their town or neighborhood according to scale. Have students measure the height, length, and width of each building and to draw the building according to a pre-determined scale (i.e. 1" = 10'). Provide students with graph paper for their drawings.

Discussion Questions

1. Why is it important for architects to know geometric shapes? (structure, function, support)

2. Can you list at least five other occupations in which a knowledge of geometry is essential?

3. What other math skills, besides geometry, are used in the construction of a building?

4. What geometric skills do you use around your house on a regular basis?

CULMINATING ACTIVITY

Invite students to assemble a "Geometry Notebook"—a collection of shapes and forms naturally occurring in nature and a collection of shapes that can be found in human-made items. For each two-dimensional or three-dimensional shape, a page in the notebook can be devoted to (a) a list of various items that exhibit that shape; (b) photographs of different examples of that shape in the community or in nature; (c) surveys of parents and other adults on how they use or see that shape in their daily lives; (d) pop-up cardboard models illustrating the shape; or (e) other examples of the shape. Students may wish to create a special book to be shared with students in grades lower than yours. A permanent display for one of the school's display cases could also be developed.

SUPPLEMENTAL LITERATURE

Books

Primary (Grades 1–3):

Anno, M. (1991). *Anno's Math Games III.* New York: Philomel Books.
Two characters, Kris and Kross, get themselves into all sorts of geometric adventures in this delightful and engrossing text.

Blackstone, S. (1998). *Bear in a Square.* New York: Barefoot Books.
Share the adventures of a big friendly bear as he discovers all kinds of different shapes.

Brown, J. (1964). *Flat Stanley.* New York: Harper and Row.
Stanley is flattened by a falling bulletin board. His adventures in his new dimension and his brother's attempts to return him to normal make an interesting introduction to plane geometry.

Bulloch, I. (1997). *Patterns.* New York: World Book.
This book teaches the skills of pattern recognition, sorting, matching, and pattern creation by means of various handicrafts.

Falwell, C. (1992). *Shape Space.* Boston: Houghton Mifflin.
A young gymnast dances her way among rectangles, triangles, circles, and squares for a lesson in geometry.

Fite, J. (1997). *Learning About Shapes.* New York: Silver Burdett.
Text and illustrations present simple geometric figures and concepts. Includes lots of comparative activities.

Hoban, T. (1986). *Shapes, Shapes, Shapes.* New York: Greenwillow.

This book, another in Hoban's delightful series, illustrates shapes in combination with each other. Again, there is much to see and much to discover!

King, A. (1998). *Exploring Shapes*. Milford, CT: Copper Beech.
Games and projects introduce 2-dimensional and 3-dimensional shapes including the square, rectangle, triangle, circle, and polygon.

King, A. (1998). *Plotting Points and Position*. Milford, CT: Copper Beech.
This book uses games and projects to introduce the concepts of coordinates and angles and how to find location and position.

Patilla, P. (1998). *Fun with Patterns*. Milford, CT: Millbrook.
Kids' observational skills are sharpened in this delightful introduction to geometric forms.

Pluckrose, H. (1997). *Shape*. New York: Children's Press.
Photographs of familiar objects introduce basic shapes of squares, circles, rectangles and triangles.

Robinson, F. (1996). *Designs*. New York: HarperCollins.
Young readers discover an exciting array of shapes and designs throughout the world.

Rogers, P. (1989). *The Shapes Game*. New York: Henry Holt.
Nine basic geometric shapes are illustrated in this delightful introduction to geometry. Colorful drawing highlight the text.

Seuss, Dr. (1988). *The Shape of Me and Other Stuff*. New York: Random House.
Readers are encouraged to use their imaginations to think about the shape of many items—those that are real, as well as those that are imaginary.

Swinburne, S. (1998). *Lots and Lots of Zebra Stripes*. Honesdale, PA: Boyds Mills.
An engaging book that will open kids' eyes to the incredible variety of shapes and patterns in the world around them.

Intermediate (Grades 4–6)

Bown, D. (1996). *Jigsaw Puzzles: Shape Puzzles*. New York: DK.
Lots of engaging puzzles highlight this book which will challenge readers' knowledge of geometry.

Isaacson, P. (1988). *Round Buildings, Square Buildings, and Buildings that Wiggle Like a Fish*. New York: Knopf.
This books looks at the different shapes buildings have and the reasons why they are designed the way they are.

Macauley, D. (1973). *City*. Boston: Houghton Mifflin.
Students will never look at their town or city in the same way after reading this book. The author takes the reader for a true "inside look" at the structure and construction of a city.

Neuschwander, C. (1997). *Sir Cumference and the First Round Table: A Math Adventure*. Watertown, MA: Charlesbridge.

Assisted by his knight, Sir Cumference, and using ideas offered by his wife and son, King Arthur finds the perfect shape for his table.

Small, D. (1987). *Paper John*. New York: Farrar, Straus Giroux.
A delightful and colorful story about a strange character who encounters an even stranger demon. A bright and creative addition to the math library.

Web Sites

http://www.mathgoodies.com
http://forum.swarthmore.edu/geopow/

MINI-THEMES

Architecture

Children often wonder about the utility of geometry in their daily lives. A mini-unit on architecture can help them understand the various ways in which shapes are used in everyone's daily lives—particularly as they relate to the buildings in which we live. The study of shapes becomes much more understandable for youngsters when they see its application in the world outside the classroom.

Activities

1. Provide each of several student groups with a camera and a roll of film. Invite each team to take a selected number of photographs of various buildings in their town or community. Have students assemble the developed photographs into one or more selected categories such as buildings of the same architectural style, buildings with squares and rectangles, and/or buildings which do not use a selected geometric shape in their design.

2. Invite students to each select a building in their town and to write a story about the construction of that building as though it might be told by the building itself—"My life while growing up."

3. Obtain the blueprints for the school (these can be obtained through the central office or superintendent's office). Invite students to discuss the various geometric shapes represented in the drawings.

4. Invite students to each design their ideal house. What shapes or designs would they use in order to complete their diagrams? Does the location of the house (i.e. beach, mountains, etc.) dictate the shapes which might be used?

References

Clinton, S. (1986). *I Can Be an Architect*. Chicago: Children's Press.
Cooper, E. (1999). *Building*. New York: Greenwillow.
Crosbie, M. (1993). *Architecture Counts*. New York: Preservation Press.
Gardner, R. (1995). *Architecture*. New York: 21st Century Books.
Grimshaw, C. (1997). *Buildings*. New York: World Book.
Kirkwood, J. (1997*). The Fantastic Cutaway Book of Giant Buildings*. Brookfield, CT: Copper Beech.

Macauley, D. (1975). *Pyramid*. Boston: Houghton Mifflin.

Macauley, D. (1973). *Cathedral*. Boston: Houghton Mifflin.

Macauley, D. (1977). *Castle*. Boston: Houghton Mifflin.

Macauley, D. (1980). *Unbuilding*. Boston: Houghton Mifflin.

Wilkinson, P. (1993). *Amazing Buildings*. New York: DK.

Wood, T. (1997). *Ancient Wonders*. New York: Viking.

Lines and Angles

Lines and angles are everywhere! Our world is filled with them and when children realize the enormous variety of lines and angles in their everyday lives, then they begin to appreciate this all-important concept. In fact, geometric principles presented in class in a two-dimensional shape achieve relevancy when demonstrated outside of the classroom in the three-dimensional world.

Activities

1. Ask each child to select one object from inside the classroom. Invite each person to add up the total number of lines in each three dimensional object, as well as the total number of angles. Students may wish to chart or graph their results.

2. Ask students to predict the number of lines necessary to draw a selected three-dimensional figure (i.e. pyramid). Provide students with straws and modeling clay (to attach the ends of the straws together) and invite them to create replicas of selected objects using only straight lines.

3. Challenge students to disprove the maxim—"A line is the shortest distance between two points." Can students figure out a situation in which that statement would not be true? Ask them to prove their ideas.

4. Invite a math teacher from the local high school to visit your class and explain the use of lines and angles in various occupations such as architect, land surveyor, draftsman, etc.

References

Adler, D. (1998). *Shape Up!*. New York: Holiday House.

Fisher, L. E. (1987). *Look Around! A Book About Shapes*. New York: Puffin Books.

Fatus, S. (1997). *Stripes*. New York: Abbeville Press.

Gundersheimer, K. (1986). *Shapes to Show*. New York: Harper and Row.

Murphey, S. (1998). *The Greatest Gymnast of All*. New York: HarperCollins.

Patilla, P. (1998). *Fun with Patterns*. Milford, CT: Millbrook.

Patilla, P. (1998). *Fun with Shapes*. Milford, CT: Millbrook.

Yenawine, P. (1991). *Lines*. New York: Delacorte Press.

Art

OVERVIEW

Note: Many of the activities and books are also appropriate or can be adapted for primary level students.

Focus

Students will develop awareness and appreciation for artists and their works.

Objectives

On completion of this thematic unit, students will be able to:

1. Identify a variety of artists and the contributions they have made to society.
2. Compare/contrast the works of different artists
3. Give examples of works of well-known artists that are recognized by our society and explain why these works are significant.
4. Evaluate their own appreciation for the arts.

HOW IT WORKS

Initiating Activity

Ask the students to identify an artist with whom they are familiar. Tell them to pretend they have been assigned to do a "Barbara Walters" type interview with him/her. Ask them to create five interview questions for this interview. Post the various artists selected by the students and ask students to sign up to be interviewed as one of the artist—other than the artist for whom they developed an interview. Allow 20 to 30 minutes to conduct interviews.

General Activities

1. Provide a painting for the students to study. Then have a discussion with them about the lines and patterns they see in the painting. What does the painting tell them? What do the colors tell them? Ask them to look for the focal point. What textures do they sense? Is there any movement?
2. Ask the students to create a "You and Me" notebook in which they save special works of art they have created and then compare their work with that of a famous artist. A three ring notebook filled with plastic sleeves can be used. Students can place their artwork on one side and a picture of the works of a famous artist (using the same style) on the other side. For example, if the student creates a piece of art that repeats the same image in repeated ways, he/she may put a copy of Andy Warhol's *Elvis I & II*, 1964 works in the notebook.

3. Provide an opportunity for the students to work in groups of 6 or 8 and assign them to look through some of the masterpieces done by great artists with the thought of selecting one of the pieces to act out. For example, if the student selects Renoir's *The Swing* to present, they would need one girl dressed in a fancy dress pretending she is on a swing, two boys dressed like farmers who are nearby and watching, and a young child standing off to one side wishing she could swing. Students would need to get appropriate props and costumes to depict the painting. Then allow time for them to present their "masterpiece" and let other students guess what artist's work is being depicted.

4. The following are the birthdates for each month for some of the great artists:

Cézanne	January 19, 1837	Rembrandt	July 15, 1606
Renoir	February 25, 1841	Warhol	August 8, 1930
Michelangelo	March 6, 1475	Arp	September 16, 1887
Leonardo de Vinci	April 13, 1452	Picasso	October 25, 1881
Rousseau	May 21, 1821	Monet	November 14, 1840
Rubens	June 28, 1577	Matisse	December 31, 1869

Encourage students to research birthdays of their favorite artists to add to this list. Then, as a class, celebrate at least one artist's birthday each month by doing all or some of these activities.
- Display some posters and/or pictures of the artists' work.
- Create a bulletin board that depicts information about artist
- Display books about the artist
- Do an art project in the style of the artist.

5. Create puzzles of great artist's work by doing the following:
   a. Glue an art print to a piece of matte board and dry thoroughly.
   b. Cut puzzle into pieces.
   c. Place puzzle pieces in an envelope or box.
   d. Allow students time to put puzzles together and identify artist.

6. Involve the students in establishing an art area in the classroom. In this area, collect books about artists such as, *The Famous Artists* series published by Barrons Ed. Series, Inc., Children's Press, or the *Weekend with Picasso* series published by Skira/Rozzoli, etc. Also, make catalogs available that include information about prints, posters, postcard art reproductions, books, etc. These catalogs can provide sources to develop matching/concentration games the students may develop. For example, cut out pictures of reproductions from catalogs and paste them on 2" x 4" index card. On another index card, write the artists name, name of artwork, type of art (abstract, impressionism, cubism), time period in which artist lived, etc. Allow students to turn cards face down and play concentration. Use this area to collect and display as much information on various artists as possible.

7. Museums and galleries around the world have web sites on the Internet. Encourage students to use the search option to find the names for indi-

vidual artists and/or museums. Establish a time for students to share their internet addresses and findings.

8. Most public libraries have a section dedicated to famous artwork in both the children and adult departments. Organize a visit to the library and ask each student to find at least one book, print, internet address, etc. to share with classmates.

9. Ask the students to select a famous artist's art technique they particularly like and one they believe is possible for them to use. For example, Warhol's repeats of the same images, Degas' chalk on cloth, Kleis' one-line designs. As a homework assignment, ask the students to create a piece of art using the technique selected. Display artwork. Be sure to ask students to identify their art techniques and artists they are copying.

Discussion Questions

1. Who is your favorite artist? Why do you like this artist? What works do you know about that this artist has created?

2. There are many great art techniques, for example, chalk, collage, painting, sculpting, printing, photography. Which of these have you or would you like to investigate? Explain.

3. Most artists do not initially make an impact with their art. In other words, their artwork does not support them financially. Often, artists are not even recognized until after their death. How do you feel about that?

4. If you were an artist, in what city would you want to live? Why?

5. In your home (room) what kind of prints, posters, and artwork do you have displayed? Do you like what is displayed? Explain.

6. Have you ever visited an art museum? If so, describe where it was and what you saw.

LITERATURE RELATED ACTIVITIES

Title: *Inspiration: Stories About Women Artists*

Genre: Nonfiction

Author: Leslie Sills

Bibliographic Information: Albert Whitman Co., Niles, IL 1989.

Summary: This book presents information and reproductions of the work of the following women artists: Georgia O'Keeffe, Frida Kahlo, Alice Neel, and Faith Ringgold.

Interest Level: Grades 2–4.

Pre-Reading Activity

Divide the students into groups and assign each of them to select one of the artists presented in this book. Ask the groups to present their authors to the class/school in a creative way—poster, play/skit, bulletin board, diorama, books displayed about artist or illustrated by artists.

Learning Activities

1. Ask students to use the first letter of at least one of the artist's names presented in this book and to write a word or phrase that describes that artist. For example ALICE NEEL:

   Artist   N

   Lovely   E

   I   E

   C   L

   E

2. Faith Ringgold has illustrated award-winning children's books such as *Tar Beach* and *Aunt Harriet's Underground in the Sky*. Obtain copies of these books. Then arrange for the students to read-aloud these books to groups of children in primary grades.

3. The lives and work of the artists presented in *Inspiration: Stories About Women Artists* are different; however, they all had a common bond of having the strength to persevere in spite of many obstacles. Ask the students to identify these obstacles for each artist and to discuss how each artist dealt with her obstacle. Do they agree or disagree with the way the obstacles were dealt with?

4. Ask the students to research women artists and to identify at least one other woman artist. Allow time for the students to provide information about each female artist, (i.e., the time period, culture, type of art, etc.).

5. The women featured in *Inspiration: Stories About Women Artists* were all born and reared in different cultures. Discuss how their cultures may have impacted their art and what influences their art may have had on their culture.

6. Read the information about the author Leslie Sills that is provided at the end of the book. Discuss the statement that she had a desire to show children "that they, too, can play; that being an artist is a viable profession and way of life." What does that mean? Do you agree? Disagree?

7. Obtain books that present each author individually such as, *Georgia O'Keefe* by Mike Venezia. This will allow students to find out more details about the women artists.

Discussion Questions

1. Which of the women artists, featured in this book, do you like best? Explain.

2. If it were possible, would you like to have a piece of artwork (created by an artist identified in *Inspiration: Stories About Women Artists*) hanging in your home? Why or why not?

3. Which of the women artists featured in this book, do you think had the most interesting life? Most difficult life? Most successful life? Explain why you selected the artist you did for each of your responses.

4. Would you recommend *Inspiration: Stories About Women Artists* to your friends? Why or why not?

Title: *Mary Cassatt*

Genre:	Nonfiction
Author:	Robyn Montana Turner
Bibliographic Information:	Little, Brown Company, Boston, 1992.
Summary:	This is a story about the remarkable life of Mary Cassatt, one of the earliest women artists. She began her career as a professional artist in 1860 and many of her paintings of children and their mothers are known around the world today.
Interest Level:	Grades 2–4.

Pre-Reading Activity

At the age of 15, Mary Cassatt knew she wanted to be an artist. Ask the students what they want to be when they grow up, how they selected that career, which influences them, etc.

Learning Activities

1. The United States paid tribute to Mary Cassatt by creating two postage stamps. Ask the students to create a postage stamp to honor a person they admire as well as one for themselves.

2. Ask the students to select one of Mary Cassatt's paintings and to recreate it. Then ask them to make changes in the painting. For example, if they select the painting, "Little Girl in the Blue Armchair" they may want to draw a cat on the armchair, a TV in one corner, etc.

3. Mary Cassatt lived from 1844 to 1926. Ask the students to make a list of things they have, such as computers, TVs, etc., that Mary Cassatt didn't have. Then ask them to select one of the items from their list that they would miss most and explain why they selected that item. Create small groups and let them discuss their selection.

4. Mary Cassatt traveled to many different places. Provide a world map and then ask the students to use the map to trace Mary Cassatt's movements.

5. On the back cover of *Mary Cassatt* by Robyn Montana Turner is a list of some other women artists. Divide the students into five groups and assign each group one of the artists to research. Allow time to complete research and then ask each group to present their artist in a creative way. After reading the book about Mary Cassatt, provide time for student to compare and contrast these women artists with Mary Cassatt.

6. Read the book, *Mary Cassatt*, written by Mike Venezia and compare/contrast it with the book *Mary Cassatt* by Robyn Montana Turner.

Discussion Questions

1. The author selected the painting, "The Boating Party" for the front cover of the book. Ask the students if they were selecting one of Mary Cassatt's paintings for the cover, which painting would they select and why.

2. Mary Cassatt had many obstacles to overcome in reaching her goal to become an artist. Discuss some of these obstacles with the students. Then ask them to identify something they have achieved or tried to achieve and what obstacles they had to overcome.

3. What do you admire most about Mary Cassatt? Explain.

4. Which Mary Cassatt painting do you like best? Least? Explain.

Title: *A Weekend with Renoir*

Genre: Nonfiction

Author: Rosabianca Skira-Venturi

Bibliographic Information: Rizzoli International Publications, Inc., New York, 1990.

Summary: Renoir, a celebrated French nineteenth-century artist, talks about his life and work as if entertaining the reader for a weekend. In addition to learning about Renoir, the reader is also exposed to what it is like to walk along the Seine River, to visit a riverside town for lunch and dancing, and to ride a train through the French countryside.

Interest Level: Grades 2–4.

Pre-Reading Activity

Inform the students that the book, *A Weekend with Renoir*, depicts what it may have been like to visit Renoir for a weekend. Ask the students to identify someone they would like to spend a weekend with (artist, politician, musician, actor, actress, etc) and to write a brief paragraph or two about why they selected the person they did and what they would expect to experience. Allow time to share.

Learning Activities

1. Renoir referred to many restaurants and famous spots in Paris and throughout France in the book, *A Weekend with Renoir*. Ask the students to recall these places as you list them on the chalkboard (Bougival, Argenteuie, LaGrenouillere, Camembert, Chatou, Montmartre, Moulin de la Galette, etc). Have the students work in pairs or small groups as they research one of these restaurants or places. Ask them to create a page for a book/brochure entitled "Renoir's Favorite Spots" by finding information on the following: name of place, location of place, brief description of place, why Renoir liked this place. Finally, put the pages together to create a book/brochure "Renoir's Favorite Spots".

2. Find someone in the class, school, or community who has visited or lived in Paris and/or France. Prior to their visit, give them a copy of the class book/brochure, "Renoir's Favorite Spots" created in Activity 1. Invite them to come to the class to present information about the city/country. Ask them to provide pictures, if possible. Also, ask them if they are familiar with "Renoir's Favorite Spots". If so, tell the class what they know about the "spot(s)".

3. The Metropolitan Museum of Art in New York City possesses one of the best collections of Renoir's work outside of France. As a class, write a letter to this museum requesting information about their Renoir collection. Display the information.

4. Renoir was considered an Impressionist artist. Form small groups of students to research Impressionism (a type of painting) and to identify other impressionist painters. Allow time to discuss their findings. Then provide paints and paper and ask the students to attempt an "Impressionist" type of painting. Allow time to share work and discuss.

5. As a group, create a bulletin board that represents Renoir. You may want to include a map of France, highlighting places where he lived and painted. Also, Renoir's prints are inexpensive and readily available. Be creative. This bulletin board could feature different artists throughout the year.

Discussion Questions

1. What do you like best about impressionist artwork? What do you like least about impressionist artwork?

2. If you lived during Renoir's life, would you have liked to spend a weekend with him? Why or why not?

3. Which of Renoir's paintings do you like best? Why?

4. Describe the kind of person Renoir was. Would you like to have someone like him as a friend? Why or why not?

Title: *Li'l Sis and Uncle Willie: A Story Based On the Life and Paintings of William H. Johnson*

Genre:	Nonfiction
Author:	Gwen Everett
Bibliographic Information:	Rizzoli International Publications, Inc., New York, 1990.
Summary:	This book is based on the actual events in the life of William H. Johnson, an African-American artist, as told by his young niece, Li'l Sis. The artist's paintings provide the illustrations in the book.
Interest Level:	Grades 1–3.

Pre-Reading Activity

William H. Johnson is an African-American artist who was successful in the art world. Ask students to identify other African-American people who have been successful in their fields and to explain their successes.

Learning Activities

1. One of William H. Johnson's paintings that are shown in the book is of the old, rickety Jacobi Hotel which Li'l Sis thought looked haunted. Display the illustration of that painting and ask the students to write a short story to accompany it. Allow time for the students to share their stories. Compile the stories into a class book of "Haunted Hotel/House Stories".

2. Uncle Willie (William H. Johnson) describes to Li'l Sis what it is like to live in a big city (New York) compared to life in a small town (Florence, South Carolina). In addition, some of his paintings depicted these differences. Ask the students to share what they would like best and least about living in a big city versus the country.

3. William H. Johnson lived from 1901–1970. Ask the students to research to find other African-American artists that lived during this period and to describe their contribution to the world of art.

4. Obtain the full biography of William H. Johnson entitled *Homecoming: The Art of Life of William H. Johnson* by Richard Powell. Allow the students time to pursue the book to find out additional information about the artist.

5. Aunt Della told Li'l Sis that Uncle Willie (William H. Johnson) liked living in Europe because people living there were friendlier to black people. Ask the students to calculate, from information provided in the book, what period of time Johnson lived in Europe. Then ask them to investigate to find out what the status of blacks living in the United States was like during that period. Do they agree with Mr. Johnson's decision to live in Europe? Why or why not?

6. Several famous black Americans (Nat Turner and Harriett Tubman) were mentioned in the book. Ask the students to research and create a list of at least five other famous black Americans who lived during this period and what made them famous. Allow time for students to share their findings.

7. The National Museum of American Art in Washington, DC has preserved over 1,000 of William H. Johnson's paintings. As a group, write the Office of Publications, National Museum of Art, Smithsonian Institute, Washington, DC 20560 and ask them to send you information about the Johnson Collection as well as a catalog of their publications.

8. Read the information on the book jacket that tells about the author, Gwen Everett. It indicates she has co-authored several museum activity guides but that *Li'l Sis and Uncle Willie* is her first picture book. Ask the students to write Ms. Everett a letter telling her what they liked about *Li'l Sis and Uncle Willie*. Mail the letters to her in care of the publisher, Rizzoli International Publications, In., 300 Park Avenue South, New York, NY 10010.

Discussion Questions

1. Would you recommend the book *Li'l Sis and Uncle Willie* to a friend? Why or why not?
2. Which of Mr. Johnson's works did you like best? Least? Explain.
3. Why do you think Uncle Will liked living in Europe more than the U.S.?
4. Explain how you think Mr. Johnson's works compare to the works of other artists you are familiar work.

CULMINATING ACTIVITY

Have an "Arts Day" open house in which local artists plus parents, school administrators, and other classmates are invited to attend. For the open house, convert the classroom into a gallery where all the art projects, created during this unit, are displayed. Be sure all pieces of art have titles and name of artist(s) identified. Serve light refreshments and play classical music for background.

SUPPLEMENTAL LITERATURE

Books

DePaola, T. (1989). *The art lesson*. New York: Putnam.
Tommy has learned to be creative in drawing pictures at home, only to become dismayed when he goes to school and finds the art lessons there are much more regimented.

Kohl, M. F., & Solga, K. (1997). *Discovering great artists*. Illustrated by Van Slyke, Bellington, WA: R. Bright Ring Publishing, Inc.
Includes instruction for art projects that corresponds to each artist's style or technique.

Muhlberger, R. (1997). *What makes a Degas*? New York: Viking Press.
This book explores such art topics as style, composition, color, and subject matter as they relate to twelve works by Degas.

Roche, D. (1998). *Art around the world: Loo-loo, boo, & more art you can do*. Boston: Houghton Mifflin Co.
Presents instructions for making art projects from around the world. For example, French stained glass, Mexican weaving, and Norwegian Viking helmets.

Venezia, M. (1994). *Diego Rivera*. Chicago: Children's Press.
Diego Rivera's life is briefly examined in this book along with examples of his works as a social realist artist.

Venezia, M. (1998). *Edward Hopper*. Chicago: Children's Press.
Briefly describes the life and works of the American realist painter, describing and giving examples of his art.

Venezia, M. (1998). *El Greco*. Chicago: Children's Press.
This book examines the life and work of Domenicos Theotocopoulous, the sixteenth-century artist who created his greatest work in Spain where he was known as "El Greco".

Venezia, M. (1993). *Georgia O'Keefe*. Chicago: Children's Press.

This book emphasizes the difficulties women faced in getting an education in art and being taken seriously as an artist.

Venezia, M. (1995). *Henri De Toulouse-Lautrec: Artist*. Chicago: Children's Press.
A biography of a nineteenth-century best known for his paintings of the lower classes.

Venezia, M. (1990). *Mary Cassatt*. Illustrated by Sarah Mollman Underhill. Chicago: Children's Press.
The book briefly examines the life and work of the American Impressionist painter, describing and providing examples of her work.

Venezia, M. (1995). *Grant Wood*. Chicago: Children's Press.
This book relates to the artistic career of an Iowan who painted people, life, and customs of the American Midwest. Wood's style of art because known as Regionalism.

Web Sites

LOANET.MIT.EDU/WEB

MINI-THEMES

Impressionist Movement

Impressionist art is an art movement that began in Paris in the 1870's. Impressionist painters include Monet, Renoir, Cassatt, Degas but there were many others associated with impressionist artwork. Impressionist painters attempted to portray the light and mood of a scene by using bright colors and small, rapid brushstrokes. There was also a post-impressionist period during the late 19th century in which artist's works followed closely that of the Impressionists. Post-Impressionists included Matisse, Cézanne, van Gogh, and Gauguin.

Activities

1. Provide illustrations or paintings that illustrate an impressionists artwork (many such illustrations can be found in books listed in reference section). Then describe how impressionists try to convey the general mood of what you see, not to produce a detailed image. Explain that this is done by using small, quick, brushstrokes of different colors close to each other to give the impression of shimmering light. Finally, provide the students with paper, brushes, and watercolor and ask them to select a photograph or poster to reproduce as an impressionist painter might do.

2. Use many different colors of tempera paint to paint a picture directly on a flat tray, cookie sheet, or pan. Work quickly so that paint doesn't get to dry. Scratch lines into the painting using a pencil or stick to represent lines trees, sky, animals, etc. Next place a white sheet of paper on top of wet painting and pat gently—don't slide the paper. Lift the paper up and see the painted picture that has been transferred onto the paper. This is called a monoprint and was a technique used by Mary Cassatt, a great impressionist.

3. Fill several small jars with approximately ¼ cup tempera paint. Use a different jar for each color being used. Then stir some textured materials into each jar. For example, add sawdust to one, crushed egg shells to another, flour in another, rice in another, sand in another, etc. Use the textured paint to paint a picture on heavy paper. Allow to dry. This was a technique used by Berthe Morisot, an early impressionist.

4. Soak a piece of white muslin in a bowl of milk. Then spread cloth out on a piece of scrap paper. Using colored chalk, draw a picture on the wet cloth—work quickly before cloth dries. When drawing is completed, flip over, face down, on a clean sheet of scrap paper. Put cloth and paper in several layers of old newspaper. Cover the bottom of an iron with aluminum foil and set on "wool" setting. Iron the back of chalk drawing to seal the chalk into the fabric. This was a technique used by Edgar Degas, an impressionist.

References

Mason, A. (1993). *Monet: An Introduction to the Artist's Life and Work.* New York: Barron's Ed. Series, Inc.

Mason, A. (1995). *Picasso: In Introduction to the Artist's Life and Work.* New York: Barron's Ed. Series, Inc.

Bjork, C. (1985). *Linnea in Monet's* Garden. New York: Harrar, Straus, & Giroux.

Harrison, P. (1996). *Art for Young People: Claude Monet.* New York: Sterling Publishers.

Harrison, P. (1996). *Art for Young People: Vincent Van Gogh.* New York: Sterling Publishers.

Loumaye, N. (1994). *Degas the Painted Gesture.* New York: Chelsea House.

Venezia, M. (1997). *Henri Matisse.* New York: Children's Press.

Renaissance Movement

Renaissance is a period in history of art mainly in the fourteenth and fifteenth centuries. It began in Italy and reached its height with the works of Michelangelo, Raphael, and Leonardo da Vinci.

Activities

1. Cut shapes (animals, buildings, people, trees, shapes, etc.) from heavy cardboard. Glue these shapes onto a piece of cardboard. Glue string or other textured materials around shapes. Then spread a sheet of aluminum foil that is larger then the piece of cardboard, over the design. Press and rub over the shapes and textures so that paper and string show through the foil. Fold extra foil edges over the cardboard edges and tape down. Lay creation on a large piece of scrap newspaper and then paint the entire surface with black tempera paint. Dry overnight and then gently rub surface with steel wool to shine the high spots. This was a technique used by Lorenzo Ghiberti, an early renaissance artist.

2. Sandro Botticelli is well known for the round art he created. Make a round art paper by tracing around a bowl, pizza pan, jar lid, etc., depending on size desired. Remember with "art in the round" there are no flat bottoms, tops, or sides so remember to think of designs that would best fit in a round setting—aquariums, planets or outer space, flowers, etc. Draw or paint picture with any art medium and display.

3. Tommasso Masaccio is a Renaissance artist who is famous for his portraits. Create a profile portrait by standing a model near a blank wall, facing sideways. Shine a slide projector or other bright light on the model so his/her shadow will reflect wall. Tape a sheet of white paper to the wall and trace around model's face, head, neck and shoulders. Turn off light and move paper to a table where details (eyes, eyebrows, mouth and other facial features) can be added plus glasses, jewelry, etc. Frame or matte the picture.

4. Michelangelo Buonarroti, a Renaissance artist, is famous for painting the ceiling of the Sistine Chapel in Rome. He did it by lying on his back. Create a similar scenario by taping a large piece of paper on the underside of a table or desk. Spread newspaper below for droppings. Then instruct the children to lie on their backs and to create a design. Remove designs and allow children to share.

References

Clouse, N. L. (1997). *Perugino's Path: The Journey of a Renaissance Painters*. New York: Wm. B. Eeerdman's Publishing Co.

Hynson, C. (1998). *Columbus: And the Renaissance explorers*. New York: Barrons Juveniles.

Morrison, T. (1996). *Antonio's Apprenticeship: Painting a Fresco in Renaissance Italy*. New York: Holiday House.

Raboff, E. (1988). *Michelangelo*. New York: Harper & Row, Publishers.

Rius, M. (1988). *Renaissance*. Hauppauge, NY: Barrons Juvenile.

Spence, D., & Krailing, T. (1997). *Michelangelo & the Renaissance*. New York: Barrons Educational Series.

Tierney, T. (1997). *Visions of Christmas: A Renaissance Nativity With Triptych Paintings*. New York: Simon & Schuster.

Venezia, M. (1991). *Botticelli*. Chicago: Children's Press.

Venezia, M. (1991). *Michelangelo*. Chicago: Children's Press.

Title Index

Across America on an Emigrant Train (Murphy), 309-310
Adding and Subtraction Puzzles (Usborne), 380
Alfie & The Birthday Surprise (Hughes), 177
Alligator and Others All Year Long (Dragonwagon), 246
Alphabet of Dinosaurs, An (Dodson), 133
America Forever New (Brewton and Brewton), 335
Amistad: A Long Road to Freedom (Myers), 344-346
Animal Monsters: The Truth About Scary Creatures (Pringle), 85
Animal Sharp Shooters (Fredericks), 85
Anno's Math Games II (Anno), 224
Ant Cities (Dorros),128
Anthology for the Earth (Allen), 288
April Fool (Christian), 166
Around the Clock with Harriet (Maestro), 244
Arthur's April Fool (Brown), 166-167
Arthur's First Sleepover (Brown), 148
Ashanti to Zulu: African Traditions (Musgrove), 222
Astronomy Activity Book, The (Schatz), 275
Astronomy for Every Kid (Van Cleave), 275
Aunt Harriet's Underground Railroad in the Sky (Ringgold),175, 201, 400

Baseball Party, The (Prager), 177
Bat Time (Horowitz), 244
Berenstein Bears Comic Valentine (Berenstein), 170
Best Birthday Party Game Book (Lansky), 177
Best Book of Bugs, The (Llewellyn), 121-122
Best Bug Parade, The (Murphy), 239
Best Way to Play, The (Cosby), 146
Big Book for Our Planet, The (Durrell, et al.), 287, 288
Big Gus and Little Gus (Lorenz), 235
Birthday (Steptoe), 177
Birthday Basket for Tia, A (Morra), 177
Birthday Bear, The (Schneider), 177
Birthday Happy, Contrary Mary (Jeram), 177
Birthday Swap, The (Lopez), 177
Black and White (Macauley), 208-210
Bow Wow Birthday (Wardlaw), 177
Boy of the Three-Year Nap (Snyder), 208
Bridges Are to Cross (Sturges), 386
Bring Me All of Your Dreams (Larrick), 320
Brown Bear, Brown Bear, What Do You See? (Martin), 130
Building (Wilkinson), 391-392

Butterflies (Delafosse), 126
Butterflies (Saunders-Smith), 126

Calamity Jane—Her Life and Her Legend (Faber), 311-312
Call of the Wild (London), 346
Cannibal Animals: Animals That Eat Their Own Kind (Fredericks), 85
Case of the Missing Birthday Party, The (Rocklin), 177
Casey at the Bat (Thayer), 325-326
Castle (Macauley), 209
Cathedral: The Story of its Construction (Macauley), 209
Celebrations (Livingston), 161-162, 176, 177
Charlotte's Web (White), 62
Charts and Graphs (Usborne), 380
Children Just Like Me: Celebrations! (Kindersley), 163
Children of the Wild West (Freedman), 303
Chinese Mother Goose Rhymes (Wyndham), 220
Chinese New Year (Brown), 164
Chinese New Year (Moyse), 164
Chocolate Dreams (Adoff), 322
Clementine's Winter Wardrobe (Spohn), 246
Clifford's First Valentine's Day (Bidwell), 170
Confetti: Poems for Children (Mora), 337
Counting Wildflowers (McMillan), 232
Cowboy and the Black-eyed Pea, The (Johnson), 305
Cowboys (Sullivan), 316
Cowboy's Handbook, The (Cody), 306, 317
Cowboys of the Wild West (Freedman), 303, 306
Crafts for Valentine's Day (Ross), 164
Cricket Magazine, 210
Cricket Songs (Behn), 322

Dances with Wolves (video), 305
Dancing Teepees (Sneve), 315
Dangerous Animals (Seidensticker and Lumpkin), 85
Day the Numbers Disappeared, The (Simon and Bendick), 223
Dinofours: I'm Not Your Friend (Metzger), 150
Dinofours: I'm Super Dino! (Metzger), 150
Dinofours: It's Class Trip Day (Metzger), 150
Dinofours: It's Time for School (Metzger), 150
Dinosaur Skeletons (Ingle), 131
Dinosaurs (Hopkins), 130
Dinosaurs and Their Young (Freedman), 139

Dinosaurs, Dinosaurs (Barton), 238
Dinosaurs: Puzzles from the Past (video), 140
Disney's Winnie The Pooh Valentine (Talkington), 170
Dollars and Cents for Harriet (Maestro), 322
Doorbell Rang, The (Huchins), 225-226
Dragon's Robe, The (Lattimore), 187
Dream Keeper, The (Hughes), 320, 321

Each Orange Had 8 Slices (Giganti), 232
Earth Words (Simon), 11
Earthquakes (Branley), 103
Earthquakes (Simon), 287
Earthquakes and Volcanoes (Watt), 12
East of the Sun and West of the Moon (Hague), 183-184
Eating Fractions (McMillan), 378-379
Eats Poems (Adoff), 322
Eleanor Roosevelt: A Life of Discovery (Freedman), 341-343
Elephants for Kids (Fredericks), 42
Exploring the Ocean Tide Pool (Bendick), 5
Exploring the Oceans: Science Activities for Kids (Fredericks), 5, 45, 51, 260-262
Exploring the Rainforest: Science Activities for Kids (Fredericks), 86
Extra Innings (Hopkins), 326

Famous Artists, The (series), 398
Farmer Boy Birthday, A (Wilder), 177
50 Simple Things Kids Can Do to Save the Earth (Javna), 18
52 Special Traditions for Family and Friends (Chronicle Books), 161
Fireflies! (Brinckloe), 119
Fireflies in the Night (Hawes), 118-120
Fossils (Howard), 132-133
Fraction Action (Leedy), 377-378
Fractions and Decimals (Bryand-Mole)a 379-381
Frames of Mind, The Theory of Multiple Intelligences (Gardner), 6
Frantic Frogs and Other Frankly Fractured Folktales for Readers Theatre (Fredericks), 188
Free Willy (video), 269
From Sea to Shining Sea (Cohn, ed.), 304

Gallery of Dinosaurs and Other Early Reptiles, A (Peters), 238
Georgia O'Keefe (Venezia), 400
Girl Who Loved the Wine, The (Yolen), 221
Giver, The (Lowry), 356-357
Going Green: A Kid's Handbook to Saving the Planet (Elkington, et al.), 19
Grandfather Tang's Story (Tompert), 390-391
Grandfather's Journey (Say), 207-208
Grasshopper Summer (Turner), 65

Great Kapok Tree, The (Cherry), 18,19
Great San Francisco Earthquake, The (video), 103
Great Women Throughout the Ages (Hazell), 349
Grouchy Ladybug, The (Carle), 121, 123

Happy New Year! (Bernhard), 168
Happy New Year, Pooh! (Zoehfeld), 167-168
Happy Valentine's Day, Miss Hildy (Grambling), 170
Her Stories (Hamilton), 200, 201
Holes (Sachar), 360
Homecoming: The Art of Life of William H. Johnson (Powell), 404
Honeybee and the Robber, The (Carle), 121
Honey, I Love (Greenfield), 320-321
How Many Snails? (Giganti), 224
How My Parents Learned to Eat (Friedman), 208
Hundred Most Influential Women of All Time, The (Felder), 350

I Am Phoenix: Poems for Two Voices (Fleischman), 321
I Discover Columbus (Lawson), 335
I Have a Dream (King and King), 175-176
I wonder Why the Sea is Salty and Other Questions About the Ocean (Ganeri), 5
I Wonder Why Triceratops Had Horns and Other Questions About Dinosaurs (Theodorou), 134
If Dinosaurs Came Back (Most), 130
If I Were in Charge of the World (Viorst), 320, 336
If You Made A Million, (Schwartz), 377
In a Spring Garden (Lewis), 322
Inside an Ant Colony (Fowler), 128
Inspiration: Stories About Woman Artists (Sills), 399
Ira Sleeps Over (Weber), 149
Is This a House for a Hermit Crab (MacDonald), 5
Island-below-the-Star, The (Rumford), 56

Jabberwocky (Carroll), 324-325
Jack London (Dyer), 346-347
Janice VanCleave's Geometry for Every Kid: Easy Activities That Make Learning Geometry Fun (VanCleave), 388-389
Johnny Tremain (Forbes) 297-298
Journal of William Thomas Emerson: A Revolutionary War Patriot, The (Denenberg), 294-295
Joyful Noise: Poems for Two Voices (Fleischman), 321, 334
Junk in Space (Maurer), 286
Jurassic Park (video), 135
Just a Minute! (Harper), 244

Ladybug (Bernhard), 122-124
Ladybug (Watts), 123
Ladybug and Other Insects, The (Jeunesse), 123
Ladybugs Ball (Heldman), 123
Land Masses (Arnold), 287

Learning Magazine, 138
Life Doesn't Frighten Me (Angelou), 328-329
Light in the Attic, A (Silverstein), 161, 165, 170
Li'l Sis and Uncle Willy: A Story Based On the Life and Paintings of William H. Johnson (Everett), 403
Lila's April Fool (Pascal), 167
Lincoln: A Photobiography (Freedman), 343-344
Little Girl and the Dragon, The (Minarik), 235
Little Grunt and the Big Egg (dePaola), 238-239
Living Monsters: The World's Most Dangerous Animals (Tomb), 85
Lon Po Po: A Red Riding Hood Story from China (Young), 181

Magic School Bus Explores the Solar System, The (video), 281
Magic School Bus Lost in Space, The (video), 281
Magic School Bus: Lost in the Solar System, The (Cole), 280-281
Magic School Bus on the Ocean Floor, The (Cole), 5
Man Who Wanted to Live Forever, The (Hastings), 244
Mary Cassatt (Venezia), 401
Meanest Thing to Say, The (Cosby), 146
Mill (Macauley), 209
Miss Rumphius (Cooney), 63
Moment of Wonder, The (Lewis), 322
Monteverde: Science and Scientists in a Costa Rican Cloud Forest (Collard, 86
Moon and You, The (Krupp), 279
Moon Book, The (Gibbons), 279
More Poetry for Holidays (Larrick), 161
Mountains and Volcanoes (Taylor), 12
Mud Flat April Fools (Stevensen), 166
Multiplying Puzzles (Usborne), 380
My Dream of Martin Luther King (Ringgold), 175
My First Book About Nature: How Things Grow (Kuhn), 145
My Mexico – Mexico Mio (Johnston), 337

National Geographic Magazine, 210
New Kid on the Block, The (Prelutsky), 322
Night on Neighborhood Street (Greenfield), 321
Nightwatch: Nightlife in the Tropical Rainforest (Riley), 86
Numbers at Play: A Counting Book (Sullivan), 226-227
Number Act (Fisher), 224

Ocean (Hirschi), 5
Ocean (MacQuitty), 5, 262
Old Bear (Hissey), 244
One Day in the Alpine Tundra (George), 287
One Day in the Desert (George), 287
One Day in the Prairie (George), 287
One Day in the Tropical Rainforest (George), 19
One Day in the Woods (George), 287

One Fine Day (Hogrogian), 184-185
100 Women Who Shaped History (Rolka and Rolka), 350
101 Valentine Jokes (Brigandi), 164
One Small Square: Seashore (Silver), 255
One Watermelon Seed (Lottridge), 224
Other Bone, The (Young), 219
Our Dynamic Earth (National Geographic Society Video), 103
Our Solar System (Simon), 277-279

Paul Bunyan (Kellogg), 240-241
Pebble in My Pocket, The (Hooper), 107-108
People Could Fly, The (Hamilton), 200
Planets, Moons and Meteors (Gustafson), 275
Plants and Animals of Long Ago (Filmstrip series), 139
Poetry of Black America, The: Anthology of the 20th Century (Adoff, ed.), 321
Pollution and Wildlife (Bright), 18
Prairie Songs (Conrad), 65
Projects with Time (Williams), 244

Quilt, The (Jonas), 304

Random House Book of Poetry, The (Prelutsky), 161
Ranger Rick's Nature Magazine (National Wildlife Federation), 116, 120
Revenge of the Small Small (Little), 235
Right Number of Elephants, The (Sheppard), 227-228
Righteous Revenge of Artemis Bonder, The (Myers), 308-309
Rumpelstiltskin (Zelinski), 179

Saint George and the Dragon (Hodges), 187-188
Salamander Room, The (Mazer), 46
Sarah Bishop (O'Dell), 296-297
Science and Children (Magazine), 102
Seven Chinese Brothers, The (Mahy), 186-187
Shaman's Apprentice: A tale of the Amazone Rain Forest (Cherry), 86
Shh! We're Writing the Constitution (Fritz), 295-296
Shipwreck Saturday (Cosby), 146
Sing to the Sun (Bryan), 321
Slugs (Fredericks), 58
Smallest Dinosaur, The (Simon), 238
Smoky Night (Bunting), 205-207
Something About the Author (Gale Publications), 354
Stay in Line (Slater), 228
Stories I Ain't Told Nobody Yet: Selections from the People Pieces (Carson), 337
Storyteller's Sourcebook, The: A Subject, Title, and Motif Index to Folklore Collections for Children (McDonald), 180
Super-Fine Valentine (Cosby), 146
Surtsey: The Newest Place on Earth (Lasky), 12

Sweetwater (Yep), 281-282
Swim Through the Sea, A (Pratt), 5, 257-259

Tar Beach (Ringgold), 175, 400
Teaching K-8 Magazine, 138
10 Bears in My Bed (Mack), 228
Ten Flashing Fireflies (Sturges), 119
Ten, Nine, Eight (Bang), 228
Then and Now (Ockenga), 246
This Changing Planet (National Geographic Society video), 11, 102
This is the Pumpkin (Levine), 165-166
Tiny for a Day (Grackenbach), 237-238
Treasure Hunt (Cosby), 146
Tropical Rain Forests Around the World (Landau), 18
True Story of the 3 Little Pigs!, The (Scieszla), 188
Tuesday (Wiesner), 210-211
26 Letters and 99 Cents (Hoban), 233
Twelve Days of Christmas, The (Kent), 228
Twelve Days of Christmas, The (Wildsmith), 228
Twelve Days of Christmas, The (Williams), 228
Tyrannosaurus Was a Beast (Mulberry), 130

Underground (Macauley), 209
Underwater Alphabet Book, The (Pallotta), 5

Valentine's Day (Nerlove), 169-170
Very Busy Spider, The (Carle), 121
Very Hungry Caterpillar, The (Carle), 121, 126
Very Quiet Cricket, The (Carle), 120-121
View From Saturday, A (Konigsburg), 359-360

Violent Earth, The (National Geographic Society Video), 12, 106-107
Volcano: The Eruption and Healing of Mt. St. Helens (Lauber), 14, 105
Volcano and Earthquake (Rose), 12
Volcanoes (Simon), 12, 106, 287
Volcanoes (Vogt), 12
Volcanoes: Fire From Below (Wood), 104

Walk Two Moons (Creech), 357-359
Watch Out for Sharks (Arnold), 5
Way Things Work, The (Macaulay), 209
Weekend with Picasso (series), 398
Weekend with Renoir, A (Skira-Venturi), 402
Westward Ho! (Carlson), 306
What If...The Earth (Parker), 13
Where do you think you're going, Christopher Columbus? (Fritz), 335
Where the Buffalo Run (Geis), 310
Where the Sidewalk Ends (Silverstein), 144
White Fang (London), 346
Why the Chicken Crossed the Road (Macauley), 209
Why Mosquitoes Buzz in People's Ears (Dillon and Dillon), 222
Wild West (magazine), 305
Will You Take Care of Me? (Bridges), 147
Wump World, The (Peet), 19, 20

Yanomami: People of the Amazon (Schwartz), 86
Your Big Backyard (Magazine), 117, 120

Subject Index

Accordion Book, 207
Active Involvement, 35
Active Learning Contexts, 35
Addition and Subtraction (mini-theme), 232-233
Afro-American Folktales(mini-theme), 200-202
After reading activities/strategies, 37-38, 55-64
    Cloze technique, 62-63
    Continuums, 55-58
    CREATIVE Questioning, 60-62
    Literature Log, 59-61
    Plot Graph, 58-59
    Story Frames, 63-64
Anecdotal records, 69
Anticipation Guide, 12-13, 43-46
Ants (mini-theme), 127-128
Architecture (mini-theme), 394-395
Art (primary unit) 397-407
    Literature related activities, 399-405
    Supplemental literature, 405-406
    Mini-themes, 406-408
      Impressionist Movement, 406-407
      Renaissance Movement, 407
Asking Divergent Questions, 51-52
Assessment, 9, 83, 99. *See also* Authentic Assessment.
Assessment Dada Planning List, 84
Attitude Chart, 140
Audio/videotapes of selected work, 71
Authentic Assessment, 65-84
Criterion Checks, 80-81
    Multiple Options, 81-84
    Nature of, 66-68
    Portfolios, 68-77
    Student Self-Assessment, 77-80
    Success Factors, 67-68

Becoming a Nation (intermediate unit), 291-302
    Literature related activities, 294-299
    Supplemental literature, 299-300
    Mini-themes, 300-302
      The Constitution and Bill of Rights, 300-301
      The Revolutionaries, 301-302
Before reading activities/strategies, 37-38
    Anticipation Guide, 43-46
    Concept Cards, 41-42
    K-W-L, 42-44

Reflective Sharing Technique, 48-50
Semantic Feature Analysis, 46-48
Semantic Webbing, 39-40
Student Motivated Active Reading Technique (S.M.A.R.T.), 40-41
Biography: Making a Difference (intermediate unit), 339-352
    Literature related activities, 294-299
    Supplemental literature, 299-300
    Mini-themes, 349-352
      Freedom Fighters, 351-352
      Women of the World, 349-351
Biopoem, 298
Birthdays (mini-theme), 176-178
Bodily-Kinesthetic Intelligence, 7
Book Planning Form, 21
Bookwebbing, 17, 19, 21

Caldecott Award, The (primary unit), 197-222
    Literature related activities, 205-212
    Supplemental literature, 212-219
    Mini-themes, 219-222
      Ed Young, 219-221
      Leo and Diane Dillon, 221-222
Caldecott Medal Winners and Honor Books, 213-218
Caldecott, Randolph, 205
Cannary, Martha Jane (Calamity Jane), 311-312
Cassatt, Mary, 401
Caterpillars, Butterflies, and Moths (mini-theme), 126-127
Censorship and Children's Literature (mini-theme), 371-374
Changing Earth, The (primary unit), 101-114
    Literature related activities, 103-109
    Supplemental literature, 109-111
    Mini-themes, 111-114
      Rocks and Soil, 112-114
      Water, 111-112
Character Analysis Frame, 64
Character Continuum, 55-57
Checklists, 69
Cloze Technique, 62-63
Collaborative Approach, 35-36
Community of learners, 5, 9
Concept Cards, 41-42
Constitution and Bill of Rights: An In-Depth Look, The (mini-theme), 300-301

Contents of portfolios, 69-75
    Anecdotal records, 69
    Audio/videotapes of selected work, 71
    Checklists, 69
    Cooperative group assignments, 74
    Examples of student work, 69
    Photographs/illustrations of completed projects, 71
    Progress notes by student, 70
    Teacher's observational notes, 69
    Tests, quizzes and/or exams, 73
    Thematic logs, 73
    Work samples selected by student, 71
    Writing samples, 74
Continuums, 55-58
    Character, 55-57
    Facts/Attitude, 56-58
    Setting, 56-57
Cooking and Eating (mini-theme), 382-384
Cooperative group assignments, 74
Cooperative Integrated Reading and Composition, 54
Cooperative learning, 4, 52-55
    Cooperative Integrated Reading and Composition, 54
    Jigsaw, 54
    Prediction People, 55
    Reader's Roundtable, 55
    STAD (Student Teams - Achievement Divisions), 53
    TGT (Teams-Games-Tournaments), 53
    Web Weavers, 55
Counting and Computation (primary unit), 223-234
    Literature related activities, 225-230
    Supplemental literature, 230-232
    Mini-themes, 232-234
        Addition and Subtraction, 232-233
        Money, 233-234
CREATIVE Questioning, 60-62, 181
Criterion Checks, 80-81
Curricular Connections (mini-theme), 333-336

Death and Dying as Part of Growing Up (mini-theme), 156-158
Decimals (mini-theme), 382
Descriptive portfolio, 68
Dillon, Leo and Diane (mini-theme), 221-222
Dinosaurs (primary unit), 129-141
    Literature related activities, 131-135
    Supplemental literature, 135-137
    Mini-themes, 138-141
        Why Dinosaurs Became Extinct, 138
        The Time of the Dinosaurs, 138-139
        Discovering Dinosaurs, 139-141
        Other Ancient Animals, 141
Directed Reading-Thinking Activity (DRTA), 50
Discovering Dinosaurs (mini-theme), 139-141
Divergent questions, asking, 51-52

During reading activities/strategies, 37-38, 50-55
    Asking divergent questions, 51-52
    Cooperative learning, 52-55
    Directed Reading-Thinking Activity (DRTA), 50
    Self-questioning, 52

Eight Human Intelligences, The, 7
Empowerment, 35
Evaluative measures, options, 80-81
Evaluative portfolio, 68
Examples of student's work, in portfolio, 69

Facts/Attitude Continuum, 56-58
Facts on File, 11
Field trips, 92-97
    mini field trips, 96-97
    possible locations, 93
    post-field trip activities, 95
    preparing a guidebook, 92-94
    tips for a successful field trip, 94
Folktales (primary unit), 179-202
    Literature related activities, 183-192
    Supplemental literature, 192-197
    Mini-themes, 198-202
        Folktales of Native Americans, 198-200
        Afro-American Folktales, 200-202
Folktales of Native Americans (mini-theme), 198-200
Fractions (intermediate unit), 375-384
    Literature related activities, 377-381
    Supplemental literature, 381
    Mini-themes, 382-384
        Decimals, 282
        Cooking and Eating, 382-384
Freedom Fighters (mini-theme), 351-352

Gardner, Howard, 6-7
Geometry (intermediate unit), 385-395
    Literature related activities, 386-392
    Supplemental literature, 392-394
    Mini-themes, 394-395
        Architecture, 394-395
        Lines and Angles, 395
Graffiti Wall, 12, 101
Growing Up (primary unit), 143-158
    Literature related activities, 146-152
    Supplemental literature, 152-154
    Mini-themes, 154-158
        Separation and Divorce, 154-156
        Death and Dying, 156-158
Guidebook, for field trips, 92-94

Hamilton, Virginia, 200
Hoban, Tana, 385

Information Frame, 64
Insects/Bugs (primary unit), 115-128
Literature related activities, 118-124
    Supplemental literature, 124-126
    Mini-themes, 126-128
        Caterpillars, Butterflies, and Moths, 126-127
        Ants, 127-128
Interpersonal Intelligence, 7
Interviews, 11
Intrapersonal Intelligence, 7
Introducing the Classics (mini-theme), 369-371

Jigsaw, 54
Johnson, William, 404
Journals, 11
Journal Entry Sheet, 74

King, Jr., Martin Luther, Day, (mini-theme), 175-176
K-W-L Strategy, 42-44, 119, 275, 344

Lesson planning forms, 31-33
Lines and Angles (mini-theme), 395
Literature log, 21, 23, 59-61
London, Jack, 346
Luchetti, Cathi, 305

Macauley, David, 385
Martin Luther King, Jr., Day, 175-176
Master Web, 40
Math-Logic Intelligence, 7
Measurement and Sizes (primary unit), 235-247
    Literature related activities, 237-242
    Supplemental literature, 242-244
    Mini-themes, 244-247
        Months and Seasons, 245-247
        Time, 244-245
Meet the Newberys (intermediate unit), 353-374
    Literature related activities, 356-362
    Supplemental literature, 362-369
    Mini-themes, 369-374
        Censorship and Children's Literature, 371-374
        Introducing the Classics, 369-371
Mini field trips, 96-97
Money (mini-theme), 233-234
Months and Seasons (mini-theme), 245-247
Multiple Intelligences, The Theory of, 6
Multiple Options, 81
Musical Intelligence, 7

Native Americans of the Wild West (mini-theme), 315-316
Naturalist Intelligence, 7
Newspaper, 11
Newbery, John, 355
Newbery Medal and Newbery Honor Books, 363-369

Oceanic Occupations, 252
Oceans (intermediate unit), 251-272
    Literature related activities, 255-265
    Supplemental literature, 265-269
    Mini-themes, 269-272
        Sharks, 271-272
        Whales, 269-271
Ogle, Donna, 44
Other Ancient Animals (mini-theme), 141

Parent and community involvement, 85-98
    Activities involving parents, 88-92
    Community field trips, 92-98
    Involving parents, 86-88
    Parent Newsletter, 91
Personal Connections, 35
Photographs/illustrations of completed projects, 71
Planning thematic instructions, 15-33
    Designing activities and projects, 27-29
    Gathering materials and resources, 24-27
        Artifacts, 27
        Literature Resources, 24-25
        Printed Resources, 24
        Technology Connection, 25-27
        Visual Resources, 24
    Implementing the unit, 29-33
        Lesson Planning Forms, 31-33
    Organizing the theme, 17-23
    Selecting the theme, 15-17
Plot Frame, 64
Plot Graph, 58-59
Poems of Everyday Life (mini-theme), 336-338
Poetry Festival, 329
Poetry Journal, 320
Poetry: The Words and the Music (intermediate unit), 319-337
    Literature related activities, 324-329
    Supplemental literature, 329-333
    Mini-themes, 333-337
        Curricular Connections, 333-336
        Poems of Everyday Life, 336-338
Portfolios, 68-77
    Advantages, students, 77
    Advantages, teachers, 77
    Contents of, 69-75. See also Contents of portfolios
    Management of, 75-76
    Rationale for, 76-77
    Types of, 68-69
Portfolio Assessment, 68-69
Portfolio Progress Sheet, 75, 80
Prediction Cards – See Concept Cards, 41-42
Prediction People, 55
Pre-reading Activities, 21
Pre-reading Strategy, 57

Progress notes, by student, 70

Read-aloud, 13
Reader's Roundtable, 55
Reader's Theatre, 108, 186, 188, 201
Reading instruction, principles of, 36
Reading Rug, 13
Reflective Sharing Technique, 48-50
Renoir, 402
Resources, 24-27
    Artifacts, 27
    Literature, 24-25
    Printed, 24
    Technology, 25-27
    Visual, 24
Revolutionaries: A Closer Look, A (mini-theme), 301-302
Rivera, Diego, 13
Rocks and Soil (mini-theme), 112-114
Roosevelt, Eleanor, 378
Rosenblatt, Louise, 36

Self-questioning, 52
Semantic Feature Analysis (SFA), 46-48, 117-118
Semantic webbing, 39-40, 115-116, 147, 160, 169, 223, 306
Separation and Divorce, Growing Up With (mini-theme), 154-156
Setting Continuum, 56-57
Showcase portfolio, 68
Space Technology: Satellites, Shuttles, Space Stations, and Colonization (mini-theme), 285-286
Space: The Final Frontier (intermediate unit), 273-289
    Literature related activities, 277-282
    Supplemental literature, 283-285
    Mini-themes, 285-289
        Space Technology, 285-286
        Third Rock from the Sun: The Earth, 287-289
Spatial Intelligence, 7
STAD (Student Teams - Achievement Divisions), 53
Stevenson, Robert Louis, 309-310
Story Frames, 63-64
Story Map, 14
Storytelling, 13
Strategies for reading literature, 35-63
Student Motivated Active Reading Technique (S.M.A.R.T.), 40-41
Student self-assessment, 77-80
Student Self-Report Form, 79
Student Teams - Achievement Divisions (STAD), 53

Teacher's observational notes, 69
Teaching thematically, 6-15
Teams-Games-Tournaments (TGT), 53

Tests, quizzes and/or exams, 73
TGT (Teams-Games-Tournaments), 53
Thematic learning, 5-6, 8
Thematic Logs, 73
Thematic teaching, 6-15
    advantages of, for students, 10
    advantages of, for teachers, 9
Thematic units, developing and using, 3-33,99
    Advantages of, for students, 4-6, 10
    Advantages of, for teachers, 3,6,8-9
    Designing activities and projects, 27-29
    Gathering materials and resources, 24,27
    Implementing the Unit, 29-30
    Planning, 8-33
    Teaching thematically, 6-15
Theme topics, 15
    Curricula areas, 6, 15-16
    Issues, 15-16
    Literary interests, 16
    Problems, 16
    Special events, 16
    Student interests, 16
Themewebbing, 17
Third Rock from the Sun: The Earth (mini-theme), 287-289
Time (mini-theme), 244-245
Time of the Dinosaurs, The (mini-theme), 138-139
Today's Cowboy (mini-theme), 316-317
Transactional approach to reading, 36-37

Unit Guide, 19, 22

Venn Diagram, 103, 141, 185, 370
Verbal-Linguist Intelligence, 7

Wall Mural, 129
Water (mini-theme), 111-112
Web Weavers, 55
Whales (mini-theme), 269-271
Why Dinosaurs Became Extinct (mini-theme), 138
Wild, Wild West, The (intermediate unit), 303-317
    Literature related activities, 306-312
    Supplemental literature, 312-314
    Mini-themes, 315-317
        Native Americans of the Wild West, 315-316
        Today's Cowboy, 316-317
Women of the World (mini-theme), 349-351
Work samples, selected by student, 71
Writing samples, 74

Young, Ed (mini-theme), 219-221

About the Authors

Anita Meyer Meinbach has worked for the Dade County Public Schools, Miami, Florida, as a classroom teacher, curriculum writer, and teacher trainer, providing seminars and guidance in curriculum development. As an adjunct professor, she has taught courses in language arts, reading children's literature and gifted education. Dr. Meinbach is the author of several textbooks and numerous resource books in reading and language arts. A frequent presenter at various workshops and professional conferences, she speaks on a variety of topics dealing with children's literature, the interdisciplinary approach to learning, curriculum development, and gifted education.

Anthony D. Fredericks is a former elementary classroom teacher and reading specialist. He is currently a Professor of Education at York College of Pennsylvania where he teaches elementary methods courses in reading, science, language arts, and social studies. He has written more than three dozen teacher resource books, including *Science Adventures Through Children's Literature,* and *Tadpole Tales and Other Totally Terrific Treats for Readers Theater.* He is also the author of a dozen children's books including titles such as *Slugs, Elephants for Kids,* and the best-selling *Cannibal Animals: Animals That Eat Their Own Kind.* He maintains a website for elementary teachers (www.afredericks.com) that includes up-to-the-minute ideas in elementary science education.

Liz Rothlein, full professor, is an Associate Dean in the School of Education at the University of Miami, Coral Gables, Florida. She is coauthor of more than 20 books about reading, language arts, environmental and multicultural issues, and of other popular resource books for using children's literature in elementary classrooms. She is the recipient of numerous teaching awards, including Professor of the year at the University of Miami, and is listed in Outstanding Elementary Teachers of America.